W9-BFU-444

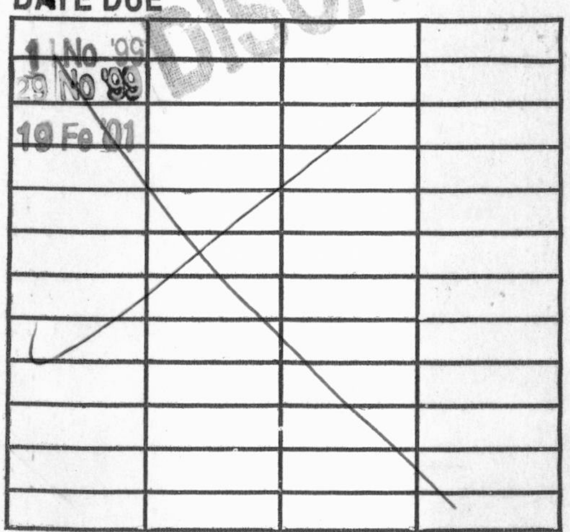
DATE DUE
1 No '99
29 No '99
19 Fe '01

THE OXFORD HISTORY OF BOARD GAMES

David Parlett

OXFORD
UNIVERSITY PRESS

OXFORD
UNIVERSITY PRESS

Great Clarendon Street, Oxford OX2 6DP

Oxford University Press is a department of the University of Oxford.
It furthers the University's objective of excellence in research, scholarship,
and education by publishing worldwide in

Oxford New York

Athens Auckland Bangkok Bogotá Buenos Aires Calcutta
Cape Town Chennai Dar es Salaam Delhi Florence Hong Kong Istanbul
Karachi Kuala Lumpur Madrid Melbourne Mexico City Mumbai
Nairobi Paris São Paulo Singapore Taipei Tokyo Toronto Warsaw

and associated companies in Berlin Ibadan

Oxford is a registered trade mark of Oxford University Press
in the UK and in certain other countries

Published in the United States
by Oxford University Press Inc., New York

First published 1999

British Library Cataloguing in Publication Data
Data available

Library of Congress Cataloging in Publication Data
Data available

ISBN 0-19-212998-8

1 3 5 7 9 10 8 6 4 2

Typeset by Pure Tech India Limited,
Pondicherry, India
Printed in Great Britain
on acid-free paper by
Bookcraft (Bath) Ltd.
Midsomer Norton, Somerset

TO

DR IRVING FINKEL

(big game hunter for the British Museum)

Contents

Preface

> I am not gamesome: I do lack some part
> Of that quick spirit that is Antony.
>
> Shakespeare, *Julius Caesar*, I. ii. 28

Just as I was reaching the end of this book archaeologists unearthed at Colchester a remarkably well-preserved Roman board game. Latrunculi was already well known in essence from scattered and incomplete remains found in all parts of the former Roman Empire, and at various times games researchers have sought to deduce and reconstruct its rules from a handful of tantalizing references to it in Latin literature. What excited the archaeologists about this one was the fact that it was set up as if at start of play. For once, they could see the size of the board (12 × 10 squares) and the initial disposition of the pieces, twelve of white glass and twelve of blue, with two of them moved forwards from their evident initial positions. The excitement of the archaeologists transferred itself to reporters and journalists, who lost no time in coming out with their misunderstandings of what the game was all about. One Chess correspondent demonstrated that it could not have been Hnefatafl, a medieval Viking game. Which was true, but he might equally well have argued that it was not Monopoly, or Scrabble, for all the enlightenment that might produce. Another floated an illustration of the game supposedly in play, showing chequered squares and diagonal moves, neither of which is actually attested before the tenth century. Yet another saw in it the ancestor of Draughts, to which it bears no plausible evolutionary relationship, though the two might just about be said to have occupied a similar ecological niche in their respective societies.

All of which goes to show that the British public's evident interest in games other than those classified as sports is not well served by readily available literature surveying the whole field on a comparative and historical basis. My aim is to fill this gap, awesome and foolhardy though such an attempt may appear. What follows is not so much a cultural history as an analytical survey conducted on historical lines. In this respect it forms a sequel to my *Oxford History of Card Games** and follows much the same approach. It focuses not on strategies or rules of procedure but rather on

* Published by OUP in hardback 1990 as *The Oxford Guide to Card Games* and in paperback as *A History of Card Games*.

mechanisms and concepts of play. To this end I have divided the games into related groups, so that each chapter describes the evolution of a particular type of game rather than the games played by a particular historical community or at a given period of time.

The only book I know of comparable in scope and purpose is H. J. R. Murray's *History of Board Games Other than Chess* (Oxford, 1952), itself a sequel to his *History of Chess* (Oxford, 1913). The former, though now revered by games researchers everywhere, was not a popular success in its day and has since become as rare as gold dust, possibly because it was just as dry to read. Furthermore, many of his conclusions have been invalidated by subsequent researches and discoveries in a field of study that has, ironically enough, been significantly motivated and directed by his pioneering work. I have to start by freely acknowledging my debt to Murray and expressing some diffidence at daring to embark on a possibly premature replacement. I say premature because I am equally aware that recent developments in the study and history of games have accelerated to such a pace, and with such lack of correlation between individual researchers and different academic disciplines (psychology, ethnology, social history, mathematics), as to make it impossible to keep up with more than a small fraction of all that's going on. Nevertheless, a start has to be made somewhere on the replacement of Murray's classic work for a younger generation, and I must admit to having enjoyed rising to, if sometimes falling before, the challenge of the publishers' invitation to attempt it.

Games are an essential aspect of cultural activity, comparable in some ways to the performing arts. All but the rarest of primitive communities have games; those of the most advanced civilizations have been correspondingly advanced in content; and, perhaps surprisingly, the playing of formal games – as opposed to 'just playing'—has throughout history been an essentially adult activity. Children have hitherto played with toys, not games. The development of board games and card games for children is historically recent and particularly characteristic of western culture, dating back not much further than the late eighteenth century. It is largely because westerners tend to perceive games as childish, and play as antithetical to work, that so little attention has been paid to them as a subject worthy of serious attention. And yet, as Michael Dummett puts it, in *The Game of Tarot* (London, 1980), 'A game may be as integral to a culture, as true an object of human aesthetic appreciation, as admirable a product of creativity as a folk art or a style of music; and, as such, it is quite as worthy of study'; and I make no apology for requoting that admirable observation by Joseph Strutt that 'In order to form a just estimation of the character of any particular people, it is absolutely necessary to investigate the sports and pastimes most generally prevalent among them. War, policy, and other contingent circumstances, may effectually place men, at different times, in different points of view; but, when we follow them into their retirements, where no disguise is necessary, we are most likely to see them in their true state, and may best judge of their natural dispositions' (*Sports and Pastimes of the People of England* (London, 1800)).

For information, help, advice, encouragement, or any combination of the four, I offer thanks to (in alphabetical order) R. C. Bell (Newcastle), Michael Dummett (Oxford), Irving Finkel (British Museum), Albie Fiore (London), Dan Glimne (Linköping), Kishor Gordhandas (Bombay), Roger Hayworth (Gibsons Games), Steve Jackson (London), Graham Parlett (Victoria & Albert Museum), Andrew Pennycook (Chesterfield), David Pritchard (Guildford), Francis Roads (London), Arie van der Stoep (Rockanje). Also to Creative Games Ltd., Gibsons Games Ltd., Hasbro (UK) Ltd., Spears Games Ltd., and Waddingtons Games Ltd., for samples. Also to Angus Phillips and Alysoun Owen, my editors at Oxford University Press, for their patience and encouragement, and to Tom Chandler for his excellent copy-editing. Also to the Bodleian Library, as much for its wonderful atmosphere as its glorious contents. And, arising therefrom, to the principal sources and authorities, listed under Abbreviations, to which frequent reference will be made throughout.

Principal References

Alfonso Manuscript A Spanish treatise on games commissioned by Alfonso the Wise and completed in 1283, republished as *Das Schachzabelbuch König Alfons des Weisen,* edited by A. Steiger, in *Romanica Helvetica,* Vol. 10 (1934). Part I Chess, II Dice-only games, III Tables, IV Alquerque, Merels, and various astronomical games. An invaluable survey of medieval board games.

Bell R(obert) C. Bell, *Board and Table Games,* (i) (Oxford, 1960, 1969), *Board and Table Games,* (ii) (Oxford, 1969), combined as *Board and Table Games from Many Civilisations* (New York, 1979). This includes invaluable potted biographies and complete bibliographies of notable games researchers, on which I here draw heavily. Author also of *Discovering Old Board Games* (Aylesbury, 1973), and many articles in *Games & Puzzles* magazine (both series). Games collector, antiquarian, historian, researcher, and inspired restorer of lost rules of play.

Culin Stewart Culin (1858–1929) Many titles, chiefly *Korean Games (with Notes on the corresponding games of China and Japan),* (Pennsylvania University, 1895), republished as *Games of the Orient* (Rutland, 1958), *Chess and Playing Cards* (Washington, 1896), *Games of the North American Indians* (Washington, 1907), republished in two volumes (respectively games of chance, games of skill) (University of Nebraska, 1992). Director of the Archaeological Museum of the University of Pennsylvania, then curator in Ethnology at the Museum of the Brooklyn Institute of Arts and Sciences. Culin's interests being primarily ethnological, his game descriptions, though comprehensive, are often lacking in clarity and technical detail.

Fiske Willard Fiske (1831–1904), multilingual polymath, diplomat, author, journalist, bookseller, etc., author of *Chess in Iceland* (Florence, 1905). Despite its title, this posthumously published magnum opus is a feast of fact and speculation on the pan-European history of Tables, Merels, Alquerque, and Draughts. The good news is that he owned a private printing press, otherwise his incomplete work, which is utterly invaluable, would never have seen the light of day. The bad news is that he died before reaching either Chess or Iceland.

Games & Puzzles: 1st series Founded by Graeme Levin, edited mainly by David Pritchard. Nos. 1–81 (monthly, May 1972–Summer 1981). In 1981 it dropped the puzzles and became *The Gamer.* In 1982 it dropped David Pritchard and expired soon after.

2nd series Revived by Paul Lamford, nos. 1–15 (monthly, April 1994–June 1995), with contributions from all the usual suspects.

Homo Ludens *Homo Ludens—Der spielende Mensch, Internationale Beiträge des Institutes für Spielforschung und Spielpädagogik an der Hochschule 'Mozarteum' Salzburg,* published by Musikverlag Emil Katzbichler, Munich and Salzburg. Scholarly papers on all aspects of games, published annually from 1991. Volume 4 (1994) is devoted to board games.

Hyde Sir Thomas Hyde (1636–1702) *De Ludis Orientalibus Libri Duo,* consisting of *De Historia Shahiludi* (1689), *De Historia Nerdiludi* and *Historia Triodii* (1694). A multilingual farrago of miscellaneous facts and speculations on games selected apparently at random from every known culture and epoch. More remarkable for its list of contents than for the contents themselves, Hyde's work exemplifies Mark Twain's definition of a classic as 'something that everyone wants to have read and nobody wants to read'.

Lhôte Jean-Marie Lhôte, *Histoire des Jeux de Société* (Éditions Flammarion, Paris, 1994). This profusely illustrated and gigantic tome (5 kg.) contains a survey of ancient and modern board games, card games, dice and tile games, first in historical sequence, and again, for reference, in dictionary form. A magnificent achievement, and quite indispensable.

Murray H. J. R. Murray (1868–1955), educationalist and schools inspector, son of the renowned philologist and lexicographer Sir James A. H. Murray. Author of two outstanding classics, *A History of Chess* (Oxford, 1913), and *A History of Board Games Other than Chess* (Oxford, 1952). Both are packed with factual detail and occasional insights, and remain invaluable despite pitfalls that have emerged with the passage of time. They are also extraordinarily dull to read, haphazardly arranged, and indexed and cross-referenced, where at all, with maddening inefficiency. More readable is *A Short History of Chess* (Oxford, 1963), published posthumously. Two versions of a history of Draughts remain in manuscript.

Strutt Joseph Strutt (1749–1802), archaeologist and antiquarian. *Sports and Pastimes of the People of England* (1801), revised and expanded by J. Charles Fox in 1903, reprinted London, 1969. Chapter 33 is on Sedentary Games (dice, Backgammon, Chess, Rithmomachy, Draughts, Merels, Fox & Geese, Solitaire, Dominoes, cards, Game of Goose, of Snake, etc.), 34 is on Chess and Tables, and 35 on Card games. Fox's helpful additions are clearly distinguished from Strutt's original material.

The Name of the Game

Proprietary games, like Monopoly, Diplomacy, etc., are customarily spelt with a capital initial, and traditional games, such as Chess and Draughts, with a minuscule. In this book, however, I follow my usual practice of capitalizing all game names regardless of their status. Consistency—that 'hobgoblin of little minds' (Emerson)—is not my primary motive. Capitals have the advantage of simplifying questionable cases like Ludo and Snakes & Ladders, which in course of time have passed from 'trade' to 'trad'. They also obviate the sort of confusion exemplified by the difference between Losing Chess, which is a game, and losing chess, which is a disgrace. The practice need not, however, apply to derivatives. Thus a chessboard and chessmen do not need capitals, as both can be used for playing games other than Chess, and are therefore generic rather than specific. I also use '&' for 'and' in such games as Snakes & Ladders, Hare & Tortoise, etc., in order to prevent one game from reading like two, especially in a list.

NOTICE

All games described as or clearly implied to be proprietary games are protected against imitation in international law by copyright, patents, trade marks, etc. Their inclusion here does not imply that they have acquired for legal purposes a non-proprietary or general significance nor is any other judgement implied concerning their legal status. Anyone seeking a licence to copy, market, or otherwise reproduce a proprietary game should contact the company concerned. The same strictures and advice apply to games of modern origin which may now or at a future date be marketed although not identified in the text as proprietary games.

Welcome Aboard

What's in a game?

There are others so continually in the agitation of gross and merely sensual pleasures, or so occupied in the low drudgery of avarice, or so heated in the chase of honours and distinction, that their minds, which had been used continually to the storms of these violent and tempestuous passions, can hardly be put in motion by the delicate and refined play of the imagination.

EDMUND BURKE, *On the Sublime and Beautiful* (1756)

I do not like this game!

Bluebottle, *The Goon Show* (*passim*)

Given our title, it would be reasonable to start by distinguishing board games from other types of game. It is not really necessary to go any further back and ask exactly what we mean by a game. Indeed, a learned journal devoted to the subject has more or less agreed that the word is used for so many different activities that it is not worth insisting on any proposed definition. All in all, it is a slippery lexicological customer, with many friends and relations in a wide variety of fields. For which very reason, of course, we cannot possibly proceed without noting some of its associations, if only for fun.

By a circuitous process of definition, a game is what you play, and to play is to do a game; therefore *game* and *play* are basically the same, except that one is a noun and the other a verb. Hardly any other language renders it desirable to start with such a simple observation. In French, *on joue à un jeu*; in German, *man spielt ein Spiel*; and so on. English is remarkable in using words from different roots for different grammatical functions.

This distinction has some fascinating side-effects. A trivial but irresistible instance is that such modern Romance words as French *jeu*, Italian *giuoco*, and Romanian *joc*, derive from the medieval Latin word for game, *iocus*, from which we also get the English *joke*. The classical Latin word is *ludus*, which also means 'school'. From this we get the game of Ludo, and, possibly, the idea of a school of playful porpoises or serious Poker-players. As for play, it not only implies practising a game but also is something you do to a piano, from which (in my case) it may never recover.

Swap the two words' grammatical functions, however, and you get a different set of meanings. *To game* is not to play but to indulge in the chance redistribution of wealth, and *a play* is not a game but a dramatic performance. We need not be deflected by this paradox, beyond noting that there are obvious relations between playing and gambling, and between a dramatic performance and a game, especially a simulation game. Many games are used for gambling—some, indeed, are not fit for anything else; but there are also many of such intrinsic intellectual interest as to appeal to players who have not the slightest interest in gambling. The relation of *gaming* to *games-playing* is therefore not one of synonymy but merely of semantic overlap. Dramatic performance is another area of overlap — one has only to think of the historically recent rise of fantasy role-playing games such as Dungeons & Dragons to see how one shades off into the other.

More paradoxes. *Play* as a noun without an article — as opposed, that is, to *a play*—does indeed denote the general activity of playing games, and can therefore often be usefully substituted for *games* (plural) as a way of retaining one word for the same idea.

Play validates itself. Its purpose and value are intrinsic. True games serve no conscious practical purpose beyond that of satisfying an urge to play which is sometimes regarded as an instinct. 'He who *must* play cannot truly *play*' declares James Carse, in *Finite and Infinite Games* (a theology book, as some have found to their surprise). They may serve some unconscious practical purpose, such as to keep mind or body in trim, or to practise some skill of value in the so-called 'real' world; but anyone who embarks on a game for any such express purpose—including that of gambling—will not be much fun to play with. They may serve some deep psychological purpose, whether consciously or unconsciously, as described by Eric Berne in *Games People Play*; but his is a psychology book (as some have found to their surprise), and his use of the word 'game' is, strictly speaking, metaphorical.

Game, however, as a noun without an article, means birds or animals hunted for sport. There is an obvious relationship between sport and play, but Avedon and Sutton-Smith[1] go further by relating it to *gam* meaning 'leg' (cf. French *jambe*, Italian *gamba*, etc.), and, of course, an unwell leg can be described as *game*. This connection may be traceable to a root meaning bent or crooked (for which the Welsh is *cam* or *gam*)—a game leg may be twisted, and the leg of running prey is continually bending and unbending.

Reference to sport recalls that activities such as football, cricket, tennis, and golf are described as both sports and games. It cannot be because they are necessarily played with legs a-bending, for Chess, Monopoly, Backgammon, Scrabble, and everything else described in this book are also classed as games but are by no means sport. Before enquiring further, we need to note a useful distinction between formal and informal games.

An informal game is merely undirected play, or 'playing around', as when children or puppies play at rough and tumble. In the school playground, informal games often engage the current heroes and heroines of urban myth, thereby exhibiting a dramatic element and showing how closely games (informal) approach the condition of plays (impromptu).

A formal game has a twofold structure based on ends and means:

Ends. It is a contest to achieve an objective. (The Greek for game is *agon*, meaning contest.) Only one of the contenders, be they individuals or teams, can achieve it, since achieving it ends the game. To achieve that object is to win. Hence a formal game, by definition, has a winner; and winning is the 'end' of the game in both senses of the word, as termination and as object.

Means. It has an agreed set of equipment and of procedural 'rules' by which the equipment is manipulated to producing a winning situation. 'Every game has its rules', says Huizinga in *Homo Ludens*. But we may go further, and say 'Every game *is* its rules', for they are what define it.

Both these defining features need qualifying and amplifying.

The first might lead us to consider one-player games a contradiction in terms. If there is only one contender, wherein lies the contest? Nevertheless, activities such as playing-card Patience and peg Solitaire feel like games and are commonly spoken of as games. They involve equipment and rules of movement; they have as their objective the achievement of a winning situation; and some, indeed, can be played almost as they stand by two or more contenders. Rather than exclude them from classification as games, it would be more sensible to regard competition as taking place between the player and the game itself—or Dame Fortune, or Lady Luck, if you prefer to personify it. A Patience game does not always come out: if it does, you win; if it does not, you lose. Similar remarks apply to so-called co-operative games, as promoted by those who cannot distinguish between competition and aggression. A co-operative game is not in fact devoid of contest, as its enthusiasts maintain: it is in effect a multi-player solitaire, since players compete as a team against the game, and either win or lose as a team. Such games might better be described as 'collective'.

The second—that winning defines the end of a game— appears to have exceptions; but closer examination shows that they are not exceptions so much as variations on a theme.

Theme. In most board games the game ends, as stated, when one contender has achieved a winning situation, such as getting home or capturing a king.

First variation. In some games, such as Tric-Trac, Pagoda, and most card games, play continues until someone reaches a target score. But this is not greatly different from the first, as it simply defines the winning situation as the attainment of that score. Alternatively, you can regard each scoring point as the end of a part-game, of which several constitute one whole game.

Second variation. In many games, especially sports or field games, play continues for a specified period of time, at the end of which the winning side is the one with the higher score. But this still amounts to reaching a winning situation, with the additional feature that time is an essential ingredient in the definition of that situation. Football, for example, does not by nature have to be played this way. It could be played the second way, up to a target score of, say, three goals; or the first way, which would be the same as setting a target score of one goal.

Reference to 'equipment' in the second part of the definition does not necessarily mean physical equipment specifically designed for games. In word-games, for example, the equipment may consist of no more than the players' organs of speech and a vocabulary of indefinite size.

Formal games are divided into sports and non-sports. There is no adequate term for the second category, unless you simply call them 'games' and then deny that term to sports such as football and tennis. They are sometimes called 'indoor' games, since sports are typically played out of doors; and sometimes 'mental' games, since sports involve physical activity, especially body-eye co-ordination. *Cassell's Book of Sports and Pastimes* (1893) quaintly refers to sports as 'manly games', but then lacks the courage of its convictions by failing to classify Chess and Draughts as 'womanly' or 'wimpish'. 'Table games', since they are typically played on tables, also will not entirely do. As for physicality, Snooker involves hand-eye co-ordination but sits uneasily on the 'sports' side of the semantic fence. None of these descriptions entirely marks them off from sports, for many sports are typically played indoors (squash), by women (hockey), or on tables (table tennis), and it would be silly to pretend that they fail to engage the mental faculties in the way that non-sports typically fail to engage the physical.

There are, in fact, several ways of distinguishing sports from non-sport games. For example, sports are 'time-bound' and games 'time-free'. In a time-bound game, such as tennis, you have only a very limited time in which to think about your next move before making it—wait too long, and the ball goes out of court. Chess, on the other hand is so notoriously time-free by nature that clock-rules have to be artificially introduced to prevent loss by boredom or old age. A simpler distinction may be made by noting that games are sports if they are sufficiently physical to require the participant's bodily presence. You can play Chess and Diplomacy by post, and card games, as James I reputedly did, by instructing your card-holding servant what to play, but you cannot play football by post, tennis by proxy, or, if it comes to that, golf blindfold.[2]

Games and Game-boards

Now, perhaps, we can return to defining a board game. 'Board' derives from a word originally meaning 'plank', and secondarily 'table', as in the phrase 'bed and board'. So, in a broad sense, a board game is any that can be played on a flat surface such as a table or floor. In practice, the term usually excludes card and dice games; unfortunately, there is less unanimity as to exactly what it *in*cludes. Before embarking on this book I asked various people what they would expect to find covered under the heading 'board games'. As expected, some immediately replied 'Chess, Draughts, Backgammon, Ludo, Snakes & Ladders . . .' and then added, as an afterthought, 'Oh, and Monopoly, Cluedo, Diplomacy, Scrabble . . .' (etc.), while others immediately replied, 'Monopoly, Cluedo, Diplomacy, Scrabble . . .' and then added, as an afterthought, 'Oh, and Chess, Draughts, Backgammon, Ludo, Snakes & Ladders . . .' (etc.). There are obviously two understandings of the term 'board game' and we ought to cover both. The question is, how best to do this, and whether to accord them equal importance or find grounds for regarding one as central and the other as peripheral to our theme.

Step one is to find a sensible way of distinguishing the two groups. Seizing upon an obvious difference, we might start by thinking of *traditional* versus *proprietary* games, or *evolved* as opposed to *invented*. Chess, for instance, is a traditional or folk game, having no creditable individual inventor and being in the public domain, whereas Monopoly has a named inventor (two, in fact, but the principle is the same), and is protected by copyright. Any games company can therefore legally produce and market a Chess set and call it Chess, but Monopoly can only be produced under licence from those who own the copyright of the written rules and the design of the board, and in whose title the name of the game is registered. The trouble with this distinction is that it produces too many areas of overlap and uncertainty to be of any great practical value. For example, Ludo and Snakes & Ladders started out as commercially titivated versions of venerable folk games, but are now in the public domain and are naturally regarded as traditional rather than proprietary. Othello is a proprietary game whose sales put yen into Japanese coffers, but is virtually identical with Reversi, a game first published in England in the late nineteenth century and now out of copyright and so in the public domain.

Try again. How about *abstract* versus *representational*? We describe Monopoly as representational because it represents in game format the sort of real-life activity supposedly involved in the world of property speculation and trading. We think of Chess as abstract because, although we are aware of its origins as a war game, we no longer think of the pieces as elements of a medieval army when we actually play it. In play, a rook is not a chariot or a howdah, a ship or a castle, or even (like the Maltese Falcon) a black bird. Rather, it is a powerful piece that moves orthogonally, comes into its own on a relatively empty board, and can deliver mate even when (apart from the King) it is the last remaining piece. The trouble with this distinction, though, is much the same as with our first: it produces too many areas of doubt and overlap. Chess, to its inventors and earliest players, was as representational as our relatively modern game of Monopoly—more so, in that they regarded it as being of educational value in the basics of warfare. Nearly all the traditional games we now regard as abstract were in their day considered representational, or at least symbolic. The simplest process of moving pebbles round a circuit of holes in accordance with the throw of dice was universally perceived as representing a real-life race, while the precursor of Snakes & Ladders was a game of moral instruction. Conversely, when playing Monopoly, we forget the deficiencies of its representational aspirations—the ancient scale of values, the simplistic purchase of public utilities, the irrelevance of enjoying birthdays and winning second prize in a beauty contest—and slip automatically into the habit of thinking of moves and transactions in abstract terms. In short, no hard and fast distinction can be drawn between abstract and representational as a classification of games. How representational a game is depends on the level at which it is being played and the extent of its player's imagination.

A better way of distinguishing the two perceived groups may be as follows:

1. *Positional games* such as Chess, Draughts, and Backgammon. The defining feature of these is not that they are played on boards, but that they are played on a pattern of significant markings, such as an array of chequered squares or a network of lines and points, whose purpose is to define the movements and positions of the pieces in relation to one another. Such designs may be printed on a board, but may equally well be (and frequently are) drawn on the back of an envelope, chalked on a table, scraped in the sand, woven into tapestry, carved in wood, burnt into

leather, incised on slabs of stone, or called up on a VDU. The word 'positional' emphasizes that the play of the game centres entirely on the relative positions of pieces on the board itself. Traditional, national, and 'folk' games are all positional, but not all positional games are traditional—new ones of varying degrees of originality are still being invented, and sometimes find their way on to the market as proprietary games.

2. *Theme games* such as Monopoly, Cluedo, and Diplomacy. Such games are commercial and proprietary rather than traditional. They may contain positional elements by virtue of being played on a board, but their defining feature is that they are representational (property trading, murder solving, international relations, etc.), and may involve elements of role-play and quasi-dramatic performances, as in fantasy games. Carried to extremes, such games may amount to simulations of real-life events conducted for the purpose of experimentation, and thus pass beyond the normal meaning of the word 'game' as something practised for enjoyment and without regard to practical consequences. Typically, the board and pieces account for only part of the equipment, and often for only a small part at that, and the play of the game centres, so to speak, 'above' the board, in the minds and interactions of the players themselves. To this group also belong word games such as Scrabble, and quiz games such as Trivial Pursuit. And right at the bottom of this barrel—say the lower 90 per cent of it—come all those promotional games, TV spin-offs, and character-merchandizing exercises, of an essentially trivial, ephemeral, mind-numbing, and ultimately soul-destroying degree of worthlessness.

The aim of this book is primarily to present an historical survey of positional board games, but extending the story to modern and proprietary games wherever they can be shown to advance or expand on a traditional idea. Whether a proprietary game is abstract or representational has no effect on its inclusion or exclusion, for it is arguable that the long-term commercial success of a theme game depends on the power of involvement of its underlying abstract structure. What makes people want to go on playing a game once its theme is past its sell-by date is the fact that it remains engaging and exciting in spite of its outdated appearance and lack of topicality. On these grounds most of the games you see this Christmas on the shelves of Toys-Я-Us will not be obtainable a year hence, except as marked-down stock.

For completeness, mention should be made of a third and possibly fourth type of game involving a board of some sort. Cribbage is the best known of several card games which make use of a specially designed scoreboard, but since no interaction takes place on the board itself, they can be equally well played by scoring on paper, and therefore do not count as board games in the sense of the term used here. There are also a number of gambling games involving a board or cloth of special design on which the stakes are placed, such as Roulette and Crown & Anchor. Again, however, no interaction takes place between the stakes or counters on the board, and the play of the game would not be affected if the design were changed. These may be described as 'stake-board' games, and, being non-positional, may be remarked upon in passing but need not be regarded as central to our theme. Finally, some games normally played with pencil and paper can be classed as board games, notably Noughts & Crosses (Tic-Tac-Toe) and Boxes. Those that can are included in this survey.

Types of Board Game

Murray distinguishes five classes of traditional board game:

1. Games of alignment and configuration, the aim being to get all one's pieces arranged in a line or other specified configuration (cf. Noughts and Crosses).
2. War games, the aim being (fundamentally) to capture or immobilize all the enemy pieces (Chess, etc.).
3. Hunt games, such as Fox & Geese, in which one player has a larger number of pieces and seeks to immobilize the other's singleton, or smaller force.
4. Race games, the aim being to be the first to get one's piece or pieces 'home', usually in accordance with the throw of dice or other lots.
5. Mancala games, in which the aim is to capture a majority of neutral pieces (beans, seeds, etc.).

This classification is based on the rationale that 'games are typical of the early activities and occupations of man—the battle, the siege or hunt, the race, alignment, arrangement, and counting'.[3] Bell follows much the same classification, reducing it to four by subsuming Murray's hunt games under the heading war games. For the purpose of this survey I attempted several different classifications, but eventually finished by rearranging Murray's five and reducing them to four. The revision is strictly formal rather than hypothetically genetic—that is, based on a relative pattern of underlying abstract principles without reference to the cultural baggage of what they supposedly represent in real life,[4] though it seems a good idea to give them simple descriptive names. My proposed headings are *race games* (no change); *space games*, which includes and expands games of alignment and configuration; *chase games*, which almost corresponds to hunt games; and (for the sake of rhyme) *displace games*. The last-named embraces all games that are won by capturing a majority of pieces, or (as in Chess) a win-defining piece. This includes both war games and bean games (Mancala; cf. German *Bohnenspiele*).

To these I add a miscellaneous fifth group, *theme games*, to cover the plethora of modern board games chiefly characterized by a thematic subject matter, such as property trading or crime detection. Murray dismissed these from consideration on the grounds that most were played with dice and so amounted to primitive race games with juvenile decorations. This was a short-sighted view, even in his own day. For one thing, many such games were not race games, or were not necessarily devoid of strategic interest if they were; for another, all thematic games are bound to employ mechanisms and procedures based on or derived from traditional abstracts, in which case they are at least interesting, and may well embody significantly new mechanisms ('ludemes'), in which case they obviously command space in an evolutionary survey such as this.

Before describing these groups and previewing their contents it may help to define some basic terms. See also Table 1.1.

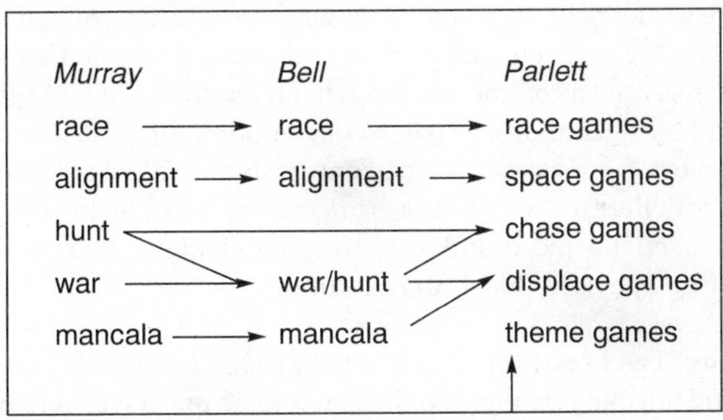

Fig. 1.1. Three types of game classification.

Piece means a gaming piece placed and moved upon a board. Murray uses the more traditional *man*, but this has developed peculiar connotations since his death, and I prefer to avoid it except in such compounds as chessman, draughtsman, tableman.

Field of action does not mean the physical surface of the board itself so much as the pattern of points or stations marked on it. A point or station is a position that may be occupied by one or more playing pieces. It may be indicated by a point, a hole, a pebble, an intersection of crossing lines, a cell defined by crossing lines, and so on. (More on this later.)

Objective or *aim* is self-explanatory. There are three main types of objective. One is to be the first to attain a winning spatial position, such as 'home' in race games such as Ludo, or the opposite side of the board in space games such as Chinese Checkers. Another is to command the board by overwhelming the opposition, such as by removing all opposing pieces as in Draughts, capturing their commander as in Chess, or (rarely) immobilizing them all. A third is to command the board by occupying most of it, as in Go, or by preventing the opposition from placing or moving a piece, as in Pentominoes.

Placement. Some games start with an empty board, on which each player in turn places a piece on any desired vacant station. If the pieces can subsequently be moved, as in Merels, the game is one of placement and movement; if not, as in Go, it is one of placement only. If a player has no free choice as to where to place a piece, as in many race games including some relatives of Backgammon, this process is better described as *entry* rather than placement.

Interaction means the way in which pieces can attack and oppose one another. This may take the form of *capturing*, i.e. permanently removing from the game, as in Chess and Draughts; *ousting*, a term I introduce to denote forcing an enemy piece to abandon its station and move somewhere else, typically off the board so that it has to be entered again (as in Ludo and Backgammon); or *blockading* or *paralysing*, i.e. preventing an enemy piece from leaving its current position, either permanently or temporarily. Rare forms of attack are *demoting*, i.e. reducing the power or value of an enemy piece, and *converting*, i.e. changing ther ownership of the captured piece to that of the capturer.

Race games The board represents a linear race track with one or more starting and finishing points, and the aim is to be the first to get one's piece or pieces from Start to Home. The track may be a simple line (Ludo, Snakes & Ladders, Backgammon), or a closed loop (The Ahl Game). It may contain short-cuts by means of branches and forks, which is precisely what snakes and ladders are. It may be folded in upon itself so as to look like a two-dimensional field (Snakes & Ladders, Ashtapada), though it remains essentially linear in the sense that a piece can move only forwards or backwards, but not sideways except at a few points specifically marked as short-cuts.

Traditionally, movement is not free but is bound by the cast of dice or other lots. This makes them games of imperfect information, albeit of a fundamentally different type of imperfection from that of playing-cards and dominoes. (More on this in Chapter 2.) A historically recent development has been the replacement of dice by freedom of movement based on calculation and strategy. My own game of Hare & Tortoise, first published in 1974, was one of the earliest to exploit this hitherto vacant niche in the board game repertoire.

Interaction consists most typically in *ousting*, i.e. sending an opposing piece back to the start of the race when landing on the station it occupies, as in Ludo and Backgammon. Some race games also involve capturing. I distinguish four groups as follows:

1. Simple race games. Each player has only one piece to move and get home. This makes them games of no choice and therefore pure chance. (Snakes & Ladders.)
2. Complex race games. Each player has a small number of pieces to get home, typically two to four. This gives some choice of play and so introduces an element of skill. (Pachisi, Ludo.)
3. Multiplex race games. Each player has a large number of pieces to get home, typically fifteen. This considerably increases the skill factor. (The Tables family, Backgammon, etc.)
4. Strategic race games. There are no dice, movement being determined by calculation and strategy. (Hare & Tortoise.)

Space games This category embraces and extends Murray's 'games of alignment and configuration', and Bell's 'positional games'. The basic pattern is that players enter or move pieces upon a two-dimensional board with the aim of getting them into a specified pattern, configuration, or spatial position. They include games of placement, movement, and both. Interaction consists chiefly in blockading. Some, such as Go and Merels, also involve capture, thus forming a taxonomic overlap with war games. I distinguish seven groups, of which several are historically recent in origin or expansion.

1. Alignment. The aim is to move or form pieces into a line of three or more (Merels/Mill/Morris, Noughts & Crosses).
2. Connection. The aim is to form a line of pieces connecting opposite sides of the board (Hex, Twixt).
3. Traversal. The aim is to be the first to get all one's pieces across the board into their corresponding positions (Kono, Halma, Chinese Checkers).
4. Attainment. As above, but the game is won by getting just one piece across (The Jungle Game, Quandary, Epaminondas).

5. Configuration. The aim is to get all one's pieces arranged in a specified pattern (Agon, Shoulder to Shoulder). Clearance, as in Solitaire, is a special case of configuration, as demonstrated by playing it in reverse.
6. Restriction. The aim is to deny one's opponent any further power of movement or placement (Do-Guti, Pentominoes).
7. Occupation. The aim is to occupy the largest amount of territory (Go, Reversi/Othello).

All space games are two-dimensional and free-moving.

Chase games This group covers more than Murray's 'hunt games'. These he defines as played on a war-game board (such as a chessboard) between two players, of whom one has many pieces and the other only one or two, and never more than four. Only the player with fewer pieces can capture. The aim of the larger force is to capture the smaller, or at least to hem it in so as to be unable to evade capture or reach safety. The aim of the smaller force is to reach a position of safety, or to capture enough of the larger force to avoid defeat. For the former it is therefore a war game, for the latter an 'attainment' space game. Thus the distinguishing feature of this group is its fundamentally bilateral asymmetry, for in all other types of game the players start in equal positions and with equal resources, enjoy equal powers of movement and interaction, and have identical objectives. Any classification based solely on mechanism and without regard to theme cannot do other than place all such asymmetrical games in the same class. My category of chase games therefore includes the Tafl group, which Murray and Bell class as war games, though Murray distinguishes it as a siege game rather than a battle game.

Displace games I retain the term 'war games' for those played mainly on two-dimensional boards in which the aim is to achieve dominance by capturing all one's opponent's material, or so much of it as to render its eventual annihilation theoretically inevitable. It is not an ideal term, as it has come to denote, since Murray's day, the specialized field of recreational board war-gaming which I here consider under the heading theme games. For traditional abstracts, however, Murray's definition is well worth quoting: 'The typical battle game is one in which two players direct a conflict between two armies of equal strength upon a field of battle, circumscribed in extent and offering no advantage of ground to either army.' Murray here contrasts 'battle game' with his 'siege' category of war game, which, as explained above, I transfer to the class of chase games. From this class also I differ from Murray in excluding the oriental game of Go or Wei-qi, which hovers on the border between space games and war games. The deciding factor in favour of classing it with space games is that it involves placement only, not movement, and therefore engages a different set of mental processes and strategic skills.

War games are mostly played on an areal or reticular grid, typically squared, and are all games of movement, except to the extent of overlap with spatial games that involve capturing, such as Go. The object is to overwhelm the enemy forces, usually by capturing all or most of them, as in Draughts, or by capturing the chief piece, as in Chess. Interaction consists in capturing pieces by various means, such as enclosure or custodianship (Latrunculi), jumping or leaping (Draughts), replacement (Chess), and so on. Murray classifies, or at least treats of, war games according to their method of capture. I prefer to classify according to whether and to what extent the pieces are functionally differentiated—that is, whether they have the same or varied powers of movement and capture.

1. Linear (and undifferentiated). A few primitive games, such as Tablan and Puluc, are played on a linear track or one-dimensional board. Bell calls these 'running fight games'. They bear some resemblance to bean games.
2. Undifferentiated. Pieces are differentiated as to ownership but not as to function throughout play. (Latrunculi, Fanorona, Alquerque.)
3. Semi-differentiated. This specifically categorizes the Draughts family as an extension of the above, in that pieces become functionally differentiated by promotion.
4. Differentiated. Pieces are differentiated as to function from the outset. The Chess family, its chief representative, is further categorized by the fact that the aim is to capture a distinctive singleton (the king).

Bean games, such as Mancala and Owari, are also games of movement and material capture. These resemble linear war games, but enjoy the distinction unique among non-solitaire games of being played with pieces that are completely neutral, being undifferentiated as to power, function, value, and even ownership. Bean games are played on a linear track, consisting of holes scooped in the ground or bowls carved from wood, and arranged in the form of a closed loop folded in upon itself into two or more rows. The holes are initially filled with pieces represented by seeds, nuts, pebbles, or similar objects. Movement consists in taking the contents of a bowl and dropping them one by one into subsequent bowls in a forwards direction. Certain configurations and positions entitle a player to capture pieces, and the winner is the player who captures most.

Table 1.1. The significant features of the five main classes of games.

Class	field	equal	movement	interaction	objective
Race games	linear	yes	dice-bound	oust	attain position
Space games	areal	yes	free	block capture	attain position make patterns gain territory
Chase games	reticular	no	free	capture	1 = attain position 2 = overwhelm
Displace games	any	yes	free	capture	overwhelm

Boards Linear, Areal, and Reticular

A linear track suitable for a race game can be made by making a line of holes in the ground or similar surface and moving a piece from hole to hole, or of solid objects like pebbles and moving a piece from pebble to pebble, or of straight objects like twigs and moving a piece from space to space between them. Its length can be increased by looping it into a circle, and the interest of the game by adding lines to form short cuts (Fig. 1.2).

Another way of increasing the length of the track is to fold it round into layers. From this it is a short step to drawing a network of lines crossing at right-angles, and moving a piece either from point to point on the intersections, or from space to space in the square cells between them (Fig. 1.3).

An areal game can obviously be derived from a linear one by first enfolding the line of points or spaces upon itself to produce a two-dimensional figure, and then agreeing that a piece can move in any rectilinear direction instead of necessarily following the originally intended linear path. (The

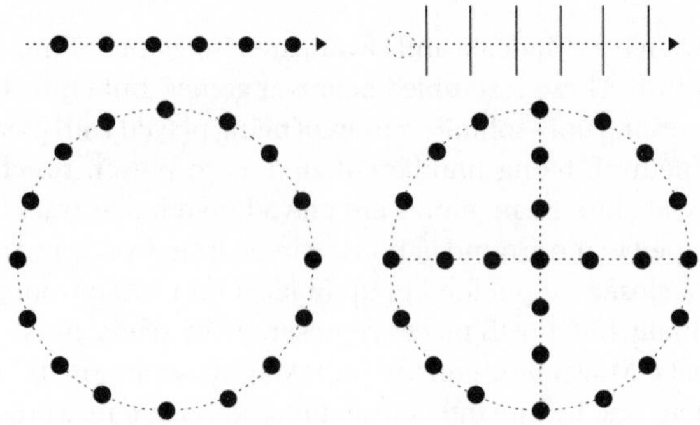

Fig. 1.2. Tracks linear and looped, movement on points or on spaces between.

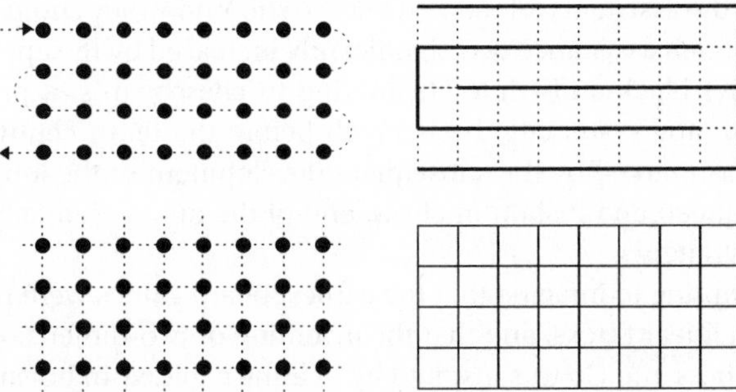

Fig. 1.3. How reticular and areal boards (*below*) may be derived (topologically, not necessarily historically) by folding a linear track in upon itself.

modern mind will naturally add 'or in any diagonal direction', but there is evidence to suggest that this is not as obvious as it appears.) Whether a game is played on the points or the cells is not necessarily significant, and one may transpose easily into the other. Chinese Chess, as Murray observes, was originally played on the cells but is now played on the points, and when the Norsemen played Tafl they happily did so on either the points of an even-celled board or the cells of an odd-celled board. However, while it is always possible to play a celled game on the points, the reverse is not necessarily true, or at least is not very practicable. Some games, notably those of the Merels and the Fox & Geese families, are played on points which are joined by diagonal lines in some directions but not in others, and it is a rule of play that a piece can only move along a line. In Fig. 1.4 for example, the fact that a piece can move between (a) and (c), but not between (d) and (b), is explicit when play takes place on the points of a properly lined board, but not when on the cells of a squared board.

Games such as this may be regarded as mid-way between linear and areal. I describe them as 'reticular', since the grids used for them have the appearance of nets or networks. They may suggest that the extension of play from orthogonal to diagonal moves took some time to effect, at first

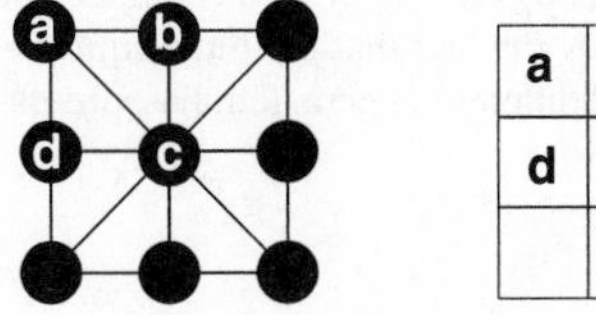

Fig. 1.4. Reticular boards (*left*) render asymmetrical moves explicit.

requiring the assistance of marked lines to show how they could and might be made. Such assistance was significantly increased by the application of (nominally) black-and-white chequering to chessboards, a practice not applied on any systematic basis much before the tenth century. Its significance is marked by the subsequent development of the long diagonal move of queen and bishop in chess, and of the quintessentially diagonal game of Draughts.

It is tempting to imagine that the earliest board games were race games played on linear tracks, and that the invention of two-dimensional games such as Chess and Go was inspired by treating a folded-in linear track as a network with freedom of movement in all directions. Murray, in fact, argues that the Ashtapada board used for Chaturanga, the Indian precursor of Chess, was originally a race game. Such developments are plausible on purely notional grounds, and may in fact have happened on some occasions, but there is no evidence to suggest that areal games invariably derived from linear ones. If we think of linear games as relatively primitive, we must mean this in terms of complexity rather than time.

The forerunners of Backgammon were played on boards consisting of two, three, or four rows of six or more squares each. Primitive war games, such as the Greek Petteia and the Roman Latrunculi, used grids of various sizes, usually rectangular but not always square, ranging in size from six to twelve in each dimension. (The one found at Colchester just as I was revising this chapter was of order 12×8.) The 8×8 board soon came to dominate and eventually to establish itself as standard for a variety of games, having the advantage of being easily produced by repeated halving, and of yielding a number of squares sufficiently small to keep track of but sufficiently large for variety of play.

NOTES

1. E. M. Avedon and B. Sutton-Smith, *The Study of Games* (New York, 1971), 5.
2. I am assured that there are, in fact, blind golfers. But even they would not think of playing blindfold.
3. Murray, *History of Board Games*, 4.
4. Any attempt to classify games by analogy with the genetic classification of the living world is inherently doomed by the fact that the ludic equivalent of genes ('ludemes') pass freely between games of different genera, families, orders, and so on.

RACE GAMES

The Role of Dice

How to be Imperfectly Informed

I govern innumerable men but must acknowledge that I am governed by birds and thunderclaps.

J. Caesar (according to Thornton Wilder, *The Ides of March*)

God does not play dice.

A. Einstein (according to B. Hoffman: *Albert Einstein: Creator and Rebel*)

All games are customarily divided into three parts: those of pure chance, such as Snakes & Ladders; those of pure skill, such as Chess; and those of mixed chance and skill, such as Backgammon. Whereas types of skill are many and various, involving such mental abilities as memory, forward visualization, manipulation of objects in space, deduction, practical psychology, and so on, chance is mainly associated with the influence on play of randomizing elements such as dice, or the shuffling of cards.

In fact, none of these perceptions is entirely unquestionable. For example, the outcome of a single Chess game between well-matched players may be influenced by such chance factors as which side of the bed either player got out of this morning, or which is suffering from dyspepsia or recovering from a divorce. If these are dismissed as irrelevant because extrinsic to the rules of the game, there is still the question of deciding who plays white and so has the statistical advantage of moving first. At the other extreme, it is well known that committed dice-players implicitly believe that the outcome depends on their skill in casting. As Dennis Tedlock remarks in respect of native American Indian dice-play:

> We might call it a 'game of chance', which is what Culin calls similar games in this book,[1] but that expresses the point of view of an observer. Meanwhile, the participants constantly think in terms of strategy, pitting their wishes against chance in momentary acts of magic, which is what we all find ourselves doing when we throw dice.

Dice are still used in modern board games normally regarded as games of skill. In board war-gaming especially, their role is not to determine movement, which instead is dictated by quasi-military skills of strategy and tactics, but rather to decide the outcome of local areas of conflict. In this respect it might be correct but would be misleadingly pejorative to describe them as elements of chance. Rather, they are elements of reality, since, in everyday life, no outcome of any significance is determined entirely by will and by skill, or is entirely uninfluenced by other 'players' or elements beyond our control. Or again, in Monopoly they certainly determine our movement at each turn, but that does not prevent it from being one of skill overall.

Ancient and traditional board games involving dice, however, are relatively simple, and of two main types. In those described as race games, the aim is primarily to be the first to get one's piece or pieces from start to home, and the distance travelled at each move is dictated by a random number generator such as dice. A good generic term for such generators is 'lots'. (Dice are not the only example—there are lots of others.) In the second the game is primarily one of dice, and the board is merely a device for recording bets placed on the outcome. I call these stake-board games, for want of a generally agreed term.

Dice-bound race games are generally classed as games of 'imperfect information', but the nature of their imperfection is quite different from that of other 'imperfect' games like cards and dominoes. In card games, information is imperfect because although you know what you yourself are holding, you do not know what cards others hold until they are played. The information you lack therefore relates to something that was determined in the past—by the shuffle and deal—and may therefore be described as 'past imperfect' information. In games where moves are determined by dice, on the other hand, you can always see what the current position is and know what resources both you and your opponents held from the outset. The information you lack is what numbers will be generated on future throws of the dice. Such games may therefore be described as being of 'future imperfect' information. In race games, you travel from the known to the unknown, so to speak, whereas in card games you travel from the unknown to the known. In card games, any plans you may be able to make for the future are based on deduction and inference from what has gone before. In race games, what has gone before is irrelevant (except in so far as it may throw light on your opponent's habits in decision-making), and any plans you may be able to make can only be based on your knowledge of probabilities. Of course, this last observation assumes comparison between games involving choice of moves and therefore the exercise of skill, such as Bridge *vis-à-vis* Backgammon. But there are both card games and race games that present you with no decisions to make and hence no skill to employ, such as certain Patience games on one hand and Snakes & Ladders on the other. In such cases the distinction between past and future imperfect information is irrelevant. In games, as in life, the purpose of information is to influence choice. If you have no choice, there's not much point in being informed.

Lots in gaming have been held to derive from a primary use in divination and soothsaying, with a secondary stage in which they are used as a way of making decisions impartially. The essential difference between these stages, according to Tylor, is the same as that between *will* and *shall.* [2] If your augurs report favourably on the bones they have cast or the cards they have turned, you may or may not decide to act accordingly ('will'), but if your belief is great you may consider yourself very wise to do so ('shall'). Thus a more superstitious ruler than Wilder's Julius Caesar would follow the advice implicit in the omens and so employ them as an impartial decision-making machine. Caesar's own officers would have cast lots in the process of 'decimating' a disgraced legion by executing one in ten soldiers. When certain other Roman soldiers cast lots to decide which of them should have the seamless (hence indivisible) garment worn by Jesus, they entered into a notional contract whereby it was agreed that one of them should 'win' something in accordance with the outcome of an uncontrollable and so impartial decision maker. Whether or not they were technically 'playing a game' is arguable. Certainly the association between gambling and playing is strong enough for religious leaders through the ages to condemn play by tarring it with the same brush as that used for casting lots.

The boundaries between soothsaying, decision-making, and gaming strike me as so blurred as to call into question the preoccupation of nineteenth-century ethnologists with showing how Amerindian gaming sticks (for example) were derived from 'divinatory arrows'. It seems more reasonable to regard lot-casting as a generalized activity that has always been employed seriously, curiously, or playfully, according to temperament and circumstance. One of these three aspects may well be genuinely anterior to the others, but the actual progression, I believe, is too remote to be demonstrable.

Binary Lots

The most primitive lots were binary in operation—like the latest computer and reprographic technology, paradoxically enough. They usually consisted of a handful of natural objects which, when thrown and allowed to fall at random, would each come to rest with either of two distinctive faces uppermost. Many cultures used arrows or staves consisting of twigs split lengthwise in two so as to fall either flat or rounded side up. Five such staves accompany a gameboard found in Tutankhamen's tomb, and three with another in the royal graves at Ur. Pyramidal dice found in other royal graves were apparently binaries, with two of their four corners marked and two left plain. The Indians of Asia have been using cowrie shells from 2300 BC to the present day, and those of the *Rig Veda* (*c.*1500 BC) used multiples of the naturally binary vibhitaka nut:

> The nuts, born where the wind blows the lofty tree,
> delight me with their rolling on the board.
> The cheering vibhitaka has brought me joy,
> like a draught of soma from Mount Mujavant.[3]

Amerindian binaries illustrated by Culin were made from such varied materials as bone, brass, cane, china, corn grain, fruit stones, ivory, leather, limestone, nuts, nut shells, pottery, sea shells, and wood. Several binary lots would be thrown together to give a reasonable number of different outcomes. Thus the six outcomes of a cubic die are paralleled by the six outcomes of five binaries, which when thrown together may fall with 5, 4, 3, 2, 1, or 0 marked or unmarked sides uppermost. 'Marked' and 'unmarked' sides are equivalent to the '1' and '0' of binary arithmetic. And yet five binary lots are not precisely equivalent to a six-faced die, for they produce a different statistical range of outcomes. With a cube, every number from 1 to 6 has an equal probability of being thrown—namely 1 in 6, or 16.67 per cent. With five binaries, however, the outcomes are:

Marked sides up	0	1	2	3	4	5
Ways of occurring (in 32)	1	5	10	10	5	1
Probability (per cent)	3	16	31	31	16	3

Table 2.1. Comparison between dice and lots.

2 × six-sided-dice			10 binary lots		
cast	coms.	prob.	prob.	coms.	cast
2	1	2.8	0.1	1	0
3	2	5.6	1.0	10	1
4	3	8.3	4.4	45	2
5	4	11.1	11.7	120	3
6	5	13.9	20.5	210	4
7	6	16.7	24.6	252	5
8	5	13.9	20.5	210	6
9	4	11.1	11.7	120	7
10	3	8.3	4.4	45	8
11	2	5.6	1.0	10	9
12	1	2.8	0.1	1	10

A similar statistical imbalance arises with dice themselves when more than one are cast at a time, but the probabilities still differ from those of an equivalent number of binary lots. This is illustrated in Table 2.1, which compares, as between two six-sided dice and ten binary lots, the eleven possible numbers yielded by a single cast, the number of possible combinations yielding each number, and its resultant probability (expressed as a percentage).

Dice yield less extreme results than binary lots, as can be seen from a graph of their relative curves (Fig. 2.1). Cubes have always tended to oust binaries where both are known, probably because they are more convenient, but perhaps also because they bring the rarer numbers more frequently into play. If you played Monopoly with 10 binaries instead of two dice, for example, the proportion of extreme throws (0–3 and 7–10, equivalent to 2–5 and 9–12) would fall from more than half (56 per cent) to little more than a third (35 per cent).

Primitive players needed no mathematical sophistication to note that the rarer binary throws are extremely rare and the commoner ones extremely common, and to attach proportionally greater rewards to the rarer casts. The actual rewards, however, tended to accord with the logic of the game rather than with that of mathematical strictness. For example, the White Mountain Apache game of 'Bounce-on-the-rock'[4] uses three sticks with flat and rounded sides as follows:

round sides up	0	1	2	3
move forwards	5	2	3	10+
comparison (× 2)	6	2	2	6

The last line shows what the moves would be if calculated in accordance with the strict probability of the throw. (Actually 3–1–1–3, here doubled to

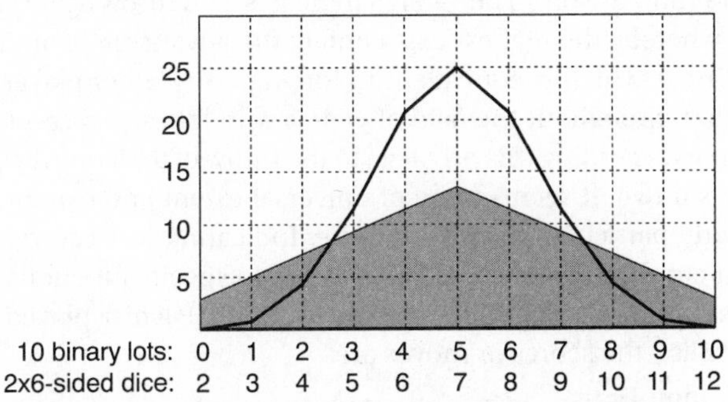

Fig. 2.1. Probability curves for binary lots (shaded area) and six-sided dice show that dice produce more dramatic contrasts and hence more exciting games.

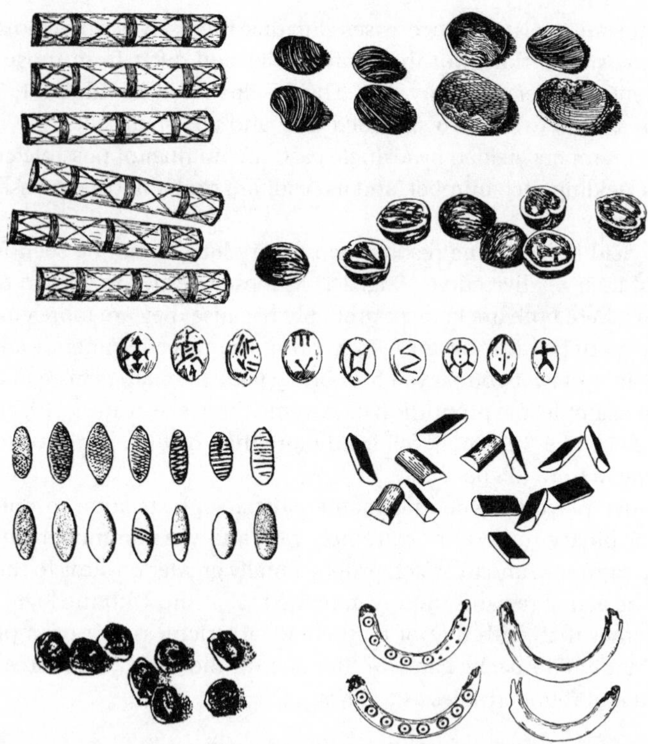

Fig. 2.2. Amerindian binary lots (from Culin): sticks (Pomo Indians, Calif.), sea shells (Hupa, Calif.), walnut shells (Yokuts, Calif.), plum stones (Cheyenne, Mont.), bone (Tanner Springs, Ariz.), wood (White Mountain Apache, Ariz.), corn grain (Choctaw, Louisiana), beaver teeth (Snohomish Indians).

clarify the comparison.) The '+' sign indicates 'and throw again'. This game element whereby the highest cast confers the advantage of an immediate second throw, which is equivalent to forcing every other player to miss a turn, recurs throughout the field of games with lots and dice—think of all those games according this privilege to the throw of a 6 if one die is used, or of doubles if two. It seems to be of universal extent and cannot be traced back to any particular game or culture. Indicating its occurrence with a plus-sign emphasizes how lots can be used to specify functions as well as quantities. In a version of the Indian game of Pachisi played with five cowrie shells,[5] the scores or moves are:

mouths up	0	1	2	3	4	5
move forwards	6+	10+	2	3	4	25+
comparison (× 2)	20	10	2	2	10	20

The Tewa (Amerindian) horse-race game of Tugi-e-pfe[6] also involves three sticks with flat and rounded sides, but elaborated in that one of them has notches incised on the rounded side. In the following table 'n' denotes that the notched stick is included among those falling round side up:

round side up	0	1	1n	2	2n	3n
move forwards	5	3	15	1	?	10
comparison (× 3)	6	3	6	6	3	6

(Culin gives no figure for the box marked (?)).

The moves awarded correspond badly with the probabilities, but it is interesting to note how closely the series 1-3-5-10-15 resembles that of the series of triangular numbers, namely 1-3-6-10-15-. A similar series occurs in the Kiowans' Ahl game[7] where the number of flat sides occurring when five sticks are thrown, 1-2-3-4-0, accords moves of 1-2-3-6-10 respectively.

We should add, as a footnote, that it is only as motors for race games that binary lots are mainly associated with primitive cultures. They remain as popular as ever today in the form of coin-tossing under such names as Odds and Evens, or Heads and Tails. Aristophanes knew it as *artiasmos*, Ovid and Livy as *par-impar*, medieval Europeans variously as *caput aut navis* (head and ship), *croix et pile* (cross and pile), *fiori o santi* (flowers or saints), *Wappen oder Schrift* (arms or writing).

Astragals

The astragal is a quaternary lot, yielding a number of outcomes intermediate between the two of binaries and the six of dice. The word comes from the Greek for knuckle-bone, those of sheep or goats having been used as playthings from time immemorial. As forerunners of the game of Fivestones, or Jacks, they are depicted in play by two young girls in a terracotta sculpture of about 800 BC in the British Museum. Their use as lots is attested from the royal graves of Palestine and by early classical writers. They are roughly cuboid, but, as two of the sides are curved and unstable, only four outcomes are possible when they are cast on a hard surface (six, however, on a yielding surface such as dry sand). The four are traditionally designated, according to the character of the uppermost face, as *flat, concave, convex,* and *sinuous.* Hyde illustrates these and labels them *supinum, pronum, planum, tortuosum,* associated respectively with the numbers 1-3-4-6. The Romans knew this device as *talus* in its natural form

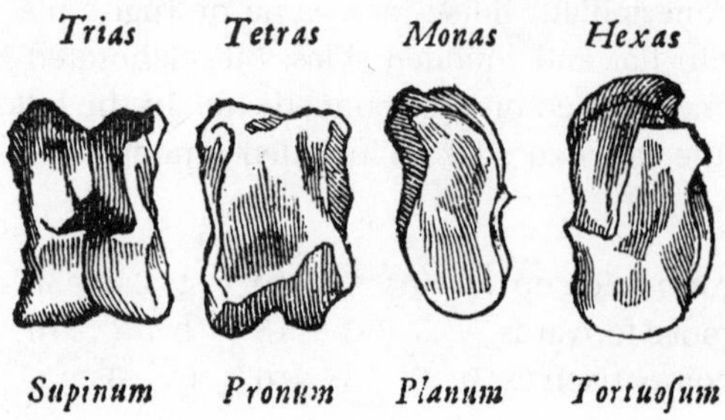

Fig. 2.3. Astragal results (3-4-1-6), after Hyde.

as a knuckle-bone, or *alea* as an artificial equivalent carved from wood or other workable material. It was they who used the numbering 1-3-4-6 for race games and pure dice games. As dice games, the aim was often to make combinations rather than totals. In a game played with four astragals, the winning throw of 1–3–4–6 was known as *Venus,* the losing throw of 1-1-1-1 as *canis,* 'dog'. Astragals were used for the Roman forerunner of Backgammon, *Ludus Duodecim Scriptorum,* the 'Game of Twelve Lines'.

Long Dice

Other quaternary lots were produced in the form of 'long dice', square in section and with four long rectangular faces—like flat-sided pastels, only less colourful. The so-called *pasaka,* or *pas,* found in the Indus valley sites of the Epic period, is still preferred for play, often with four of them linked together on a spindle. The Epic long dice are marked 1-2-3-4; those used later for Dice Chess have 2-3-4-6, Chaupar has 1-2-6-5 or 1-3-4-6, and two found in the lake village at Meare 3-4-5-6.[8]

Long dice are not necessarily four-sided but may present any larger number of flat, oblong faces equivalent to the number of sides of their polygonal cross-section. The Korean Game of Dignitaries employs a pentagonal long die, with from one to five nicks carved into its longitudinal edges and painted red.[9]

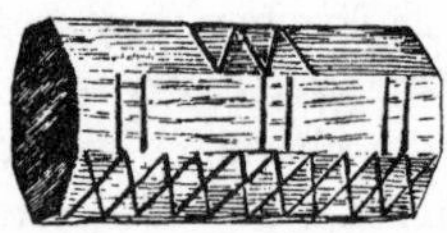

Fig. 2.4. Long Lawrence (after Culin).

A traditional English long die of carved wood, as described by Alice Gomme,[10] was designated Lang Larence, or Long Lawrence. It was either square or octagonal in section, with four sides bearing distinctive markings, the whole series being repeated in the case of the eight-sided Lawrence, which of course rolled better. The markings were:

1. Three transverse cuts, one at each end and one in the middle.
2. Five diagonal cuts at alternating angles producing a series of four linked Vs.
3. Six transverse cuts produced by doubling those of the three cuts.
4. Ten Xs linked at the corners to produce a trellis pattern running the full length of the side—reminiscent of the gridiron on which St Lawrence died and hence possibly the origin of its name.

That it was used for playing a version of Put & Take (a teetotum game; see below) is indicated by the fact that 'The sides are considered to bear the names "Flush", "Put doan two", "Lave all", "Sam up one".' R. C. Bell's remarkable collection of gaming paraphernalia includes a Long Lawrence, which he found in a junk shop.

Cubical dice

Herodotus credits the invention of cubical dice to the Lydians of Asia Minor. Murray endorses this, none being known from Egypt before the seventh century BC, and those found subsequently mostly belonging to the Roman period. They reached India in the sixth century AD as instrumental to the Persian game of Nard, but never displaced the *pasa* in native Indian games.

Etruscan dice are variously numbered with the pairing of opposite sides as (1-2)(3-4)(5-6), (1-2)(3-5)(4-6), (1-3)(2-4)(5-6), but the ancient Greeks

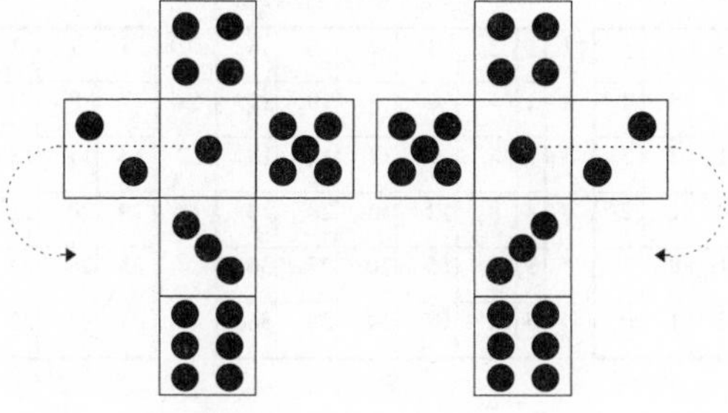

Fig. 2.5. Left- and right-handed dice.

made opposite sides total 7, a tradition that has received virtually universal acceptance. Such universality is probably due to the intuitive feeling that the arithmetically most symmetrical arrangement ensures the most even distribution of weight—as indeed would be the case if the spots were to be incarnated as solid inserts like blobs of lead. Curiously, no such universality attaches to the right- and left-handedness of dice. A die is right-handed if, when you look at the corner surrounded by the lower numerals, the numbers 1-2-3 read in clockwise rotation, and are left-handed otherwise.

In practice, I can find no reference to any such left–right standardization, and the several dozen I have immediately to hand from various sources are about equally divided between the two. From a practical viewpoint, of course, it makes no difference: any literal weight that might be attached to the spots would be equally balanced regardless of handedness. Even so, the traditional superstitiousness of gamblers leaves one surprised to find no mention in the literature of gaming of the presumably *sinister* implications of left-handed dice.

The traditional English names of the six sides of a die are Norman French, or Anglo-Norman, namely *ace, deuce, trey, quater, cinc, sice.* These are long since lost in respect of dice, but the first three survive through being transferred to playing-cards. 'Ace' remains universal in extent, but *deuce* and *trey* are now heard only in gambling games such as Poker, and more in American than in British parlance.

A variety of different totals and statistical effects can easily be produced by varying the markings or methods of combining the throws of ordinary cubical dice. For example, taking the differences instead of the totals of two standard cubes (first table) gives a skewed range of outcomes from 0 to 5—or, if you call doublets 6, a different pattern of outcomes of 1 to 6 from that of throwing a single die. Multiplying the faces of two dice instead of adding them (second table) produces a skewed and incomplete range of products

	1	*2*	*3*	*4*	*5*	*6*
1	0	1	2	3	4	5
2	1	0	1	2	3	4
3	2	1	0	1	2	3
4	3	2	1	0	1	2
5	4	3	2	1	0	1
6	5	4	3	2	1	0

	1	*2*	*3*	*4*	*5*	*6*
1	1	2	3	4	5	6
2	2	4	6	8	10	12
3	3	6	9	12	15	18
4	4	8	12	16	20	24
5	5	10	15	20	25	30
6	6	12	18	24	30	36

	1	*2*	*3*	*4*	*5*	*6*
0	1	2	3	4	5	6
6	7	8	9	10	11	12
12	13	14	15	16	17	18
18	19	20	21	22	23	24
24	25	26	27	28	29	30
30	31	32	33	34	35	36

Fig. 2.6. Two six-sided dice can be used in more varied ways than by mere addition. These are the results of subtraction, multiplication, and equiprobable distribution.

from 1 to 36, while all numbers from 1 to 36 can be produced with equal probability by numbering one of two dice with every multiple of 6 from 0 to 30 (third table).

Some games of the Backgammon family are played with three dice, and employ various devices to reproduce the effect of three if only two happen to be available. Other effects are produced by changing the shape of the die. Any of the five Platonic solids can and have been used: the tetrahedron with four triangular faces, the cube with six squares, the octahedron with eight triangles, the dodecahedron with twelve pentagons, and the icosahedron with twenty triangles. Many of these are exploited in modern board war games and fantasy role-playing games, where, for example, '3D10' is a common shorthand for 'use three ten-sided dice'; but even the Alfonso manuscript of 1283 calls for such oddities as seven- and eight-sided dice—and that for so-called Great Chess played on a 10 × 10 square board.

Teetotums

The original teetotum was a cubic die threaded on a spindle so that only four of its sides were capable of falling uppermost. It was used for a popular sixteenth-century German gambling game, illustrated as a children's game in the bottom left-hand corner of Pieter Bruegel's painting *Kinderspiel* (1560). The device was known by its French name *toton*, evidently a corruption of the Latin *totum*, and its four sides bore the initials P-N-J-F, or A-R-J-F. Each in turn paid a stake to the pool, spun the toton, and followed the instruction specified by the letter falling uppermost as follows:

P (French *piller*, 'plunder') or A (Latin *accipe*, 'receive'): the player retrieves his stake.
N (Spanish *nada*, 'nothing') or R (French *rien*): a stand-off.
J (Middle French *jocque*, 'game'): the player doubles his stake.
F (French *fors*, 'out'): the player sweeps the pool and may retire.

Under the name Dreidel (or German Kreisel), the game remains popular with Jewish children during the eight days of *Hanukkah*, the Festival of Lights, or Purim.[11] The sides bear the Hebrew initials of the message *Neš gadol hayah sham*, 'a great miracle happened there' (or, in examples from Jerusalem, 'here', which is P for *poh*).[12]

N = nothing
H = win half the pool
S = add a stake to the pool
G = sweep the pool

Its English counterpart appears in the early eighteenth century as a square piece of board with a spindle through the centre, allowing it to be spun like a top. Three sides were blank and one marked with a 'T'—whence its name, originally written 'T-totum'. Stakes accumulated so long as blanks turned up, and the resultant pot was won by whoever was lucky enough to spin it to the T position. The square can be transposed into any regular polygon, and by the end of the century six-sided teetotums were regularly included in family board games in place of dice, in order, it was said, to protect the family atmosphere from the taint of the gaming table or gambling den. They are also cheaper to produce, of course. Specially marked six-sided devices of this kind were made in the nineteenth century for Put-and-Take, with additional instruction involving two counters. The sides were marked:

Put 1 = Put a counter in the pool
Put 2 = Put two counters in the pool
All put = all put 1 counter in the pool
Take 1, Take 2, Take All (self-explanatory).

Stake-Board Games

This survey cannot very well end without mention of some dice games which, though played on gaming boards, do not qualify as positional board games. Probably the best known of these to British players is the Royal Navy game of Crown & Anchor, which is also much played in Australia and may be encountered in the United States and India. Crown & Anchor is played

Fig. 2.7. Crown and Anchor.

with three dice whose six faces are marked with a spade, a heart, a club, a diamond, a crown, and an anchor. The board is typically printed on a piece of oilcloth for lightness and portability—as suggested by the earlier name of the game, 'Sweatcloth'—and is divided into six staking compartments with the same markings.

Punters stake on any of the six compartments and the banker casts the three dice from a cup. The stake on a given symbol wins at even money if it turns up on one die, at 2 to 1 on two, and at 3 to 1 on all three dice. Despite the banker's more than generous edge of 8 per cent, the game remains popular largely because the odds appear deceptively favourable in the eyes of an unsophisticated punter. Sweatcloth, played with ordinary dice and a board marked with six numbers, reached America towards the end of the eighteenth century and subsequently became the casino and carnival game known as Chuck-a-Luck, or Bird-Cage, from the appearance of the pivoted cage in which the dice were held and rotated. It was said of Wild Bill Hickock and his like that they loved the game 'probably because they never had enough upstairs to figure the odds against them'.[13] Chuck-a-Luck is the game so memorably shaken by Gloria Grahame for Robert Mitchum in *Macao* (RKO, 1952).

A substantially similar game is played by the Chinese under the title Hoo-Hey-How, or, more picturesquely, Fish-Prawn-Crab,[14] the six compartments and dice-sides being marked respectively with a fish, a prawn, a king crab, a flower, a butterfly, and a woman. More elaborate than both is an eighteenth-century game of Italian origin but perhaps best known, for musical rather than gaming reasons, under its German title *Eulenspiegel,* or 'Owlglass' (Italian *Il nuovo piacevole gioco del pelato chiù,* French *Jeu de la Chouette,* Dutch *Uilenbord*).

Stake-board games can be traced back to the sixteenth century. Johannes Amos Comenius (1592–1670) distinguished between dice games in which the aim was to throw the highest numbers, and those in which dice were thrown through a funnel onto a board marked with various numbers.[15] The Cluny Museum in Paris houses such a board, divided into twenty numbered compartments reminiscent of Roulette. Better known is the sixteenth century German game of Glückshaus, whose rules survive and from which the games described above derive.

Glückshaus is basically the same game as one called Pinke (Yiddish for 'purse') played on an ad hoc chalk-drawn board. It has eleven compartments numbered 2 to 12. Each in turn throws two dice. If the compartment corresponding to the cast is empty, the caster places a stake on it; if not, he wins the stake already there, leaving it empty again. This does not apply to compartment 7, the commonest throw, on which stakes are left to accumulate. Throwing a double-1 entitles a player to sweep all the stakes except that on compartment 7, while a double-6 sweeps the board entirely. This game remained popular in one form or another down to the nineteenth century, in a variety of designs and often incorporating the figure of Harlequin, which also provides the French name of the game.[16]

A similar board of 1583 has ten compartments in the spaces formed from a doubled cross, and these have background decorations reminiscent of playing-cards, with King equivalent to 12 and marriage to 7. As there is no 4, a player throwing it simply does nothing. A later example has on the back of it the design for a similar game known as 'Merry Seven' (*Die Lustige Sieben*), which includes compartments for doublets and sequences. Many games of this sort overlap with card games. The classic German game of Poch, for example,[17] is played with a staking board on which are marked possible outcomes of various simple manipulations with cards, though it would require little alteration to make a game equally playable with dice. The National Museum of Bavaria, Munich, houses a delightfully attractive board for a game called Card Roulette, in which the forty-eight cards of the old German pack (lacking Aces) are painted into a design consisting of four concentric circles divided into twelve radial segments.

A well-known dice board game requiring more elaborate equipment is Shut the Box, also called Trick-Track, said to have been a favourite game of sailors up and down the Normandy coast for more than two centuries.[18] The essentials are a surface on which two dice are thrown, integral with a row of boxes numbered 1 to 9 and having hinged lids. At start of play all boxes are open, the aim being to shut as many of them as possible. Each in turn throws two dice, and may shut the box corresponding in number to the total thrown, or the two boxes equivalent to the individual numbers, provided both are open. His turn continues until he either wins by getting all the boxes shut, or makes a throw whose numbers or total are already shut. When the total values of the open boxes amount to six or less, a player throws only one die. At the end of a turn, the total value of any open boxes is added to that player's penalty score, and if this brings it to 45 or over he withdraws from play. The winner is the first to shut all the boxes, or, if no one does, the last remaining in play.

These and many other stake-board games are non-positional, in that it makes no difference to the play in what order the staking compartments are arranged. The possible derivation of positional board games from stake-board games therefore seems inherently unlikely.

NOTES

1. Dennis Tedlock, in his introduction to a reprint of Culin, *Games of the North American Indians* (Lincoln and London, 1992), i, *Games of Chance*, 23.

2. E. B. Tylor, *Primitive Culture,* ch. 3. Quoted in E. M. Avedon and B. Sutton-Smith, *The Study of Games* (New York, 1971), 70.
3. Translation by A. L. Basham in *The Wonder that was India* (New York, 1954). Cited by Wayne Saunders, 'Counter Space (Part 1)', in *Game Times,* 25 (Dec. 1994).
4. Culin, *Chess and Playing-Cards,* 713.
5. *Qanoon-e-Islam,* 1832, cited by Tylor in Avedon and Sutton-Smith, *The Study of Games,* 81.
6. Culin, *Chess and Playing-Cards,* 762–3.
7. Ibid. 731.
8. Culin, *Games of the Orient,* 76.
9. Ibid. 77; Irving Finkel confirms their continued existence.
10. Alice Bertha Gomme, *The Traditional Games of England, Ireland and Scotland* (London, 1894), v. i. 326.
11. F. V. Grunfeld, *Games of the World* (UNICEF, Zurich, 1982), 142.
12. I am grateful to Irving Finkel for the parenthetical note.
13. Remark credited to Major A. Riddle, President of the Dunes, Las Vegas. See entry in Carl Sifakis, *The Encyclopedia of Gambling* (New York, 1990).
14. Bell, *Board and Table Games,* ii. 90; E. Glonnegger, *Das Spiele-Buch* (Ravensburg, 1988), 60.
15. W. Endrei, *Spiele und Unterhaltung im alten Europa* (Budapest, 1986), 31.
16. Glonnegger, *Das Spiele-Buch,* 58; Grunfeld, *Games of the World,* 140.
17. D. Parlett, *The Oxford Guide to Card Games* (Oxford, 1990), 87.
18. Grunfeld, *Games of the World* (UNICEF, Zurich, 1982), 143.

Getting Home

Race Games from Nyout to Ludo

It seemed to him no extraordinary mark of court favour to play Pachisi with the king.

Kipling and Balestier, *The Naulahka*

The race may not be to the swift nor the battle to the strong, but that's the way to bet.

Damon Runyon

A race game is one in which players start with one or more pieces at one end of a linear track, advance them in accordance with the throw of dice or other lots, and win by being the first to get from start to home. The use of lots makes it a game of 'future imperfect information' as already defined. A 'simple' race game may be defined as one in which you have only one piece to move and get home, as in Snakes & Ladders. Such a game depends entirely on chance, there being no choice of which piece to move or how far to move it. A 'complex' race game is one in which you have several pieces, typically four, as in Ludo and its Indian ancestor Pachisi. Such a game is one of skill to the extent that you have at least the choice of which piece to move for any given throw, if not to subdivide it. And I would describe as 'multiplex' race games of the Tables family, notably Backgammon, in which you have a large number of pieces, typically fifteen. These are games of higher skill, in that you have a choice of which piece or pieces to move, can subdivide throws between as many pieces as there are dice, and, in its latest incarnation, are confronted with the further choice of doubling.

All cultures that have games at all have race games, and all three types are of extremely ancient date. As befits games with a significant element of chance, most are gambling games by nature. Many are dressed up with thematic devices to impart an element of fun and drama to the proceedings. This occurred especially in late medieval Europe with a class of games represented most classically by the Royal Game of Goose, in which the various stations that pieces may land on in the course of travel—let's call them 'hazard squares'—dictate special payments to or from the player, or cause a piece to advance or retreat by a dramatic amount. This has provided a template for thematic family race games in which the theme (say horse-racing) is reflected in the pseudo rationale for each hazard (say 'jockey found giving hot tip'), as well as for political satires run by newspapers at Christmas or election times ('caught napping with Chief Whip—lose seat and return to Start').

Race from Dice?

It seems intuitively obvious that race games evolved from dice games. Telescoping the evolution of games from ages to seconds and from various parts of the world to a single notional tribe, one envisages first the use of lots primarily as a form of religious divination and secondarily as an exercise to discover whom Fate has appointed to win the stakes being played for. Interest then begins to centre on the play itself, and the outcome is delayed by making it dependent upon a longer series of throws, thus heightening the tension and excitement of play. This requires a tally to be kept of the mounting total, either by collecting objects as counters, or by marking out a sort of abacus and moving a single counter along or around it. As binary lots precede dice, it is soon found that the more extreme totals occur more rarely than those of middling value, and their significance is marked by doubling or otherwise increasing their nominal value, or having them confer an extra throw, or both. This stage is found in many Amerindian games recorded by Culin, some being played with scoring objects and some by moving pieces around a scoring track. The transition from score-keeping to the movement of pieces—or 'counters', as they are appropriately called—is well expressed by Erasmus:

> [Consider] the implication in the change to stationary tallies. As long as tally sticks are employed, the dice will remain the centre of attention, the dynamic elements in the game. But as soon as the tallies become stationary, and a counter is moved along them, a new dynamic element has entered the field of play. Attention can now very easily switch to the counters, the dice becoming merely the instruments to give them motion. When this happens, the counting may become secondary to the race between the counters. Whether the players use one or several apiece makes no great difference... Once the counters have become the centre of attention, the dice game is open to countless variations and modifications of play.[1]

Thus the sight of pieces moving around a track inevitably invites a representational comparison with, for example, athletes, or horses, or mounted warriors. This in turn produces a positive feedback effect. As an effect on pieces, landing on an occupied square may result in 'capturing' or 'killing' the occupant. As an effect on spaces, certain of them may be regarded as gateways, bridges, or natural obstacles and their real life effects then translated into gaming terms. In real life a river is an obstacle, so if you reach one in the game you miss a turn. Conversely, a river with a bridge is no longer an obstacle, so if you reach a bridge you get another turn.

Further interest is introduced by increasing the number of pieces controlled by each player, so that, in effect, a number of different part-games are played simultaneously. Herein lies the source of the Tables family, such as Ludo and Backgammon. This potentially increases the amount of player interaction, and, in so far as it gives players a choice of which counter to move at any given time, also potentially increases the skill factor.

Murray, it must be said, was sceptical of all this:

> Culin is… responsible for the view that race-games were invented to keep a record of the successive throws of lots by means of counters shifted along a track, the length of which corresponds to the winning score. This view is repeated by G. Marin ('An ancestor of the game of Ludo', in *Man,* lxii (1940), 64.) But in none of the Indian race-games which he describes, nor in the American Indian games given by Culin, is the purpose of the game merely the summation of a number of throws of the lots. At any moment of these games a player's total may be cancelled if he reaches a point already occupied by his opponent, or otherwise complicated by the existence of crosscut cells. It is precisely in these additional hazards that the charm of these race-games consists.[2]

Such doubts seem based on evidence too negative to demolish Culin's reasonable view. The absence of race games representing a mere summation of totals (and Tatsungin, described below, is little else) is surely due to the fact that they would have proved as dull as a mere repetition of throws without a board, and been rapidly displaced by games with more interesting rules. As Lhôte says, 'Le tableau est bien sûr un support pour la marche des pions, mais en même temps et surtout un instrument pour visualiser le comptage des points, ce qui est le propre de l'abaque'.[3]

Primitive Race Games

The simplest race track is a straight line. Lengthening the track to revitalize the game by delaying the outcome necessitates deforming the line into a playing area of more convenient size and shape to accommodate the circle of players and interested bystanders. The simplest deformation is to loop it into a circle (Fig. 3.1*a*). Some circle games include crosses, consisting of two diameters crossed at right angles and thereby providing possible short cuts (1*b*). A distinctive series of oriental games deforms the circle itself into a cross, as if by pushing it inwards towards the centre from the four cardinal points (1*c*). This is not the same as a cross-and-circle game with the circle

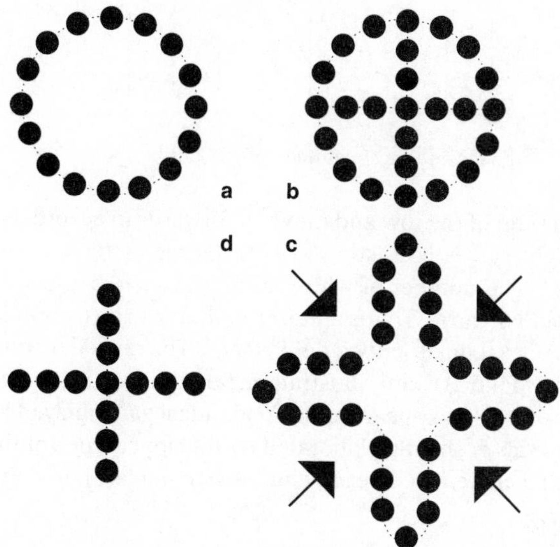

Fig. 3.1. Linear tracks in basic formations (*a*) Circle, (*b*) Cross and circle, (*c*) Circle deformed into a cross (dual carriageway), (*d*) Cross and circle without the circle (single carriageway).

removed (1*d*), as the latter produces what might be called a single as opposed to a dual carriageway. (On a single carriageway a piece travels only in one direction. On a dual carriageway, it travels one way along one carriageway, then turns round and travels back on the other.)

Formally, primitive race games are well represented by those of the Amerindians, of which we have a collection of accounts excellently preserved by Stewart Culin, though the accounts themselves vary considerably in quality. Amerindian sedentary games were remarkably similar despite being spread over the vast area of central and northern America and divided among multitudes of cultural and linguistic stocks. All were played with binary lots consisting, according to situation, of bone, fruit-stones, shells, nuts, and so on, but most typically of flattish wooden staves marked on one side and plain on the other, with markings often suggestive of divinatory arrows. The games themselves, though widely played to satisfy individual gambling interests, often had a ceremonial or symbolic value too. There were two main types.

Tatsungin (Paiute Shoshone, Pyramid Lake, Nevada). Eleven spaces are indicated by placing ten sticks vertically in a row. Each of two players enters

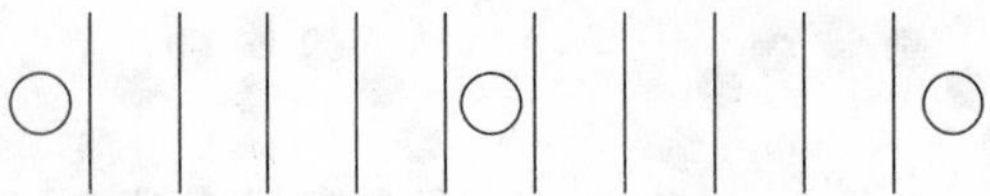

Fig. 3.2. Hopi game resembling Tatsungin (after Culin).

a piece at his end of the row and moves it forwards in accordance with the throw of eight staves consisting of split pieces of reed, their flat faces coloured red. The number of white (round) faces falling uppermost dictates the length of move. This is almost too simple to be true, unless there is more to the rules than described here. (It could be related to 'running fight' games such as Puluc.) Culin[4] illustrates a board (Fig. 3.2) marked on a slab of sandstone for what appears to be an identical game played by the Hopi Indians, and this is slightly elaborated by the appearance of three spaces marked with a circle, one at each end outside the last bar, and one in the central space.

Totolospi (Hopi Indians) was played by two or four players on two linear 10-space tracks crossing at right angles, the central crossing point being marked with a circle. Three staves are thrown, each being unmarked on the flat face and dotted on the round, and each moves his single piece one step only on the throw of three identical faces, any other throw being valueless. A similar but more elaborate game was played on a squared-up loop with a single branch (Fig. 3.3).

Zohn Ahl. 'Ahl' or 'Awl' designates a range of similar games formerly played throughout North America and Mexico, sometimes as a form of divination. It is characterized by a looped track of forty spaces marked by forty lines

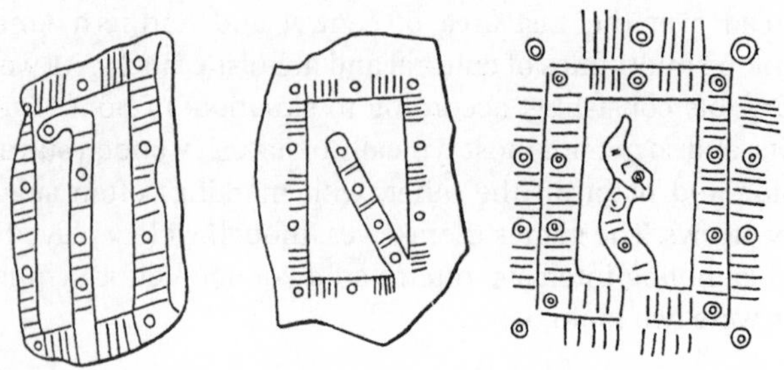

Fig. 3.3. Totolospi boards (from Culin)

drawn on a piece of cloth or hide, or by forty stones arranged in a square or circle of up to 2 metres in diameter. In the centre of the circle is a flat stone, the *ahl* stone, upon which a bundle of staves is vertically dropped or thrown so as to bounce off it. Culin records[5] a version played by White Mountain Apache women and called Sé-tich-ch, meaning 'hit' or 'bounce on the rock'.

The track for Sé-tich-ch has its forty stones arranged in four distinct quadrants of ten each. Four or six play in two teams, each of which moves two sticks around the circuit, the two teams moving in opposite directions (cf. Backgammon), as determined by the throw. The lots are three sticks with one side flat and one side rounded. These are held vertically and bounced violently by their ends off a flat rock in the centre of the circuit. The distance moved is determined by the number of rounded sides falling uppermost as follows:

rounds up	0	1	2	3
move forwards	5	2	3	10+

The rules are incomplete. Each side's two sticks may have been used to record both the current position and that from which it was counted, as at Cribbage, and the game was presumably won by completing a circuit. In view of known related games, it is equally possible that two sticks were specific to the four-player game, so that six players would have used three per side, and two one each.

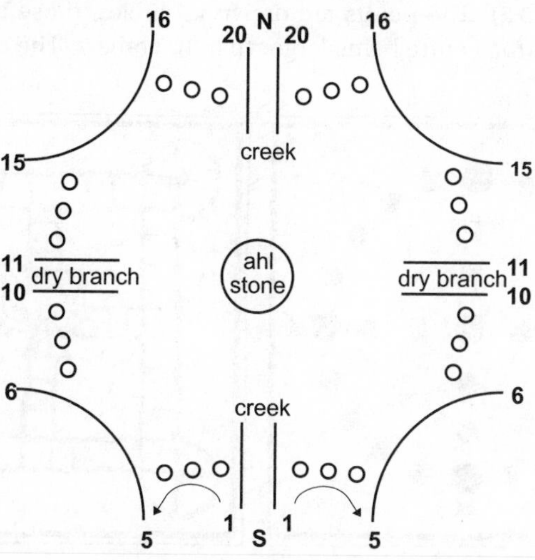

Fig. 3.4. Ahl game as played by Kiowa women.

Much the same game was played by the Kiowa women of Oklahoma. Part of James Mooney's account of it, reported to Culin, runs:

The players sit on the ground around a blanket marked in charcoal with lines and dots and quadrants in the corners, as shown in [3.4]. In the centre is a stone upon which the sticks are thrown. Each dot, excepting those between the parallels, counts a point, making 24 points for dots. Each of the parallel lines and each end of the curved lines at the corners also counts a point, making 16 points for the lines, or 40 points in all. The players start at the bottom, opposing players moving in opposite directions, and with each throw of the sticks the thrower moves her awl forward and sticks it into the blanket at the dot or line to which her throw carries her. The parallels on each of the four sides are called rivers, and the dots within these parallels do not count in the game. The rivers at the top and bottom are dangerous and can not be crossed, and when the player is so unlucky as to score a throw which brings her upon the edge of the river (i.e. upon the first line of either of these pairs of parallels) she falls into the river and must lose all she has hitherto gained, and begin again at the start. In the same way, when a player moving around in one direction makes a throw which brings her awl to the place occupied by the awl of her opponent coming around from the other side the said opponent is whipped back to the starting point and must begin all over again. Thus there is a constant succession of unforeseen accidents, which furnish endless amusement to the players.[6]

Nyout a Korean cross-and-circle game of classic elegance and simplicity, was first described in English in 1895 by Culin,[7] who over-enthusiastically embraced it as the ancestor of all race games, if not even of Chess.

The board is a cross and circle with twenty peripheral points and a cross of nine (Fig. 3.5). The points are drawn as circles, those at the cardinal points and in the centre being larger than the others. The cardinal points

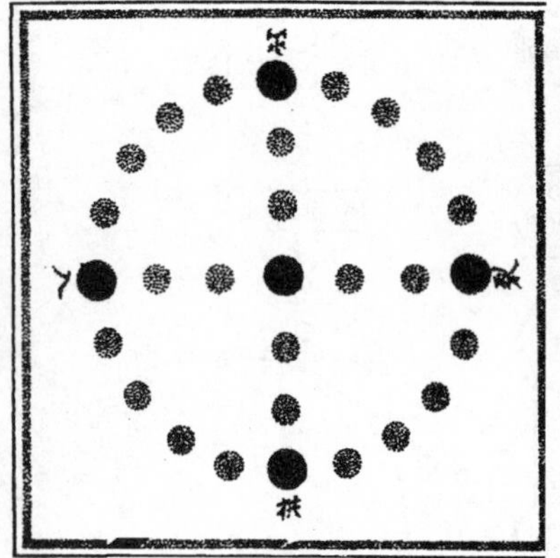

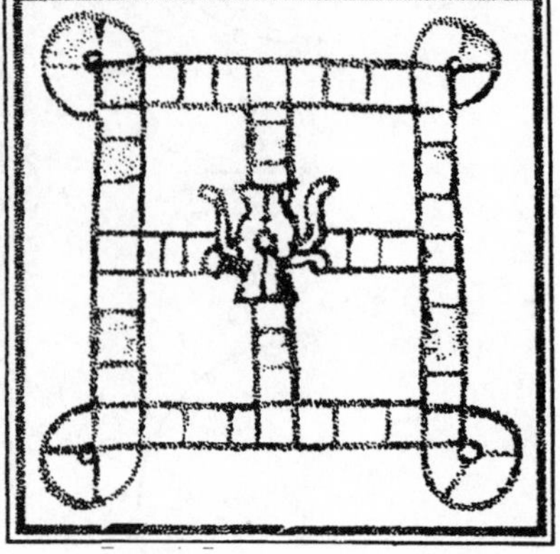

Fig. 3.5. Nyout (Korea) and the Mayan game (Central America).

are labelled with Chinese characters as follows: north = *c'hut* ('exit'), west = *yap* ('enter'), south = *kung* ('encircle'), east = *lít* ('cut through'). The lots are four binaries consisting of wooden blocks made by splitting sticks (typically chestnut), one side being flat and white, the other convex and blackened. These are thrown through a ring of straw about 5 cm. in diameter, projecting horizontally from the top of a stick about 30 cm. high stuck in the ground.

Two or more players start each with four pieces called 'horses', initially in hand. The aim is to enter one's pieces into the game and be the first to get a previously agreed number of horses to complete a circuit. Two players aim to get either one or all four of their horses around, as agreed, and three players three horses each. Four play in partnerships, each side having four horses.

Highest throw moves first. Any throw entitles a player to enter a horse through the point to the immediate left of North, from which it proceeds in an anti-clockwise direction. Distance is determined by the number of white sides falling uppermost as follows:

white sides up	0	1	2	3	4
name of throw	*mo*	*to*	*kai*	*kel*	*nyout*
forward move	5+	1	2	3	4+

A block falling on one end counts as black. A throw of *mo* or *nyout* awards another throw. You must take this before moving a piece, but are not obliged to move the same piece for each throw.

If one of your horses lands on another, you stack them together and thereafter move them as a unit, though counting them as two. The same happens if two or more of your horses moving as a unit land on another, so that it is possible for all four to form a single moving entity. If a single or compound horse of yours lands on that of another player, the latter is ousted and has to start the race again, and you get another turn. If a single or compound horse of yours lands on a cardinal point by an exact throw, then on your next turn you may move it along the radius to the centre point and thence northwards to the home point (north). From the west and south points such a move offers a short cut, while from the east it enables you to avoid landing on a space in the north-east quadrant at which you might be vulnerable to capture. In any case, the move is optional.

You needn't make an exact throw to get home, but must throw more than is necessary to reach the home point. In other words, a horse landing exactly on the north point is not borne off the board until the next throw, and remains subject to capture.

The origins of the game, though uncertain, seem other than Korean. Culin says a similar game is recorded from third-century China.[8] There is also a tradition that the twenty-nine points represent the Chinese general Hiang Yu (d. 201 BC) and his twenty-eight horse soldiers, who aided his escape after his defeat by the Prince of Han. On more elaborate boards the twenty-eight points other than the centre bear Chinese characters that read as an ode relating to this battle, said to have been written by a south Korean scholar. The direction of reading suggests that the home point was originally the centre rather than the north. Despite these connotations, the Chinese themselves regarded the game as foreign. Assuming the names of the throws listed in the table above to be numerals, they are certainly neither Korean nor Chinese, but those for one, two and three are reminiscent of Finnish and Lappish.

Classical and literary allusions notwithstanding, Nyout is (or was) regarded as a low-class gambling game and forbidden to the well-brought-up children of all self-respecting families.

The Mayan game. Similar cross-and-circle boards have been found inscribed on stones datable to the seventh century AD in Mayan archaeological sites at Palenque, Teotihuacan, Chichen Itza, and other parts of Central America. Nothing is known of the games played on them, but the track design is topologically identical with that of Nyout.[9]

Cruciform Games: Pachisi, Chaupar

Pachisi—meaning 'twenty-five', the highest possible throw—has been described as India's national board game from the fact that it is of great extent and antiquity in its presumed country of origin. It is basically a four-player race game played on a distinctive cruciform board, which will be readily recognized from the traditional pattern of its two well-known western derivatives, the British Ludo and the American Parcheesi. Two points must be made immediately, to avoid misunderstandings. One is that the western derivatives are deliberately simplified children's and family games played all-against-all, whereas Pachisi itself is a relatively skill-demanding partnership game, rather like a four-handed Backgammon. The other is that many western descriptions of Indian Pachisi confuse and conflate it with the closely related game of Chaupar (properly Chaupaḍ; also rendered Chaupur, Chaupat, Chausar, etc.). The most obvious difference is that Pachisi is played with binary lots in the form of cowrie shells and Chaupar with quaternary lots in the form of long dice. Pachisi has been called 'the poor man's Chaupar',[10] partly from an age-old use of cowries as currency by the poorer Indian classes, and partly because Chaupar is distinctly more complex and was thus perceived as the more aristocratic of the two. It remains to add that both have lost the status they once enjoyed. Upper-class and cosmopolitan Indians seem to regard it as a trivial pastime game if they acknowledge its existence at all, judging from Wayne Saunders's helpful study made with the assistance of games researcher Kishor Gordhandas of Bombay.[11] Grunfeld's *Games of the World* (1975) reproduces photographs of its play by women at a social centre in Amritsar and by girls in Udaipur, Rajasthan; and boards are still to be found scratched in stone on benches in Indian village squares and temple complexes. It has, in short, reverted to its status as a folk game, being played more in rural areas than in the relatively westernized towns and cities, and thus usually remaining free from the cultural tyranny of official rules, exclusive clubs, and national tournaments. Similar games are played throughout south-east Asia; and Irving Finkel, who collects games on behalf of the British Museum, has acquired a contemporary embroidered Pachisi cloth from Syria, where it is apparently still played by Muslim women.

The golden age of Chaupar coincided with the Mogul dynasty (1526–1857), as apparent from the large boards marked out with inlaid marble on palace courtyards at Agra and Allahabad. The Emperor Akbar (1542–1605) played the game on this scale, directing from a central dais the movements of sixteen slave-girls from the harem dressed in the traditional four colours of the various pieces. Abul Fazl, Akbar's vizier and historian, asserted that the Hindustani predecessors of the Moguls had enjoyed the game from times of old,[12] but as to its actual antiquity there is no firm evidence. The earliest claimed representation of Chaupar is the carving of Shiva and Parvati at play in the cave temples of Ellora, specifically in cave 21, whose carvings date from the late sixth or early seventh century; but only the dice can be seen—there is no sign of a suitable board. Murray[13] cites a work of the Sung period claiming that *t'shu-p'u* was invented in western India and reached China in the third century AD. Given the known antiquity and Indian origin of Chess, a first-millennium origin for Pachisi or Chaupar seems plausible. Another plausibility is that cruciform games were developed from the 8 × 8 Ashtapada board of more certain antiquity, perhaps as a way of clarifying the routes to be followed.

As there is no universally accepted standard form of the game, the following description of Pachisi—based on that of Wayne Saunders and Kishor Gordhandas—must be regarded as typical rather than definitive.

Equipment. The board consists of four arms of 8 × 3 squares radiating from a large central square, the *char koni* ('all square'), which is both Start and Home. The arms may be chequered red and white. Certain squares are cross-cut to represent forts or safe houses, where pieces are

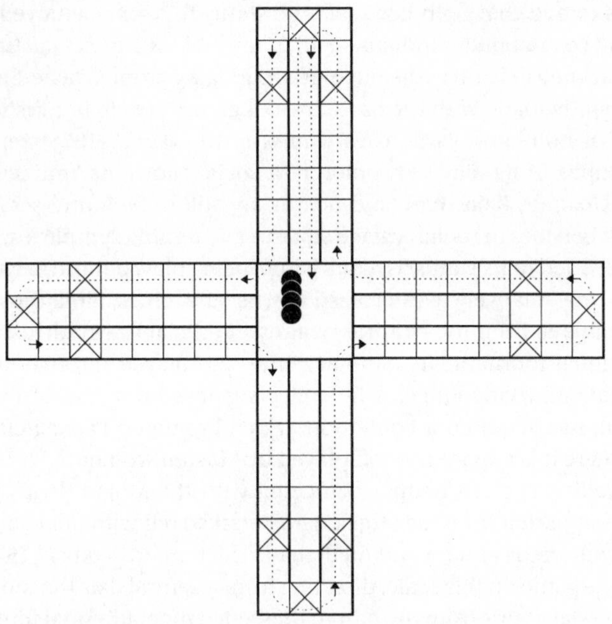

Fig. 3.6. Cruciform board for Pachisi and Chaupar.

immune from capture. Four play in partnerships, each sitting at one end of an arm facing his or her partner.

Players. Each starts with four distinctively coloured wooden pieces in hand (or, in some versions, on the centre square). Shaped like beehives or spinning tops, they are known as *goti*, 'horses'. Black and red oppose green and yellow.

Movement. Each in turn throws a number of binary lots, typically six or seven cowrie shells. The number of shells falling mouth up specifies the length of move according to any of these schedules:

mouths up →	0	1	2	3	4	5	6	7
if five cowries	25+	1	2	3	4	5+		
if six cowries	25+	10+	2	3	4	5	6+	
if seven cowries	7	11+	2	3	4	25+	30+	16

Object. Each player aims to enter his pieces one by one at the centre and move them down the central pathway of his own arm, around the perimeter of the board in an anti-clockwise direction, then back up the central pathway of his own arm and into the *char koni*, a distance of eighty-four spaces. The partnership getting all eight of its pieces home first wins. Players may move their partner's pieces as well as their own.

Play. Whoever throws highest plays first, and the turn to play passes to the right (anti-clockwise). The first player throws again, enters a piece in the *char koni*, and moves it down the arm the appropriate number of spaces.

Graces. On this and all subsequent turns, a player throwing a grace (marked '+' in the table) may, after moving the appropriate distance, either move any one of his own side's pieces already in play exactly one square forwards, or enter a new piece of his own (but not his partner's), and in either case then throws again. Throwing three grace numbers in the same turn usually incurs a penalty, but there is no agreement about what it is—possibly because the commonest one, which is to annul the two previous throws by restoring the position that obtained before them, can cause dispute as to what that position was.

Refusing. A player throwing an undesirable number may pass his turn without moving.

Capturing. A piece whose move ends on an unprotected square occupied by an enemy piece ousts the latter from the board, requiring its owner to re-enter it when possible. Making a capture entitles the player to another throw, in addition to any conferred by a grace. However, a piece occupying a safe house is immune from capture, and no enemy piece may make a move that would bring it to the same square.

Doubling up (optional). Some varieties of the game permit the doubling up of like pieces, as in Chaupar (see below).

Blockading (questionable). This feature appears only in some western sources and is of doubtful authenticity. If two partners get a piece each on the same square, these form a blockade which no singleton enemy piece may pass or land on so long as they remain together. However, an enemy doubleton can pass such a blockade, and, if it lands on it, sends both pieces back to the start (unless the blockade is on a safe house).

Homing. A piece that has completed its circuit may be moved towards home along the appropriate central arm, but may only reach home upon an exact throw. (If a one is required, this can be done by throwing a grace.) It is permissible, however, for a player to by-pass his home row and make another circuit of the board. Note that if a piece reaches the safe house at the end of the third arm in its journey, it may remain there, immune from capture, until a throw worth 25 enables it to reach home in one turn.

Unlike western board games, Pachisi is played in partnerships, requiring co-operative rather than individual play. There is no point in rushing to get your own pieces home before your partner, because the opponents will then enjoy the advantage of two throws to your partner's one and will be able to set up blockades or make repeated captures by virtue of their numerical superiority. If you get three of your pieces home and find your partner lagging, you may find it advisable to bypass the homeward path with your fourth piece and go round again. This prevents the opponents from playing twice in succession and may enable you to guard your partner's pieces.

An interesting and perhaps evolutionary relationship between Pachisi and Korean Nyout lies in the fact that their tracks are topologically identical. Four of the 'safe houses' correspond to the cardinal nodes of Nyout, which also confer advantage, albeit of a different sort. If, as has been suggested, Nyout was originally played from centre to centre rather than from north to north, then the two games may share a common ancestor.

Chaupar (Chaupaḍ) a more complex game played on the same board, differs in a number of significant respects, of which the following are, again, typical rather than definitive.

Black and yellow oppose red and green, and movement is governed by the throw of two long dice marked 1-3-4-6, or, more interestingly, three marked 1-2-5-6, giving these possibilities:

totals	3	4	5	6	7	8	9	10	11	12	13	14	15	16	17	18
ways of getting	1	3	3	1	3	9	9	3	3	9	9	3	1	3	3	1

A throw may be split between more than one piece, but may not be passed in whole or part unless no legal move is possible. There are no grace moves or additional throws.

Entry. There are no rules of entry, since play begins with pieces arranged in fixed positions. Different sources give different arrangements. Abul Fazl specifies squares 6-7-9-10 from the centre. Reiniche specifies 6-7-23-24, with the last two poised to ambush the two about to emerge from the right-hand opponent's arm.

Capture. There are no safe houses, and cross-cut squares (assuming play on a Pachisi board) have no significance. Making a capture does not produce an extra throw (a rule deduced *ex silentio*). Sources are equivocal about where a captured piece must be re-entered. Logical possibilities are (*a*) from its original start position, (*b*) from hand or from the *char-koni*, equivalent to 'the bar' at Backgammon.

Doubling. If a piece finishes on a square occupied by one of its own colour, the two may be doubled up and moved as a unit. Such a doubleton cannot be captured (or, therefore, landed on) by an enemy singleton. Three or even all four may theoretically be compounded in this way, and no such compound may be captured by a smaller one.

Blockading. The dubious blockading rule of Pachisi is not appropriate to Chaupar.

Homing. An exact throw is required to get home. By an interesting variation of the rules that substantially affects the strategy, all the blacks must be got home before the yellows start homing, and all the reds before the greens. A player whose pieces are all home continues to throw, the results counting for his partner. By some accounts, a player can elect to bypass the homeward arm and begin a second circuit, or even, having got a piece home, play it out again for another circuit.

Chaupar's greater depth (or at least complexity) derives from the possibility of splitting dice throws in a way denied a binary game like Pachisi. Saunders points out that the twenty possible combinations of three quaternaries all have native technical names equivalent to such westernisms as boxcars, snake-eyes, naturals, etc. How our minds reel (he adds) when we read Abul Fazl's description of the web of intricacies Akbar added to the Court game for the edification of his subjects: 'A throw consisting of a six, a five, and a one is called kham (raw); and in this case, two pieces, provided they are together on the same field, may each be moved six fields forwards, and every single piece twelve fields ... There are many other rules for particular cases.'

Murray briefly describes a number of other Pachisi congeners culled from various sources,[14] of which the Thai game of Len-doat used a board strongly reminiscent of Tables (Fig. 3.7; the numbers are not part of the board). A description of the game by one Captain Low is quoted verbatim by Murray, probably because it is barely intelligible:

26	25	24	23	22		21	20	19	18	17
5	4	3	2	1						16
6	7	8	9	10		11	12	13	14	15
15	14	13	12	11		10	9	8	7	6
16						1	2	3	4	5
17	18	19	20	21		22	23	24	25	26

Fig. 3.7. Len-doat (Murray)

Two persons each take a side of the board. There are five cowrie shells for a dice, each of the players has three pieces – each throws in turn, and if no. 1 or no. 5 casts up, the thrower continues to throw and to play until another number comes up. The chief object is to pass through all one's squares to those of the opposite party without interruption, taking his men if they can be overtaken by throwing a corresponding number and leaping over them if the number cast exceeds. He whose pieces are thus returned to the space whence they set out, wins the game. Nos 6, 15, 17, 26 on each side are castles, and the piece holding one of these cannot be taken. The pieces which have been taken are re-entered again by casting the dice. No. 1 enters one, no. 5, the whole are out, but the intermediate numbers do not enter any.[15]

If both players are, in fact, circuiting the board in like rotation, there can be few opportunities for capture. This apparent cross between Pachisi and Tric-Trac raises the intriguing question whether it is a colonial hybrid, or a descendant of some game ancestral to both the cruciform and the Tables families.

Western Derivatives

Parcheesi, the American equivalent of Ludo, is of all western derivatives the least divergent from its Indian model. As befits the folding-board method of games manufacture developed in the nineteenth century, the board is a square that has been filled out by using the corner spaces between each pair of arms as individual players' starting-points.

From two to four play as individuals; optional partnerships are only mentioned in passing in older sets. Pieces start in the corner spaces. Two dice are thrown. A piece can only be entered on a throw of 5 on either or both (1 + 4, 2 + 3). With more than two pieces in play, the number thrown can be split. Both numbers must be played if possible. Doublets give an extra throw. Furthermore, when all four pieces are out, both the numbers showing and their complements are played, as in Russian Backgammon. (A throw of 2-2, for example, is equivalent to a four-dice throw of 2-2-5-5.) If a third doublet is thrown in succession, the player may not move but must send his leading piece back home and end his turn. Two pieces of the same colour (but not more) may occupy the same space. They are then immune from capture and prevent any other piece from passing them. But this applies for one turn only, for a doubleton cannot move as a singleton, even on a doublet throw. Landing on an enemy piece sends it back home and earns the bonus of moving any other piece twenty spaces forwards, provided this can legally be done. A piece occupying a square marked with a circle is immune from capture. Getting home requires an exact throw, and allows the player to move one other of his pieces ten spaces forwards if possible.

The origins of Parcheesi are still being explored. Martin Gardner's inauthentic story crediting its invention to Sam Loyd,[16] who supposedly lost millions by selling it outright for $10, probably derives ultimately from the publicity machine that was Loyd himself—the P. T. Barnum-cum-Ely Culbertson of his day. Better documented is John Hamilton of the Hudson River Valley, who marketed and in 1867 claimed copyright to a version called Patcheesi, later changing it to Parcheesi because in the mouths of many it wafted misleading associations with pot cheese (cottage cheese). Hamilton is said to have sold the rights in 1868 to Albert Swift, a New York fancy-goods manufacturer, who in 1870 passed it on (together with a clerk named John Righter) to Elisha Selchow, a supplier of boxes for boxed games. The trademark followed in 1874, and by 1900 Parcheesi was the company's biggest selling product, a role it continued when Selchow & Righter concentrated on games in the 1920s. Similar boards illustrated in *Gameboards of North America*[17] appear to date from about 1850s, leading Wayne Saunders to ask whether there may not have been 'traditional' American versions before then, much as Monopoly was fine-tuned on home-made boards long before it became a commercial success.[18] Pertinently, he adds

> We can't explain the overwhelming popularity of the game here by appealing merely to the fortuitous decisions of a small paper goods concern in the mid 1800s. The scant historical record we have at present suggests greater powers at work, if only because the game couldn't have taken off as it did had the little decisions that were made not reflected a larger world waiting to receive them.

Ludo, first published in England around 1863, is a positively childlike offspring of Pachisi. From two to four play, each with four pieces, and without partnerships. Each enters pieces from a corner area next to the arm of his homing track. Only one die is thrown, pieces may only enter upon the throw of a six, and any throw of a six is rewarded with an extra turn. Two pieces of one colour may not occupy the same square. Pieces are immune from capture only when on their home stretch, and they need an exact throw to get home.

Equally simplistic are such other European versions as Mensch Ärgere dich nicht (Germany, 1910), Parchis (Spain), and Le Jeu de Dada, or Petits Chevaux (France). A late nineteenth-century German game called Eile mit Weile, dressed up with a travelling theme, remains popular in Switzerland, as does its Italian equivalent Chi va Piano va Sano![19]

Chinesenspiel, 'the Chinamen's Game', is a nineteenth-century German game antedating many western Pachisi variants. The board is a cross-and-circle formation, but deformed into a squared perimeter connected at the four corners by two crossing diagonals, thereby suggesting a cross between Nyout and Pachisi. Each player takes one of four distinctively coloured pieces shaped like Chinese figures and places it on the appropriately coloured corner square. Four sides of the cubic die bear a spot corresponding to one of the playing colours and the other two are blank. If you roll your own colour you advance your piece one step and throw again. If you throw an opponent's colour your turn ends without a move. A white confers no move but entitles you to throw again. It takes 28 steps to get round, and five to reach Home at the central intersection.[20]

Sorry! (Waddingtons, in UK) plays a variation on the Pachisi theme by replacing dice with cards drawn from a shuffled pack, disguising its origin still further by replacing the cruciform track with a peripheral square one. The five of each card numbered 1 to 11 (omitting 6 and 9) not only specify distances but also carry specific bonuses and penalties, such as 'Move backwards' or 'Split between pieces'. Additionally, five 'Sorry!' cards entitle the player drawing one to enter a piece on a square occupied by any enemy piece, sending the latter back to Start. The game is so called from a requirement to apologize for ousting an opponent's piece—a nice idea, spoilt only by the lack of a penalty for failing to do so. (One feels there should be a modernized version called 'Have a Nice Day'.)

Coppit (Spears, in UK) is the English version of an evident Nyout/Pachisi derivative invented in 1925 by a German, C. Neves, and known in Germany as Fang den Hut!, in France as Chapeau, Chapeau, and in the US as Headache. The chief variation is that the pieces are hollow cones, like dunces' caps. If you land on an opponent's hat you capture it and move the two as one. Several hats may be captured in this way, and the pile belongs to and is moved by the player who made the last capture and whose hat is therefore uppermost. The aim then is to get your pile to your home square and unload your booty of hats. Coppit is therefore a capturing game rather than a simple race.

Malefiz (Ravensburger, Germany). A good modern derivative of the Pachisi principle is Das Malefizspiel, invented in 1959 by Werner Schöppner. Malefiz is the equivalent of 'Old Nick'. Each of up to four players starts with five pieces at one end of the board (Fig. 3.8), and the winner is the first to get at least one piece home, on an exact throw, to the furthest point at the opposite end. A single cubic die is used, and a piece may be moved the given length in any direction—forwards, sideways or backwards—provided

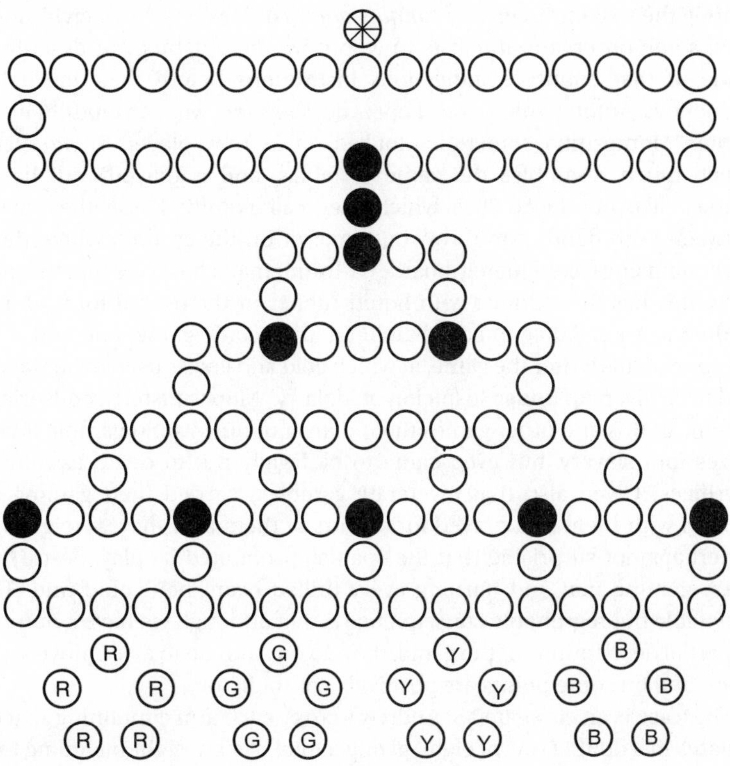

Fig. 3.8. Das Malefizspiel (Werner Schöppner).

that it does not change direction in one move. A piece if landed upon goes back to the start. Certain points are initially occupied by neutral blockading pieces. A blockade may not be crossed, but must first be landed upon by an exact throw. The player who does so may then move it and replace it on any other point on the track. The fun and originality of Malefiz lies in the increase of tactical skill afforded by the choice of routes and the constant reformatting of routes by the transfer of blockades.

Patolli of the Aztecs

Algunas vezes mirauia Monteççuma como jugauan al Patoliztli, que parece mucho al juego de las tablas.

F. L. de Gomara, *Istoria de las Indias* (Saragossa, 1552)

Among the sixteenth-century *conquistadores* of Mexico's Aztec civilization were some observant annalists to whom we are indebted for describing some of that country's indigenous institutions before their inevitable extinction. Among them was Lopez de Gomara, who around 1540–50 wrote: 'Montezuma sometimes looked on as they played at *patoliztli,* which much resembles the game of tables, and is played with beans marked like one-faced dice which they call *patolli.* These they shake between both hands and throw on a mat or on the ground, where there are certain lines like a merell-board . . . ' Torquemada observes that the mat, or *petate,* has lines drawn with liquid rubber in the overall form of a St Andrew's cross. Sahagun calls Patolli an aristocratic game, and adds: 'By the time of this writer the game, at which gold and jewels used to be staked, had been given up under suspicion of idolatry.' More sinisterly, adds Diego Durán, 'at this and other games the Indians not only would gamble themselves into slavery, but even came to be legally put to death as human sacrifices'. Given also that inveterate gamblers carried their gaming kit around with them and prayed for favours of them as if they were gods, it is perhaps not surprising that the Spanish prohibited its play, destroying every gaming mat and burning every drilled bean they could find. The inevitable but regrettable consequence is that although we have a number of partial descriptions of the game, they do not sum up to a definitive set of rules, and on some points are positively contradictory.

The track is an elongated St Andrew's cross, each arm containing sixteen squares in a double row of eight, giving a total of sixty-eight including four at the intersection. The ends of the arms are rounded, and towards the end of each an adjacent pair of squares are marked off with a cross. On one arm each cross separates the outermost three pairs of squares from the innermost four, and on the other it separates the outermost two pairs from the innermost five. Each of two active players plays for a team with an interest in the outcome. The two sides are red and blue, each with six pieces of their own colour. Details of entry and movement are unknown, but the lots were five binaries consisting of beans (*patolli*) left blank on one side and marked

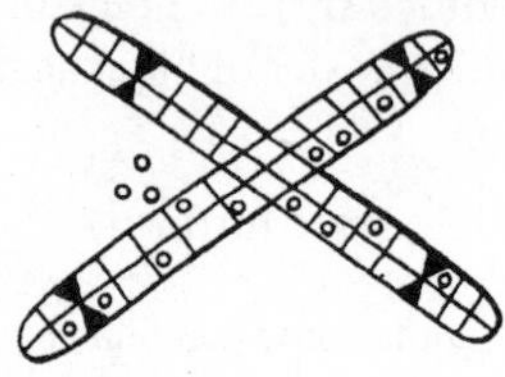

Fig. 3.9. Patolli (Durán, via Murray).

on the other with a white spot made by drilling a hole. Durán gives some idea (not very clear) of how many spaces were moved in the case of from one to five marked sides falling uppermost. He omits zero, but elsewhere refers to an unexplained move of 20. Assuming this is the move for zero, the schedule is comparable to that of Pachisi:

holes uppermost	0	1	2	3	4	5
move forwards	20	1	2	3	4	10

This description of the board matches a drawing by Durán. It conflicts with other illustrations, but may be taken as reliable partly because it appears to be drawn for the specific purpose of illustrating the game, and partly because Durán's account is thought to be based on an Aztec original. What remains unclear is whether the pairs of squares marked with crosses are actually playing squares or, as some illustrations seem to suggest, blacked out triangles which separate spaces but are themselves not landed upon, in which case the length of the track is only sixty steps. Either way, these markings are so placed as to produce a board of mysteriously asymmetric design. In this connection it may be significant that the number of squares on the internal side of the cross-marks totals forty, a figure prominent in Amerindian race games such as Zohn Ahl, while the number at the four extremities totals ten.

Nothing further is known of the play,[21] and we might well have left the game there were it not for the remarkable role it has played in anthropological and ethnological argument.

E. B. Tylor, one of the first anthropologists to appreciate the cultural significance of games, was so struck by what he regarded as startling similarities between the Mexican Patolli and the Indian Pachisi that he wrote several scholarly papers with such titles as 'On the Game of Patolli in Ancient Mexico and its probably Asiatic Origin', and 'On American Lot-Games, as Evidence of Asiatic Intercourse Before the Time of Columbus'.[22] He thought it incredible that two games could have sprung up independently on opposite sides of the globe that had in common such significant features as moving pieces around a cruciform track, some with cross-marked squares, and motivated by the cast of five binary lots, of which the rarer throws permitted exceptionally long moves. Here was an incontrovertible argument for the theory of cultural diffusion beloved of nineteenth-century anthropology. Tylor further argued that the circular race games of many North American Indian tribes—such as Zohn Ahl—resulted from additional diffusion, but with an element of degradation, in that the doubled cross was simplified to a single circular track with four cardinal points marked off, and in some cases omitted altogether to yield nothing more than a lot-casting game. The fact that at least one such game was called Patol clearly shows its lineage.

The alternative explanation of parallelism rather than diffusion is well argued by Erasmus.[23] In addition, Tylor fails to note that the Pachisi and the Patolli tracks are fundamentally different. The Pachisi track is severely symmetrical, the Patolli track uniquely asymmetrical; yet the Patolli track, if opened out, is nothing but a circle, whereas the Pachisi track, as we have seen, is topologically a cross and circle design.

Square Games

A linear racetrack can be so folded in upon itself as to produce a squared-up grid. Heavily marked delineation may indicate a pathway varying between a spiral and a ploughed furrow (Fig. 3.10*a, b*). In these, players may move in parallel motion from a common Start to a common Home, or—especially when two play—in contrary motion, each player's own Start being the other one's Home. The latter is characteristic of Backgammon, though both are found in the Tables family (Chapter 4). The furrow is also typified in Snakes & Ladders (Chapter 5).

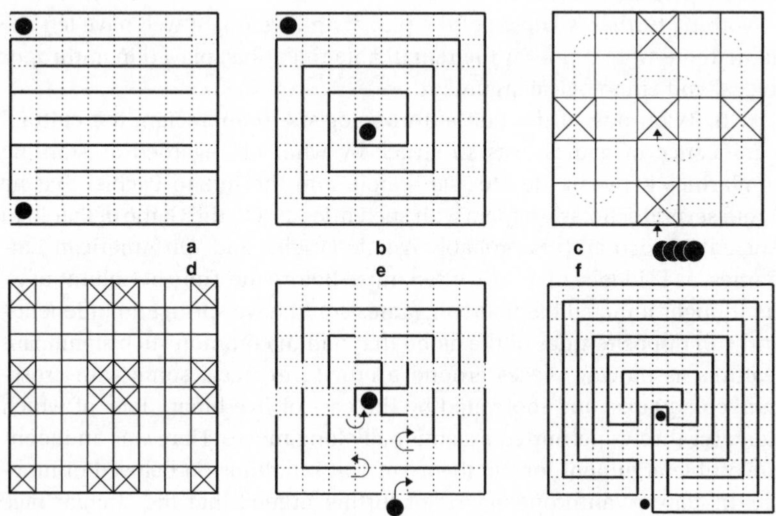

Fig. 3.10. (*a*) Ploughed furrow (boustrophedon). (*b*) Squared spiral. (*c*) Thaayam, showing one player's route. (*d*) Ashtapada board. (*e*) Same, showing South's route. (*f*) Squared-up classical labyrinth.

The fourth and fifth illustrate the Indian board known as *ashtapada*, or 'eight-footed'. If it was designed for a race game, as Murray believes, it may be for the purpose of turning a two-player spiral into a game for four players. Each of these would start at a different point, all, however, being reflections and rotations of the same point. The most obvious purpose of the cross-cut squares would be to clarify each player's route to the centre by marking his turning-points. Another would be to mark safe houses, squares on which pieces were immune from capture. It is plausible, if speculative, that cruciform games like Pachisi arose as a means of visually simplifying the individual pathways.

Ashtapada is not recorded as a race game in its own right, but its nature may be suggested by better-attested east Asian games played on similar boards.

Thaayam ('Dice') is described by R. C. Bell[24] as played by women and girls in Southern India as one of several pastimes practised when they spend much of their time out of doors frightening birds off the ripening rice. Three or four usually play, marking a board on the ground and using twigs for pieces. Four binary lots are made by stripping the dark skin off three sides of cubical tamarind seeds, and the throws are:

whites sides up	0	1	2	3	4
move forwards	8+	1+	2	3	4+

(Alternative lots, such as cowries, or two flat sticks marked 0-1, 2-3, figure in variants.)

A turn may consist of several casts, ending on a cast of 2 or 3. Pieces are then moved in accordance with all the numbers cast, being divided among them or allotted to a single piece at the caster's discretion. An ace entitles the player to enter a piece on her first square, or to advance another piece one square. No other throw permits an entry. Numbers cast before the first qualifying ace are lost. Pieces are moved around the board as shown until all reach the centre, for which an exact throw is required. When all are in place, they are borne off individually, each in turn upon the throw of an ace.

Several pieces of the same colour may occupy the same square simultaneously. If a piece lands on a square occupied by one or more enemy pieces of different colours, they are ousted and have to be re-entered in the usual way. All cross-cut squares are safe houses, and may be occupied by any number of pieces without capture. If a player gets two of her pieces on the opposite crosscut (eight from the start), she may declare them a twin, and thereafter move them as one, but only half the distance indicated by the throw. If this is an odd number, the odd one is lost. Tripletons are not allowed. Twins and singletons may occupy the same square simultaneously, but singletons oust only singletons and twins only twins. Whether ousted twins are entered singly by one ace, or as twins by means of two aces thrown in the same turn, is a rule that must be agreed beforehand. A twin upon reaching the centre reverts to two singletons.

Murray describes several similar games played on boards of various odd-square sizes. The 5 × 5 is used for Sadurangam, Siga (Southern India and Sri Lanka), Tammam (Somalia), and Gavalata (Southern India), which has an extra cross-cut on each of the four squares lying diagonally between the centre and each side cross-cut. Ashta-kashte is a 7 × 7 game from Bengal, and Saturankam or Siga a 9 × 9 game (Southern India and Sri Lanka). More are described by Parker in *Ancient Ceylon*.

The distinctive 'boustrophedon spiral' pathway followed in games of this sort brings to mind the winding track of the classical labyrinth, which is found throughout Europe and the Indo-European areas of Asia. This design is recorded in the epic saga of the *Mahabharata,* which dates back to the first millennium BC, and the remains exist of an actual stone labyrinth near Kundini, Madras. It is known in Hindu tradition as *kota,* meaning fort or city, which is also the name of the crosscut squares giving immunity from capture in the relevant games. The labyrinth has been inscribed on stone walls as a good luck charm, is found as a traditional body tattoo in Southern India, and, carved on a pebble, is used as a *yantra* for concentration in childbirth.[25] The possibility of ancestral relationships between games and mazes remains to be explored. While there is no evidence to link the *kota* labyrinth with the basis of a race game, the fact that players were acquainted with its distinctive pattern would at least make it easy for them to pick out the path to be travelled on the squared grid. Equally fortuitous is the appearance of a swastika—an Indian good-luck symbol—at the centre of the *ashtapada* board drawn here in such a way as to reveal the separate routes.

NOTES

1. Charles John Erasmus, 'Patolli, Pachisi, and the Limitation of Possibilities', *Southwestern Journal of Anthropology,* 6 (Winter 1950), 369–87 (as reprinted in E. M. Avedon and B. Sutton-Smith, *The Study of Games* (New York, 1971), 109–29).
2. Murray, *History of Board Games,* 234.
3. Lhôte, 133.
4. Murray, *History of Board Games* after Culin.
5. Ibid.
6. Culin, *Games of the North American Indians,* i. 127.

7. Culin, *Korean Games* (Philadelphia, 1895), reprinted as *Games of the Orient* (Tokyo, 1958), 66 ff.
8. Ibid. 72. Bell says 3rd-cent. Korea, but this may be a misreading.
9. See Bell, *Board and Table Games from Many Civilisations*, Pt. 1, p. 3, and Erwin Glonnegger, *Das Spiele-Buch* (Munich, 1988), 21.
10. Norman Brown, 'The Indian Games of Pachisi, Chaupar, and Chausar', in *Expedition*, 6 (1964), 32–5. Cited by Wayne Saunders, 'Counter Space (Part 1)', in *Game Times*, 25 (Dec. 1994).
11. Wayne Saunders, 'Counter Space', in *Game Times*, 24–7 (1994–5), Journal of the American Game Collectors Association, kindly sent me by Kishor Gordhandas.
12. Norman Brown, 'The Indian Games of Pachisi, Chaupar, and Chausar', in *Expedition*, 6 (1964), 32–5. Cited by Wayne Saunders, 'Counter Space (Part 1)', in *Game Times*, 25 (Dec. 1994).
13. Murray, *History of Chess*, 120; but Irving Finkel tells me that he has been unable to trace the citation and questions its validity.
14. Murray, *History of Board Games*, 132–40.
15. Ibid. 138–40.
16. In Gardner's introduction to the Dover edition of *The Mathematical Puzzles of Sam Loyd* (New York, 1959).
17. Bruce and Dorinna Wendel, *Gameboards of North America* (New York, 1986).
18. Wayne Saunders Part 2, *Game Times* 25 (Dec. 1994), 547
19. These and others are illustrated in Glonnegger, *Das Spiele-Buch*, 14–17.
20. See Grunfeld, *Games of the World* (UNICEF, Zurich, 1982) 32–3.
21. A proposed reconstruction is offered by Bell, *Board and Table Games from Many Civilisations*, i. 7–8.
22. The former in *Journal of the Anthropological Institute of Great Britain and Ireland*, 1878. The latter is more accessibly reprinted in E. M. Avedon and B. Sutton-Smith, *The Study of Games* (New York, 1971), 77–93, together with long extracts from original Spanish texts. See also 'Backgammon Among the Aztecs', *Macmillan's Magazine*, Dec. 1878.
23. Erasmus (n. 1 above).
24. Bell, *Board and Table Games*, i. 17–20.
25. N. Pennick, *Mazes and Labyrinths* (London, 1990), 33 and 52.

The Tables Turned

*Backgammon—from Ur to Us**

Choice books, safe horses, wholesome liquor
Billiards, backgammon, and the vicar.

Soame Jenyns (1735)

The only athletic sport I ever mastered was Backgammon.

W. Jerrold, *Douglas Jerrold* (1914)

Backgammon is the chief western representative of a distinctive family of race games best referred to as Tables. This derives from Latin *tabula,* whose primary meaning of 'board' or 'plank' developed various specific applications including one precisely equivalent to our modern English 'board' game. From its plural *tabulae* derive also Spanish *tablas,* Italian *tavoli,* Greek *tablē, tavli,* German [*wurf*]*zabel,* Scandinavian *tafl,* Anglo-Saxon *tæfel,* Gaelic *taibhleas,* Welsh *tawl[-bwrdd],* and so on. There are two reasons for the plural. One is that *tabula* came to denote each quarter of the board rather than the whole surface, individual quarters being significant to the play. The other is that the boards often comprise two separate halves hinged together for ease of manufacture, storage, and portability. *Tabulae* also denotes the pieces moved along the board and is properly rendered into English as 'tablemen', or 'men' for short, though I will continue to call them 'pieces' for consistency. (Yes—I did consider 'table-persons'.)

Tables differ from most of the race games hitherto described in two main respects. First, they are *multiplex* games, each player having a large number of pieces, typically fifteen. Second, they are essentially *two-player* games, and hence bilaterally symmetrical. Whereas most race games are played on radially symmetrical tracks, such as a square, a circle, a cross, or some combination of the three, Tables is played on a rectangular board with each player sitting at one of its long sides. These features are evidently related. The unknown ancestor may have originated in a desire to expand the length and interest of play by increasing the number of pieces and the

* *From Ur to Us* was the splendid title of an article by R. C. Bell in *Games & Puzzles.* I wish I had thought of it.

consequent degree of choice on offer at each move. With more than two players, the result would be self-defeatingly complex. A rectangular board is thus the inevitable concomitant of an essentially linear game for two.

Backgammon as Archetype

The general nature of Tables is best understood from a summary of traditional English Backgammon.

The track comprises twenty-four 'points', twelve on each side and six in each table (quarter). They are not numbered or lettered, but the lettering shown here is traditional, convenient, and applicable to all games of the family.

White and Black each start with fifteen pieces posted in groups of two, three, and five, as illustrated. White moves all his pieces anti-clockwise from (a) to (z), Black clockwise from (z) to (a). Each player's first aim is to get all fifteen pieces moved round to his inner table, regardless of how they are distributed among its six points. Having done so, his final aim is to 'bear' them off the board—i.e. move them to an imaginary 'home' point lying immediately beyond (z) or (a). Thus, for example, White needs a 6 or better to bear a piece from (t), 5 or better from (v), and so on. The first to bear all his pieces wins a single game; or, if his opponent has not borne any, a double game or *gammon*; or, if his opponent has any pieces remaining in the winner's inner table, or still in capture, a treble game or *backgammon*. (The modern game scores differently, as explained later.)

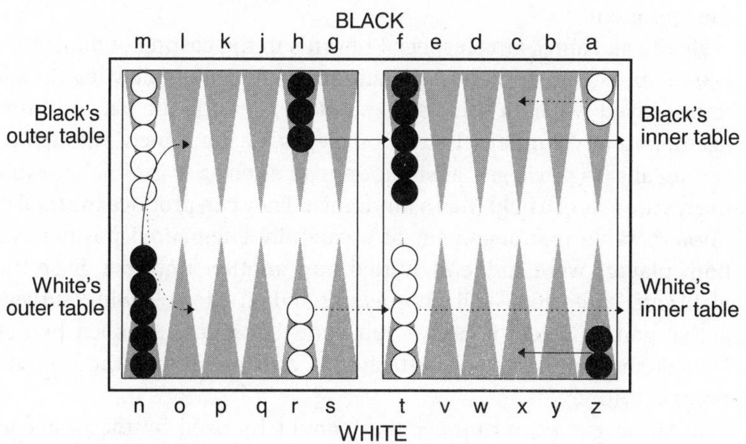

Fig. 4.1. Anatomy of Backgammon.

Each in turn throws two dice, and moves one piece forwards by one number, then either the same or a different piece forwards by the other. Doublets are played twice. Thus, for example, 3-3 counts as 3-3-3-3, the four moves being taken by one piece or divided ad lib between two, three or four pieces. All legally possible moves must be played. It is legal to move to a vacant point, or one occupied by one or more friendly pieces, or one occupied by an enemy singleton (a *blot*).

Hitting a blot forces its owner to remove it to the *bar* (the vertical division between the inner and outer tables). That player may then not move until he has been able to re-enter it. White re-enters from (a) and Black from (z). An ace thrown entitles White to enter it on (a), a deuce on (b), and so on, provided that the point in question is legally occupiable. If not, his turn ends, and on subsequent turns he cannot move any piece already on the board until any and all captured pieces have been re-entered.

This pattern is typical of a vast family of games, which differ from one another in one or more of the following basic respects:

Dice. All historically recorded forms of Tables are about equally divided between two- and three-dice games. Some are played with either number, and a nominally three-dice game would often be played with two in the absence of three, a notional third throw being assumed for the sake of argument. The third figure was set in various ways. It might be set permanently at six or at one; it might be held to duplicate the higher number shown on the two real dice (*majoret*), or the lower number (*minoret*); or it might be any number freely chosen by the caster, or by the opponent.

Nearly all games attach special rewards to the casting of doublets, or, where applicable, triplets. Backgammon is typical in allowing doublets to be played twice. In some games doublets entitle the player to throw again, and in yet others the two privileges are combined—though they are not always privileges, as situations can often arise in which too many moves are less of a help than a hindrance. They can produce the total and unpredictable rearrangement of a carefully engineered position, as if both players were suddenly hurled into another universe. Even more elaborate extensions will be encountered in the following survey of actual games. There is also a sub-family of games, typified by Acey-Deucey, in which privilege attaches to a throw of 2-1, the nominally poorest throw.

In some games, a number that cannot be used by the caster may instead by played by his opponent. This can be particularly devastating in games involving long series of moves initiated by a throw of doublets.

Pieces. In all modern Tables games White and Black have fifteen pieces each, and the usual—but not invariable—aim is to be the first to bear them all. Very rarely is the aim to get them all piled up on (a) or (z). This is probably because the process of 'homing' on the last space in other race games usually necessitates an exact throw, which would be unnecessarily tedious in a game of fifteen pieces, rendering it more logical to sweep them off with any sufficient throw. Thus a piece on (x) can be borne by any throw of three or higher, and one on (z) by any throw at all.

Direction of play. In most of the race games hitherto described all or both players move their pieces in parallel motion—that is, in the same direction, clockwise or anti-clockwise as the case may be, even if, as in Chaupar, they start from different points. A significant feature of Tables is that about half the recorded games of the family are played in 'contrary motion', as in Backgammon. In other words, the two sides start from opposite ends of the 24-point track and come into contact with each other head on. This makes for a relatively violent game at first, though there eventually comes a point at which all the pieces have passed each other and can head for home unhindered—a situation described as 'a running game'.

There still remain, however, a number of games played 'in parallel'. Some of these start at the same point, with both sides entering at (a) and bearing from (z). This produces a game of constant interaction, more reminiscent of a steady-state universe than the expanding-contracting universe of Backgammon and other contrary games. Others start from opposite positions, White playing anti-clockwise from (a) to (z) (north-east to south-east), and Black also anti-clockwise but from (n) to (m) (south-west to north-west). Other combinations of starting-point and direction of travel are possible, and these provide a convenient basis of classification. The distinction between parallel and contrary motion is fundamental, providing two types of game quite different in feel and strategy.

Initial arrangement. Theoretically and primitively, both players start with fifteen pieces 'in hand', i.e. off the board, and enter them one by one at their respective starting-points. Thus a throw of 2-5 entitles White to enter a piece on (b) and (e). Games in which the two players have different entry points often start with all fifteen pieces piled up on the starting-point. This is almost identical with the previous situation, the only difference being that they are all one point further ahead than they would be if started off the board on a notional point zero. (Compare games of Patience, of which some specify extracting the Aces and setting them out to build on, while others specify setting the Aces out as and when they turn up in the deal. Same difference, to quote a cliché.)

Many games, however, start with the fifteen pieces in peculiarly conventional arrangements. That of Backgammon, for example, as shown above, often bemuses beginners, until they discover the catch, which is that they have to get all fifteen of their pieces into their inner table before they can start bearing them. The effect of this dramatic starting position is to speed the game up by starting at the sort of position that might be reached half-way through a game where all fifteen started in hand, thus leading to more rapid interaction and conflict. Other games begin with quite different but equally startling opening positions.

Interaction. The following rules apply to most members of the Tables family, though some gain a peculiar distinction by running counter to one or more of them:

1. You may move a piece to a vacant point.
2. You may move it to a point occupied by one or more of your own pieces.
3. You may move it to a point occupied by a blot (enemy singleton).
4. You may not move it to a point occupied by more than one enemy piece.

It follows that one of the aims of play is to hold as many points as possible by 'piling' them with at least two pieces, and that conflict may arise over points occupied by only one piece.

Singletons are variously treated:

1. In most games, hitting a blot forces it off the board. In some games, including Backgammon, it must be re-entered before any other piece of that colour is moved, though some allow it to be held out as long as its owner wishes.
2. In some, it *pins* the singleton and holds the point. That is, the pinning piece may not itself be hit or pinned, but may be piled upon by others of its own colour. The pinned singleton then remains frozen to the spot until exposed again by the removal of all the enemy pieces holding it down.
3. In a very few, singletons are invulnerable and simply hold the point they occupy, preventing the other player from landing on it.

Allocation of moves. In all games, each number thrown not only must be used if legally possible, but also must be used to the full, unless the piece so moved is borne off the board before completing its run. The numbers thrown may be allocated individually to the appropriate number of pieces or combined in the movement of one piece. If combined, they must nevertheless be considered as individual moves and are accordingly bound by the rules of play. For example, suppose you throw 5-3 and wish to move a piece to a legally occupiable point eight ahead. You may move either five forward and then three, provided that the fifth point is legally occupiable, or three forward and then five, provided that the third point is legally occupiable. If, however, both the third and fifth points are held by your opponent, you cannot move forwards at all. This rule significantly affects the play, for if you can establish control of six or more consecutive points—called, in Backgammon, a 'prime'—your opponent will be incapable of moving a piece past them, and will be held back in play for as long as you can maintain the block.

Tables games clearly increase the proportion of skill to chance compared with other dice-motivated race games. For one thing, you are presented with a multiplicity of choices—typically thirty or more—in the allocation of throws to pieces. For another, you are not merely rushing to get home first, but, rather, to set up positional situations which will tend to advance your own interests while retarding those of your opponent. Indeed, there are some games of the family that can be won by achieving a certain position rather than by bearing off. Finally, whether you play for money or for graded wins, you must always consider whether a game might not be more cheaply resigned early rather than played to a possibly more costly conclusion, which is a matter of mathematical judgement.

Forerunners

Bilateral race games, the possible ancestors of Tables, are most at home in western Asia, and probably originate there. The Middle East, in particular, has yielded many artefacts, illustrations, and literary references—in one case, even, a clay tablet details the rules of play in cuneiform script. The following are of particular interest to the probable development of the Tables family.

The Royal Game of Ur. The remains of the city-state of Ur, home of the biblical Abraham and capital of the Sumerian Empire in the third millennium BC, lie some 105 miles (168 km.) west-north-west of Basra in modern Iraq. Ur is also the home of the oldest complete set of board-gaming equipment ever found. Excavated by Sir Leonard Woolley in 1926–7, its royal tombs yielded (among other things) four gaming boards, identical in layout though varying in richness of materials and decoration. The board consists of twenty squares, some decorated with rosettes (Fig. 4.2).

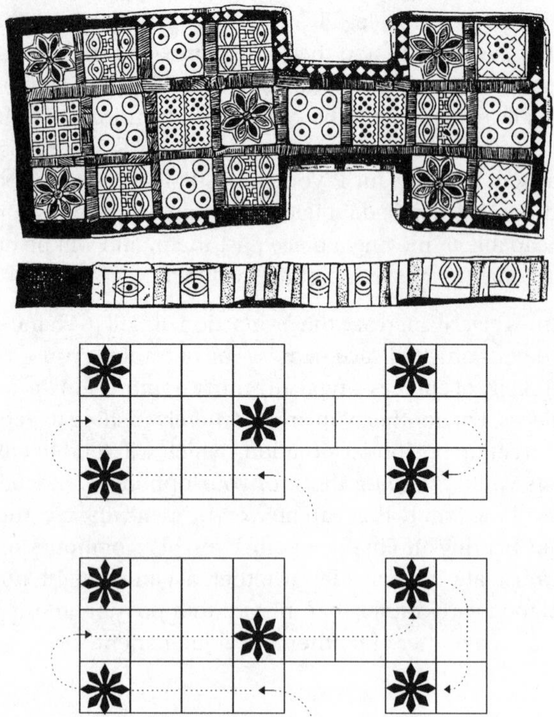

Fig. 4.2. The Royal Game of Ur.

The accompanying equipment comprised fourteen pieces in two different colours, thus seven per player, and six binary lots, evidently three per player, in the unusual form of tetrahedrons (four-sided pyramids), each with its four corners snipped off and with two of the resultant exposed surfaces marked by a treatment of inlay. Casting three lots gives an equal chance of their landing with a plain or marked tip uppermost, giving four possible results from 0 to 3. Irving Finkel's reconstruction, published as a boxed game by the British Museum,[1] is based on a late inscription and involves five individually distinguished pieces per player. Black and White enter them one at a time in the squares lying respectively above and below the central rosette, moving them first towards the rosette at the extreme left, then on to the central track and towards the extreme right, finally diverging again (Black to north and White to south) to complete the circuit on or notionally beyond the final rosetted square. The players' pieces were safe on their own side of the board, but in traversing the centre line would have been subject to ousting. Landing on a rosetted square gave a piece immunity from attack. By an unusual stroke of good fortune, a cuneiform tablet dating from 177/176 BC gives most of the rules for the game, lacking only an indication of the direction of travel. The fact that the first two rosettes encountered by each player are four steps apart suggests that the number of marked tips dictated the length of the forward movement, with zero representing four and conferring a second throw. R. C. Bell proposes a detailed and more elaborate mode of play.[2] Murray counters the apparent oddity that the final rosettes are six spaces apart instead of four by suggesting that the full game consisted of twenty-eight moves, following the route shown for White in Fig. 4.2 (bottom), with a return to home for bearing off. This more plausibly sets all the rosettes at four points apart.

The Game of Twenty. A similar board to that of Ur, known as the Game of Twenty from the number of squares, is often found on one surface of Egyptian gaming boxes, with the better-known game of Senet on the other. Such a game is known from about the middle of the second millennium BC in Babylon, with later examples from the third century BC in Mesopotamia and Iran.[3] It became popular in Egypt from the advent of the New Empire, but is depicted in a tomb at Beni-Hassan from the early twelfth century BC. An inscription identifies it as *aseb*, a non-Egyptian word of presumed Babylonian origin. The game itself is thought to have originated in India. It looks, in fact, like a sort of two-hand Pachisi. Each player had five pieces, entered them from the single end of the arm, and, after struggling for position and no doubt sending enemy pieces back to the start, aimed to get them on to the four squares on either side of the opposite end, thence to bear them off. An oft-reproduced illustration from a New Empire papyrus in the British Museum depicts a lion and an ibex at the play of Twenty (Fig. 4.4).

In the 20th dynasty (*c*.1185–1070 BC) the Twenty is supplanted by a similar board expanded to thirty-one squares, though only three examples of it are known.[4] Players may now have started at opposite ends of the board rather

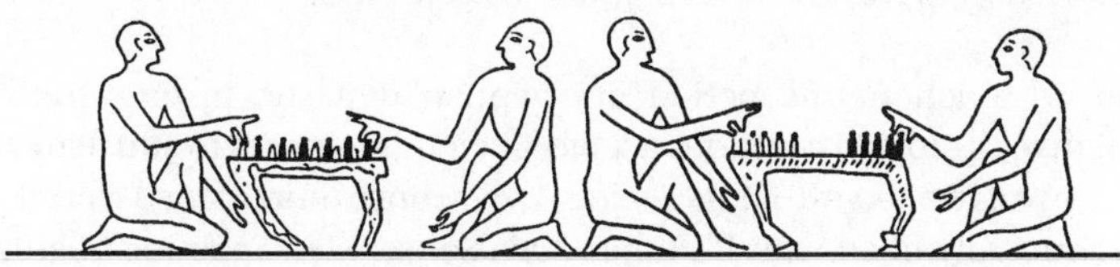

Fig. 4.3. Senet and the Game of Twenty, from the Benihassan tomb.

Fig. 4.4. Ibex and lion at the Egyptian Game of Twenty.

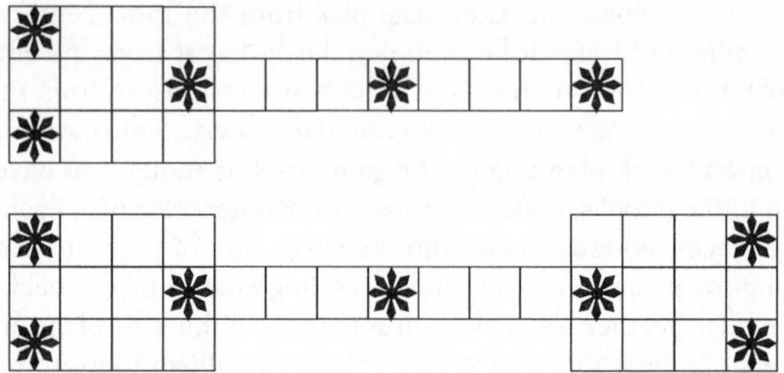

Fig. 4.5. The Egyptian Game of Twenty (*above*), and the Double Game (*below*).

than merely on opposite sides, and moved in opposite directions—in 'contrary' rather than 'parallel' motion—resulting in an enhanced degree of interaction more similar to that of Backgammon.

Senet. Throughout the period of Egyptian dynastic history, from the thirtieth to the fourth centuries BC, there occur references to and depictions of a two-player board game called *s'n't*, whose unrecorded vowels are conventionally filled with E's to produce Senet. Many gaming boards are also found—some scratched on a stone surface, some moulded in clay, some forming part of a well carpentered gaming table, suggesting

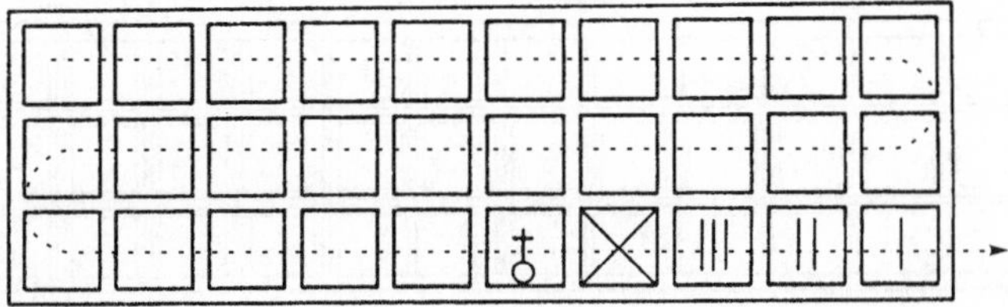

Fig. 4.6. Senet.

popularity with all social classes—consisting of thirty squares arranged in three rows of ten. The pieces are of two contrasting designs for the two players, ranging from simple geometric figures to heads of lions and heads of demons, and vary between five and seven a side, eventually settling down to five in the New Kingdom (18th–20th dynasties, *c.*1550–1150 BC).

Of the thirty squares on the board, five invariably bear hieroglyphs, and some or all of the others may be similarly decorated. This suggests that the five marked squares are of particular significance to the play. The fact that they are not symmetrically arranged suggests that the pathway is to be regarded as linear and that both players started from the same end of the track. The specially marked squares always occur in the same positions and with the same markings. Since all appear at one end of the track, it seems likely that this is the further end—that is, squares 26 to 30. Square 30 often bears a hieroglyph that might be taken to indicate 'home', or the goal of the race. Square 15 is also often specially marked. Illustrations suggest that the players started with their five pieces occupying alternate squares in the first row of ten. The presumed aim was to be the first to get all one's pieces 'home' and borne off the board, either from square 30 or from a notional square beyond. The fact that some boards have raised intersections and that the pieces are evidently unstackable shows that a square could only be occupied by one piece at a time. Forward movement was dictated by the cast of four binary lots, giving five possible outcomes. It was probably desirable to get all five of one's own pieces in a consecutive line so that the opponent would be unable to pass them. 'Square fifteen (House of Rebirth) and square twenty-six (the Beautiful House) had positive significance, while square twenty-seven, a field of water, was to be avoided. Landing on that square sent the pieces back to square fifteen, where the hieroglyphics frequently referred to rebirth. From the last three squares one had to throw the exact number to bear men off from a notional thirty-first square.'[5]

Timothy Kendall's reconstruction of the game is widely approved.[6] The track of thirty squares, called houses, is folded into three rows of ten, such

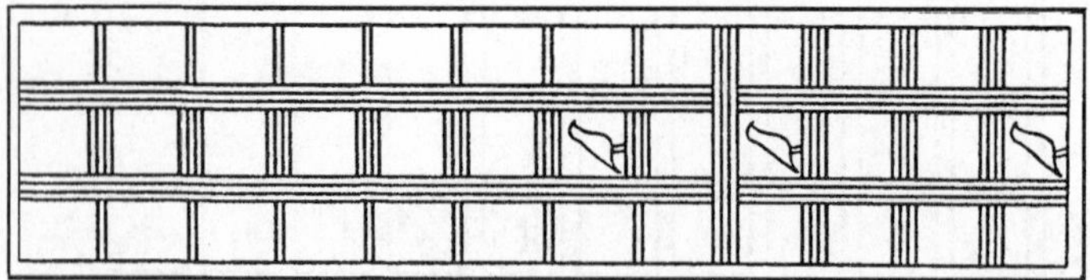

Fig. 4.7. The thirty-six square game from Ak-Hor (after Murray).

that forward movement traces the shape of a reflected S. Each player starts with seven pieces arranged on alternate houses of the first fourteen. Four binary lots, consisting of split twigs called fingers, with one side plain and one decorated, determine the length of move as one per plain face uppermost, or five if none so fall. Throws of 1, 4, 5 entitle the player to another throw. Landing on a house occupied by an enemy piece returns the latter to the house from which the move was made. The 15th, or House of Rebirth, and the last five houses, all bear symbols. The 26th, House of Happiness, cannot be passed but must be landed on by an exact throw. Upon reaching 27, the House of Water, a piece must return to the House of Rebirth (15). Alternatively, or compulsorily if 15 is occupied, its owner must home it by throwing a 4 before he can make any other move. Houses 28, 29, and 30, require an exact throw of, respectively, 3, 2, 1, to enable a piece to get home —or be 'born(e)', in both senses and spellings of the word. Failing an exact throw, it retreats 27. The first to get all seven home wins.

Similar gameboards are found in neighbouring cultures in the Sudan, in Cyprus, and in Phoenicia, and the game is mentioned by Plutarch (*De Iside*, 12). A variant with 3 × 12 squares, found in a tomb at Akhor, though evidently an expansion of the twenty-square game, could almost be regarded as a precursor of Tabula, the ancestral Backgammon of the Romans.

Shields, Palms, Dogs & Jackals. Remains are found of yet another and perhaps older game of thirty squares—or, more accurately, points, as they usually consist of holes into which pegs are fitted like those of a Cribbage board. Its original name being unknown, it enjoys a variety of contemporary aliases taken from the design of the board or pieces. The board itself is found in the form of a shield, a double axe-head, or a modern bagatelle board, and one, from Deir-el-Bahri, bears the design of a palm tree. For these reasons it has been called the Shield Game or the Palm-Tree Game. It is also known as the Game Dogs & Jackals, or Hounds & Jackals, from the

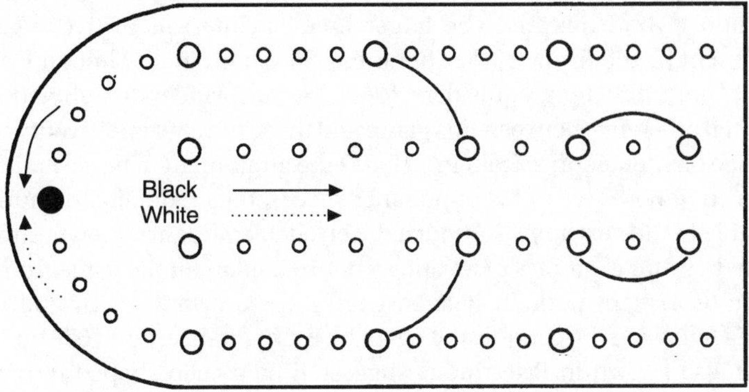

Fig. 4.8. Fifty-Eight Holes, or Dogs & Jackals (generalized).

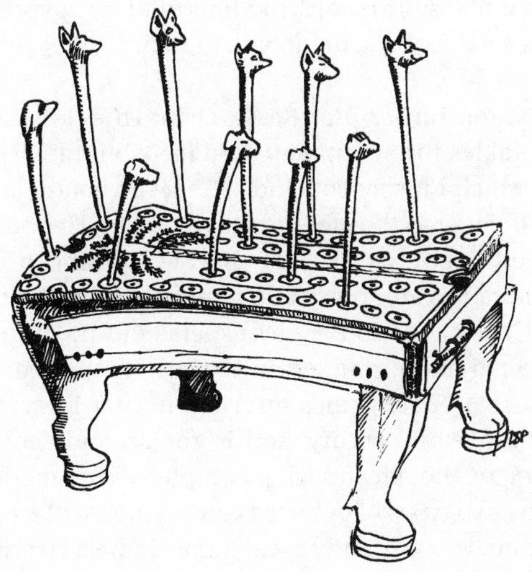

Fig. 4.9. Dogs & Jackals, or the Palm Tree Game, from a tomb of the 12th dynasty (1800 BC), showing pieces as pegs fitting in holes.

design of the pieces by which the two players are distinguished, each having five. Roland May[7] considers it best referred to as the Game of fifty-eight holes, this being the only self-evident factor common to all.

The two players each started with his five pieces in the first five holes and followed the paths marked here with arrows, turning the corner at the right-hand edge, then proceeding leftwards to the apex shown here solid—a distance of twenty-nine steps each, the thirtieth being Home and common to both players. The larger holes at intervals of five suggests movement by the throw of four binaries. The semi-circular lines are short cuts in both direction, equivalent to snakes and ladders combined. The essential difference between this game and those of Senet and Twenty is the absence of interaction, except in so far as the attainment of home entitled a player to remove one of his opponent's pieces, thus reducing the number available in the next game.[8] About a dozen such boards are known, supplemented by four examples of an apparent descendant of the game from the Coptic (Christian) period.[9] Related games are known from Ur and from Assyria following the conquest of Egypt by Esarhaddon around 675 BC. That it was also known in Palestine is suggested by a cello-shaped terracotta plaque from Gezer, whose thirty perforations on each side more probably supported a race game than acted as 'a highly conventionalised representation of the Queen of Heaven'.[10]

Imaginative but plausible reconstructions of these Egyptian games have been made by several experts, notably R. C. Bell.[11]

Grammai and **Duodecim Scripta.** Research into the classical contribution to the origin of Tables throws up few hard facts but much circumstantial evidence, from which Murray concludes 'that the board games of Greece and Rome are affiliated to the older games of Egypt, Ur and Palestine, and that they reached Greece by way of the Mediterranean islands'. If the remains of Greek games are sparse and unenlightening, literary references to them in the Classical period are less sparse but no more illuminating. They were collected and examined in the first century AD by Suetonius, whose book on Greek board games survives only in a few extracts made by Eustathius in the twelfth century, and in the second century by Pollux, whose *Onomasticon*, though surviving complete, is no model of clarity.

Plato mentions two types of of board game. Petteia, played with pebbles on a squared board, was evidently a war game. Kubeia clearly refers to dice and may mean either dice games in general or a particular game played with them, possibly a race game akin to Tables. Philemon, in the fourth or third century BC, uniquely mentions a game called Diagrammismos, which Pollux later says 'used to be called Grammai'. *Grammai* means drawn marks, or lines, and Austin plausibly equates this with the more frequently mentioned Roman game of Ludus Duodecim Scriptorum, or just Duodecim Scripta, 'the Twelve-Line Game'. No written description is known, but such a game appears to be depicted on the back of a silver mirror found at Palestrina and dating from the third or second century BC. The illustration (Fig. 4.10) shows a young couple seated at a gaming board consisting of

Fig. 4.10. Duodecim Scripta, as depicted on the back of a Roman mirror.

twelve straight lines in a row, looking at first blush rather like a shove-ha'penny board. With no pieces in view, play either has just ended or is about to start. The youth seems poised to cast a die or dice, and is making the untranslatable utterance 'OFEINOD', to which the girl responds 'DEVINCAMTED', perhaps roughly equivalent to 'I bet I beat you'. Nothing further is known of this game, and one need not take too seriously Oswald Jacoby's suggestion that the scene depicts a bout of Strip Backgammon.

Duodecim Scripta clearly relates to many more elaborate gaming boards surviving from all parts of the Roman Empire, including Britain. These are 3 × 12 boards consisting of two halves separated by a blank or decorated 'bar' equivalent (Fig. 4.11). The cells are usually represented by symbols such as circles, square, vertical bars, monograms, leaves, crosses, crescents, and suchlike, or by letters of the alphabet, which may even, with a nod to word-gamers, spell out an appropriate epigram composed of six six-letter words.

The first epigram reads 'To hunt, to bathe, to play, to laugh—this means to *live*!', the second 'Get out of here—you haven't a clue how to play. Push off, fathead!'

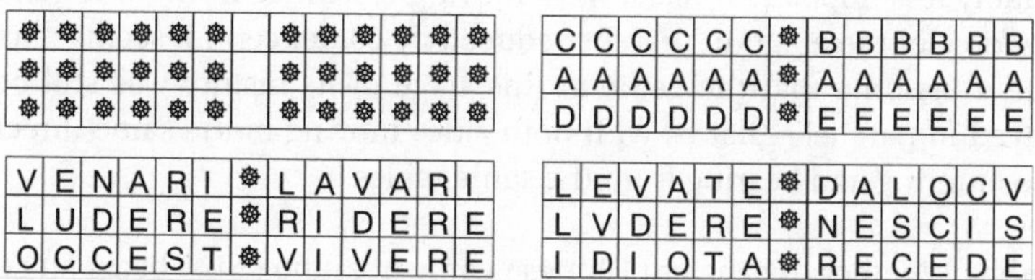

Fig. 4.11. Elaborations of Duodecim Scripta.

Duodecim Scripta could have derived from the 3 × 12 extension of the Egyptian Game of Thirty. It was played with three dice (*tesserae*) and fifteen black and white pieces. Though precise details of play are lacking, it evidently belongs to the Tables family in all major respects. The board marked merely with the letters A to E, found at Ostia, leads Murray to suppose that 'the men were entered in A, moved through the tables B, C, and D, and were borne from E when the player had brought all his fifteen men to that table'.[12]

Alea, described in a seventh-century work of Bishop Isidore, is Duodecim Scripta reduced from three rows to two. The date of this change is unknown, but the new game became popular in the first century AD, being especially favoured by the Emperor Claudius (r. 41–54). 'So addicted was his devotion to dice,' says Suetonius (in Robert Graves's translation), 'that he published a book on the subject, and used to play, while out driving, on a special board fitted to his carriage which prevented the game from upsetting.'

Tabula. *Alea* previously meant lots in general, whether dice or astragals, and subsequently attached itself to the game described above. While it continued to denote that game in literary texts of the early medieval period, on the practical front it was replaced by the more specific name Tabula. As such, it passed into Byzantium and thence entered Greek as Tablē, whence the modern Greek Tavli and all the western European variations on the word Tables.

Tablē is the subject of four epigrams by Agathias of Myrine, one of which concerns an embarrassing position fallen into by the Byzantine Emperor Zeno (r. 475–81). The position as reconstructed by Becq de Fouquières[13] is shown in Fig. 4.12.

Zeno, moving White anticlockwise from (a) to (z), throws 2–5–6. Unable to move any from (f), (j), or (y), he necessarily splits the doubletons on (k), (t), (v), leaving no fewer than eight blots. Since his position would be notably less hopeless if Black were moving clockwise from (z) to (a), and the force of the epigram thereby reduced by 60 per cent, it seems reasonable to assume that the game at this stage of its history was still being played in parallel—that is, with both sides moving in the same direction and entering and bearing from the same tables.

Liubo. Whether the ancient Chinese game of Liubo ('Six') bears any relation to early forerunners of Tables is a tantalizing question. This prestigious game of the Han period (206 BC–AD 220) was said by a contemporary

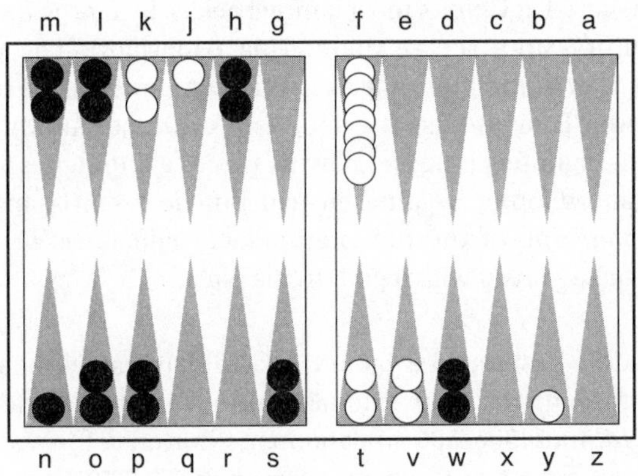

Fig. 4.12. Zeno's game.

historian to have been played as early as the twelfth century BC, in the reign of King Wuyi. Practically all is known about it apart from that most vital component, the rules of play. Information gathered from the survival of complete sets, from contemporary illustrations, passing references, and, especially, from a ceramic model in the British Museum of two men playing the game, yields the following description.[14]

Two players face each other from opposite sides of a square board. The board, typically of stone, consists of eight large rectangles surrounding a slightly smaller central square. Each rectangle is filled with elaborate carvings prominently featuring T and L shapes, abstract curves, and snakes. These may conceal positional subdivisions of the board, as eight rectangles seem insufficient for what is assumed to be some kind of race game. Each player has six pieces, and (presumably) moves them in accordance with the throw of lots. In most relics and representations these are twelve split bamboo rods, though some are associated with dice of either six or eighteen faces.

The game is mentioned in a fifth-century AD Chinese translation of the Indian *Brahmasutra*, but by this time appears to have been obsolescent. If it was some kind of race game, as most believe (though it looks more like a stake-board game), perhaps its demise was caused by the more exciting challenge of Shuang-liu (Nard; see below).

'The most ambitious Liubo players of antiquity stopped at nothing in their desire to play the ultimate contest', says Oliver Moore of the British Museum's Department of Oriental Antiquities.[15] 'In China "mountains are gods", and it is thus not surprising that the most sublime legends about

Liubo were located at China's most famous peaks. By far the most evocative is a 3rd-century story set at Mount Hua (Huashan). The Qin dynasty philosopher Han Fei relates that King Zhao of Qin ordered his workmen to climb Mount Hua and use the abundant cypresses and pines to make throwing rods eight feet long and playing pieces eight inches long. Han Fei does not state whether a game ensued but he records an inscription, perhaps left on one of the mountain's sheer cliff faces or on a tablet: "King Zhao once played with a god in this place".'

Nard is a Middle Eastern race game virtually identical with Backgammon. The name of the game, in its extended form Nardshir, first occurs in the Babylonian *Talmud* (300–500 AD), and in its shortened form as early as the Middle Persian romance *Chatrang-Namak* (*c.*650–850 AD), which retails the story of how Chess entered Persia from India and led to the invention of Nard in return. The Chinese game of Shuang-liu, 'Double Sixes', certainly resembles Nard, and may date from the fifth century AD. Following their seventh-century conquest of Persia, Nard was adopted by the Arabs and became as popular throughout the Muslim world as might be allowed by individuals' observance of religious restriction. The eighth-century founders of the schools of Muslim jurisprudence strictly forbade it and attached legal penalties to Nard players. The game also spread northwards in Georgia, to the Kalmuks of Central Asia, the steppes north of Astrakhan, and into the Deccan, but failed to displace games of the Pachisi family in the affections of the Hindus. Shuang-liu also spread from China throughout the Orient, including Korea (*Ssang-ryouk*), Japan (*Sunoroku* or *Sugoroku*), and elsewhere. Nard also travelled westwards, entering Europe through the Moorish conquest of Spain and in the baggage of crusaders returning from the east.

Nard as described in the Alfonso MS of 1283 is recognizably ancestral Backgammon, but in the absence of earlier rules one can only assume that it was substantially similar. Murray notes that *nard* is the Iranian for a wooden block or cylinder and *shir* means 'lion', and takes these as referring to the respectively plain and carved pieces with which the game was played, as were ancient Egyptian race games.

Fiske[16] distinguishes three periods of development, to which it seems logical to attach an anterior fourth covering the classical and prehistoric varieties, producing the following scheme:

1. Grammai and other classical games, including Tabula.
2. Nard, from its invention or earliest appearance in south-west Asia prior to the ninth century AD.

3. Tables, the European game in all its variations from around the turn of the first millennium.
4. Backgammon, Trictrac, and other sophisticated games from the fifteenth century on.

What remains unclear is whether European Tables is better regarded as a continuation of Tabula or as an import from Nard-playing Islam, or how the two might be combined. Fiske seems to ascribe more to Nard than to Tabula, possibly because the latter was played with three dice as opposed to the two of Nard and Tables, yet all his evidence rather favours a continuation from Tabula. The identity of modern Nard with Backgammon does not help, as the Iranian game may represent a back-borrowing. The matter is complicated by the fact that Tables is mentioned two centuries earlier than Chess. It appears, for example, in the Exeter MS, a collection of Anglo-Saxon verse dating from the tenth century. Fiske quotes a ninth-century German gloss of *ludere tabulis* as *za spillone zaples*. The first German mention of Chess occurs in the *Ruodlieb*, an eleventh-century Bavarian epic, and thereafter Chess is generally referred to as *Schachzabel*, as opposed to *Wurfzabel*, as if Chess were regarded as a novelty bearing some relation to a game already known as *Zabel*. There is also the curious fact that the Byzantine equivalent was always known as Taula, implying an import from the west, whereas one might have expected it to have acquired the game, as it did Chess, direct from the Arabs and under its Arabic name.

Games without Movement

The following survey of games played 'within the tables' begins with a small number of games suitable for children.

Eureika is a Levantine children's game forming an introduction to the Backgammon board. Starting with tripletons on their first three points and doubletons on the next three, each in turn throws two dice. There are no moves or captures, the winner being merely the first to bear all off. The Alfonso Manuscript describes a forerunner, *Doblet*, played with twelve pieces each, starting doubled on all six points.

Los Doze Canes (Los Doze Hermanos), also in Alfonso, is the reverse of Doblet. Starting with twelve pieces in hand, each in turn throws two dice and enters pieces on the appropriate points of one table only, the other three being disregarded. A singleton is vulnerable, and, if captured, must be re-entered on the same point before another entry is made. The winner is the first to get doubletons on all six points.

Doublets, a Tudor game subsequently described by Cotton[17] and Holme,[18] is Eureika with restrictive refinements. With two dice, doublets conferring a second throw, the aim is first to bear off all pieces in excess of one from any point, and then the remaining singletons. Hyde and Cotgrave[19] respectively equate and associate this with the French game of *Renette* ('The Queen's Game'). Rabelais mentions an extended form, *Tables Rabattuées,* in which, having borne all your pieces, you must then re-enter them and restore the original arrangement in order to win. In *Ofanfelling,* an eighteenth-century Icelandic game, each starts with doubletons on the six points of one table, and the winner is the first to unpile all one's pieces, then repile them, and finally bear them.

Paumecary (French *paume carie*) denotes two games, one a variety of Buffa (see below). The other was a fourteenth-century English game played only on the six points of one table, either by two players or by two teams of two or three. In team play, all the members of one team threw before the turn passed to the other. With two dice, doublets conferring a second throw, the aim is to get all twelve pieces entered and then bear them. Singletons can be captured and must then be re-entered. 'When either side has borne all its men it proceeds to help bear the other side's men, smacking the losers' hands for each of their men so borne' (Murray).

Catch-Dolt, or *Ketch-Dolt,* mentioned in the sixteenth–seventeenth centuries, is a jocular extension of Paumecary. Black seeks to enter fifteen pieces in the north-east table, White likewise in the south-east, and the first to bear them wins. Cotton explains the title by noting that if you duplicate either or both of the numbers thrown by your opponent on his previous turn, you may not enter one of your own men, but instead must take the one your opponent has just entered on the equivalent point. Failing this, you are *dolted,* and lose the game outright.

Games of Parallel Movement

Puff and Buffa. Games of parallel movement are invariably played anticlockwise. In the Puff family, both start with all fifteen pieces in hand and start from the same table.

Buffa Cortese is an Italian game described in Alfonso, together with its Spanish equivalent *Pareia de Entrada.* It was later known as just *Buffa,* or *Buf,* became popular in Germany under the name *Puff[-Spiel],* and is recorded in England under the name *Paumecary* (which also applies to a game without movement, see above). Two or three dice are thrown, doublets give a second throw, and a throw unusable by one player may be used by his opponent. Singletons are captured, and the game won by bearing.

Lange Puff, a later German development, and known in English as *German* or *Russian Backgammon*, is distinguished by a remarkable variety of doublet treatments. Typically, doublets are played twice, then their reverse doublets are played twice and the player throws again. (The reverse of *n* is 7 minus *n*.) A second consecutive throw of doublets repeats the process, but not a third. The English game does not give a second throw or allow the play of reverse doublets to be used for bearing off. A throw of 2-1, or 'deucey-ace', however, entitles the player to play any desired doublet.

Recontrat (Alfonso) is a variety of Buffa in which pieces are entered and bear from diagonally opposite tables, White playing from north-east to

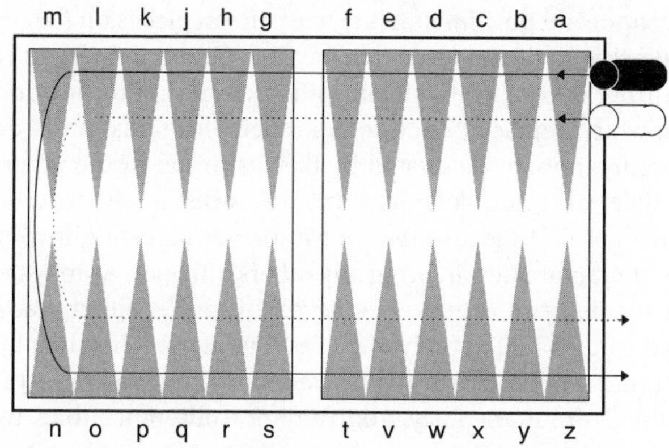

Fig. 4.13. Puff.

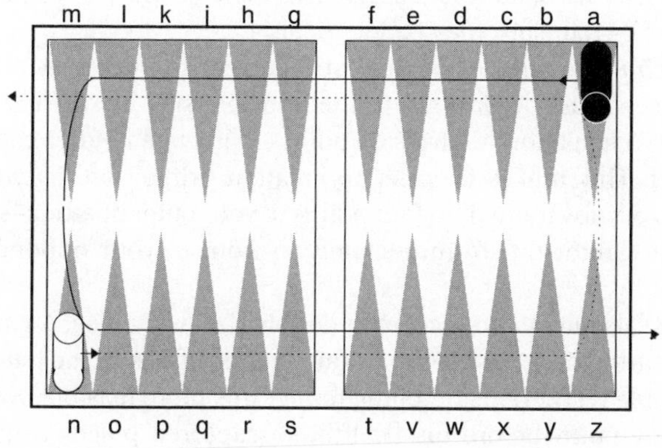

Fig. 4.14. Jacquet.

south-east, and Black from south-west to north-west. (Murray's uncharacteristic misreading of the phrase *que llaman los romanos recontrat*, 'which the Romans call Recontrat', has resulted in a general rendering of the game's name as 'Los Romanos Rencontrat'.)

Verquere group. Verquere is the name given by Seymour in the 1754 *Court Gamester* to a form of Tables known as *Verkehren* in Germany, *Verkeer* in the Netherlands, *Revertier* in French, meaning '(to) return'. Substantially similar are the Spanish *Chaquete*, French *Jacquet*, Italian *Giacchetto*, and the modern Turkish *Moultezim*. These games of parallel movement are distinguished from the Puff group by the fact that both players start from diagonally opposite positions, White with fifteen pieces on (a) and bearing from (z), Black with fifteen on (n) and bearing from (m). In Scandinavia, the game is further developed by the introduction of various positional wins.

Jacquet, which replaced Trictrac in French affections in the early nineteenth century, only to be ousted by Backgammon in the late twentieth, uses two dice, with doublets played twice. A distinctive feature is that a player must get one piece— his *courier* or *postillon*—right round to the fourth quarter before he can bring any others into play. As may be appreciated from the diagram, whoever achieves this first is better placed to start attacking the other's main body of pieces (Fig. 4.14). Piling is subject to the constraint that neither player may have more than two points of his entry table doubled simultaneously, and may not pile more than two on his twelfth point. A win counts double if the opponent has borne none (*marcia*), and treble if the winner at no time constructed doubletons on six consecutive points (*marcia per punto*). In *Jacquet de Versaille*, double-6 counted as six sixes, double-5 as five fives, and so on. The game of *Jacina*, mentioned by Rabelais, may be identical.

Moultezim is a form of Jacquet still current in Turkey. A player's first moved piece must be brought to the opposite side before any more can be moved. A singleton controls its point—it may be neither captured nor landed on. This makes it easier to create a prime, but, as you are not allowed to occupy more than four points in your outer board (n–s in White's case), you cannot do so immediately in front of your opponent's entry point.

Verquere also uses two dice, with doublets played twice. A game can be won by bearing or by achieving certain end positions in the bearing table. Considerable restrictions on piling render this more feasible. Neither may pile on any point before his twelfth, so captured pieces cannot be re-entered on occupied points. In the English game, a player with more than six pieces to re-enter is *johned*, and loses double. In *Brädspel*, the Swedish equivalent, the higher throw must be taken first, throws may not be combined to re-enter a piece, and wins are graded from least to most spectacular as follows:

1. Bearing all first.
2. Getting five each on the last three points (*enkelt kronspel*, or 'single royal').
3. Getting three each on the last five points (*dobbelt kronspel*).
4. Getting respectively three, five and seven on the last three points (*trappspel*).
5. Getting all fifteen on the last point (*uppspel*).
6. Leaving the opponent with more to re-enter than points available (*jan*).
7. Leaving the opponent with no points on which to re-enter (*spräng-jan*).

Kotra, the Icelandic equivalent, adds to these wins for getting three each on the last three points and two each on the previous three,[20] and for getting seven and eight on the penultimate and last respectively. *Piprjall* is a form of Kotra in which throwing a double-x entitles all doublets to be played in order from x-x down to 1-1 inclusive, while 1-1 itself does the same in reverse up to 6-6.

Barail and Myles. The following games resemble Puff in that both play from north-east to south-east, but differ in starting with all thirty pieces on the board in more or less dramatic initial arrangements. Some use three dice, others two with a notional third throw of six.

Cab e Equinal (Alfonso MS). In one variant, White has fifteen on (g) and Black fifteen on (h); in the other, White has 14 on (g) and one on (t), Black 14 on (e) and one on (d).

Laquet, also in Alfonso, and there said to be 'recently invented', more bizarrely equips White with one on (a) and 14 on (z), Black one on (m), two on (t), and three each on (vwxy). Two dice are used, and an unusable throw may be used by the opponent. Unusually, no captures are made.

El Seys, Dos e As (Alfonso MS) is so called ('Six-Deuce-Ace') because White starts with three on (a), four on (b), eight on (f), while Black has five each on (c,d,e). A curious rule decrees that a captured piece be re-entered in the table diagonally opposite the one it was captured in.

Barail, a sixteenth-century Italian game perhaps equivalent to the *Sbaraglio* mentioned by Cardano in *De Ludo Aleae*, is much the same, except that White starts with one on (k) and fourteen on (l), Black with fifteen on (m). It is described under the name *Baralie* in an English MS in the British Library, with two dice and a notional throw of six.

Myles is the name given by Strutt to a related game recorded in the same English MS. White has five on (m), four each on (r,s), two on (x); Black has three each on (n–r).

Chase the Girls. Some of the most unusual Tables games are of Scandinavian development. Among them is the Icelandic *Að Elta Stelpur* (Chase the Girls), which involves movement around the board but is won by capturing instead of bearing. As the title suggests, it is more of a chase game than a race game. Each player starts with six pieces, one on each point of his left-hand table. Both move endlessly anti-clockwise. No point may be occupied by more than one piece. If you land on one of your own, you move it to the next vacant point beyond. If you land on an enemy piece, you capture it. The first to lose all his pieces loses the game.

In the first half of the game movement is conferred only by throws of six, one, and doublets:

6-6 = move four pieces 6 points each.
6-x = move one piece 6 points.
1-x = move one piece 1 point.
x-x = move two pieces *x* points each, and throw again.
x-y = no move.

The second half begins when one player has only one piece left. This is called a *hornaskella*, or 'corner rattler', because it can move only to the corner points of each of the four tables—in effect, it is 'blind' to the four central points of each table. For a corner-rattler only:

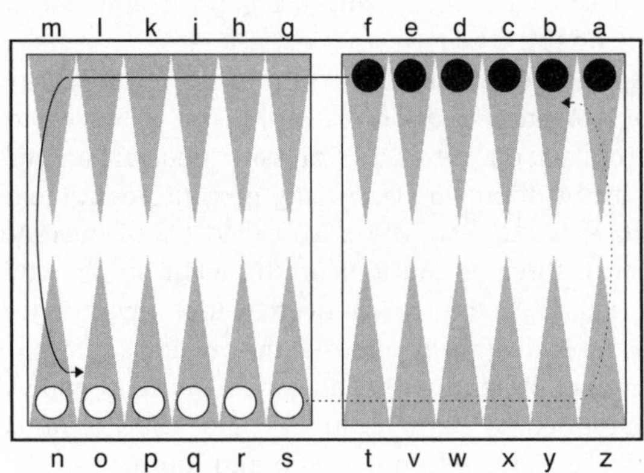

Fig. 4.15. Chase the Girls.

1-x = move to the next corner point.
6-x = move to the next corner point but one.
1-1 = move to the next corner point but one.
6-1 = move to the next corner point but two.
6-6 = move to the next corner-point but three (= no move!)
x-x = no move, but throw again.
x-y = no move.

It follows that a corner-rattler can only capture and be captured on a corner point. Even then it is invulnerable if sandwiched between two enemy pieces, one lying on each of the true points immediately before and behind it. See R. C. Bell for a more detailed practical guide to the game.[21]

Games of Contrary Movement

Gegenpuff and Acey-Deucey. In games of contrary movement both players move their pieces in opposite directions, as in Backgammon. A few of them start with an empty board.

Acey-Deucey is one of the few Tables games other than Backgammon practised by English-speakers, being especially popular in the US navy. It derives from a game recorded in Germany as *Gegenpuff* or *Contrabuf*, and is variously known in Britain as *French, Dutch,* or *Double Backgammon.* As the German name implies, it amounts to *Lange Puff* played in contrary motion (*gegen* = against, contrary), otherwise resembling it in that both players start with fifteen pieces in hand and enter from opposite tables.

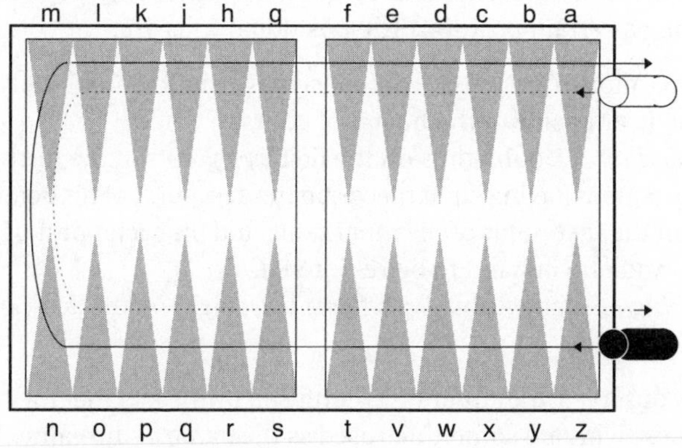

Fig. 4.16. Gegenpuff, Acey-Deucey.

A feature of Dutch Backgammon is that a player must enter all fifteen pieces before moving any off their point of entry, and may not capture singletons until at least one of his own pieces has reached his bearing table.

Acey-Deucey, the Navy game, starts with fifteen pieces in hand and plays like Backgammon, except that you are allowed to move a piece on the board even when you have one in hand to re-enter. Its most startling feature is the privilege attaching to the throw of 1-2. It entitles you to move 2-1 first, then play any doublet (four moves) of your choice, and then to throw again. Such a throw also automatically doubles the stake, and in some circles the final pay-off varies with the number of losing pieces left unborne.[22]

Buff de Baldriac, described in the Alfonso MS, is an apparent forerunner distinguished by the unique peculiarity that players enter and bear from *adjacent* tables, Black moving clockwise from north-west, White anti-clockwise from north-east. This leads to a game of perpetually aggressive encounter, practically abolishing the running game.

Ludus Anglicorum, Plakoto. Other games of contrary motion start with each player's fifteen pieces piled on their entry point, White on (a), Black on (z).

Ludus Anglicorum, described in an undated manuscript in the British Museum, is equivalent to the Spanish *Emperador* (Alfonso MS), Italian *Testa*, French *Tieste* and *Impérial*. It uses three dice if available, otherwise two and a notional throw of six, or else the player or his opponent chooses a throw for the notional third die. Neither may enter a piece on a point occupied by another of its own, and neither may pile any point on his half of the board (cf. Jacquete and Verquere). A player wins by bearing all or by achieving a certain position. The positional wins are:

- *Bareta* (Alfonso MS only) = Six consecutive doubletons—only possible on the further side of the board, of course.
- *Limpolding* = Doubletons on the first five points of the further board, the opponent having eight pieces on the ace-point of his bearing table, one on the first point of his inner table and on each point of his entry table, and one in hand to be re-entered.
- *Lurching* = As above, but with fewer than eight on the ace-point of the bearing table.

As Murray observes, the situation is confused by the fact that the names for some of these wins are sometimes used as the name of the game. There is a French reference to *la Limpole*, and frequent mentions in the sixteenth century of a game called in English *Lurch*, French *Lourche* or (mistakenly) *l'Ourche*, German *Lurtsch*. The word *Jan* is either a variant of *Jean* or has become confused with it. In Trictrac it means both a table and a winning position—the latter reflected in the term *johned* used in Seymour's *Court Gamester.* Scandinavian card games recognize a degree of loss called *jan*, equivalent to our *lurch* (American *skunk*) in Cribbage.

Medio Emperador, mentioned in Alfonso, is, as the name implies, a version of Emperador speeded up by ignoring two tables.

Garanguet is a French game of this type still occasionally described in French game-books. A triplet is played triply and a doublet doubly, but only if its sum exceeds the throw of the third die.

Plakoto,[23] current in Greece, and *Tavli*[24] in Cyprus, start with fifteen white pieces on (a) and 15 black on (z). The aim and the use of doublets are as in Backgammon. The significant difference is that a player hitting a blot does not thereby oust it but pins it so that it cannot move. Each player controls all those points on which he maintains two or more pieces, or one or more pieces pinning an enemy piece down. A pinned piece cannot move until exposed by the removal of all enemy pieces holding it down.

Gioul,[25] widespread in the Levant and perhaps of Turkish origin, resembles Plakoto in all but two significant respects. First, singletons are neither captured nor pinned, but control their points, as in Moultezim. Second, doublets are played four times, as in Backgammon, but, if less than 6-6, are then followed by all consecutive higher doublets up to and including the sixes. Throwing a double-1 therefore initiates a series of twenty-four moves. There is, however, a catch. If, in the course of all these moves, you reach one you cannot legally fulfil, then your turn ends, and your opponent continues the series up to 6-6 from and including the move you could not make. If he also reaches a premature halt, the rest are cancelled and he makes his normal throw.

Backgammon. Backgammon is the chief member of a group of games of contrary motion, the players entering and bearing from directly opposite tables, and each starting with fifteen pieces in a conventional opening arrangement. Several direct precursors are described in the Alfonso manuscript of 1283.

Quinze Tablas was played with three dice. Each player starting with doubletons on his first seven points and a singleton on the eighth. Variants were played with smaller numbers of pieces.

Todas Tablas means much the same thing, namely, that 'all [15] tablemen' are in play. It is matched by French *Toutes Tables* and Italian *Tavole Reale*, and is essentially the game described by Cotton under the name *Irish*. The initial arrangement is that of Backgammon.

Fallas, described in Alfonso, was played with three dice, or two and a notional third permanently set at one. It shares with the Barail group a dramatic opening position, White having two on (a) and thirteen on (t), Black two on (z) and thirteen on (f). It is recorded in France as *Faille* and in England as *Fayles* or *Fails*. Murray identifies this with *Minoret*, described as the leading variety [of Tables] in the Romagna in 1600.

Imperial, a fourteenth-century English three-dice game, has each player start with five pieces on each of three points. According to Murray, White starts on (f,g,h), Black on (p,s,t)—an extraordinarily asymmetrical arrangement. The same manuscript mentions *Provincial*, a more balanced variant, in which each player starts with eight on his sixth point and seven on his seventh.

Backgammon means 'the back game'. The latter half derives from an older *gamen*, and if its newer spelling evokes a side of bacon this is probably due more to the corruption of a bad speller than to that of an undisciplined punster. The earliest reference to it recorded in *The Oxford English Dictionary* is from one of Howell's letters, *c*.1645, observing: 'Though you have learnt to play at Baggammon [note the spelling and hence the presumed pronunciation], you must not forget Irish, which is a more solid and serious game.' The earliest reference in the *OED* to this immediate forerunner is from Richard Tarlton, *Newes out of Purgatorie* (1588): 'Her husband that loved Irish well, thought it no ill trick to beare a man too many.' Cotton's descriptions of both games suggest that Backgammon is merely a souped-up form of Irish made by introducing a revolutionary new rule whereby doublets count double, which, as he observes, 'makes a quicker dispatch of the game'. It also increases the incidence of more dramatic and correspondingly profitable wins, which in the earliest form of the game occurred at four levels. You won a single game by bearing off all your men before your opponent has finished bearing off, a double if you finished on a doublet throw, a triple, or *backgammon*, if you finished before your opponent had borne off any, and a quadruple if you did this on a doublet throw. Hence the game took its name from the newly invented triple win made when the loser is 'backward in the game', or 'backgammoned'.

The idea of degrees of win was not in itself entirely new. Earlier varieties of Tables included a double win or 'lurch' made before the opponent had borne off any men. Jacoby and Crawford[26] seem to think this an error arising from confusion with Cribbage, so perhaps we should note that the word derives from the earlier French game of Lourche, and thence in turn from a German word meaning left-handed, with a general flavour roughly equivalent to our 'wrong-footed'. Hence 'the lurch' in Cribbage, together with our metaphorical 'in the lurch', has its origin in a Tables game, not vice versa. By a later development, the increased win for a final doublet was abolished; the original backgammon (triple) was reduced to a double and renamed a simple gammon; and the backgammon triple win redefined into its present form. And so the game remained until a similar speeding up was effected by the introduction of the doubling die in the early twentieth century.

Backgammon and its immediate ancestors were popular at all levels of society, though in Britain it was never considered 'royal' as the game of Chess was, and it seems to have been especially associated with the professions and the bourgeoisie, and with the clergy in particular. Cotton places it second after Irish in his *Compleat Gamester*, and Hoyle in 1743 makes it the subject of an immediate sequel to his incredibly successful *Short Treatise on Whist*. Joseph Strutt, however, could later write, in *The Sports and Pastimes of the People of England*:

> At the commencement of the eighteenth century Backgammon was a very favourite amusement, and pursued at leisure times by most persons of opulence, and especially by the clergy, which occasioned Dean Swift, when writing to a friend of his in the country, sarcastically to ask... 'In what esteem are you with the vicar of the parish; can you play with him at Backgammon?' But of late years (1800) this pastime is become unfashionable... The tables, indeed, are frequently enough to be met with in the country mansions; but upon examination you will generally find the men deficient, the dice lost, or some other cause to render them useless. Backgammon is certainly a diversion by no means fitted for company, which cards are made to accommodate in a more extensive manner; and therefore it is no wonder they have gained the ascendancy.

Strutt's explanation of the game's eclipse is questionable, for if cards were its cause they could have eclipsed it just as easily up to five centuries earlier. An alternative possibility is the rise at this period of proprietary race games of the Goose family, which compete for the same ecological niche and have the advantage of accommodating a more sociable number of players.

The twentieth-century renaissance of Backgammon dates from the introduction of the doubling die in one of the American clubs in the 1920s. This stake-raising device has six sides numbered 2-4-8-16-32-64. Play starts for a single stake. Either player, when about to throw, may offer to double the stake by passing the die with its '2' uppermost to the opponent's side of the board. If the opponent resigns, the doubler wins a single game; if not, play continues at doubled stake. Subsequently, the doubled player, on his turn to throw, may offer to quadruple by passing the die with its '4' uppermost across the table... and so on, following the same principle. It is still possible to win a 'gammon', thereby doubling the amount shown on the doubling die, but the thrice-valued 'backgammon', which gave the game its name when first introduced in the seventeenth century, is now generally disregarded, except by prior agreement.

Trictrac. As Backgammon is the classic Tables game of the English-speaking world, so Grand Trictrac was that of the French—until, that is, its displacement in the twentieth century first by Jacquet and subsequently by Anglo-American Backgammon. It differs from most forms of Tables in that the aim is not so much to bear off as to score points for achieving certain positions and making certain moves. A game can end with one player's pieces being borne, but more usually does so by the attainment of a target score before a bearing-off position is reached. Originating in France probably around 1500 (it is mentioned by Rabelais), it may have been inspired by point-scoring systems associated with card-play. The rules were not fixed until the reign of Louis XIV, and further development in the eighteenth century produced the elaboration known as Grand Trictrac, which has changed little since its classic exposition by the Abbé Soumille in 1738.[27]

A possible ancestor of Trictrac, albeit not recorded before the seventeenth century, may be reflected in the game of *Tourne-Cas*. Each starts with three pieces in hand, enters them from the east, White in the lower table and Black in the upper, and moves them to the west. The winner is the first to get all three piled on his *coin de repos*, his twelfth or westernmost point. Pieces are entered and moved in accordance with the throw of two dice. Movement is restricted by the fact that only one piece may occupy one point at a time (other than home), and that no piece may overtake another. The two side's pieces remain on opposite tables, but one can capture another by landing on the point directly opposite. Variants and similar games included Toc (France), Toccateglio (Italy), Tokkadille (Germany) and Schuster (Sweden).

NOTES

1. See also Irving Finkel, 'La tablette des règles du jeu royal d'Ur', in *Jouer dans l'Antiquité* (Marseille, 1992), 154.
2. Bell, *Board and Table Games*, i. 24.
3. See Timothy Kendall, 'Le Jeu des Vingt Cases', in *Jouer dans l'Antiquité* (Marseille, 1992), 148–53.
4. Wolfgang Decker trans. Guttmann, *Sports and Games of Ancient Egypt* (Cairo, 1993), 131.
5. Ibid. 128.
6. Timothy Kendall and Roland May, 'Le Jeu de Senet', in *Jouer dans l'Antiquité* (Marseille, 1992), 130–47.

7. Roland May, 'Le Jeu de "58 trous"', in *Jouer dans l'Antiquité* (Marseille, 1992), 156–8.
8. Timothy Kendall (above, n. 3), 160.
9. Decker, *Sports and Games of Ancient Egypt*, 135.
10. R. Macalister's suggestion, in *History of Civilisation in Palestine* (1921), cited by Murray, who also illustrates it (*History of Board Games*, 23).
11. In Part I: of his *Board and Table Games from Many Civilisations.*
12. Murray, *History of Board Games*, 31, with 'D' misprinted for 'E'.
13. Of several reconstructions, that by Becq de Fouquières is favoured by R. G. Austin in 'Zeno's Game of Table', *Journal of the Historical Society* (1934), 202–5.
14. Based on Lhôte, 173–4 and 528, and Moore (next reference).
15. Oliver Moore, 'Winning Throws in Games with Gods', *The British Museum Magazine*, no. 25 (Summer 1996), 18–21.
16. Fiske, 173.
17. Charles Cotton, *The Compleat Gamester* (London, 1674; facsimile repr. Cambridge, 1972), 161–2.
18. Randle Holme, *The Academy of Armory* (1688; vol. ii, ed. I. H. Jeayes, London, 1905), 63.
19. Randle Cotgrave, *A Dictionarie of the French and English Tongues* (1611).
20. Murray says 'three each on each of t, u, w, x, y, z', but this makes eighteen. For further details, see Murray, *History of Board Games*, 127.
21. A less telegraphic account of this game appears in Bell, *Board and Table Games*, i. 37–8.
22. The Diagram Group, *The Way to Play*, (London, 1975), 25.
23. So Oswald Jacoby and John R. Crawford, *The Backgammon Book* (New York, 1970), 212. It appears as *Plakato* elsewhere, which makes less sense.
24. *Tavli* is described by R. C. Bell in *Games & Puzzles* 1st ser., 30 (June 1975). I was always under the impression that the game is so called in Greece, but the boxed game I bought in Greece under that name proved to be Backgammon.
25. Ibid.
26. Jacoby and Crawford, *The Backgammon Book*, 28.
27. Abbé Soumille, *Le Grand Tric-trac* (Avignon, 1738; 2nd edn. 1756).

Back to Square One

Snake, Hyena, Snakes & Ladders, and the Royal Game of Goose

The pictures plac'd for ornament and use,
The Twelve good rules, the Royal Game of Goose.
Goldsmith, *The Deserted Village* (1770)

There is a family of race games distinguished by the following features. First, each player moves just one piece from Start to Home ('simple' race games as previously defined). Second, the basically linear track is elaborated with actual or implicit short cuts, in that landing upon a specially marked space causes a piece to be suddenly advanced by an extra large amount—or rather, and more often than not, relegated 'Back to square one'.[1] Third, the game is decorated, both visually and conceptually, with a supposedly real-life theme providing a rationale for these sudden spurts of good or bad fortune. Thus ladders, in the Indian ancestor of Snakes & Ladders, represent personal qualities that carry you virtuously forwards towards Nirvana, while snakes—by far the more numerous—are vices that correspondingly impede your progress towards moral perfection.

The classic European game of this type is the sixteenth century so-called Royal Game of Goose. From it have sprung more thematic board games than from any other archetype, since it provides a simple mechanical template on which to build an unlimited number of apparently new games by simply varying the theme and decorations. This is why no Christmas edition of a newspaper is complete without its cartoonist's topically satirical game based on throwing dice and moving either forwards or backwards to become Prime Minister, or Public Enemy Number One, as the case may be. The best-known traditional or folk game on this theme, which has a goosy feel about it but is not in fact related, is the Indian game already referred to, from which derives the late nineteenth-century children's game of Snakes & Ladders.

Goose is sometimes referred to by its contemporaries as (the game of the) Snake—not because it features such a creature, but because its linear track takes the form of a spiral, like a coiled snake. As it happens, the players' pieces start on the outside and proceed counter-clockwise to the centre. Also as it happens, many relics survive of an ancient Egyptian gaming board having the form of a coiled snake, with its head in the centre, and so arranged that the passage from tail to head runs counter-clockwise. Furthermore, the outer end of a Snake board in the Louvre is carved into the shape of a bird whose head and feet unmistakably resemble those of a duck—or could it be a goose? It would take more than a flight of fancy spanning more than 4000 years of unrecorded ludic history to imagine a thematic link between these two groups of games. Nevertheless, on formal gounds alone, this is the point at which to introduce Mehen, or the ancient game of Snake.

Mehen: The Egyptian Snake Game

A score or more of such coiled boards are known. All depict a snake coiled in the same direction and divided into a number of rectangular segments—sometimes raised, sometimes indented—equivalent to the spaces of a race-track. They are made of various materials, range in size from 26 to 40 cm., and contain varying numbers of segments. Unlike Goose, but not surprisingly, the segments are plain and undifferentiated, making it doubtful whether short cuts were inherent in the board, though they could have been dictated by particular lot casts. Nor, in the absence of any contemporary documentation, is it certain that a race game is in question. That it is a game of some sort is indicated by the equipment either found with it or illustrated in tomb paintings. One of the oldest is a picture in the tomb of Hesy, a royal official, found at Saqqarah and dating from about *c.*2650 BC. It depicts equipment neatly laid out for three games, those of Mehen, Senet, and M'n. (Senet we have met. M'n, known from only two examples, consists of sixteen vertical lines or spaces in a row, and could be anything.) The Mehen equipment comprises 3 lions and 3 lionesses, each associated with six spheres of about 1 cm. diameter, resembling marbles. How they were used remains a mystery, and it has to be said that none of the surviving pieces are small enough to fit on the individual spaces of the boards they are associated with.

A curious feature of the Snake game is its apparent disappearance from the Egyptian record for a space of almost 2,000 years. One of the three or four oldest known boards bears the name of Aha, second king of the First Dynasty. This dates it to about 3000 BC. Artefacts and representations continue until about 2300, and remain absent until about 700 BC.[2]

Hyena

A children's game of the Baggara Arabs in Sudan, though of unknown antiquity, is thought to be a linear descendant of the Snake.

Li'b el Marafib, 'the Hyena Game',[3] takes place on a track drawn in the sand in the form of a square spiral and marked off into an indefinite number of points representing days of travel. Each player's piece represents his or her 'mother'. She enters at the starting point, which is one of the corners, and travels forwards by the throw of lots until she reaches the central point, representing a well. There she washes her clothes before retracing her steps back to the village (starting point).

When a player's mother reaches the village she releases a hyena, represented by the same piece and moved supposedly by her son. The hyena then travels to the well and back, but at twice the speed of a mother, each throw being counted double. At the well it pauses to drink, then travels back to the village. On the way, it 'eats' any mothers it may overtake, and these are removed from the board. The game ends when all remaining mothers have been eaten, or when the hyena reaches home. The player with the hyena wins, but there are degrees of winning and losing, and a player whose mother gets eaten is mocked by those who successfully return their mothers to the village.

The motors are three binary lots consisting of split sticks about 15 cm. long. They fall either bark or flat side up, and the number falling flat side up counts as follows:

flat sides up	0	1	2	3
move forwards	6+	T+	2	3+

Every throw is followed by another, except the 2, which ends the turn. The 'T' marked for one white side up stands for *taba*. A *taba* is followed by another throw but produces no movement. Instead, the player marks a credit in the sand for each *taba* thrown. *Tabas* confer certain graces and are deleted as the appropriate number are used up. Thus it costs you:

- One *taba* before your mother can leave the village and start on her journey.
- One *taba* to complete each day's journey short of the well, which must otherwise be reached on an exact throw. For example, if you are four days short, and throw a zero, entitling you to six days' movement, you cannot take it, but may instead get home by cancelling four *tabas* if you have them.
- Having reached the well, four *tabas* before you can start to move your mother back—two to wash clothes and two to get started. Any forward numbers you throw while awaiting your *tabas* may be noted down and used towards the return journey when you have enough *tabas* to start it.

- Ten *tabas* for your hyena to drink at the well. Not until these have been paid may it move off and start eating mothers.

Snakes & Ladders

Snakes & Ladders bears no evolutionary relationship to the game of Snake, but on formal and thematic grounds this is the place to take account of it. Many regard it as the most characteristically English children's game, which is true to the extent that, unlike Ludo/Parcheesi, it plays no part in the children's repertoire of either the rest of Europe or the USA. In fact, the English version is a degraded form of a game that is characteristically Asian, and evidently introduced by colonials returning from India, the jewel in the crown of the nineteenth century British Empire.

The track consists of 100 serially numbered squares forming a boustrophedon pathway in a field of 10 × 10. Certain pairs are connected, some by a snake with its head on one square and its tail on another, others by a ladder with its head on one square and its foot on another. There are typically twelve snakes and eight ladders, leaving 64 squares unaffected by either.

Any number may play. Each starts with a single piece in hand, and enters and moves it forward in accordance with the throw of one or two dice—if two, both must be thrown. The full value must always be taken if possible. An additional throw is conferred by a six if one die is used, or a double if two. Two or more pieces may occupy the same square at once. A piece landing on the head of a snake is 'eaten' and promptly travels to the lower-numbered square occupied by its tail. A piece landing at the foot of a ladder is promoted and promptly rises to the higher-numbered square at its head.

Home must be reached on an exact throw. If the throw is greater, the piece moves to 100 and then travels backwards until the count is fulfilled. If this brings it to the head of a snake it is 'eaten' in the usual way. The first to reach home wins, and the others may play for position.

Rules vary. Murray (1952) says it is played with two dice on an 8 × 8 board, but the one-die game on a 10 × 10 board seems to have been commoner from the start and is now universal. Many players demand an opening throw of six before a piece may be entered, the initial distance travelled being that of the next number thrown on the same turn in accordance with the usual entitlement. Bell says landing on an occupied square sends the occupying piece back to Start, but other rules require the second piece to return to the square it departed from, in effect forcing the omission of a turn, unless a six was thrown. Pritchard[4] reports that if a throw would take a piece beyond 100 it merely stays put.

Snakes & Ladders first appeared in Britain at the close of the nineteenth century. In 1892 F. H. Ayres published a version played on a circular spiral of 100 steps, and the following year R. H. Harte produced one played on a serpentine route contained within a square frame.[5] An unnamed but virtually identical game is described, in a British Patent specification of 1893, as consisting of

> a board whose squares are numbered and linked together forwards and backwards according to any arbitrary arrangement in combination with pieces and with a roulette teetotum dice or other means for the chance determination of numbers as specified.[6]

This has downward arrows instead of snakes. A similar patent of 1895 depicts a route connected by bridges, monkeys, grasshoppers, and rivers. Bridges are equivalent to ladders, and rivers are impassable except by means of bridges. Monkeys are equivalent to snakes, and landing on a grasshopper reverses a piece's direction of travel. Snakes and ladders featured in the 1895 game of Kismet, published by Globe Games (shortly to be renamed Chad Valley), described by Topsfield as 'essentially a product of the the Georgian and Victorian tradition of edifying morality games of the type of Virtue Rewarded and Vice Punished (1818) and The Game of Human Life (1790)'. Many varieties of Snakes & Ladders were published from the turn of the twentieth century, but the end of Victoria's reign saw

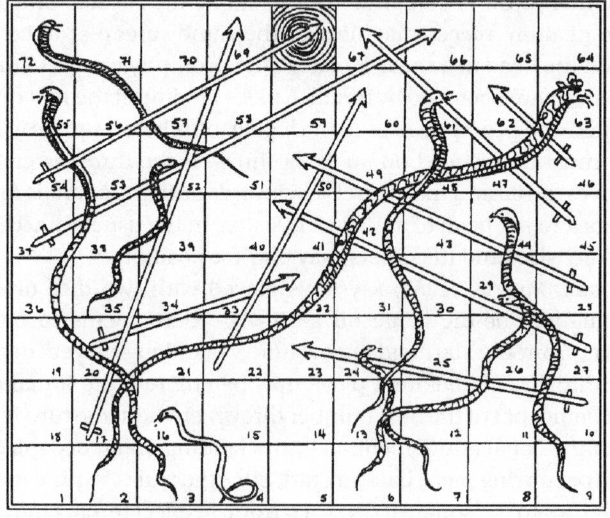

Fig. 5.1. Nagapasa, Nepalese Snakes & Ladders.

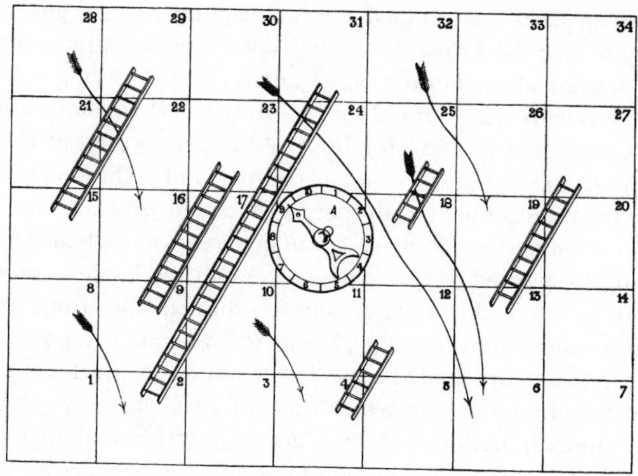

Fig. 5.2. An early form of Snakes & Ladders, patented in 1893.

the gradual loss of moral exhortations, and the inter-war years the loss of Indian decorative motifs or, indeed, any reference at all to the jewel of the imperial crown.

The Asian original, known from India, Nepal, and Tibet, and occurring in Vaishnaite (Hindu), Jain, and Muslim versions, is known in Hindi as *gyá n chaupaḍ*, 'the Chaupar of knowledge', and the Nepalese as *ná gapá sa*, 'Snake Dice'. It is one of moral instruction, in which the player pursues a sort of Pilgrim's Progress from the lower levels, associated with earthly desires and vices, to the higher, associated with increasingly more ethical and spiritual values, eventually reaching Vishnu, or Nirvana, or an equivalent peak experience. Movement is by the throw of dice or lots. A variety of boards dating from the eighteenth and nineteenth centuries are hand-drawn and painted on paper or cloth, and it is presumably only their flimsiness that has militated against the survival of earlier examples. Yet earlier examples there must have been, in view of the great variety of sizes, designs, and relative scales of values. The family of games is thought to go back perhaps to the thirteenth century AD, From the existence of examples lacking the snake-and-ladder short cuts it is possible that they were originally absent, and introduced at a later date to make the game more exciting. The numbers and relative proportions of snakes and ladders vary considerably, but in design remain fairly constant, with few local exceptions and departures.

Andrew Topsfield[7] has studied the surviving boards and groups them according to size. All follow the underlying pattern of a boustrophedon pathway starting at the bottom of the board and proceeding upwards in layers. They range in size from 72 squares, in eight rows of nine, through 81 (9 × 9), 84 (9 × 9 plus 3), 100 (10 × 10), 124 (in three sections of 40, 41, and 43), up to 342 and 360 squares. Not all boards number the squares, but all associate them individually with specific vices and virtues, trials, tribulations, and rewards. A modern version in my possession (thanks to Kishor Gordhandas) is printed on cheap paper in Hindi and English and entitled Tantric Snakes & Ladders, 'your journey through life, from existence towards liberation and knowledge, Karma to Brahman'. Every square from 1 to 84 is individually labelled, since 'All creatures are divided into eighty four genes or the moulds in which they are cast. These are eighty four perfect postures or *siddhasanas*.' Four ladders jump from fulfilment to bliss (14–44), self-realization to liberation (47–83), basic awarenesss to divine reality (50–84), recluse to transcedental [*sic*] knowledge (58–79). Eight snakes drop from source of light to cosmic sound (78–52), dissolution to self expression (76–2), resolution to law of causation (67–16), divine mother to fulmination (61–42), aloofness to illumination (48–10), cosmic time to the world (45–9), power of elimination to repetition of a sacred formula (13–8), and 'awful' to 'lowest plane of existence' (17–1).

Oriental Promotion Games

Hyde, in *De Ludis Orientalibus*, describes a Chinese gambling race-game played on a more or less spiral board.[8] Shing kun t'o, or the game of Mandarin Promotion, from the Ming dynasty (1368–1616), has a track of 98 irregularly sized segments in a rectangular spiral running clockwise to the central Imperial Palace. The various compartments represent ascending grades in the civil service hierarchy. The action is determined by the combinations, rather than the totals, of throws of six dice. The first throw determines which of several social origins the player comes from, and thus his entry-point and the career opportunities open to him. The aim is less to reach home first than to progress in such a way as to gain more riches according to the various levels reached. A modern version of the game still exists.[9] Culin describes a reduced form played in the succeeding Manchu dynasty, and some related games of Korea, Japan, and Tibet.[10] The Korean Tjyong-kyeng-to, 'Game of Dignitaries', is a Buddhist promotion game with spaces bearing the names of various conditions of existence, while the Tibetan Srid-pai khorio, 'Circle of Life', accords players 'different positions in the various heavens and hells' (Murray). These may bear some relation to

Indian morality games of the Nagapasa (Snakes & Ladders) type. Ba xian tu, the Game of the Eight Immortals, is the Chinese equivalent of Goose, and may derive from it.[11]

The Arabic Astronomy Game

We may here conveniently note in passing a circular gambling game described in the Alfonso MS of 1283 under the misleading title Los Escaques (Chess). Murray adds its Arabic name al-Falakiya and its Iranian name Kawakib ('Stars'). Seven players each move a piece representing a planet (the Moon, Mercury, Venus, Earth, Mars, Jupiter, Saturn) in accordance with the throw of a seven-sided die, and payments are made according to the astrological relationships so formed—trine, sextile, opposition, and so on. It is not a race game but a stake-board game of movement, having no defined ending.

The Royal Game of Goose

Francesco I de' Medici, grand-duke of Tuscany from 1574 to 1587, and regarded by some as a bit of a playboy, is known to have sent to the dour and mirthless Philip II of Spain a game called Gioco dell'Oca, thus bringing into the light of history one of the most fascinating games of all time.[12] In many ways, it may be said to usher in that modern period of board-gaming characterized by the introduction of illustrative and thematic elements to what had hitherto been primarily symbolic and mathematical. Unlike most board games of its time, Goose was little more than a lottery, being entirely governed by chance and invoking not the slightest element of skill or true player interaction towards the winning of stakes. Perhaps because of its deep symbolism and close involvement with Fate and Fortune it has the advantage, for descriptive purposes, of remaining remarkably constant in the essential details of its design and procedure.

The track is an elongated spiral of spaces numbered 1 to 63 with 'home' at the centre. Each player starts with (typically) twelve counters and places an agreed stake in the centre pool, which is an enlargement of 63. Starting with a distinctive piece initially placed on a notional 'zero' space, each in turn rolls two dice and moves it forward the number of spaces equivalent to the total cast. Some spaces are blank, and some marked with eventualities requiring whoever lands on them to move elsewhere, or add a stake to the pool, or both. The pool is won by the first to arrive at 63 on an exact throw.

The standard eventualities, appropriately illustrated, are:

Goose. Typically on 5, 9, 14, 18, 23, 27, 32, 36, 41, 45, 50, 54, and 59. A piece landing on a goose may move forwards again the same distance. If this brings it to another goose, it moves the same distance again, and so on, until it reaches a non-goose space.

Nines. 26 and 53 depict two dice headed respectively 6-3 and 5-4. Casting either of these combinations on the first throw of the game entitles you to move immediately to the space so marked. This prevents a piece from getting home in one throw from scratch, as landing on 9 on the first throw would result in completion of the circuit by the constant repetition of goose steps.

Bridge. On 6, sometimes 5. Pay a stake to the centre and move to 12.

Tavern (inn, alehouse). Typically 19. Pay a stake for your drink, and miss two turns (sometimes three).

Spring or well. Typically 31. Pay a stake for a wash and miss two turns, but move again if another player lands on the same space sooner.

Maze or labyrinth. Typically 42. Get lost, pay a stake, and return to 29.

Prison. Typically 52. Pay a stake and remain there until another player lands on it (by some accounts), or (by others) until another player makes the same cast as the one that got you there. The former seems excessively drastic.

Death. Invariably on 58, this is illustrated by a skeleton or a grave. Pay a stake, remove your piece from the board, and start again on your next turn.

Goblet. Invariably on 62. Pay a stake for 'tasting' and miss a turn.

If a piece lands on an occupied space, the occupant moves back to the space from which the usurper came, and both players pay a stake.

Home must be reached on an exact throw. If you throw too many, your piece proceeds to 63, then reverses direction and keeps going to the full extent of the throw. If this brings it to an eventuality space the eventuality applies in the usual way. In more drastic versions of the game, an overshoot required the player to go back to the beginning and start again. For obvious reasons, this may be associated with another alternative rule reducing the number of dice cast at each turn from two to one when a piece attained 57.

If more than three play, it may be agreed that the first home wins half the pool plus any odd unit, and the second and third half the remainder each.

Rules of play vary little in wording and arrangement from country to country. They are traditonally embodied in twelve numbered paragraphs, whence Oliver Goldsmith's reference (see epigraph, above).

They were so well known that many boards bear just the pictures without any associated verbal instruction. The non-eventuality spaces originally

Fig. 5.3. An Italian game of Goose, source undated.

bore just the number, being left otherwise blank; inevitably, however, designers took to filling them with scenes from everyday life, or philosophical or mythical subjects. Although 63 was the standard number of spaces, many games were produced with other numbers, though the significant ones, such as the well on 31, tended to remain constant.

Goose is thought to be of Italian and specifically Florentine origin. In 1612 the doctor of Louis XIII of France noted in his diary that the infant king enjoyed playing it—which may seem unlikely for a 2-year-old, but acquires interest from the fact that his mother, Catherine de' Medici, was a native of Florence. In any case, the game seems to have spread with remarkable rapidity. The Graz Museum houses a German equivalent dated 1589, engraved on stone by Michael Holzbecher, which is identical in all respects with the classic game except for the replacement of geese by the figure of Fortuna. In 1597 John Wolfe registered 'The newe and most pleasant Game of the Goose' at Stationers Hall, London, thereby acquiring the dubious equivalent of copyright. One of the earliest surviving examples is a French game printed at Lyon in 1601.

What inspired the invention of Goose? Formally, it loosely resembles its contemporary Chouette ('Owl')—a simple stake-board game, with no movement of pieces, but with outcomes determined by combinations resulting from the cast of three dice. Rabelais lists a Chouette as one of the games played by Gargantua (1534), but with no indication of its nature. Geese subsequently metamorphosed into other characters. In Italy a 78-space version called Il Guioco del Barone enjoyed considerable popularity up to the nineteenth century.[13] In northern Europe the key figure popularly became a monkey, producing a variety of so-called Affenspiele from the early nineteenth century on. From about the end of the eighteenth century Goose ceased to have much connection with royalty, the aristocracy, or even adulthood. Its point and purpose as a gambling game were overtaken by more exciting lotteries. Serious gamblers outgrew the need for mythic symbols and pretty pictures in the hard business of losing money, and bequeathed the tradition to their children for play with counters. Strutt in 1801 gives a bare and unenthusiastic description of a game he characterizes as childish and out of date, and a contemporary *Académie des Jeux* deems it too dull and old hat (*ancien*) to be worth explaining.

Games of Life, Bliss, and Moral Instruction

Variations on a theme of Goose are recorded from an early date. An obvious English derivative was John Garrett's possibly satirical Royal pass-tyme of Cupid or the Most Pleasant Game of the Snake (1690). The spaces, though decorated, were not marked with eventualities, the only remarkable occurrence being that if a piece reaches an occupied space, the previous occupant is removed and must be entered again from the beginning.[14]

As time went on the original meanings and symbolism were forgotten, and printers shifted their attention to the expanding domestic market for moral and educational games that would instruct and inform the young.

Anxious to eschew the slightest hint of gambling, many dispensed with that most natural and essential piece of equipment, dice, in favour of the teetotum. A notice accompanying the game of Human Life (1790) says the teetotum is 'to avoid introducing the Dice Box into private families'. By 1807, however, The Game of the Jew provides in its rules for the use of two dice or a twelve-sided teetotum.[15] Purists will note that, mathematically speaking, such a teetotum is by no means equivalent to two dice. It would need 36 sides to achieve the same effect, and would still fail to make the right noise when used. The eventual return to dice was inevitable.

The pieces used to move around the board were called 'pillars', and the boards themselves were paper sheets printed by means of copper or steel engraving, water coloured by hand, and mounted on canvas or linen (like maps). Lithographs began to replace engraving by the middle of the nineteenth century. The mounted boards were then folded and inserted into slip cases, decorated with patterned paper and finished with a label identifying the contents.

Culin (1895) gives a long list of Goose-derived games held in the Museum of Archeology and Paleontology, University of Pennsylvania.[16] Whitehouse, in *Table Games of Georgian and Victorian Days*, classifies such games according to thematic groups. The twenty-six geographical games in his collection are typified by A Journey through Europe, or the Play of Geography, invented by John Jefferys and sold at his house in Chapel St, Westminster. Dated 1759, the game has no compunction about the inclusion of dice, nor about its provenance, being 'played in all respects the same as the Game of Goose'. Some flavour of its particularities may be gained from the following: 'He who rests at No 77, London, wins ye play, shall have the honour of kissing Ye King of Great Britain's hand and shall be knighted and receive ye compliments of all ye company in regard to his new dignity' (Mr Pooter would have played this with relish.) On the other hand 'He who rests at 48 at Rome for kissing ye Pope's Toe shall be banished for his folly to No 4 in the cold island of Iceland, and miss three turns.'

Wanderers in the Wilderness, an undated game by Edward Wallis, has nothing to do with relegated football teams, being based instead on the exploration of South America. A player whose piece arrives at no. 22 is enjoined to 'Hark at the horrid sounds that proceed from the forest! It is the death roar of a Jaguar which an immense Boa Constrictor is in the act of crushing to a jelly.'

Other geographical games overlap with and form a transition to historical games. Whitehead describes sixteen such games, still reproducing the format of Goose, but with spaces now decorated with pictures of events, persons, or battles, and bearing dates and descriptions of each. From 1791 comes the less than pithily titled Royal Genealogical Pastime of the Sovereigns of England from the Dissolution of the Saxon Heptarchy to the Reign of His Present Majesty George the Third. How one would set about creating a demand for such a game in 15 seconds of TV prime time provides an interest subject for speculation. The title would have to be shortened for a start, perhaps to something as eye-catching as A Universal History of Chronology, a new game by Edward Wallis dated 20 May 1814. Wallis, however, was not without an eye for publicity. In The Royal Game of British Sovereigns, his Home square bears the legend: 'The Present edition of this game was published at Wallis's Juvenile Repository, 42 Skinner Street: whoever arrives here first is recommended to proceed instantly to the publishers to purchase another game equally instructive and amusing.'

Thirty-odd games of a miscellaneously 'instructional' nature include an Arithmetical Pastime (1798), a Grammatical Game in Rhyme, and What, Why, and Because (1850). All are race games, mostly spiral. Their moral-instructional tone is epitomized in the note relating to space 6 in Pleasures of Astronomy: 'The County Gaol—this is the place for those who attend to the motions of Billiard Balls more than to the motions of the planets.'

A separate category of 'games of moral improvement' include The Game of Human Life (1790), Swan of Elegance, Virtue Rewarded and Vice Punished, and Mansion of Bliss (pre-1818). In the first of these, directly ancestral to Milton Bradley's classic Game of Life, one notes with interest that manhood commenced at 13, old age at 49 (Daisy Ashford, it may be remembered, in *The Young Visiters* declares 'Mr Salteena was an elderly man of 42'). It may come as a surprise to discover that some games were designed for no more than amusement, such as The Adventures of Lord Pudding and his Companions on the Journey through Switzerland in 64 Stages. Some of these began to wander from the original Goose format. Funnyshire Fox Chase ends with the demise of the fox rather than with the attainment of a home position, while My House to Furnish involves a board and 35 cards.

The modern board-game industry may with little exaggeration be said to be built on the back of Goose. As Lhôte remarks, 'Comme celle des jeux de cartes, l'imagerie du jeu de l'oie se révèle inépuisable.' In the nineteenth century their proliferation by hundreds, thousands, eventually millions, saw the establishment of many well-known companies. As Love points out in *Great Board Games* (1979), America led the field, as with most popular entertainments. One of the earliest American games was Mansion of Happiness (1843), based on the Mansion of Bliss referred to above, a moralistic Goose variation devised by Anne W. Abbott, a clergyman's daughter. Milton Bradley was established in 1860, initial success built on The Game of Life.

Selchow and Righter, of Scrabble fame, entered the games business in 1867. In 1878 J. W. Spear, a German (*né* Spier) who had emigrated to the United States in the 1840s, then settled in Britain before going back to Germany, founded the British games company that still bears his name, most of the original production taking place in Nuremberg. The American firm of Parker Bros started in 1883, the English of Chad Valley in 1897.

The Race of Life, though nominally reminiscent of The Game of Life, was patented in 1893 by Seth Middleton Baines of Leicester, hosiery manufacturer. It is delicately described as a race game in which 'certain squares are marked with various words'. The clockwise spiral track starts on the square marked, naturally enough, Start of Life, and ends—somewhat ominously, as Bernard Kew remarks[17]—with the words 'the Race of Life is ended'. Some squares are devoted to diseases. You are thereby set back six squares when landing on croup, measles, whooping cough, mumps, erysipelas, influenza, or bronchitis. Landing on scarlet fever, typhoid fever, diphtheria, broken leg, or smallpox, forces you back to the nearest infirmary or hospital square, there to miss a turn. Rheumatism induces a delay curable only by throwing an ace, while consumption sends the unfortunate player right back to Square One. Less drastic are spaces representing coughs and sore throats, which merely set you back by a stated number of squares, though one of the cough squares, rather unkindly, gives you consumption. On a more positive note, however, The Race of Life is blessed with a number of bonus squares representing doctors, medicines, pills, and powders. There is even a vaccination square, which advances you to a point safely beyond the perils of smallpox. These all serve the happy effect of more rapidly propelling you towards the End of Life. And, in case you can't get out of the game fast enough, you will find the ultimate remedy on a square marked 'Suicide'.

NOTES

1. According to Brewer's *Dictionary of Phrase and Fable*, this derives not from board games but from diagrams used to assist football commentaries in the early days of radio. Pity.
2. See Timothy Kendall, *The Ancient Egyptian Game of the Serpent* (London, British Museum, 1993); also Lhôte, 108–13, 117–18, 552, and Gisèle Pierini, 'Le Jeu du Serpent', in *Jouer dans l'Antiquité* (Marseille, 1992), 125–9.
3. Murray, *History of Board Games*, 143; Bell, *Board and Table Games*, 1–12.
4. David Pritchard, *The Family Book of Games* (London, 1983), 162.
5. Erwin Glonnegger, *Das Spiele-Buch* (Ravensburg, 1988), 54.
6. Patent No. 5586. See 'Bernard Kew' (Barry Quest), *Games & Puzzles*, 1st ser. 25 (June 1974), 8–11, illustrated.

7. Andrew Topsfield, 'The Indian Games of Snakes and Ladders', *Artibus Asiae* (Institute of Fine Arts, New York University), XLVI: 3 (1985) 203–26.
8. Hyde, *Mandragorias*, 70 ff. See Murray, *History of Board Games*, 144–6.
9. Irving Finkel has one, but I discovered this too late to include a description.
10. See Culin, *Games of the Orient*, 77–8.
11. Lhôte, 401, quoting Jacques Pimpaneau, *Chine, Culture et Traditions* (Paris, 1988), which contains a chapter devoted to games.
12. The gist of this opening is borrowed from Giampolo Dossena, *Giochi de Tavolo* (Milan, 1984), 78. That such a gift was made is asserted by Pietro Carrera in *Il Gioco degli Scacchi* (1617).
13. Erwin Glonnegger, 'Brettspiele des Volkes', in *Homo Ludens*, iv (1994), 184–5.
14. Murray, *History of Board Games*, 143.
15. Whitehouse, *Table Games of Georgian and Victorian Days* (1971).
16. Culin, *Chess and Playing Cards*, 843–8.
17. 'Bernard Kew', *Games & Puzzles*, 1st ser. 26 (July 1974), 16.

No Dice

Hare & Tortoise

The most ingenious race game yet devised.
Intellect Games (Blurb)

He who hesitates comes first.
Proverbs. (Not.)

Strategic race games, in which progress is determined solely by judgement and calculation and not by the throw of dice or draw of cards, is a logical category of games but one that has remained entirely empty until the late twentieth century. In fact, I know of only two, of which the second, Hare & Tortoise, was invented by me and first published in 1974. Not until several years later did I become aware of the earlier game of Bantu, published by Parker Bros in 1955.[1] The track consists basically (but with some pleasing asymmetrical divergences) of a number of positions arranged in four concentric circles, and so designed as to be vaguely reminiscent of a village of African huts seen in plan. Further decorative motifs support the Bantu flavour, which, however, is entirely irrelevant to the essentially abstract nature of the game. Each player has four distinctively coloured pieces, numbered 1-4, which are entered into the circular track at the four cardinal points and required to travel clockwise towards home. Those numbered 4 are entered furthest away, and must cover the full circuit of four quadrants in all. The others are entered correspondingly closer to home, those numbered 1, for example, having only one quadrant to complete. Each in turn either enters a piece of his own colour, or moves such a piece already entered. The distance it moves is that of the number it bears (from 1 to 4), but if two or more pieces, not necessarily of the same colour, occupy a row of spaces in the same radial arm, and consequently the same distance from home, then the distance to be moved by each is the total of all their values. Thus if four pieces lying abreast of one another are numbered 2-3-4-3, any one of them moves 12 spaces forwards, thereby reducing by its own value the distance that may be covered by the next of them to be moved; and so on.

If Bantu vanished without trace, Hare & Tortoise, having appeared in a dozen different languages and sold several millions copies since it first appeared, is still available in Germany, where it has achieved the status of a minor classic. So far as I am aware, it remains the only one entirely fitting this unique category.[2]

Stripped of its faunal and floral associations, the game runs as follows. The aim is to be the first to advance one's piece from Start to Home, a distance of 64 steps. Movement is not dictated by lot. Instead, each player is initially equipped with cards of various denominations representing a total 65 units of energy. At each turn you may move any distance forwards to an unoccupied square, provided you can pay for it. The cost of movement increases geometrically with the number of spaces moved. To move

2 forward costs 3 units (1 + 2)
3 forward costs 6 units (1 + 2 + 3)
4 forward costs 10 units (1 + 2 + 3 + 4)

... and so on. To generalize, the cost of moving *n* forward is $(n^2 + n)/2$, or 'triangular *n*'. From the Start, therefore, you can get Home in 64 moves by the expenditure of 1 unit at a time. On the other hand, you could get nearly a quarter of the way round on the first two turns, leaving you well in advance but utterly played out, having spent either all 65 units on moves of ten and four, or 64 on moves of seven and eight. The spaces you land on bear symbols representing different ways of acquiring more energy. Many of these vary the amount you regain in inverse proportion to your current position in the race—10 if in the lead, 20 if lying second, 30 if third, and so on up to 60 if six play. It therefore pays to hang back. Furthermore, payment is made only when you leave the square, not when you land on it. Hence players may hinder one another's progress by using an intervening move to go past an expectant traveller, so altering his or her position in the race, and either reducing or annulling their entitlement.

It was at this point in the originally abstract development of the game that the title Hare & Tortoise naturally suggested itself, since skill consists in not haring ahead so fast as to run out of energy too soon, nor in lagging tortoise-like behind so as to be unable to catch up when necessary. The game is therefore almost entirely one of energy management and player interaction. Given this theme, it will not be surprising to find that the units of energy are designated carrots and lettuces. Each player starts with 65 carrots and three lettuces, and is obliged on three occasions during the course of the game to convert a lettuce into carrots on the appropriate squares, it being illegal to reach home with an uncashed lettuce (or, as an additional constraint, with a surfeit of carrots).

Having now devised a convenient symbolic language, we can continue the description. The various methods of carrot retrieval are indicated by the types of square landed on, as follows.[3]

Lettuce squares (total 5). Land on, do nothing. On the second turn, encash lettuce for carrots at the rate of 10 times your current position in the race. On the third turn, you must move away.

Carrot squares (11). You may, but need not, miss one or more turns and either draw or discard 10 carrots at each.

Number squares (nine of 2, seven of 3, five of 4). Land on, do nothing. On your next turn draw carrots equivalent to 10 times your position in the race before moving off, but only if your position then corresponds to the number shown.

Flag squares (3). Same as number squares, each one counting for positions 1, 5, or 6.

Hare squares (13). Draw a hazard card and obey the instructions printed on it. (This is known as 'jugging the hare'.) Some instructions vary according to your position, generally favouring tortoises rather than hares. This is the only true hazard element in the game, being provided for players who enjoy taking a chance. Those who prefer pure skill simply avoid landing on them. None of the instructions are strong enough to exert a decisive influence on the game as a whole.

Tortoise squares (10). These squares may only be reached by moving backwards instead of forwards. Such a move entitles you to draw 10 carrots for each square traversed.

You may not reach home if you have any lettuces uncashed, or if the number of carrots remaining unused exceeds 10 times your final position—i.e. 10 for the first home, 20 for the second, and so on.

Hare & Tortoise was developed, with hare-like rapidity, in November 1973, and first published by Intellect Games (UK) in 1974. In 1979 Ravensburger produced the German edition under the title Hase und Igel—literally 'Hare & Hedgehog', this being the Grimms' equivalent of Aesop's originally reptilian fable. (The story-line differs too. Tortoises plod while hares take naps, but hedgehogs blatantly cheat.) This edition was the first winner of the Game of the Year Award presented annually by a consortium of commercially independent games journalists and critics. It has sold some 2 million sets in Europe and appeared in a dozen different languages, including at least two in pirated editions. Further English-language editions were published by Waddingtons in 1981 and H. P. Gibson in 1988, all with slight variations. If the game has not realized its full potential—by failing, in particular, to make any impression on the American market—this may be due to the fact that it looks like a children's game but is in fact an adult game, so misleading both age-groups. As Lhôte observes, 'Undoubtedly the game suffers from its presentation—the hare and tortoise imagery, beloved by La Fontaine, excites no great passion in the 20th century. It would have been more judicious to apply the same principle to a racing-car game.'[4] Ironically, when I first developed this mathematical mechanism (in 1968) it was for a Space Race game played on a hexagonal grid rather than a linear track.

Such are the ironies and vicissitudes of the games-inventing life.

NOTES

1. See Phil Orbanes, 'Bantu—the Great Game that never made it', *Games & Puzzles*, 1st ser. no. 68 (March, 1978), 8–9.
2. A point made independently by Lhôte, 527, and E. Glonnegger in *Das Spiele-Buch* (Ravensburg, 1988), 74.
3. This description applies to the German edition published by Ravensburger since 1979. Other editions vary slightly both in layout and in the treatment of hare squares.
4. Lhôte, 527.

SPACE GAMES

All in a Row

Games of Alignment and Linear Connection: Noughts & Crosses, Merels, Renju, Hex, Twixt, etc.

The fold stands empty in the drowned field,
And crows are fatted with the murrion flock;
The nine men's Morris is filled up with mud.

Shakespeare, *A Midsummer Night's Dream*, II. i. 96

Oft we may track his haunts...
By nine-peg-morris nicked upon the grass

Clare, *Rural Muse* (1835)

Noughts & Crosses remains in Britain the lowly but liveliest survivor of an ancient and world-wide family of games in which the aim is to get three or more pieces in a line. The European games are typically played on the points of a double-square diagram, with or without added diagonals (Fig. 7.1*b*, *c*). In many countries a line of three is called a mill, so it will be convenient to refer to this figure as a single mill board. The board is often extended by the addition of one or two concentric squares and suppression of the centre point, producing the double mill of 18 points (*e*, *f*) and the triple mill of 24 points (*g*, *h*), in each case with or without diagonals.

The European family as a whole is traditionally and best referred to as Merels, ultimately from the Low Latin *merellus*, plural *merelli*, meaning a token, counter, or gaming piece, from which derive the equivalent Italian *Smerelli* and French *Merelle*, formerly *Marelle*. (*Marelle à cloche-pied* is the French for Hopscotch.) It was the Norman French version of this name that accompanied larger varieties of the game reaching England in the wake of William the Conqueror. Hyde, in 1694, lists a variety of games as bearing, *apud Anglos*, an equal variety of names, beginning 'Bushels, Marlin, Three Men's Morals, Nine Men's Morals, Nine-Penny Miracle, Nine-Pin Miracle...'

Such variety emphasizes the popularity and rusticity of the game already evinced by Shakespeare in *A Midsummer Night's Dream* (see also Fig. 7.3). Of particular interest is the fact that 'Morris' has come to stand most typically for the English attestations of the game. Shakespeare's mention of the village green suggests an alternative origin in the Morris of dancing,

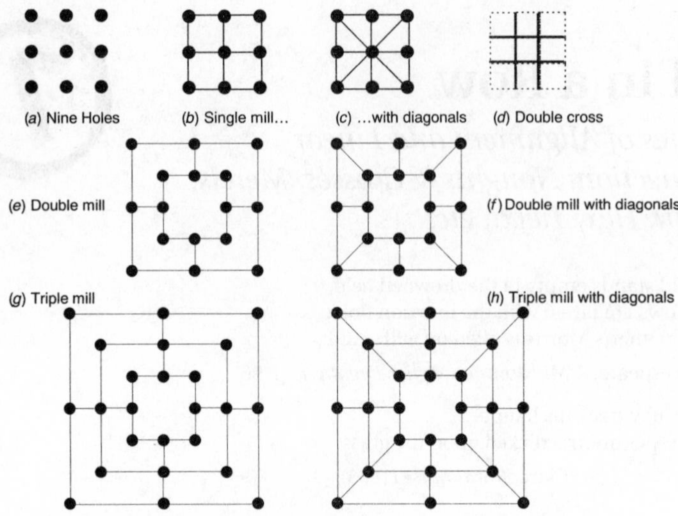

Fig. 7.1. Mill boards of various sizes, and ad hoc diagrams for Nine Holes and Noughts & Crosses.

Fig. 7.2. Celtic cross with an incised mill-like labyrinth at Glencolumcille, Co. Donegal.

Fig. 7.3. The rusticity of Merels is apparent from this detail from the *Suite des Nobles Pastorales,* an early sixteenth-century tapestry in the Louvre, Paris.

but the name of the dance is a corruption of 'Moorish', not 'Merels'. Perhaps, however, the coincidence of game and dance in the same cultural context has favoured the survival of Morris over Merels.

In medieval Europe, Merels achieved a social status hardly inferior to that of Chess and Tables, with which it formed a distinctive trinity. The aristocracy could afford richly worked gaming boards with surfaces marked for Chess on one side and Merels on the other, and opening out to reveal a Tables (Backgammon) board inside, thus accounting for the distinction made in older books between games 'within' and 'without' the tables. The tradition of producing double boards with chequered squares on one side and a triple mill on the other survived well into the twentieth century and is not entirely defunct today, though Merels itself has suffered a steep decline. The later Middle Ages saw a marked increase in the sophistication of indoor games, certainly after and possibly under the influence of card games, which entered Europe in the later fourteenth century as upper-class intellectual activities from which mindless gambling games were only a subsequent spin-off. As Chess took flight with the Queen's empowerment, and Tables enhanced its appeal by evolving into Backgammon and Trictrac, so Merels sought to expand its domain by a process of enlargement and complexity. In this it ultimately failed. Its basic problem is a lack of depth and variety. Well-matched players soon find the game losing interest, and cannot be encouraged by the knowledge that the whole strategy tree has been solved by computer—in fact, it is rather less complex than Connect-4, one of its modern descendants.[1] It will be interesting to see how Morris fares as a resuscitated fossil in the World Merils Championship (*sic*), which takes place every year at the Ryedale Folk Museum, Hutton-le-Hole, Yorkshire.[2]

In essence, Merels is a game of placement and movement played by two on a reticular board, each player's aim being to get three of his own pieces aligned in a horizontal or vertical row. Variation occurs in the size of board and number of pieces, and some games also allow alignments on the diagonal. To counter the relative simplicity of the exercise, the basic game was successively enlarged in both size and duration. In the larger games, a player making a line of three removes an enemy piece from the board, and play continues from the new position, eventually ending when one player has only two pieces left. The capturing feature does not, however, require Merels to be classed as a war game. Rather, a single game should be seen as a series of part-games, each culminating in the formation of a line, and followed by a game played from the same position but with a reduced complement of pieces. It is a space game rather than a war game because it is the making of lines that engages the attention—capturing a piece is merely the reward for so doing.

Games of Placement

Noughts & Crosses is as Cotton said of Whist in 1674, a game, 'so well known in England, in all parts thereof, that every child almost of eight years hath a competent knowledg in that recreation'. Each in turn enters one of his own symbols, in Britain a nought or a cross, into one of the spaces of a 3×3 grid made by drawing a double cross (Fig. 7.1*d*) with the aim of getting three in an orthogonal or diagonal line. (Curiously, despite the order implied by the title, the player who goes first almost invariably starts with an X.) Translated into board-game terms, both start with five pieces in hand and each in turn enters one on any vacant point or space. The game was formerly known as Tit-Tat-Toe, Tip-Tap-Toe, or Tick-Tack-Toe (the current American term), from the butcher-boy rhyme recited by a successful player upon completing such a row. Similar rhymes occur in other languages. The Swedish equivalent, played with noughts and ones, is called Tripp-Trapp-Trull, a line followed by *Min qvarn är full*, 'My mill's full'. The Dutch rhyme, *Boter, melk en kaas, Ik ben de baas* ('Butter, milk, and cheese, I am the Big Cheese') reinforces the traditionally rustic nature of the game.

Correct play is bound to end in a tie, 'As any fule kno',[3] traditionally credited as a win to Old Nick, or Old Tom (the Devil). Murray and others credit one A. C. White with pointing out that the first player has only three distinct moves, that only 12 different positions are possible after the opponent's response, and that, with correct play, the first player has the advantage but the second can always force a tie. In fact, every child almost of 8 years knows by intuition or experience that the centre is always the best square to play to and a middle-of-edge always the worst. This is easily demonstrated by marking each cell with the number of lines of three of which it can form part, thus:

3	2	3
2	4	2
3	2	3

The rest is obvious, though it takes John Horton Conway and two other high-powered mathematicians two pages of text to analyse all possible lines of play exhaustively.[4] And, as Martin Gardner points out,[5] many players who consider themselves unbeatable will all too often go for a draw against a weak player instead of so playing as to maximize their chances of cashing in on a weak move. What, for example, is X's best move in this position, following an eccentric opening?

1	**X**	3
4	5	6
7	**O**	9

Other ways of extending the game produce more interesting variations. One is to make the board three-dimensional and play in a cube of $3 \times 3 \times 3 = 27$ (the first player has a forced win), or even $4 \times 4 \times 4 = 64$ smaller cubes. A slightly simpler version of the order-3 cube is a non-transparent variety in which cubes are placed only on the six outer faces, so that, in effect, six different games are played simultaneously.

Connect-4, first published by Milton Bradley in the 1970s (1976 in the UK), remains a classic example of updating a traditional game into commercial format with greater interest but no loss of integrity. The players sit each side of a vertical board consisting of forty-two spaces in seven columns and six rows. Each in turn drops a disc of his own colour into the slot at the top of a column, allowing it to fall to the base or on to a partly built column of pieces. The aim is to get four of one's own colour in any unbroken orthogonal or diagonal line. Fig. 7.4 shows a win for Black after White's failure to play his eighth piece to the central column.

Foxo. Other variants are based on the replacement of two by three distinctive pieces or signs. A good pencil-and-paper example is described by Peter Newby under the name Foxo.[6] On a 5×5 grid, each in turn of two players designated O and X writes the word FOX from left to right, top to bottom, or both (diagonally). At least one letter must be new, but either or both of the others may be already in position. A player scores a point for completing a line of three of his own letter, which is then lined through, and cedes a point if he happens to align three of his opponent's. The 'F' is neutral and confers no score. The winner is the player with the higher score when no new FOX can be entered. Foxo is not really a word game, of course. It would be interesting to play it on a chessboard with pieces of three different colours, as there may be more to it than its inventor has realized.

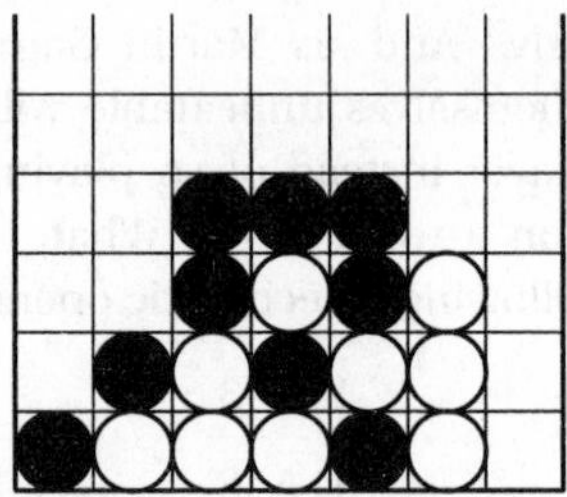

Fig. 7.4. Connect-4.

Beer Squares, an ad hoc variant by Dan Glimne, is played on a grid of 3×3 beer mats with up to nine glasses of beer undifferentiated as to ownership. Starting with an empty grid, each in turn either (*a*) places on any vacant beer mat a glass that may be still full of beer, or half consumed, or empty, or (*b*) takes up any non-empty glass already in position and reduces its level to either half (if it is still full) or zero. The winner is the first player to complete a line of three glasses containing the same quantity of beer, i.e. one, half or zero. The advantage of this game is that it is bound to end in a win. The disadvantage is that it gradually becomes harder to distinguish who the winner is.

Linop, by Alex Randolph, is one of the most attractive and inventive of modern abstracts based on getting three in a line by placement only. The board is a grid of 5 × 5 points connected by lines as shown in Fig. 7.5. There are six pieces in each of four different colours, of common ownership. Each in turn places a piece on any vacant point. The aim is to be the first to get a third piece of the same colour on the same line, regardless of their actual positions and whether or not interrupted by spaces or pieces of another colour.[7]

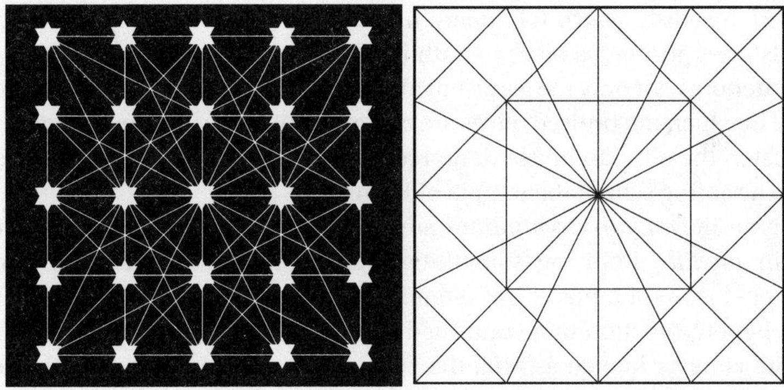

Fig. 7.5. Linop, by Alex Randolph (*left*) invites comparison with a late nineteenth-/early twentieth-century alignment game of placement and movement (*right*), from Albert Rossel, *Dix-huit jeux du temps passé* (1968).

Games of Placement and Movement

Nine Holes, the European precursor of Noughts & Crosses, was, paradoxically, more advanced than its pencil-and-paper derivative, in that it was a true board game involving not merely the placement but also the movement of pieces. It was played on a grid of 3 × 3 = 9 points or holes, or on the corners and junctions of a quartered square (Fig. 7.1*a, b, c*). Starting with three pieces in hand, each in turn enters one on to a vacant point, aiming to make an orthogonal line of three. Assuming neither does so, the players continue by alternately moving a piece of their own to any vacant point until the game is won or both tire of an endless draw. Much played by scholars, monks, and clerks, it produced a plethora of scratched or incised diagrams still to be found in the cloisters of originally monastic cathedrals, from Westminster Abbey down. In 1699 a Manx ecclesiastical court punished two men for 'making nine holes with their knives after evening prayers'.[8] Some of the incised nine holes are well worn, demonstrating the long popularity of the game—or pastime, as it might be more accurately and literally designated.

Mills and Merels. In France, Spain, and Italy the line is known as a 'line' (*file, filetto*, etc.), more commonly 'table' (Latin *tabula*) in the Middle Ages, but in Germany and countries deriving their game from the German one it is more graphically designated *Mühle*, 'mill', or its equivalent or cognate—Danish *Mölle*, Icelandic *Mylna*, Russian *Melnitsa*, Hungarian *Malom[-jatek]*, Swedish *Qvarn* (cf. 'quern'), and so on. The image is that of two millstones grinding a piece to nothing between them. The Spanish *alquerque* denotes not only the game but also, as Murray says, 'that part of the oil-mill in which the bruised olives are laid out, which has channels or grooves to catch the oil'—an image reinforced by the crossed circle design incised into a roofing slab of the temple of Kurna (Fig. 7.6).

Hyde, in *De Ludis Orientalibus*, supposed *Mühle* to be a corruption of the Latin *medius*, implying something effected in the middle, and hence the enclosure of a piece; but the milling imagery seems too apt to justify the hypercorrection of a confirmed classicist. Even in English, where the game is never known as Mill, the centre contained a circle referred to in some areas as the 'bushel'.

The Smaller Merels or **Three Men's Morris** is a development of Nine Holes played on a single mill with diagonals (7.1*c*). Each starts with three pieces in hand and plays as at Nine Holes, but now a piece can move to an adjacent vacancy, though only along a line. This restriction is countered by the fact that a winning line may be either diagonal or orthogonal. The Alfonso MS of 1283 demonstrates a forced win for the first player if he starts at the centre, and for this reason it is traditional, at least in France, to

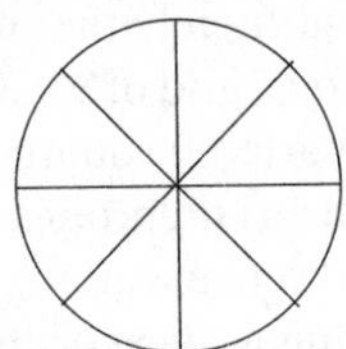

Fig. 7.6. Circular diagram, Kurna.

prohibit that opening move. The Smaller Merels feels, in play, more like a blockading than an aligning game, a resemblance underlined by the fact that it (or Nine Holes) is recorded in India under the name Tre-Guti, the linear 'Three Game', as distinct from Do-Guti, the blockading 'Two Game' (see Chapter 10). The Smaller Merels is world-wide in extent and its characteristic diagram is found in the archaeology of Egypt, Greece, Rome, Ceylon, and China. Some twenty-one books were written on *kiu king*, 'the six men game', in the Swei-shu dynasty (581–617), and that name survives as a term for the central part of the Chinese chessboard to which the general and counsellors are confined. The Smaller Merels is not known in Britain before the Norman Conquest, but is widely attested thereafter, with occurrences of board 7*c* on the cloister seats of many English cathedrals. The Irish equivalent, recorded by Hyde as Cashlan Gherra, was widely played in the early nineteenth century.

Five (or **Six**) **Men's Morris** was popular in Italy (*Smerelli*), France (*Merelle à Six Tables*), and England (Fivepenny or Fipenny Merills) up to about 1600, when it was displaced by Nine Men's Morris and its Continental equivalents. It was played on the double mill with or without diagonals (Fig. 7.1*e*,*f*), though diagonals affect only movement since a diagonal line of three is impossible. Note that an orthogonal line is valid only if all three points are connected by a line. You cannot make a line of three from the middle of an outer edge towards the centre, as a centre point is deliberately omitted. The central space, known as the bushel or pound, is a prison for captured pieces.

The games played on them involve not only placement and movement but also capture. Each player starts with five or six pieces in hand and enters them in turn on any vacant point. A line of three does not end the game, but entitles its maker to capture an enemy piece, which is placed in the pound and cannot be re-entered. When all are on board, play continues with each moving a piece to an adjacent vacancy connected by a line. A player reduced to two pieces loses the game.

Murray's son, as Surveyor of Antiquities in Nigeria, witnessed the play of this game by Yoruba in the late 1920s, noting that, in addition to the normal method of capture, a player who secures two men on any line connecting corresponding points on both squares takes one of his opponent's men'.[9] In effect, this amounts to making a diagonal line of only two pieces. Murray Sr. also records, from a correspondent in *Notes & Queries*,[10] a curious triangular variant played in nineteenth-century Wiltshire under the name Sixpenny Madell. Each player has six pieces to enter on a diagram consisting of three concentric triangles with lines connecting corresponding angles (Fig. 7.9). In a rather unclear passage, Murray argues that the mid-points of the sides of the triangles must be regarded as points either additional or alternative to those of the corners, and cites experiment as showing that the game works better with lateral instead of corner lines. It is interesting to compare, as follows, the numerical complexity of Sixpenny Madell with that of Three, Six, and Nine Men's Morris, with P = number of points, L = number of possible lines of three, orthogonal only, T = total number if diagonal lines also permitted:

	P	L	T
Three Men's Morris	9	6	8
Six Men's Morris	16	8	—
Sixpenny Madell	18	12	15
Nine Men's Morris	24	16	20

The Larger Merels or **Nine Men's Morris** is played on a board extended to twenty-four points by the addition of yet another enclosing square, to which diagonals were added by 1400 (Fig. 7.1*g*, *h*). It is illustrated in a manuscript written at Cerne Abbey in the second half of the thirteenth century, and is found incised or scratched in the stone of many English cathedrals and abbeys from the Norman Conquest on.[11]

The main effect of the larger board was to increase the number of pieces—to nine on (*g*), eleven or twelve on (*h*)—and hence the length and complexity of play. It also encouraged the evolution of refinements applied to significant positions or events that might be reached during the course of play. Many such rules must have been devised and lost in course of time, but the flavour of the more refined game may be had from this description of the early nineteenth-century German game *Das Doppeln Mühlespiel*:[12]

The game is played on board [Fig. 7.1g], each player starting with nine pieces in hand. In Phase 1, each in turn places a piece on any vacant point. A player who forms a mill (line of three) captures by removing any enemy piece from the board and placing it in the central pound. In Phase 2, which begins when all uncaptured pieces are in position, each in turn moves a piece to any adjacent vacancy connected by a line. Again, making a mill entails a capture. When one player's forces are reduced to three he embarks upon Phase 3. This entitles him at each turn to move any one of them to any vacant point on the board, whether or not connected to its current position. If both players are reduced to three, the game is drawn. Otherwise it is a win when one player reduces the other's forces to two. It is a double win (*kleiner Matsch*) if the loser failed to make any mill (capture any piece) before reaching Phase 3, and a treble win (*grosser Matsch*) if he never made a mill at all.

This description includes the term *Zwickmühle* for the devastating situation in which one player is able to alternate the same piece between two mills and so make a winning series of captures. The word literally means 'pinch-mill', and retains a currency of usage as the German equivalent of 'a Catch-22 situation'. More elaborate terms are listed for the Icelandic version of the game as described by Ólafur Davídsson.[13] This also is played with nine pieces on a triple mill without diagonals. It includes an additional rule prohibiting the capture of a piece currently forming part of a mill, and credits a win—or, in some circles, a half-win—for so blockading the other player that he is unable to move. *Svikamylna,* obviously cognate with *Zwickmühle,* is a position enabling you to make a mill at every turn. *Krossmylna,* or *vængjamylna,* is four pieces forming a cross enclosing a vacant central point, thus enabling a mill to be made by moving any one of them to the centre. Even more powerful is the *rennihestur,* though it is not well defined and there is no agreement as to its meaning. Murray says the cross-mill was known as a 'running Jenny' in Yorkshire.

Nicholas de Nicholae, a resident of Northern Italy who wrote a treatise on games under the pen-name Bonus Socius (for he's a Jolly Good Fellow, evidently, *socius* meaning a fellow of an academic fraternity), ascribes high status to Marelli, describing the pieces as being red and gold rather than black and white. Although his diagram suggests the Larger Merels, his text seems to imply the use of six differentiated pieces: *luna, stella, scutum, crux, quadratus, rotundus.* These may refer to configurations of pieces rather than the pieces themselves—thus *crux* may relate to the Icelandic *krossmylna.* Alternatively, since the appropriate astrological signs appear on diagrams of that period, they may have served as a form of notation, or even simply of decoration.

The triple mill with diagonals (Fig. 7.1*h*) is first illustrated in an early fifteenth-century Arabic text.[14] As described by Moulidars in *La Grande Encyclopédie des Jeux* of 1840, the diagonals were used for movement only, diagonal lines being invalid. Phase 3 of the game, in which a piece could jump to any vacant point, began when a player was reduced to four pieces.

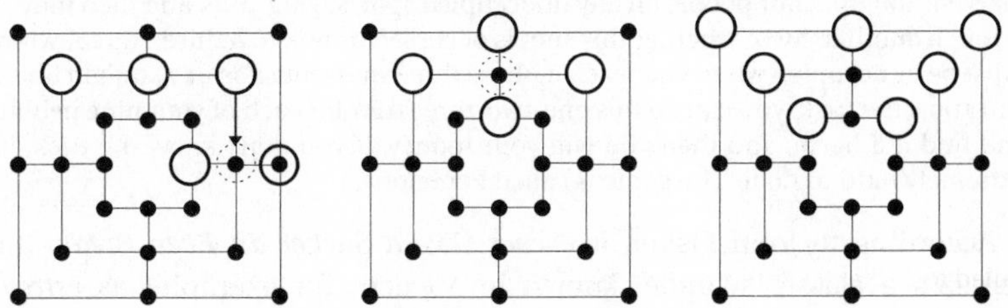

Fig. 7.7. *Left to right*: pinch-mill, cross-mill, and a possible interpretation of *rennihestur.*

Carried to America by British settlers, Twelve Men's Morris became the standard American form of the game, with diagonal lines of three permitted.

Shah is a variety of the game recorded in the early twentieth century in what is now Somalia.[15] Each player has twelve pieces which are entered on the triple mill without diagonals. During entry rows may be made but no piece captured. With entry complete, every point is occupied. If any rows were made during entry, the player who made one first now begins by removing any one of his opponent's pieces; if not, whoever entered the last piece starts by capturing an enemy piece. If at any time the player in turn cannot move, his opponent makes a second move to give him a piece to play, but he may not capture on this move even if he makes a row. The winner of a game scores his win by placing a pebble in the pound. If a series of games is played, the loss of a game cancels all previous wins. Four successive wins constitute a *gal*, 'pool'; five, *gabad*, 'girl'.

Lest the triple mill be thought a medieval invention, it remains to add that it occurs (without diagonals) in the Egyptian temple at Kurna (fourteenth century BC), twice in Ceylon from not later than AD 100, and in a Neolithic burial site in County Wicklow, Ireland.[16]

Origins. Mill boards are of ancient date. The fourteenth-century BC triple mill at Kurna is accompanied by others that may bear some ludic relation. They include a circular version of the diagonal single mill (Fig. 7.6) and a design that in other contexts would be a pentagram (Fig. 7.8). The only problem is uncertainty as to whether the game played on them was one of alignment—they could equally well be blockading games like Do-guti and Mu-torere (Chapter 10). The pentagram is used for a solitaire which Murray declared to be still current in Crete,[17] citing this description made in 1938:

> 'You have nine pebbles, and the aim is to get them each on one of the ten spots marked. You put your pebble on any unoccupied spot, saying 'one', and then move it through another, 'two', whether this spot is occupied or not, to a third, 'three', which must be unoccupied when you reach it; these three spots must be in a straight line. If you know the trick, you can do this one-two-three trick for each of your nine pebbles and find it a berth, and then you win your money. If you don't know the trick, it's extremely hard to do it. The game is called Pentalpha.'

According to John Fisher, in *Never Give a Sucker an Even Break*, this remains a classic swindle, known in Mexico (for example) as *estrella mágica.*

If Greek board games derived from those of Egypt, this could relate to the mysterious *pente grammai* of Sophocles. Or it could be used for a version of

Fig. 7.8. Pentalpha.

the simple Merels. Each in turn enters a piece on one of the ten points, and then, assuming that neither has allowed the other to make three in a row, moves one to an adjacent vacant point, winning the game by either making three in a row or leaving the other no move.

Ovid several times refers to what appears to be a three-in-a-row game, as in his *Ars Amatoria* (iii. 355–6; cf. *Tristia*, ii. 481–2):

Parva tabella capit ternos utrinque lapillos
In qua vicisse, est continuasse suos.

(On a little game-board each in turn moves [one of] three pebbles, the winner being the first to get their own three connected.)

Since blockading occurs in many advanced members of the Merels family, it may be that both types of game evolved together, using the same boards.

Alquerque. No written or physical evidence attests the continuity of alignment games from classical civilization through the Dark Ages of Europe. Since three-in-a-row games first appear here around 1100, one might naturally look to an Arabic inspiration for their eventual discovery, or rediscovery, as the case may be. Sure enough, the Alfonso manuscript of 1283 contains a section devoted to several games sharing the name Alquerque, of which two are varieties of Merels. Alquerque is primarily a war game, i.e. one of movement and capture, played on a board consisting of four diagonally crossed squares united in a single square (Fig. 7.10). What Alfonso calls *Alquerque de Tres* is the Smaller Merels or Three Men's Morris (7.1*c*), while *Alquerque de Nueve* is the equivalent of Nine Men's Morris played on the triple mill (7.1*g*). The latter includes an an optional variant played with dice, which govern the placement of pieces on the board. In addition, certain throws, namely 4-5-6, 3-3-6, 2-2-5 and 1-1-4 (all totalling significant multiples of three), entitle the thrower to enter three in a row and make a capture. With all available pieces on board, play continues in the normal way.

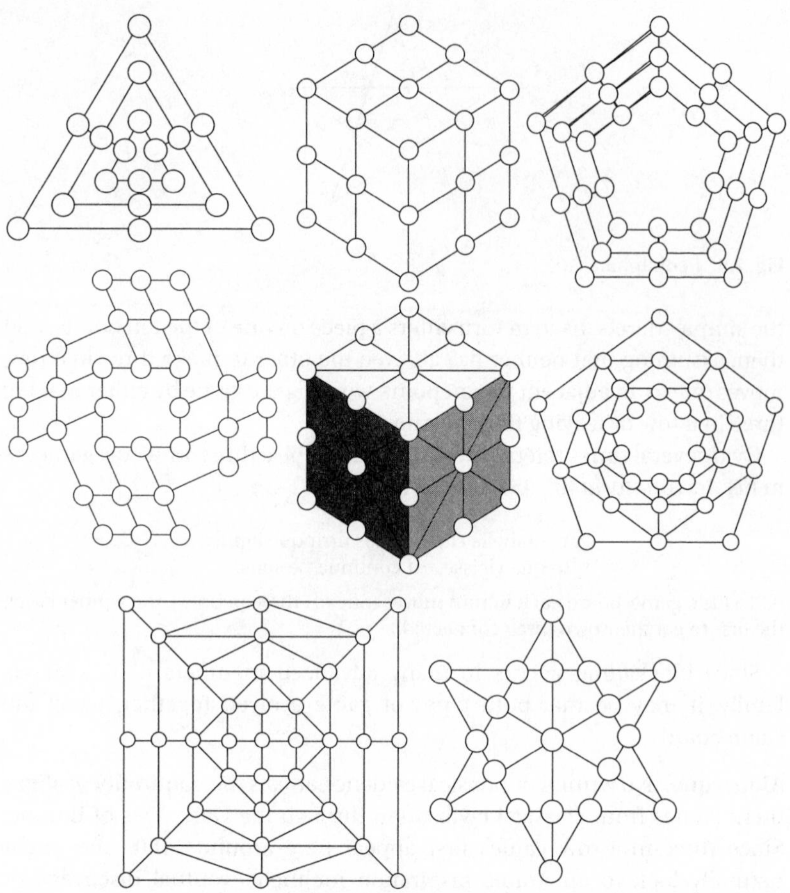

Fig. 7.9. Many geometric variants have been devised for the play of Merels. The concentric triangles were used for the nineteenth-century 'Sixpenny Madell' (Murray). Beneath it is 'Windmill', in which lines of three must be straight (not angled). In the lower of the two 'cubes', a line of three is valid only if entirely contained in one of the three visible faces of the cube. The central point may not be occupied except to complete a line of three, or to prevent the opponent from completing a line of three on his next turn. The last two are some of the many designs used for Mongolian games such as Zirge.[18]

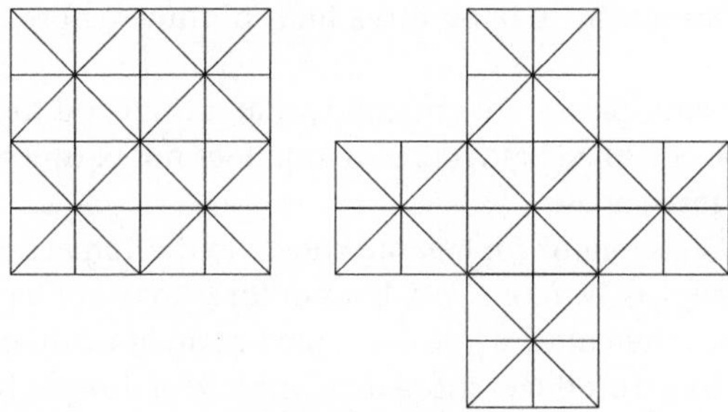

Fig. 7.10. Quadruple and quintuple Alquerque.

What sort of game Alquerque originally denoted remains obscure. A tenth-century Arabic work refers to an inhabitant of Mecca keeping sets of Chess, Nard (proto-Backgammon), and *Qirq* for entertaining guests, but as *Qirq* itself does not derive from Arabic roots it probably represents a borrowing from some other culture,[19] leaving us in the dark as to whether it originally denoted a war game, chase game, or game of alignment. As Murray remarks, the modern Arabic name of the game is *Dris*, and *Qirq* may originally have meant nothing more precise than a lined board. Fiske (1905) quotes unnamed Spanish lexicographers as proposing *al-kar(i)k* = 'the space in an oil-mill into which the must of the olive is placed'. This seems to link neatly with the 'mill' series of titles—perhaps too neatly, however, and suggesting some benefit of etymological hindsight.

Shiva (Murray) and **Dara** (Bell) typify a number of three-in-a-row games played in various parts of Africa on a grid of 5 × 6 or 6 × 6 points, squares, or, usually, holes in the ground. Two players each have twelve or thirteen distinctive pieces and enter them one by one in alternating turns of play. With all entered, each in turn moves one of his pieces one step only in an orthogonal direction. Making a row of three—neither more nor fewer—entitles a player to remove an enemy piece. The player who is first reduced to two loses.

Regional variations relate to methods of entry and alignments of more than three pieces. One such game is used for divination. In a Gold Coast game called *Wari* (misleadingly, as Wari normally denotes a form of Mancala), a line of four does not entitle any capture to be made, nor does a line of three produced by removing one from a line of four.

In *Kare*, or *Karnum* (Nigeria), moves are made diagonally, but lines of three must be orthogonal. Neither player may make a line of more than three, and once a line has been made none of its pieces may move again. A player wins outright by making three lines of three before his opponent makes one.

In *Dala* (Sudan), pieces are entered two at a time and the four central points must be occupied first. A line of four does not permit a capture, but reducing it to three does.

In *Dili*, the Hausa name for a game known to the Tamacheq (Sahara) as *Dra* and to others as *Wali* or *Kyoti*, lines of three may not be made during the entry phase. Thereafter, a line may not contain more than three pieces, and if a single move produces more than one line of three only one capture can be made. The winner scores a double game if he has not lost any of his own pieces, and a session is usually scored up to ten games.

The Tuareg game of *Alkarhat* is used for divination. 'A holy man presides, and the winner of three games running carries the alternative submitted for divine decision' (Murray, from whom all these games and blessings flow).

Trebles is a cross between Shiva and Twelve Men's Morris played on a chessboard.[20] Each player has twelve pieces, which are played alternately to the central 6×6 squares. Making an orthogonal line of exactly three of your own pieces entitles you to remove an enemy piece. Pieces once placed may be moved one step orthogonally at each turn. The loser is the first player reduced to two pieces.

Five-in-a-Row Games

Renju, meaning 'row of gems', is the modernized version of an old Japanese game played ('by women and children') with black and white stones on a Go board. The original was first described in English in the 1880s, under such names as Go-bang, a corruption of Go-ban, 'five board', and Go-moku, 'five stone'.[21] *Indoor Games and Recreations,* published by the Religious Tract Society in 1889, carries an article on Go-ban by one Herr Meyer, while *Cassell's Book of Sports and Pastimes* credits a certain Mr Cremer, Jr., with having introduced Go-bang to Modern Civilization. Both also include a chessboard variant, which in fact is Hasami Shogi (see below). A subsequent proprietary American version known as Pegity involved placing pegs in holes, whence the title.

In its raw form, each in turn places a stone on a vacant point or cell until one player makes a line of five. A line of six or more, made by connecting two part-lines, is invalid. If neither succeeds, each in turn moves one of his pieces to an orthogonally adjacent vacancy until one of them wins or both die of boredom. With correct play, Black, who starts, cannot lose. In the twentieth century various attempts have been made to improve the game by countering Black's advantage, notably by Shuroku (1900s) and Takagawi

(1930s). The rule of three and three[22] prohibits either player (or just Black, who has the advantage of opening), from making two lines of three of which each is capable of being converted into a line of four. In Mobile Renju, play must jump to another part of the board when a limited number of stones have been initially placed.[23] In Go-moku, or Ninuki (Korean) Renju, two adjacent stones of the same colour can be captured by enclosure, thus: ●○○●.[24]

The currently 'official' version is played on a 15 × 15 board with fifty stones each.[25] Black may not so play as to create simultaneously two or more open lines of three or two or more open lines of four, nor make an overline. The latter—a line of six or more stones—is not prohibited to White, who thereby wins. An open line of four is four in an unbroken row, and an open three is one that can be converted into an open four by adding one stone. Black can therefore only force a win by creating a simultaneous 4-3 (Fig. 7.11).

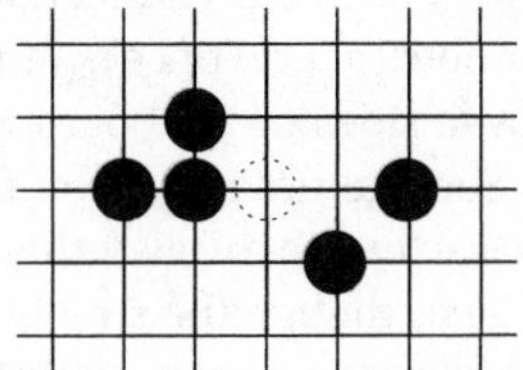

Fig. 7.11. Renju. Black, with a 'broken' four-three (i.e. not open), wins by playing to the dotted point, threatening on the next move either a winning horizontal five, or an open four on the diagonal.

In effect, Black and White are playing to different rules. A match is therefore usually two games, one with each colour. This inelegant procedure is rendered even more artificial by a rule permitting White to specify one of twenty-four possible 3-stone openings. (There are actually twenty-six arrangements of B-W-B, discounting rotations and reflections, but two certainly lose for Black.) Renju may yet undergo further refinement. It remains, however, popular enough to support a number of professional players who compete in well-publicized national and regional tournaments, a rating system similar to that of Go, with *dan* and *kyu* grades, and the inevitable governing body (Nihon Renju-sha).

Hasami Shogi (Bell[26]) is a relative played on one quarter of a Go board, or any other 9 × 9 squared grid. Starting with eighteen pieces on his two back rows, each in turn may move a piece any distance orthogonally, or jump an adjacent piece of either colour to the necessarily vacant square beyond. An

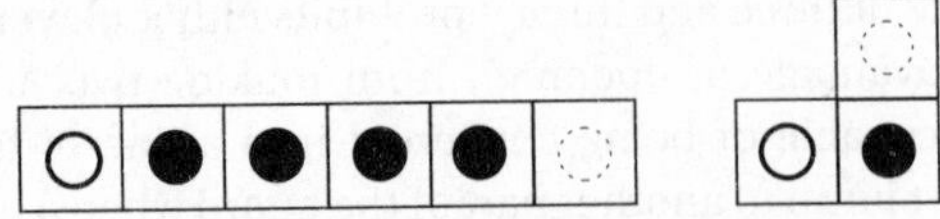

Fig. 7.12. Hasami Shogi.

enemy piece, or an unbroken orthogonal line of enemy pieces, may be captured by custodianship (left), as may a piece occupying a corner square (right). The aim is to get five of one's own colour in an orthogonal line other than in either of the initially occupied rows.

Games of Linear Connection

Alignment games took a different turn in the twentieth century, resulting in what might be called games of linear connection. Each in turn places a piece on a bilaterally symmetrical grid of cells or points, and the winner is the first to connect opposite sides of the board with an unbroken line of pieces of his own colour. Such games may be of placement, movement or capture, or all three. Some can end in a draw, others offer a winning strategy to the player who moves first, though the strategy may be so hard to find (unlike that of the lower-order Merels) as to maintain interest over years of play. That there can be no winning strategy for the second player is said to have been formally proved by Hales and Jewett[27] by means of the 'strategy-stealing' argument. It assumes, for the sake of argument, that the second player has a winning strategy. Then the first player starts with a random opening move, pretends to himself that the second player's first move is the first move of the game, and himself follows the supposed winning strategy, or makes a random move if the required strategic move is impossible. It follows that if the second player had a winning strategy then so would the first, since an additional piece on the board cannot be other than advantageous. This conclusion needs to be qualified by the proviso that it applies only in the case of complete symmetry between the respective winning positions of the two players.

Hex is the classic of its type, if not the earliest. It was invented in the 1940s by the Danish mathematician and poet Piet Hein, then a Princeton University student, and became so popular in Denmark as to be published in the form of notepads containing grids for play by pencil and paper. In this form the grid consists of equilateral triangles arranged in a lozenge shape, with play taking place on the intersections. As a board with counters it is

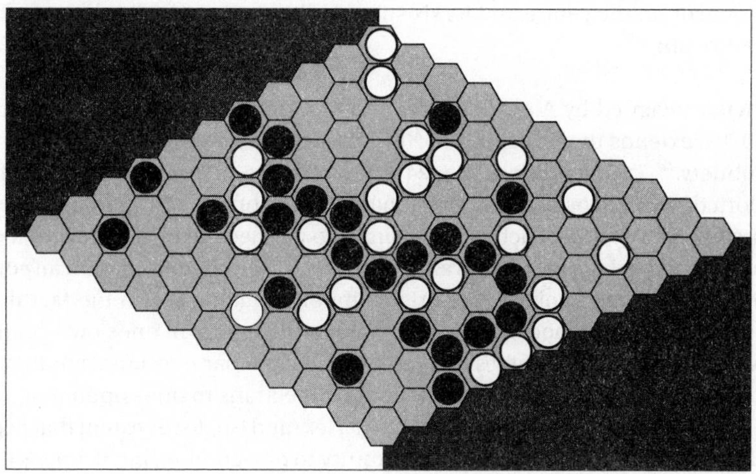

Fig. 7.13. Hex, by Piet Hein. Black has connected.

more attractively arranged as a hexagonal grid with counters placed in the cells. Either way, the standard size is order 11, i.e. with eleven points or cells to a side, but this can be varied ad lib: seven is a good size for beginners, more than eleven renders the game too complex for everyday play. Black and White start with an indefinite number of counters of their own colour and each in turn places one counter in any vacant cell. There is no movement or capture. The winner is the first player to complete an unbroken line of counters of his own colour connecting the two opposite sides of the board assigned to that colour. Two counters occupying contiguous cells are considered 'connected' for this purpose. A draw is impossible, since every cell is traversed by three routes instead of the two that would be the case in a squared grid.

The mental challenge of this game lies in avoiding the obvious manœuvre of placing counters on contiguous cells to start with. The player who has only one line in mind and plays obviously towards its completion is easily countered by an intelligent opponent. The real strategy lies in placing pieces in such a way as to allow of several possible connective routes depending on the countering moves of one's opponent. Thus the initial placement of pieces by an expert player may appear to the inexpert as random and pointless as those of a Go master.

The first player theoretically has a forced win, but it is hard to find on the standard board, and increasingly so on larger ones. It being plainly advantageous to seize the centre, some players prohibit opening on the centre alone, or on the centre and its six surrounding points, or anywhere on the centre line.[28]

Twixt, invented by Alex Randolph and first published by 3M in the early 1970s, extends the principles of Hex into a game of remarkable depth and subtlety.[29] The board is a 24 × 24 array of holes into which pegs can be slotted. Two opposite sides of the board are notionally black (actually red), the other two white. Each player's aim is to connect his two opposite sides with an unbroken line of pegs and connectors. Neither may play on an edge of his opponent's colour. The originality of the game lies in the fact that connections are made by laying a bar across two pegs of one's own colour which are exactly a knight's move apart. Since no bar may cross another, a single connector denies nine potential connections to one's opponent.

The strategy of Twixt resembles that of Hex (and Go) to the extent that pegs should not be placed in obvious proximity to one another, but deepens the idea in that single pegs do not in themselves constitute part of a connecting line. Fig. 7.14 shows a position after 25 moves. Black looks well placed at first sight, but closer examination shows that the pegs marked (x) require three more bars and two pegs to connect, which White can easily prevent. The area between Black's x's and White's z's is probably no-man's land, and

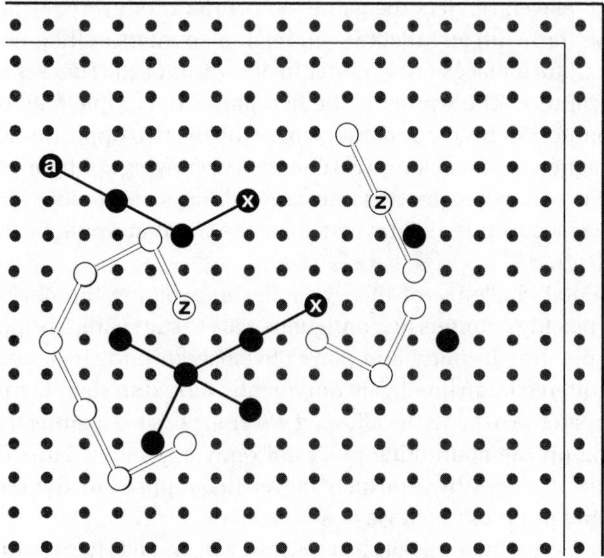

Fig. 7.14. Twixt. White is playing vertically, black horizontally.

White may do better to play somewhere north or west of Black's (*a*). Twixt is not easily available, but can be converted into a pencil-and-paper game by playing on squared paper. A dot of one's own colour represents a peg, and two such squares a knight's move apart are joined by ruling a straight line between them.

Another member of this family is Sid Sackson's Network, which has the slight advantage of being played with small material on a chessboard, though it is not one of his better games. Each player has ten counters or draughtsmen of his own colour. Two opposite sides are designated white and the other two black. Each plays a piece in turn and the winner is the first to connect his two sides by means of a notional line passing through at least six pieces of his own colour. The game is too full of rules and restrictions to justify detailed description here.[30]

Thoughtwave. To avoid the expense of solid pieces, a number of proprietary connection games involve flat tiles that can be simply pushed out of a punched card. Each tile has part of a linear track printed on it, and the aim is to lay tiles in such a way as to connect opposite sides of the board. These can be jollied up by the addition of thematic decorations. Two particularly pleasing ones that spring to mind are Nile (Spears, 1972) and The Great Downhill Ski Game (Waddingtons, 1975).[31] Its most abstract and challenging embodiment is to be found in Eric Solomon's game of Thoughtwave (Intellect Games, 1975).[32] This is played on a plain 10×10 board with two opposite sides red and two blue. Each player starts with 24 tiles of his own colour, of which two are crossroads, six T-junctions, five single lines, and one a dead end. Each in turn plays a tile to any vacant square, provided that it correctly matches track to track or blank to blank of any adjacent tile already in place, and each aims to form a pathway connecting his own two sides of the board. The most significant feature of the game is that the pathway may consist of tiles of either or both colours, so that each tile played may count as well for the opponent as for the one who placed it. In Fig. 7.15, Black has successfully connected. The type of thinking involved is similar to that of Hex and Go.

Connections, at time of writing the latest variation on a theme of Twixt, is essentially the same as Bridg-it, first published in the USA in 1960.[33] White aims to connect right and left, and Black top and bottom, by placing line-bearing plastic tiles connecting two points of their own colour. Design and production values compensate for some lack of originality.

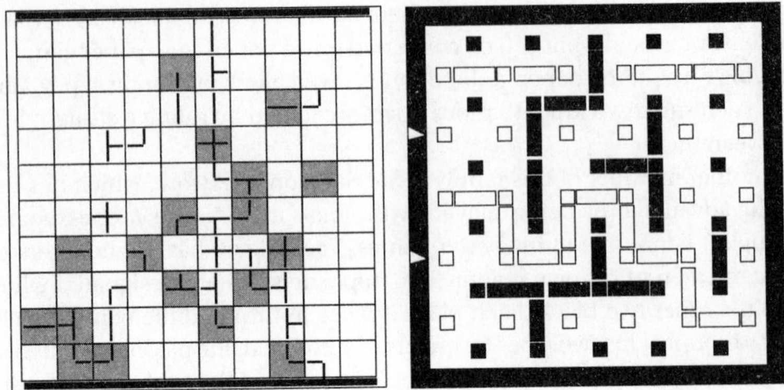

Fig. 7.15. Thoughtwave (Eric Solomon), Connections (Tom McNamara).

NOTES

1. See L. V. Allis, 'Beating the World Champion: the State of the Art in Computer Game Playing', in *New Approaches to Board Game Research*, IIAS Working Papers, 3rd ser. (Leiden, International Institute for Asian Studies, 1995), 155–71.
2. See *Games & Puzzles*, 2nd ser., no. 6 (Sept. 1994), 4.
3. Catchphrase of Molesworth jun. in G. Willan and R. Searle, *Down with Skool.*
4. E. Berlekamp, J. H. Conway, and R. K. Guy, *Winning Ways* (New York, 1982), 670–1. Chapter 22, 'Lines & Squares' (667–93), is devoted to games of alignment and configuration.
5. Martin Gardner *The Scientific American Book of Mathematical Puzzles and Diversions*, cited by Allis (n. 1 above). I seem to have lost my copy. Better than seizing the centre is X in 4 or 6, giving O four losing moves in six possible replies.
6. Peter Newby, *Pears Word Games* (London, 1990), 149–51.
7. Source: H. Bücken, and D. Hanneforth, *Klassische Spiele ganz neu* (Reinbek bei Hamburg, 1990), 64.
8. Murray, *History of Board Games*, 39, quoting correspondence from W. Cubbon in *The Times*.
9. Ibid. 41.
10. G. E. Dartnell, *Notes & Queries*, 8th ser. 12. 333.
11. Murray, *History of Board Games*, 44, gives a list, and identifies the manuscript as MS Trin. Coll. Cambridge, O.2.45, f. 2*b*.
12. *Archiv der Spiele* (Berlin, 1819–21), vol. 2 (1820), 21–7, quoted by Fiske, 129–31.
13. Ólafur Davídsson, *Islenzkar Skemtanir* (Copenhagen, 1888–92), quoted by Fiske, 138 ff.
14. al-Firuzabadi's *Qamus*, pre-1414 (Murray, *History of Board Games*, 43 n).
15. R. G. Drake-Brockman, *British Somaliland* (London, 1912), 129; cited by Murray, *History of Board Games*, 48.
16. Murray, *History of Board Games*, 44.

17. L. S. Sutherland, quoted in Murray, *History of Board Games*, 28.
18. Windmill and pentagons from Bücken and Hanneforth *Klassische Spiele ganz neu*; cubes suggested by David Parlett; Zirge from Assia Popova, 'Analyse formelle et classification des jeux de calculs mongols', *Études Mongoles*, 5 (1974), via Lhôte, 645, and see also p. 97.
19. Murray, *History of Board Games*, 37. The document referred to is the *Kitab al-aghani*.
20. Stephen Addison, *100 Other Games to Play on a Chessboard* (London, 1983), 47–8.
21. G. A. Hutchinson (ed.), *Indoor Games and Recreations* (London, 1889), 204–7; *Cassell's Book of Sports and Pastimes* (London, 1893), 394–5.
22. Edward Lasker, *Go and Go-moku* (New York, 1934 and 1960), 206.
23. Yasunari Kawabata (trans. Edward G. Seidensticker), *The Master of Go* (London, 1972), 98 and endnote 21, 187. The text implicitly credits Tagaki Rakusan with this rule, evidently inspired by the *ko* rule in Go.
24. Kawabata, *The Master of Go* 59, and E. Glonnegger, *Das Spiele-Buch* (Ravensburg, 1988), 141.
25. Source: David Pritchard, 'Renju', *Games & Puzzles* 1st ser. 76 (Spring 1980), 26–7.
26. Bell, *Board and Table Games from Many Civilizations*, ii. 97.
27. Berlekamp *et al.*, *Winning Ways* ii. 679.
28. See Rodney Headington, 'The Game of Hex', *Games & Puzzles*, 16 (Aug. 1973), 8–9.
29. For an extensive appreciation and analysis see David Wells, 'Twixt', *Games & Puzzles*, 1st ser. 18 (Oct. 1973), 4–7.
30. Sid Sackson, *A Gamut of Games* (London, 1974, first published USA 1969), 135–41. Also described, but less cogently, under the name 'Connection', in Addison, *100 Other Games*, 46–7.
31. Nile reviewed in *Games & Puzzles*, 1st ser. 6 (Oct. 1972), 26, The Great Downhill Ski Game in *Games & Puzzles*, 38 (July 1975) 24.
32. Thoughtwave review in *Games & Puzzles*, 1st ser. 36 (May 1975), 26; see also Eric Solomon, 'How to play Thoughtwave', *Games & Puzzles*, 38 (July 1975), 4–6.
33. Andrew Pennycook tells me it is the same as Gale, first described by Martin Gardner in *Scientific American*, (Oct. 1958), and republished, with a complete solution, in 'Bridg-it and Other Games', *New Mathematical Puzzles and Diversions* (1966).

Across the Board

Games of Attainment and Traversal: Halma, Chinese Checkers, etc.

Over there! Over there!

US marching song (George M. Cohan)

Ils ne passeront pas!

French defensive cry (Gen. R.-G. Nivelle, 1916)

A distinctive branch of the family of space games is one in which two players confront each other with a collection of pieces, which may be identical or functionally differentiated but are the same on both sides, and aim to be the first to get one piece, or the whole group, over to the opposite side of the board. It must be emphasized that this is a purely formal classification and not an evolutionary one, most of its members being relatively modern. Those in which the aim is to get just one piece across I refer to as games of *attainment*, and designate as games of *traversal* those in which it is to get all across, or as many as remain after capture. Games of attainment are essentially linear, in that the winning piece will have traced a line connecting one side of the board to the other. This puts them in a logical relationship with games of linear connection such as Hex and Twixt, the chief difference being that they are games of attainment, involving movement rather than placement. They also resemble race games, in that the object is to get 'home' first, the chief difference being that they are played on two-dimensional grids and are games of perfect information, movement being determined by strategy rather than lot. Both they and games of traversal may involve capture, but this does not make them war games, since win or loss is determined not by the capture of material but by the attainment of a positional objective, making capture only the means to an end and not an end in itself.

It would be logical to start with games of attainment, but games of traversal are older and therefore perhaps ancestral, so let us take the historical path instead.

Games of Traversal (Massed Positional Attainment)

Five-Field Kono is a primitive example from Korea. 'The players move one square at a time, either backward or forward, diagonally across the squares' (Culin, verbatim.[1] He does not mention orthogonal moves.) The winner is the first to finish with all his pieces occupying the starting points of those of his opponent. There are no captures.

Tablan, described by R. C. Bell[2] as a traditional game still played in Mysore, shares the same objective but involves more complex play. Reaching the back rank, however, is not the primary object of the game, as captures are involved and the winner is the player who succeeds in getting more pieces home than his opponent. The fact that a win is determined by the amount of material taken classifies Tablan as a 'linear war-game', or what Bell calls a 'running-fight' game, and the only reason for mentioning it here is to suggest a possible origin for traversal games.

Halma, the earliest modern proprietary game of its type, was invented in 1883 by Howard Monks, an English surgeon, who named it from the Greek for 'jump'. It has also been known as Hoppity, in hopes of appealing to a classically uneducated market. Lhôte, unaware of this word, wonders whether the game might not owe something to the Hopi people of North America.[3] More usefully, he notes the existence of a similarly marked 20×20 board dating from the late eighteenth century that could have been used for just such a game.

Black and White each start with nineteen pieces in each of two adjacent corners of a 16×16 chequered board (Fig. 8.2). The winner is the first to transfer all his pieces to his opponent's equivalent starting places. A turn consists of a single step in any direction, or a short leap over a piece of either colour to the necessarily vacant square beyond. Jumps may be

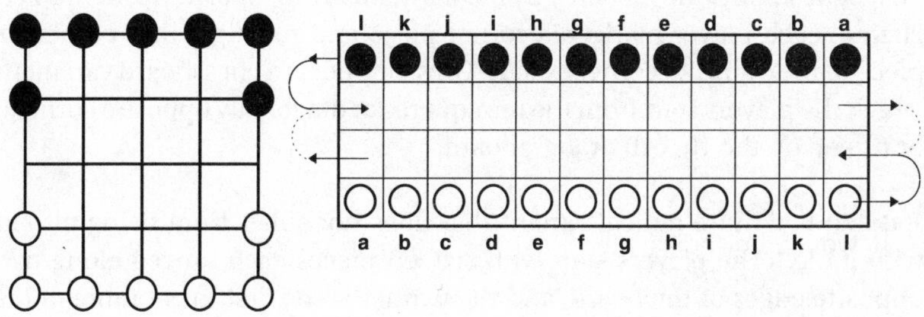

Fig. 8.1. *Left*: Five-Field Kono; *right*: Tablan.

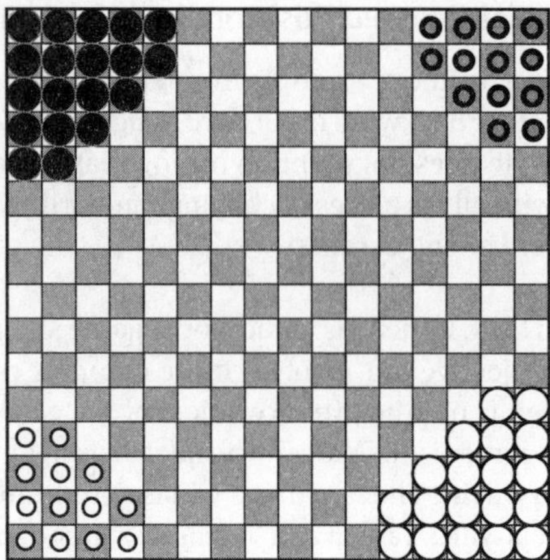

Fig. 8.2. Halma: Two players start with nineteen pieces each (*top left, bottom right*), four with thirteen each (omitting the inner line of six from each group of nineteen).

enchained, but steps and jumps may not be combined in one turn. Jumped pieces are not captured. To prevent a cussed player from exploiting a theoretical loophole, it may be decreed that a player wins when all the opposing base points are occupied, at least one of them by a piece of his own colour. If four play in partnerships, each starts with thirteen pieces of a distinctive colour in a subset of the corner squares and aims to transfer all his pieces to the diagonally opposite corner.

Several variations have been proposed. Colour Halma is based on the fact that the board is chequered, and varies the powers of movement according to colour. A piece that starts on a dark square must remain throughout on a dark square, moving only one step diagonally and being prohibited from jumping, whereas a piece starting on a light square must similarly remain on a light square, moving only by means of an orthogonal jump. In Marked Halma, each player marks his corner piece and must get that particular piece to the opposite corner exactly. Grasshopper is a chessboard variant in which the players start from the ten squares of diagonally opposite corners, or fifteen on the 10×10 draughtboard.

Rakado is a more radical variant that does not suffer from being played with a die.[4] The players start with sixteen pieces each ranged along two opposite edges of the board, and the winner is the first to get more of his pieces to the opposite side than his opponent. Each plays in turn by rolling the die and moving any of his pieces orthogonally forwards by the distance shown. A six confers another turn. A piece may jump but not land on one of its own colour, but may not jump an enemy piece. Captures are possible but not necessarily desirable, as they reduce the number of pieces required by one's opponent to achieve his objective. A piece is captured by landing on it by an exact throw. For this purpose only, the direction of travel may be forwards, diagonally forwards, or sideways. If one or more captures are possible it is obligatory to make at least one of them, otherwise a piece that could have captured is itself removed from play. The furthest line must be reached on an exact throw, which may or may not yield a capture, and the piece so moved must then remain in place.

Salta, an obvious Halma derivative even to its title, which merely comes from a different language, was invented in 1899 by Düsseldorf-born musician Konrad Büttgenbach and exhibited at the Monte Carlo Chess Tourney in 1901. It is played on a 10 × 10 chequerboard, Black and White having each fifteen pieces arranged on the dark squares of their nearest three rows as if for Draughts. (A variant called Pyramid has four in the back row, three in the second, two in the third, and one in the fourth.) All fifteen pieces are individually distinguished, those in the back row being stars, in the second row moons and in the third row suns, and those in each row being also numbered 1 to 5 from left to right. As the symbols confer no distinct powers, the pieces might just as well be numbered 1 to 15. Pieces are moved as at Draughts, either one space diagonally forward or by a short diagonal leap but without capture, and the winner is the first to get each of his pieces on to the starting square of his opponent's correspondingly numbered piece. Aggressive marketing secured for the game a wide popularity in several countries, but it did not last long. Even a picture of its inventor playing Salta with Sarah Bernhardt in 1901[5] does little to enhance its appeal to modern audiences, especially as both are fully clothed.

Chinese Checkers is the longest surviving member of this family, having attained a status comparable to that of Ludo and Snakes & Ladders. The board is a six-pointed star ruled into equilateral triangles and the game is played on the intersections using pegs which slot into holes, though it could equally well be presented as a hexagonal grid and played in the cells. Each of the six 15-point external triangles represents a player's home base and is distinctively coloured. If two play, each starts with fifteen pegs of his own colour occupying a base directly opposite that of his opponent. If more than two play, each starts with ten pegs of his own colour, omitting the inmost line of five. Three occupy alternate bases, and more than three occupy whichever bases they please. If four or six play in

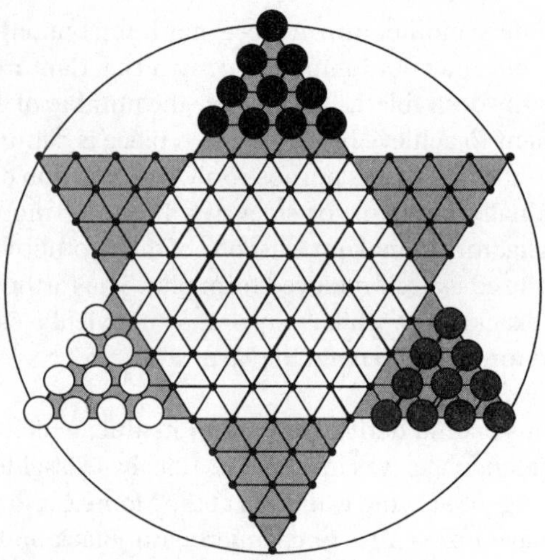

Fig. 8.3. Chinese Checkers—initial array for three players.

partnerships, each player's base should directly oppose that of an opponent. Six may play as three opposing partnerships of two or as two teams of three. The winner is the first to get all his pieces across the board to occupy the base directly opposite. In partnership play, it is the first team partnership to do so. Each in turn moves a piece to any vacant adjacent point, or jumps an adjacent piece of any colour to land on the necessarily vacant point in a straight line beyond. A non-jump move completes a turn. A jump move may be followed in the same turn by any number of further jumps that may be possible and desired, changing direction as often as necessary. Jumped pieces are not captured.

Chinese Checkers, or *Tiau-qi*, 'the jumping-game', was first published in the West in 1892 by Ravensburger[6] under the name *Stern-Halma* (Star Halma). Its subsequent success over 'square' Halma is due partly to its more attractive appearance, partly to the catchier title it later acquired in America, and perhaps largely due to the fact that it can be played by up to six. Film buffs may like to spot its unbilled appearance in Billy Wilder's *Double Indemnity* (1944).

Permutations is a beautiful French game by Charles Truex published in 1979.[7] The 144 squares (Fig 8.4) are in three colours, and each player has twelve pieces, four of each colour, the two sides being distinguished by shape. The winner is the first to get all his pieces across to the back rank. A piece moves in any orthogonal or diagonal direction either one space, or over an unbroken line of pieces of any shape or colour, provided always that

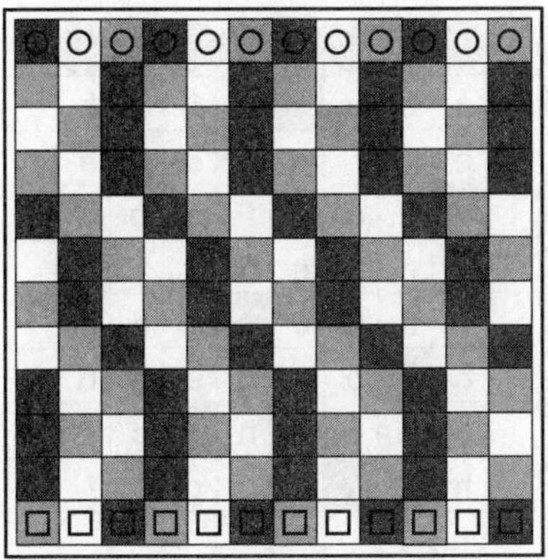

Fig. 8.4. Permutations.

it starts from and lands only on a cell of its own colour. One or more moves of either or both sorts may be enchained in one turn.

Colorado, an unpublished game of my invention, is played on a 10×10 squared board of which the central 8×8 and two opposite rows of eight constitute the 10×8 field of play, enabling the board to be used in either orientation. The squares of the 8×8 field are charged with eight different colours arranged in such a way that no two of the same colour are orthogonally aligned. Black and White each start with eight pieces on the nearer edge, and the winner is the first to get all his pieces, or as many as remain after capture, to the opposite side of the notional river (Colorado). Eight pieces of a third colour, representing rocks, are placed on all eight squares of any agreed colour. This gives sixteen different games, since each colour forms a distinctive pattern and the board may be placed in either orientation. Each in turn moves one of his pieces in a straight line, orthogonally or diagonally, in any direction. It must move as far as it can until it reaches a piece of its own colour, or a rock, or the edge of the board, and must then stop on the square before it. If it reaches an enemy piece, it must capture it by replacement. Naturally, a player who is foolish enough to capture all his opponent's pieces loses the game.

Games of (Singleton Positional) Attainment

Attainment games appear to be entirely modern and proprietary, and it will suffice to mention a few that illustrate the principle well.

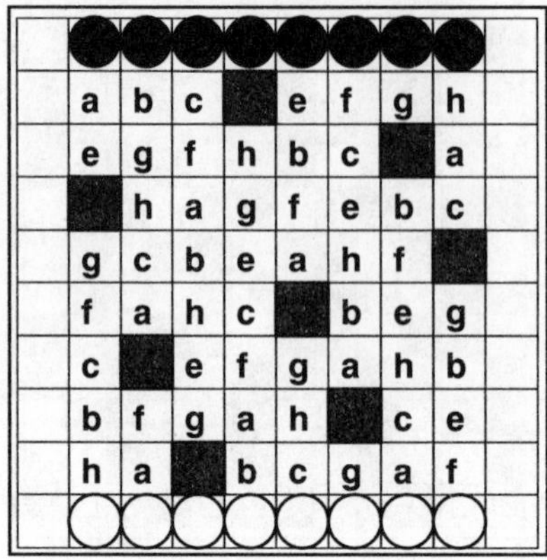

Fig. 8.5. Colorado, with rocks on colour 'd'.

Epaminondas, by American games inventor Robert Abbott, exhibits a classical elegance that puts it at the forefront of this family. Indeed, if the playing public were better educated in games appreciation it would occupy a position well above that of Chinese Checkers or Reversi/Othello. The simple pieces are of little power and value in themselves, but become strong when combined in straight lines called phalanxes. (The game is named after the Greek hero whose novel military tactics led to the liberation of Thebes from the Spartans in 379 BC and the subsequent unification of Boeotia. I believe it was later renamed Phalanx.) A notable merit of this unjustly neglected game is that of immediate visual clarity, the absolute and relative power of any piece or phalanx being readily apparent throughout.[8]

The board is a grid of 168 squares in twelve ranks of fourteen each. Black and White each start with twenty-eight pieces occupying their home ranks. (It is playable on a chessboard with sixteen pieces each.[9])The aim is to be the first to position a piece on the opponent's home rank in such a way that it cannot, on the opponent's next move, be either captured or matched by an equal move.

White starts. An individual piece, whether isolated or part of a phalanx, moves one square in any direction, like a Chess king. Two or more like pieces forming a connected line, whether orthogonal or diagonal, constitute a phalanx. A phalanx may move in either of the two directions (forwards or backwards) that it delineates. It, or whatever smaller portion of it may be moved, moves any distance up to the number of pieces it contains.

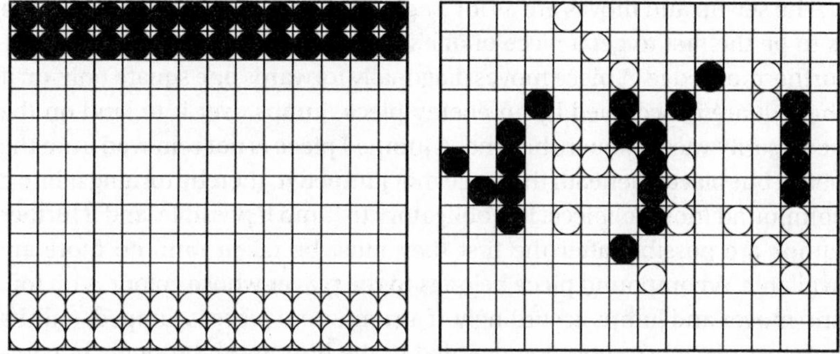

Fig. 8.6. Epaminondas. *Left*: Opening position. *Right*: White has moved a diagonal phalanx of three on to Black's home row. Black can counter by moving his left-hand vertical phalanx of four down to White's home row. If White then moves his right-hand phalanx of two vertically to the back rank, Black could prevent defeat by moving his diagonal phalanx of three to capture its head. White must first destroy this phalanx by moving his central phalanx of three vertically, capturing its centre piece. Black, however, can defend again with his right-hand vertical phalanx of four; and so on.

If only part of a phalanx is moved, its maximum distance is similarly dictated by the number of pieces actually moved.

A moving phalanx stops when its head reaches the maximum permissible distance, an edge of the board, a piece of its own colour, or the head of an equal or longer enemy phalanx. If it reaches the head of a shorter enemy phalanx in the same line of travel, or a singleton which may or may not form part of a phalanx differently aligned, it captures that head or singleton by replacement, together with any and all members of that phalanx aligned behind it.

When a singleton or the head of a phalanx reaches the opposing home row, the opponent may stave off defeat either by capturing it, or by correspondingly moving a singleton or head of a phalanx to the opposite home rank. If he cannot do so, he has lost. If he can, play continues, and pieces occupying their opponent's home row may not for the rest of the game be either moved away or captured. The game ends when either player, upon his turn to move, has more pieces occupying his opponent's home rank than vice versa.

Pasta, by Alvin Paster, and first reported in *Computing News* (15 March 1956), bears some relation to the Draughts variant Lasca (see Chapter 15).

The set-up and moves are as for Anglo-American Draughts, and the aim is to be the first to get a piece of one's own colour across the board to the furthermost edge. A piece moves diagonally forwards one square only, or, if that square is occupied by an enemy piece, jumps over it to land on the necessarily vacant square beyond. A jumped piece is not removed from the board but placed beneath the piece that jumped it, thereby turning it into a compound (double) piece. It is obligatory to jump if possible, and if further jumps are possible after the first they must be taken until no more are available. A compound piece belongs to the player whose colour is on top, and moves and jumps accordingly. If a compound piece is jumped, only its topmost piece is removed and added to the bottom of the single or compound piece that jumped it. It is not permissible to move without capturing if a capture can be made, but, given a choice of multiple captures, it is not obligatory to make the longest series.

A pile headed by one piece of a given colour moves forwards only. If headed by two or more, it counts as a 'king' of that colour, and can move and capture diagonally backwards as well as forwards. A player who gets a king on to the furthermost rank only wins if it can legally stay there. If it can make a backwards capture from that position it must do so, and play continues.

A pile headed by three or more pieces of a given colour is known as a *chiang*. It has no special power beyond the tactical advantage of enticing the opponent into a forced capture without losing its kingly power of movement.

'The game commonly opens with an exchange of jumps designed to produce kings', writes Fred Gruenberger.[10] 'This has been variously characterized as the Dance of the Wild Loons, the Gooney-Bird Dance, and Yo-yo-ing... Games can be terrifically fast at times, taking as little as one minute and as few as seven moves. [But] Innocuous-looking jumps can create more jumps to form a totally unexpected chain reaction, running in some cases to as many as twenty forced moves. It is thus extremely difficult to see more than a few moves ahead.'

Quandary. This delightful two-player abstract published by Spears Games in the 1970s, and still one of my favourites,[11] introduces a novel form of interaction—that of exerting direct control over the movement of enemy pieces, even to the extent of temporarily immobilizing them. The board is a grid of 12 × 12 multi-coloured squares arranged more or less at random. That is to say, there are eighteen in each of eight colours, and no two squares of the same colour are next to each other, but beyond that there is no apparent pattern to their distribution. Starting with four pieces

n	b	y	w	g	m	b	o	y	p	b	o
g	m	o	p	y	n	w	p	m	w	n	g
o	n	g	b	w	o	g	y	o	g	m	p
m	p	w	y	p	b	m	n	w	b	y	n
y	b	n	o	g	n	w	o	p	m	w	b
w	g	m	p	b	m	p	y	n	o	g	y
m	o	w	n	y	w	g	m	b	y	p	o
p	y	b	g	o	b	n	p	g	n	m	w
b	n	o	w	m	g	o	b	w	o	y	p
o	g	m	y	n	p	w	g	y	m	b	n
y	w	o	p	b	m	n	o	p	w	g	y
g	b	n	m	w	g	p	y	m	n	o	b

Fig. 8.7. Quandary, with colours neutral, blue, yellow, white, green, magenta, pink, and orange, more or less randomly arranged. From this initial position, Black can move to a pink, blue, neutral, or green square (five possibilities), or White to pink, magenta, or neutral (also five, but his rightmost piece is immobile).

arranged on four random squares of his home rank, each in turn moves one of his pieces forwards one space orthogonally or diagonally—provided, that is, that the square is vacant and that it is of the same colour as one of the squares lying orthogonally ahead of any opposing piece. For example, if the squares immediately ahead of your opponent's pieces are green, yellow, pink, and blue, then you may move any of your pieces orthogonally or diagonally forwards on to a square of any of those colours. Of course, if your opponent's four pieces are all immediately behind a blue square, then you can only move to a forward blue square, which there may not be, thus causing you to miss a turn. Additional rules, requiring the board always to be placed in the same orientation, and dictating the starting squares by a draw of numbered cards, are needless fripperies, and best ignored.

Trippples (with three Ps), published by Aladdin Games shortly after Quandary, plays a variation on the same theme of directly controlling the movement of enemy pieces. The two players have only a single piece each, which start on adjacent corner squares, their aim being the first to get their piece across the 8×8 board to the diagonally opposite corner. Before any move is made, however, the remaining fifty-six squares—corner and centre squares being excluded—are covered with directional tiles. Each of the fifty-six tiles shows three arrows pointing in three of eight compass orientations (N-NE-E, N-NE-SE, N-NE-S, etc.), and each is unique, there being exactly fifty-six combinations of three from eight. There are three phases to the play. In Phase 1, each in turn takes a tile from the stockpile until they have twenty-eight each. In Phase 2, each in turn places a piece on any vacant valid square. In Phase 3, finally, each in turn moves his piece from one square to another. From its initial corner position, the piece can move freely to any of the three immediate squares. Thereafter, it may move to any adjacent or appointant tile, only in one of the three directions indicated by the tile on which the *opponent's* piece currently stands. Much of the planning of the game takes place in Phase 2, when it is possible to think ahead to the sort of route that one's opponent might be forced to take.[12] In practice, the game is less appealing than Quandary, in that it lacks visual clarity (not to mention desirable colour), and the choice of three directions for one piece is distinctly less satisfactory than the choice of four pieces offering up to three moves each.

Conquest, published in 1976,[13] is worth remembering. The board is 9 × 8 and each player starts with nine pieces arranged on his back rank. These are large dice, constructed in such a way as to pass from square to square on the grooved plastic board, so that each move automatically turns the die over on to its next successive side. Eight dice are orthodox, with opposite sides totalling seven and left-handed for both players. The ninth has a single spot on each side. This is the Key Piece (equivalent to a Chess king), and occupies the centre or Key Square of the back rank. The primary aim is to get one's Key Piece across the board and on to the opposing Key Square, but capturing the opposing Key Piece is a 'sudden death' winning alternative. A piece moves by rolling from square to square in any orthogonal direction, and it may (but need not) turn through one right-angle (only) at any point in its move. The distance it moves is from one to six spaces, as determined by the number of spots initially uppermost. It cannot pass over an occupied square, but may land on one, thereby capturing the occupant. Conquest was an excellent game, but too original to remain successful in Britain (I believe it lasted longer in Germany). Within a short space of time it was repackaged and re-titled 'George *v.* Mildred', after a domestic TV comedy series—a true kiss of death.

The Jungle Game. R. C. Bell describes[14] this contemporary Chinese game sent him in the 1960s by a correspondent in Hong Kong, but knows nothing of its ancestry. The board design suggests some influence of Chinese Chess, and the perfection of the game—it 'plays well'—suggests a solid period of experimentation and refinement; yet the concept as a whole appears too sophisticated to have much of a history behind it.

The 7 × 9 board represents a jungle terrain. The two central blocks of six squares (shaded) represent river. Each player has a den, indicated here (Fig. 8.8) by R for Red's den and B for Blue's. The three squares adjacent to each den (shaded) are traps. Each player has eight pieces representing animals bearing values from 1 to 8 thus: rat, cat, wolf, dog, panther, tiger, lion, elephant. The initial arrangement is shown in Fig. 8.8.

The aim is to be the first to occupy the opponent's den on the far side of the board with any of one's own animals. Each in turn moves one of his animals one space orthogonally to a square that is either vacant or occupied by an opposing animal of equal or lesser value.

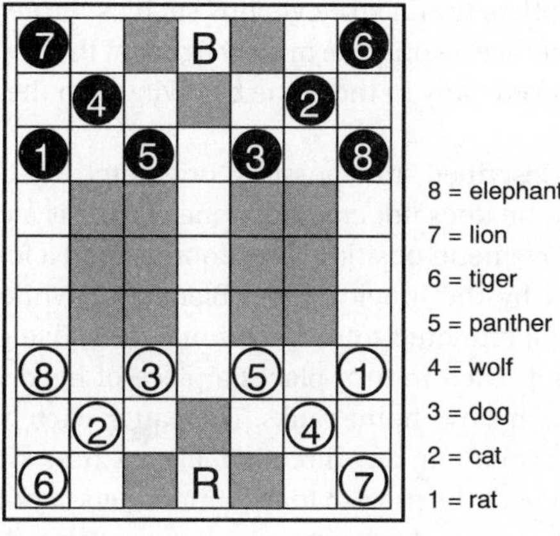

Fig. 8.8. The Jungle Game

River squares. Only a rat (1) may enter river squares. A tiger or lion (6, 7) adjacent to a river square may leap orthogonally over the river to the nearest square beyond, provided that (*a*) it is legally occupiable, and (*b*) the animal's passage over the river is not impeded by a rat.

Traps. An animal entering an enemy trap (on the far side of the board) assumes a value of zero as long as it remains there, but resumes its normal value on moving away. It may enter a trap on its own side with impunity.

Capture. An animal moving to a square occupied by an opposing animal of equal or lower value 'eats' it, and the latter is removed from play. However, a rat (1) can eat an elephant (8) by notionally entering its ear and gnawing its brain. A rat when in the river can neither be eaten by any animal on adjacent dry land, nor attack the opposing elephant. One rat can attack the other, however, so long as both are in the river. An animal occupying an enemy den, being temporarily valueless, can be eaten by any opposing animal.

Dens An animal may not enter its own den. Entering the opponent's den, however, wins the game.

The 'attainment' objective is a vehicle of exploration for the novel idea of larger-valued pieces capturing equal or smaller ones. Of several adaptations and borrowings made by western inventors, by far the best is Eric Solomon's version[15] entitled The Business Jungle, in which the hierarchy runs: office boy (1), trainee, clerk, salesman, executive, director, managing director, chairman (8), and the two areas of river are translated into typing pools. Solomon offers useful strategic tips such as 'Protect the office-boy: he is your best defence against the mighty figure of the opposing chairman. This can be achieved early in the game by diving into the typing pool.'

Breakthrough, described and possibly originated by Stephen Addison (since, unusually, he does not credit anyone else),[16] is a chessboard game of placement, movement, positional attainment, and a form of interaction possibly inspired by the Jungle Game. Black and White each start with sixteen pieces differentiated into six commanders, five generals and five majors. In Phase 1, each in turn places a piece of his own colour on any square in either of his two home ranks. Thereafter, each in turn moves one of his pieces one square in any direction, like a Chess king. Capture is by replacement, but with the proviso that commanders capture only generals, generals only majors, and majors only commanders. A piece failing to capture when able is huffed. The winner is the first to place a piece of his own on his opponent's home rank—presumably without being promptly captured, though the author says nothing one way or the other.

The same principle found expression in the game of Advice published by Alick Elithorn in 1976. Each player aims to get his Citizen across the board with the help or hindrance of Priests, who captured Lawyers, who in turn captured Psychiatrists, who in turn captured Priests.

NOTES

1. Culin, *Games of the Orient*, 102.
2. Bell, *Board and Table Games from Many Civilisations*, 87–9.
3. Lhôte, 496.
4. E. Glonnegger, *Das Spiele-Buch* (Ravensburg, 1988), 203.
5. Reproduced ibid. 206.

6. Illustrated ibid. 204.
7. From Lhôte, 577.
8. See Robert, Abbott 'Under the Strategy Tree', *Games & Puzzles*, 36 (May 1975), 4–5, and David Wells's comments on 'conceptual clarity' in his review of Epaminondas in *Games & Puzzles*, 42 (Nov. 1975), 18–19.
9. See S. Addison, *100 Other Games to play on a Chessboard* (London, 1983), 44–5.
10. F. Gruenberger, editor of *Popular Computing*. His article for that magazine was republished in *Games & Puzzles*, 57 (Feb. 1977), 16, with a follow-up in no. 59 (April 1977), 17.
11. Generously, but inaccurately, Lhôte (590) credits me with the invention of Quandary. I merely reviewed it, in *Games & Puzzles*, 1st ser. 15 (July 1973), 36–7.
12. From the games review by David Wells, in *Games & Puzzles*, 42 (Nov. 1975), 18.
13. Published by Denys Fisher Toys, and reviewed by David Parlett in *Games & Puzzles*, 1st ser. 48 (May 1976), 20–1.
14. Bell, *Board and Table Games from Many Civilizations*, 69–70.
15. Eric Solomon, 'The Business Jungle, or Goldberg v. Silverstein', *Games & Puzzles*, 1st ser. 11 (March 1973), 10–11.
16. Addison, *100 Other Games to Play*, 45.

Making Arrangements

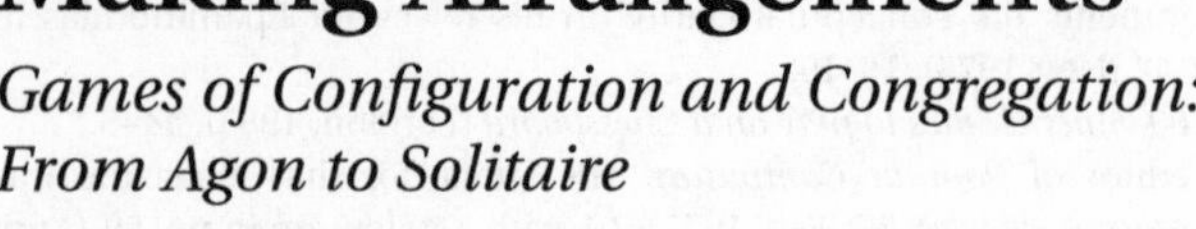

Games of Configuration and Congregation: From Agon to Solitaire

There is a dark
Inscrutable workmanship that reconciles
Discordant elements, makes them cling together
In one society.

Wordsworth, *The Prelude* (1850)

Never mind the weather,
Never mind the rain
Here we are together
Whoops! She goes again . . .

Well known: untraced

Another class of space games explored in recent years is that in which players aim to get their pieces into a given configuration, or, at least, into a congregation of any shape so long as every piece is adjacent to at least one other of its partners. They are variously games of placement, movement, or both. Interaction consists almost entirely in blocking, though some also involve capture.

Agon or **Queen's Guards** may be the oldest of its type. It appears, in company with Backgammon, Fox & Geese, Nine Men's Morris, and Solitaire, in the section headed 'Minor Skilled Games' of *Cassell's Book of Sports and Pastimes* (1890), where it is described as 'amusing and ingenious'. White and Black each start with a Queen and six plain 'guards' arranged on the hexagonal board of Fig. 9.1, *left*. The winner is the first player to attain the position of Fig. 9.1 *right*, that is, with his Queen in the centre hex surrounded by her six guards as shown.

Each in turn moves a piece to an adjacent hex, either sideways to one of the same colour, or inwards towards one of opposite colour, but never backwards towards the perimeter. Pieces may not jump or pass each other, nor may a piece move to a hex lying between two enemy pieces so that it is sandwiched between them in a straight line. Any piece finding itself so enclosed as the result of an enemy move is ousted and placed on any vacant peripheral and unenclosed hex of its owner's choosing. A

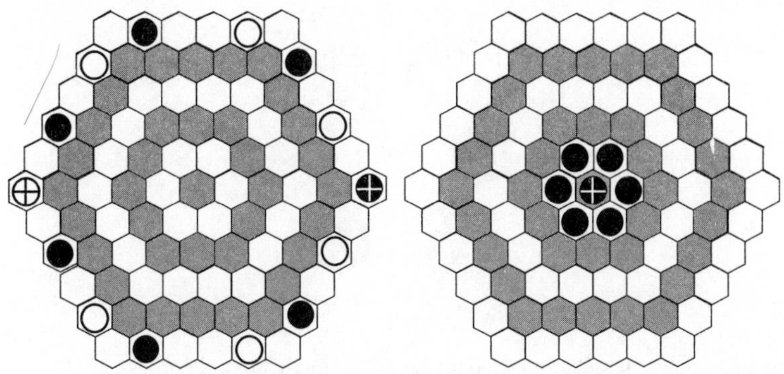

Fig. 9.1. Agon, or Queen's Guards. *Left*: Initial array. *Right*: Winning configuration.

Queen, however, if so ousted, may be placed on any vacant and unenclosed hex. If two or more pieces are ousted in one move, their owner must move them one at a time on succeeding turns, each removal counting as a turn. They may be taken in any order, unless one of them is the Queen, who must be taken first. The game is forfeited by a player who entirely surrounds the centre hex with guards, leaving the Queen outside, since neither can then attain the objective. As a variation, the game may be made one of placement and movement, each in turn entering first the Queen and then a guard on any unenclosed peripheral hex, and not moving until all are in place.

Agon could equally well be classed as a game of positional attainment or of blockade and restriction. Surprisingly, it appears to be at least a century older than its appearance in Victorian books. Lhôte notes that two tabletops with its distinctive pattern executed in marquetry can be positively ascribed to the Parisian furniture-maker Adam Vaugeois, and so dated to the 1780s.[1] He surmises that it is the earliest abstract game to be played on a hexagonal grid, an idea that may have been inspired by experiments being made in the contemporary development of war simulation games. The game itself, however, is not described earlier than 1872, and Moulidars in 1888 supposes it to have originated outside France. A similar Victorian game was published by J. Jaques of London under the title Hexagony.

Kensington, invented by Brian Taylor and Peter Forbes in 1979, is a pleasing game of shifting configurations that achieved a brief vogue before passing the way of all abstracts promoted with such claims as 'the game is apparently quite simple but in point of fact turns out to be several times more complex than Chess'. It is played on a tessellation well-known to

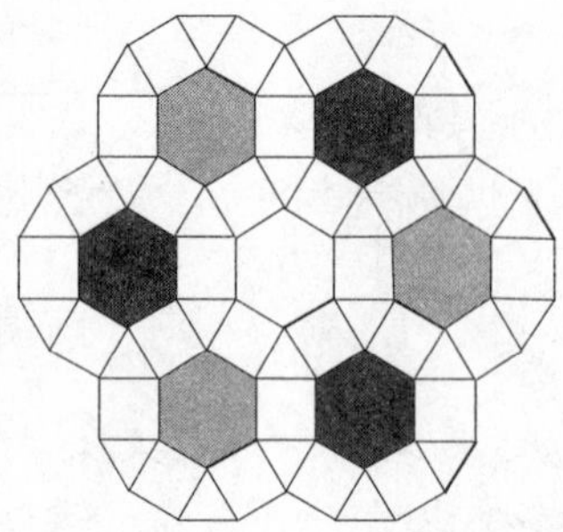

Fig. 9.2. Islamic tessellation used for Kensington (Taylor and Forbes).

mathematicians, which the inventors found in a volume of ancient Islamic patterns they bought in the street market of Portobello Road, Kensington, London. The board consists of seven hexagons with peripheral squares and triangles (Fig. 9.2). The inner hexagon is white and the outer hexagons coloured alternately red and blue. The game is one of placement and movement. Starting with fifteen appropriately coloured pieces each in hand, each in turn places a piece on the corner point of any square or triangle. Occupying all three points of a triangle or all four points of a square entitles a player to reposition, respectively, any single or any two opposing pieces ad lib. The winner is the first to occupy all six points of the central hexagon or of a hexagon of his own colour. There are versions for four and six players.

Pattern-Making

Pagoda (Shuti). A relatively unexplored extension to the family is that of placing pieces in such a way as to form regular or symmetrical patterns. The best of few examples is Valentin Siena's Pagoda, published in the mid-1970s by F. X. Schmid, and said (without further reference) to be based on an 'ancient oriental game called Shuti'. Two players, Green and Red, each have fourteen pieces of their own colour designated stones (square) and columns (round). Each in turn either places a piece on a vacant square, or removes one of his stones for play elsewhere on a subsequent turn, or moves one of his columns to any other vacant square of the same colour as the one it was on. The aim is to form and score for various types of 'building'. A building consists of four pieces of the same colour, at least one of which must be a stone, occupying the four corners of a square or

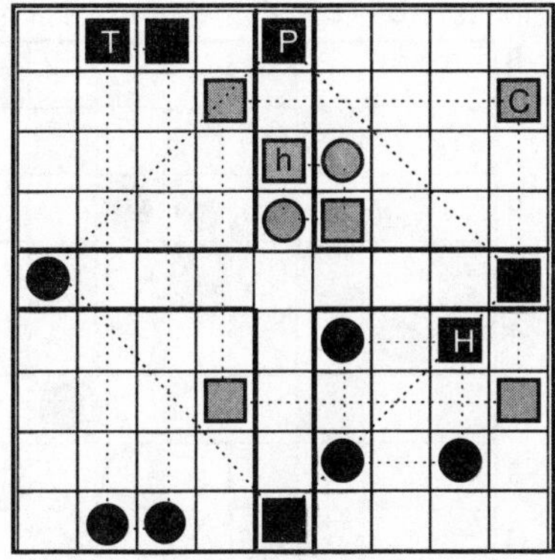

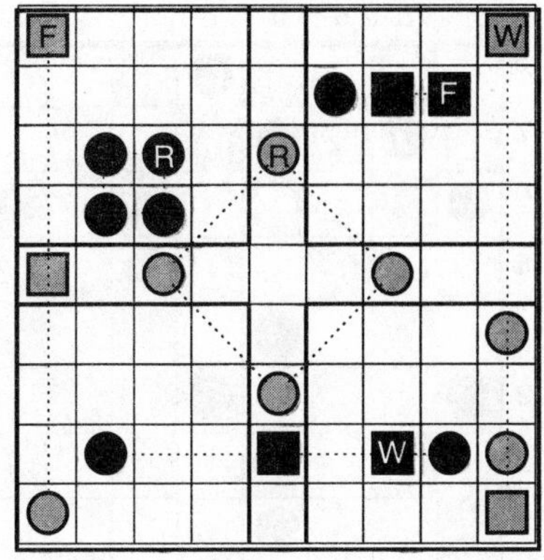

Fig. 9.3. Pagoda. *Left*: Scoring configurations: Hut, House, Tower, Castle, Pagoda; *Right*: Penalty configurations: Fence, Wall, Ruin

rectangle. The score for a completed building is the sum of the values of its individual stones. It varies with the type of building so created, is doubled for each stone occupying a square of the opponent's colour, and is doubled if consisting entirely of stones. Four columns at the corners of a rectangle constitute a 'ruin', which scores zero. The basic value of a stone in a hut is 1, in a house 5, a castle 10, a tower 11, a pagoda 15. A pagoda is the only scorable square formed on a diagonal, and its four pieces must occupy the arms of the central orthogonal cross. Penalty scores obtain for making a 'wall', which is four pieces of one's own colour orthogonally aligned, or a 'fence', which is three in symmetrical alignment—i.e. with the same distance between the centre piece and each of its neighbours. A piece is captured and lost for ever if it finds itself equidistant between two enemy pieces in one orthogonal direction and two in the opposite direction, the four enemy pieces thereby forming a 'cross' centred on the capturable piece.

As there is even more to this attractive game than described above, it is hard to believe that the inventor has not expanded considerably on its supposed ancient oriental model.

Squares. An unusual variation on pattern-making is Martin Gardner's chessboard game of Squares. Black and White each in turn place a piece of their own colour on any vacant square. The aim is to avoid getting four of one's own pieces arranged in such a way as to mark the corners of a square, of any size and orientation. The first to do so loses. Fig. 9.4 shows how difficult it can get to spot danger points. White, for example, would lose by playing to g3 (dotted outline).

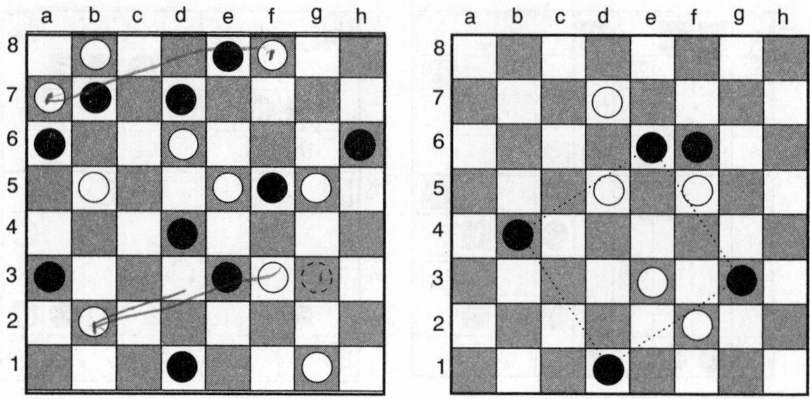

Fig. 9.4. Squares (*left*): White would lose by playing to g3, completing a square with a7-b2-f8. In Kvartal (*right*), Black plays g3, capturing a white piece on either d5 or e3.

Kvartal, a comparable but hitherto unpublished game by Mikhail Arnautov and Andrew Pennycook, involves the capture—or, more accurately, ousting—of enemy pieces by enclosing them within a square of any size and orientation (Fig. 9.4 *right*). Each in turn places one of initially nineteen pieces of his colour on any vacant cell. If a fourth piece is played in such a way as to complete the corners of a square, of any size and orientation, then any opposing piece whose centre is enclosed within that square, or crossed by one of its notional edges, is captured and returned to its owner. It is not permissible to complete such a square, however, unless one such capture is thereby made. If several pieces are enclosed, only one may be captured, but the capturer may freely choose which. A player who has just lost a piece may not immediately play to the square in which it was lost. (This is equivalent to the *ko* rule in Go.) The winner is the first to have no piece in hand when it is his turn to play. The inventors admit that after a few moves Kvartal requires the aid of a computer as track-keeper and referee.

Entropy, invented by Eric Solomon and published in the 1970s by Skirrid International, is a game of conflict over the forces of order and chaos (entropy). It is played on a 5 × 5 grid with twenty-five pieces, five each of five different colours. Two players, the Maker and the Breaker, each play in turn. The Breaker places a piece on any vacant square, and the Maker may then slide any piece any distance in an orthogonal direction, provided that it does not jump over an occupied square. The Maker's object is to ensure that the coloured pieces form as many symmetrical lines as possible at end of play, while the Breaker's is to hinder him as much as possible. With all twenty-five pieces on board, the Maker scores, in respect of each row and each column of five, one point for any two or more colours forming a linear pattern. For example, a line of colours a-b-b-c-b would score 2 for the b-b subset and 3 for the b-c-b. A line consisting of five of the same colour would score a total of 30, this being the sum of 2 for each of four pairs, 3 for each of three triplets, 4 for the two overlapping lines of four, and 5 for the line of five. Players alternate roles in successive games. As I write, Entropy is about to be republished in an enlarged format, with seven pieces in each of seven colours, and a 7 × 7 board.

The Puzzle of Oz is a solitaire of my invention designed to make use of some pieces the manufacturer happened to have available for another game (Plugnorth Ltd., 1981). The board is a trellis of twenty-five squares and the pieces five each of five different colours. These are drawn one by one from a bag or box and placed on a vacant square. The object is to finish with all in place and no two of the same colour next to each other either orthogonally or diagonally. The first four pieces drawn must be placed on the four corners in rotation, and each subsequent piece orthogonally adjacent to another already on the board.

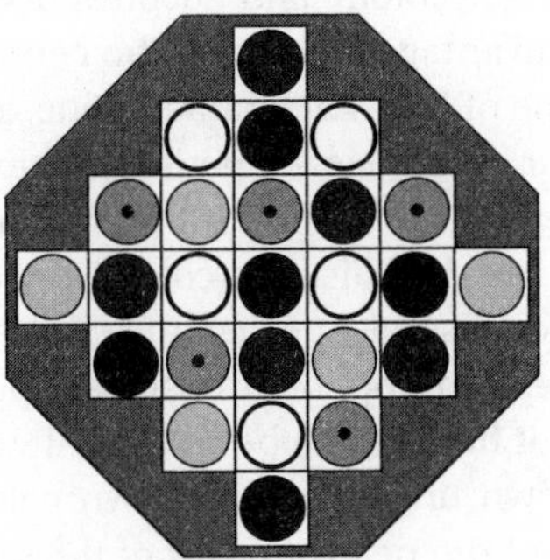

Fig. 9.5. Oz (Parlett): a successful outcome.

Congregation

Another possible objective is to get all one's pieces connected into a single group of any size, shape or orientation. So far as I know, the first published proprietary game based on this theme was one of my invention.

Shoulder to Shoulder I devised in response to an urge to produce an abstract game for three players instead of the universal two or four.

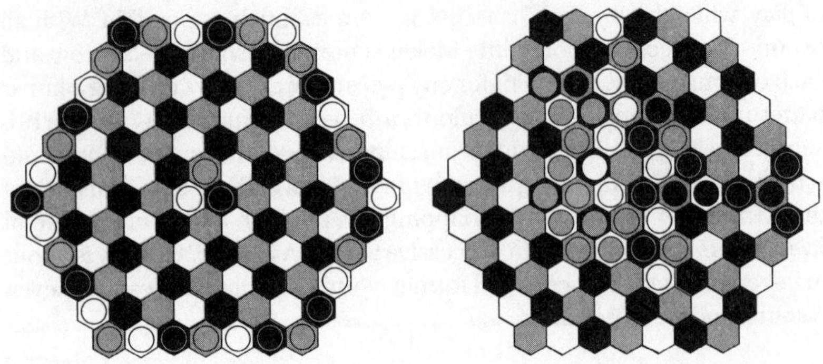

Fig. 9.6. Shoulder to Shoulder (Parlett). *Left*: Initial array. *Right*: Grey has connected. White scores three penalties for groups of 7, 3 and 2, Black four penalties for groups of 8, 2, and two singletons.

Originally called Triton, it was published in 1975 (by Intellect Games) as Shoulder to Shoulder, the title of a then current television series about suffragettes. It is played on a point-centred grid of 114 hexagons. Centring it on the junction of three hexagons rather than one yields the same number of hexes of each colour and so prevents any one player from gaining a presumed advantage by seizing the centre—an idea that could benefit Piet Hein's game of Hex. Each of Red, Blue, and Green starts with a piece of his own colour on the eleven perimeter hexes of the same colour and a twelfth on the central hex of that colour, which is marked with a spot. Each in turn moves a piece of his own colour any distance orthogonally, provided that it does not pass over an occupied cell. It may land on a vacant cell of any colour except an opponent's central 'spot' hex, though it may pass over a spot hex if it happens to be vacant. Alternatively, a player may move a piece of his own on a hex of its own colour (only) by a single diagonal move to one of the nearest hexes of the same colour. This move enables a trapped piece to 'squeeze' its way between two orthogonally adjacent pieces of any colour.

Play ends as soon as one player's pieces form a single connected group or line, each being adjacent to at least one other of its colour. The other players each count a penalty point for each singleton or group formed by their own pieces. A session is three games, each in turn having the first move, and is won by the player with the overall lowest score. I have never determined whether a game could theoretically fail to reach a conclusion with perfect play, but the experience of several hundred games suggested that, for all practical purposes, somebody would always win.

Action Lines,[2] by Claude Soucie, is a chessboard game based on the same theme. Though involving both movement and capture, strategy is directed by the goal of being the first to unite one's pieces in a single group. Black and White each have twelve pieces of their own colour on opposite sides of the board as shown in Fig. 9.7.

A piece moves in any straight line, orthogonally or diagonally, provided that the distance it traverses is precisely equal to the number of pieces (of both colours) in that line, and that it lands on a vacant square or one occupied by an enemy piece, which it thereby captures. It may, in moving, pass over any number of friendly pieces, but not any enemies. An unusually pleasing element of strategy derives from the fact that it is not desirable to make too many captures, as each capture reduces the number of pieces required for the opponent to win. In the extreme case, the capture of one of two last remaining pieces would result in the opponent's winning with a 'group' consisting of a singleton! It is, of course, possible to draw by making a move that simultaneously produces two winning groups.

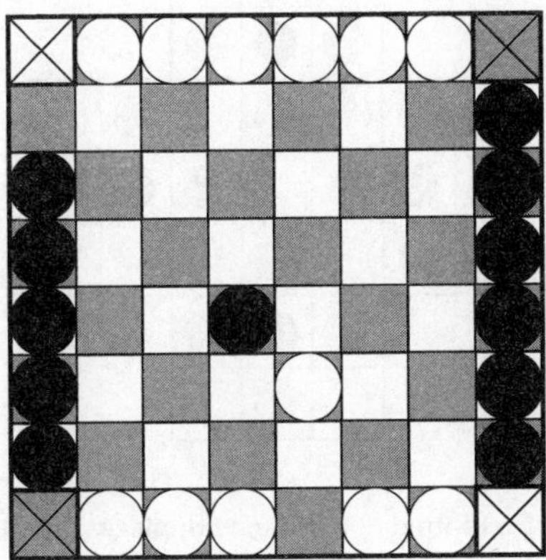

Fig. 9.7. Action Lines (Soucie). White's first move was necessarily of two squares, thereby creating three lines of power three. Black has responded with a diagonal move of three.

Clearance Games

Clearance games, in which the object is to clear the board of pieces, may be regarded as games of 'null configuration', or negative games of arrangement. The classic example is Solitaire, known in America as Peg Solitaire to distinguish it from Card Solitaire, or Patience. As the name implies,

Solitaire is primarily a one-player game, and so less of a game than a puzzle for the purposes of our present survey.[3]

Solitaire. Fig. 9.8 shows the 33-hole board traditional in England and Germany, with four additional squares in dotted outline that yield the 37-hole board customary in France and Sweden. Four types of piece are shown differentiated by colour because, although in their physical embodiment all pieces appear identical, in actual play the procedure of movement-by-capture restricts the movement of any given piece to a subset of the thirty-three holes—just as each of a player's two bishops in Chess is restricted to the thirty-two squares of a given colour. In Solitaire, the pieces here shown as white are each restricted to movement over twelve holes, those shown as light and dark grey have access to only eight each, while those shown black are restricted to five (nine on the 37-hole French board).

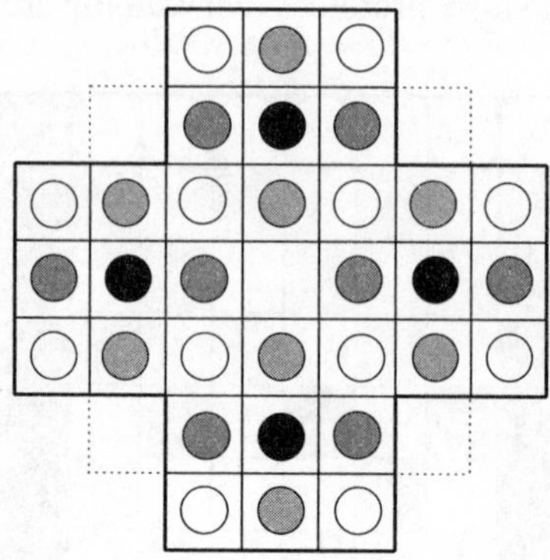

Fig. 9.8. 33-hole Solitaire (dotted = 37-hole) with pieces differentiated as a guide to play.

In the standard game, the player starts by removing any one of the thirty-three pieces and continues by removing each of the other thirty-two by a process of capturing. A capture is made by causing a piece to jump over a piece occupying an adjacent cell to land on the necessarily vacant cell on its further side, like the capture in Draughts but orthogonal instead of diagonal. The aim is to clear the board of all pieces except (of course) the one making the last capture, and to do so in such a way that the final piece is left occupying the cell made vacant at the outset. It being easy to forget where one started, it is usual to specify starting and finishing in the centre. Alternatively, start anywhere ad lib, but always finish in the centre; or, to make it a little easier, start anywhere and finish in any one of the central nine cells. In fact, a wide range of puzzles and problems have been devised, their varying aims and requirements requiring equally varying degrees of skill in forward planning. One of the most spectacular is called 'Man on the watch'. For this, the player specifies in advance which piece is to be last on the board, and may not move it until it is ready to make its final sequence of capturing moves. An additional object may be to make this sequence as long as possible. Another approach, dubbed Colourtaire, has been to differentiate the pieces by colour and specify initial layouts from which the colours are to be removed in a predetermined order. An obvious variant is to aim to finish with the remaining pieces forming a predetermined pattern or configuration.

The value of differentiating the pieces will now be apparent. If your aim is to finish in the centre, you dare not, in course of play, capture all four (or five) of the black pieces, since your final move must be to the centre, which only a black piece can occupy. At the other extreme, it should be fairly easy to set as your target one of the cells shown initially occupied by a white piece, provided that you are careful not to remove all the whites in course of play. Beginners can help themselves by playing with pieces marked or coloured according to the above scheme in order to help them keep track.

Solitaire may be played on square, hexagonal or virtually any other tessellated grids of any order. Those of particular interest so far known to have been explored are detailed in Beasley's indispensable study of the game.[4]

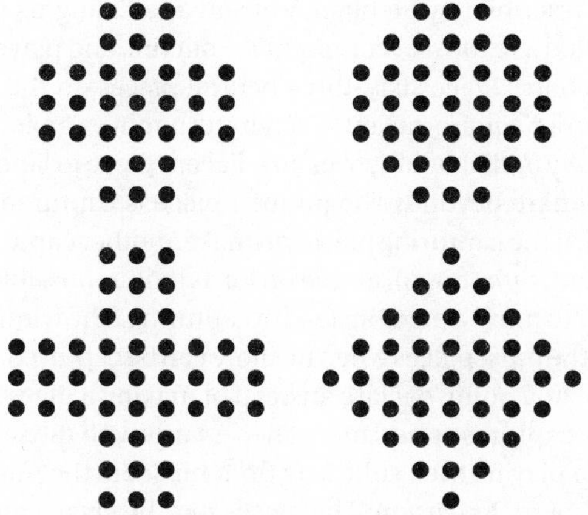

Fig. 9.9. Solitaire boards of various sizes (33, 37, 41, 45).

Attempts are often made to derive a two-hand competitive game from Solitaire. A logical approach is for each in turn to make a capture until one player has no move to make, thereby losing. (This makes it a game of restriction: see Chapter 10.) The winner scores a point for each piece left untaken and a game is played up to a previously agreed target score. In Interruption, by David Ramsay, 'the board is set up with the centre hole vacant. Player A starts the game by making single moves; i.e., capturing one peg with each move. Player B may interrupt this game at any point and must then reduce the board to as few pegs as possible. Again a points system may be used; suppose player B interrupts after n moves and ends with m pegs on the board, his score could be n-m.'

The game can be made more interesting by differentiating the pieces as to ownership or intrinsic value, or both. Many such games have been devised, but none has reached the status of a classic.

Leap-frog is listed by Murray as a similar game played by any number of players on a squared grid of any size, typically of order 15 to 18. Each in turn removes one piece ad lib; thereafter, each in turn makes one or a sequence of captures as at Solitaire. Play ceases when no more captures are possible, and the winner is the player who took most pieces. Unfortunately, Murray does not explain how, when one player's turn comes to an end, the next player is to proceed, since, by definition, no more captures are then possible. This is, in any case, a capturing game rather than one of null configuration.[5]

Acquisitions, described by Stephen Addison as a Draughts variant (p. 72), could be regarded as a form of competitive Solitaire, and played equally well on a Solitaire board. Place sixty-three neutral pieces on the draughtboard leaving one corner square vacant. Each in turn moves a piece in a straight line, orthogonally or diagonally, over an adjacent piece to land on the necessarily vacant square beyond. The jumped piece is captured and removed from the board. If the capturing piece can make another capture, it may do so (or, by agreement, *must* do so), and so on for as long as possible. It is not legal to miss a turn or to move a piece instead of capturing. The winner is the player who has taken the most pieces when no more can be captured. *Optional rule*: A player may at any point 'declare' instead of making a play. The other then makes as many captures as he can, not necessarily with the same piece, and, when unable to play further, subtracts from his score the number of pieces remaining on board. *Extension*: The pieces may be given values written on self-adhesive labels and attached to their faces. The winner is then the player capturing the highest value of pieces.

Origins

The origin of Solitaire has been ascribed to clerics, as suggested by its German titles *Priesterspiele* (Priests' Game) and *Nonnenspiele* (Nuns' Game), though they also call it *Grillenfang* (Crickets' Capture), by the same token suggesting invention by grasshoppers. The 1799 *Encyclopédie Méthodique* says it was first played by Amerindians with arrows after returning from the hunt; and Joseph Strutt reports the most popular theory: 'It is said to have been invented by an unfortunate man who was several years kept in solitary confinement at the Bastille in Paris.' More bizarrely, a German (DDR) newspaper of 1986 credits it to the shepherds of Malagasy, where the game is widely played.[6] In fact, Solitaire seems to have appeared first in the seventeenth century at the court of Louis XIV, being depicted in several engravings from the last decade of that century. One, dated 1697 (possibly in retrospect), is by Claude-Auguste Berey and shows *Madame la Princesse de Soubize jouant au jeu de solitaire*, which she does at the 37-hole French board. Since the Solitaire board is the same as that used for the older game of Fox & Geese and its equivalents, themselves played on boards deriving from the Merels-type game of Alquerque, Solitaire may have originated in an attempt to play Fox & Geese by oneself, or to practise it for future contests. In 1710 Leibniz describes it in a paper written for the Berlin Academy, beginning 'Not so very long ago a distinctive type of game became widespread under the name *Solitarium*, a game that I play on my own but as if with a partner to act as a witness and referee.'[7] The 33-hole board is first mentioned in 1779 by J. C. Wiegleb in Volume I of *Unterricht in der natürlichen Magie*, together with the 37- and 45-hole boards (the latter with each of the four arms increased from six to nine holes). An early English reference occurs in a letter written in 1746 by Hugh Walpole to George Montagu, enquiring 'Has Miss Harriet found out any more ways at *solitaire*?' Beasley's fear that this may refer to card Solitaire is groundless—Patience dates from the late eighteenth century, did not reach England until the nineteenth, and was not called Solitaire when it did. The first serious English study of Solitaire was made in 1920 by Ernest Bergholt. In the *Complete Hand-book to the Game of Solitaire on the English Board of Thirty-three Holes*, Bergholt opened up what he called 'nearly a virgin field of enquiry', lamenting that it had fallen into an undeserved neglect 'wholly due to the fact that no one up to the present has ever investigated the possibilities of the subject or provided the person of average intelligence with any adequate guide to the numerous and fascinating problems for which the game affords scope'.

Perhaps the boldest suggestion as to the origin of Solitaire is that of Becq de Fouquières, who believes it to be the subject of a passage in Ovid:

Reticuloque pilae leves fundantur aperto
Nec, nisi quam tolles, ulla movenda pila est[8]

The passage briefly describes five games as appropriate pastimes for girls: dice, Latrunculi, *pilae leves*, Duodecim Scripta, and Three in a Line. The third of these, says Peter Green in his translation,[9] 'Is so out of place in this sequence of dice-and-board games that one suspects textual transposition or interpolation. What it describes—something nowhere else referred to in ancient literature—is a number of "smooth balls" being emptied into a net, the object being to move one without disturbing the rest. How this was done is not at all clear. It suggests that popular, and far more comprehensible, children's game known as spillikins.' Becq de Fouquières, also noting its inappropriateness, interprets the passage as follows.[10] 'On dispose, dit Ovide, de petites boules (*pilae leves*) sur une table à cavités (*reticulo*) qu'on a devant soi; et l'on ne peut mouvoir aucune boule, à moins qu'on n'en enlève quelqu'une (*nisi quam tolles*)'—'Little balls (*pilae leves*) are placed in the holes of a board (*reticulo*) in front of one, and no ball may be lifted unless you make a capture (*nisi quam tolles*)'. In short, Solitaire!

Against this passage, in the Bodleian Library's copy, is a pencilled note in Murray's distinctive handwriting, evidently disagreeing with his conclusion and querying as a possible alternative 'some game like spilikins?'.

One could sometimes wish that Murray had had a little more romance in his soul.

NOTES

1. Lhôte, 384, citing *Grands Ébénistes et menuisiers parisiens du XVIIIme siècle*, an exhibition catalogue published by the Musée des Arts Décoratifs (Paris, 1955–6).
2. S. Addison, *100 Other Games to Play on a Chessboard* (London 1983), 47. It is called Lines of Action in S. Sackson, *A Gamut of Games* (London, 1974), 34.
3. Relevant articles in *Games & Puzzles* (1st ser.) are: R. C. Bell, 'Fox & Geese and Solitaire', 17 (Sept. 1973), 4–5; John Maltby, 'The Solitaire Revival', 30 (Nov. 1974), 8–9; David Ramsay, 'Solitaire', 31 (Dec. 1974), 6–13, and 32 (Dec. 1974), 6–11.
4. John D. Beasley, *The Ins and Outs of Peg Solitaire* (Oxford and New York, 1992).
5. Murray, *History of Board Games*, 93.
6. E. Glonnegger, *Das Spiele-Buch* (Ravensburg, 1988), 196.
7. Gottfried Wilhelm Leibniz, *Miscellanea Berolinensia* i (1710), 24; quoted by Beasley (*Ins and Outs of Peg Solitaire*).
8. Ovid, *Ars Amatoria*, iii. 361–2.
9. Peter Green, *Ovid: The Erotic Poems* (Harmondsworth 1982), 392.
10. L. Becq de Fouquières, *Les Jeux des Anciens* (Paris, 1873), ch. 18.

Restrictive Practices

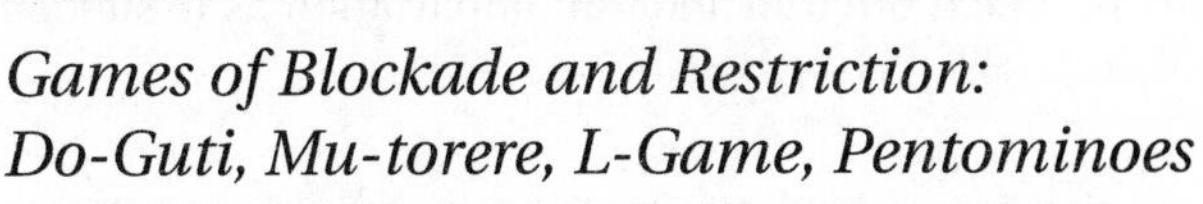

Games of Blockade and Restriction: Do-Guti, Mu-torere, L-Game, Pentominoes

On with the dance! let joy be unconfined . . .

Byron, *Childe Harold's Pilgrimage*

A number of games are based on the following pattern. Each of two players in turn places or moves a piece on the board in such a way as to restrict the other's subsequent power of placement or movement. The first player unable to continue play loses. (Or, by previous agreement, wins; but even where this is practicable—it renders some games endless—this amounts to the same game played with reverse strategy and so does not count as a substantial variant.) Such games are usually regarded as variants of games played with similar pieces on similar boards, but the mental processes involved are distinctive enough to justify classifying them under an equally distinctive heading. They are sometimes generically referred to as 'Nim'. This comes from an Old English word meaning 'take' (cf. German *nehmen*), and is normally applied to a branch of recreational mathematics typified by the game of Matchsticks. In its simplest version each of two players in turn removes one, two, or three matchsticks from a row of thirteen, and the player who takes the last match wins, or loses if so agreed in advance. In the more classic version, once known as the Marienbad game from its dramatic role in the film *l'Année dernière à Marienbad*, fifteen are arranged in a triangle consisting of three rows of three, five, and seven matches respectively, and each in turn may take any number from any row. The substantial role played by Nim in recreational mathematics is underlined by the fact that a mighty tome in two volumes entitled *Winning Ways*, by three eminent mathematicians,[1] analyses virtually all known games in terms of it.

Nim-type board games fall into two broad classes. In games of placement, the board starts empty and each in turn places a piece until one player cannot add another without breaking a rule of restriction. In games of movement, there is an initial array of pieces and each in turn moves one until the other cannot move.

Games of Movement

These are the older branch. They may share an origin with alignment games such as Merels, which often include immobilization as a 'sudden death' alternative win.

Do-guti. The most primitive, indeed minimalist, game of this type is one widespread in Asia, known in India as *Do-guti*, 'the Two[-piece] Game', in China as *Pong Hau K'i*, in Korea as *On-moul-ko-no*, in Thailand as *Sua tok tong*, and so on. In essence, the board is a diagonally crossed square with one side missing.

Each player starts with a piece on each of two adjacent points parallel to the missing side, or, in some versions, enters them alternately into play, then moves a counter to an adjacent point, the aim being to immobilize the opposing pieces. Murray classifies this with the blockading division of war games.

Mu-torere. A more elaborate version of the same game, or at least one more heavily disguised, is *Mu-torere*, which is said to be the only indigenous board game of the Maori,[2] and is played on the stellar grids illustrated below. Starting with four pieces, one on each of four adjacent points, each in turn moves a piece to an unoccupied adjacent point, the centre-point being adjacent to all. The first move must concede a vacancy to the opponent, and the game is eventually won by immobilization. Bell expands on this by noting that a piece may not be moved to the centre if currently flanked by two vacancies, and adds the unsurprising news that the game, if properly played, goes on for ever.

Fig. 10.2 shows two representations of Mu-torere. The second, from Gould via R. C. Bell,[3] more clearly identifies itself with the single mill board with diagonals, and even more so with its Ancient Egyptian circular precursor from Kurna. Indeed, it is hard to tell which sort of game the circular board was used for. Perhaps both were played on the same board,

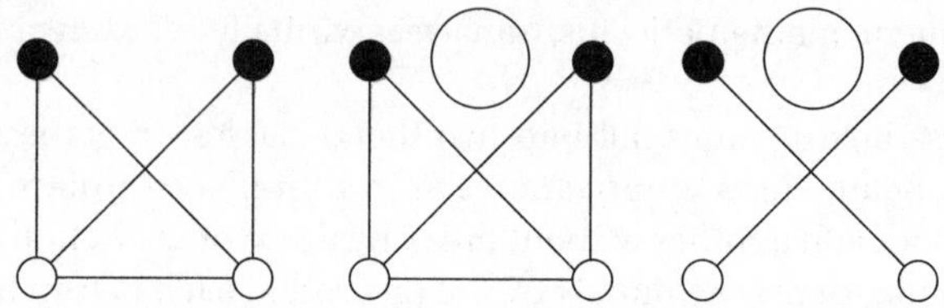

Fig. 10.1. Do-guti (Punjab), On-moul-ko-no (Korea), Sua tok tong (Thailand).

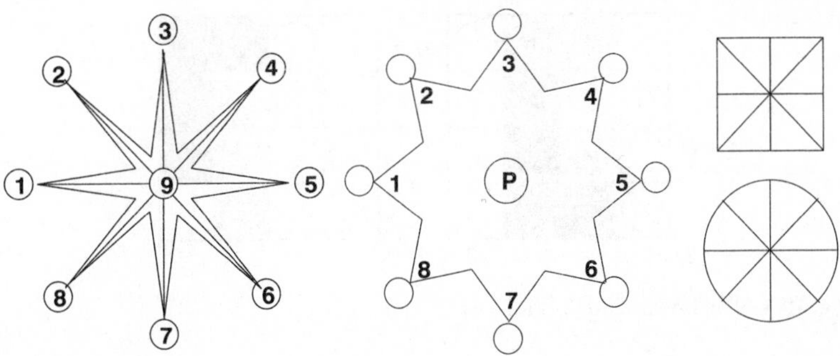

Fig. 10.2. Mu-torere (*left*: after Murray; *right*: after Bell; the centre point is called and labelled *putahi*).

and the blockading or immobilizing aspect of the larger Merels perpetuates a common point of origin.

The L-Game. The opposite extreme of sophistication from the relative simplicity of Do-guti and Mu-torere is represented by a game invented by Edward de Bono, the latter-day exponent of lateral thinking. His account of its genesis in *Games & Puzzles* magazine bears reproduction.[4]

The L-Game came to be designed deliberately in the following manner. One evening I was having dinner in Trinity College, Cambridge, and happened to be seated next to the famous mathematician Professor Littlewood. We got to talking about computers and the difficulty of putting Chess on a computer. We agreed that the number of pieces and the inherent complexity of the game made this difficult. As a creative challenge I undertook to design the simplest possible classic game: a game that would be simpler than Noughts & Crosses and yet would be indeterminate and capable of being played with skill. The L-game was the result. It is so simple that each player has only one playing piece, which he must move each turn. In addition there are two neutral pieces which do not belong to the players but may be moved by either player. The playing pieces cover ten of the sixteen squares of the board—and yet the asymmetry of the playing piece ensures that a huge variety of moves are possible. When I first invented the game I played against a well-known Chess player and won on the first move. We played again and I won on the second move. And yet against a Japanese master of Go the game went on for almost two hours before I finally won (and he had never seen the game before). The game requires a sense of spatial perception rather than sequential moves.

To this it need only be added that the start position of the standard game is shown in Fig. 10.3 (*left*). Each in turn must move his L-piece to any different position on the board, turning it over if desired, and then may (but need not) move either one of the neutral pieces to any vacant square. The first player unable to reposition his L-piece loses. Black has lost in Fig. 10.3 (*right*).

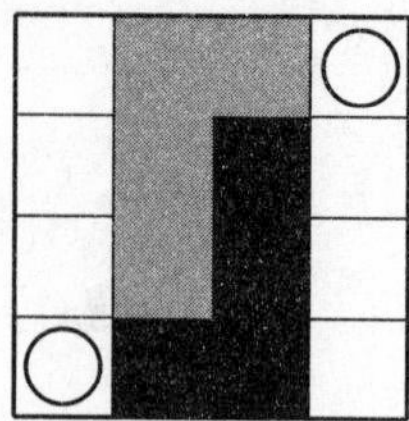
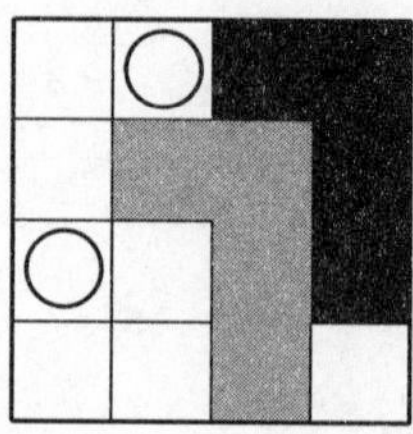

Fig. 10.3. The L-Game (de Bono).

This undeniably fascinating game gave rise to the sort of equally fascinating correspondence that only ever appeared in *Games & Puzzles* and of which the British games world has been starved since its demise. At the trivial level, one reader objected to de Bono's use of the word 'classic'—surely, he claimed, such an epithet can only be the verdict of history, or at least of players other than the inventor? (A more charitable opinion would be that de Bono meant 'classical' but got the wrong word.) More mathematically inclined readers went into computations of all possible positions with a view to devising a winning strategy. The last word came from D. H. Fremlin of Essex University:

> Sir, I found Edward de Bono's description of his L-game most interesting. While he vigorously claims that it is 'sophisticated' he is a little coy about whether it is 'difficult'. Actually the 'classic' game is fairly limited. There are 18368 possible positions in this game, but these fall into 2296 classes of 8 positions which differ only by a rotation or a reflection of the board and are plainly equivalent. Of the 2296 classes, 1261 (including the original position) are draws, 1006 are wins for the first player, and 29 are wins for the second player. I enclose a list of the 29 exceptional positions. Fifteen are outright wins, as the next player cannot move (de Bono's figure of 10 terminal positions refers to the 10 different ways in which the L-pieces can be arranged; my figure of 15 includes differences in the neutral counters), 3 are wins after one move each, 3 after 2 moves, 5 after 3 moves, and 3 after 4 moves. The fact that there are so few makes it practicable to memorise them all. You now have to look one move ahead to ensure that your opponent cannot move into one of the 29 positions and win.

Several variations were proposed, for various reasons. De Bono himself suggested a scoring variant in which the starting position was decided *ad hoc*, and a subsequent reader proposed as an alternative object that of so placing your L-piece that it precisely replicates the position and orientation of your opponent's, on different (of course) but equivalent squares.

Pentominoes. A domino can be regarded as consisting of two squares stuck together. Given that the first syllable is vaguely reminiscent of the

Greek for 'two', recreational mathematicians call a shape made of three squares stuck together a tromino, of four a tetromino, five a pentomino, and so on. Trominoes come in two forms, linear and L-shaped, and tetrominoes in four. There are, discounting rotations and reflections of the same configuration, twelve possible pentominoes, as shown in Fig. 10.4 (NB the identifying letters used in this figure will be continued throughout the section). These form the basis of many varied and fascinating mathematical puzzles, many of them fully explored by the American mathematician Solomon W. Golomb, who coined the word 'pentomino' and designated each of them by a letter of the alphabet. The best known puzzle is that of so arranging them as to form the equivalent of a chessboard. Since each pentomino covers five squares, their placement on an 8×8 board will leave four squares uncovered, and one challenge of the puzzle is to find a solution whereby these four occur in symmetry, such as all four in the middle, or one at each corner. Another of Golomb's puzzles was to discover the minimum number of pieces required to saturate the chessboard—that is, to be so arranged on it that none of the other seven will fit anywhere in the remaining space. Such puzzles are, by nature, solitaires, but the saturation problem led Golomb to devise a two-player competitive game of disarming simplicity but unrivalled fascination—namely, each in turn places a piece on the board in any position and any orientation, and the first player unable to do so loses. This has long been one of my favourite games, and was the subject of the first series of articles I wrote for the earliest editions of *Games & Puzzles* magazine.[5]

Golomb's Game, also known as Quin, can be played more or less at random for the first few moves, but quickly calls for considerable powers

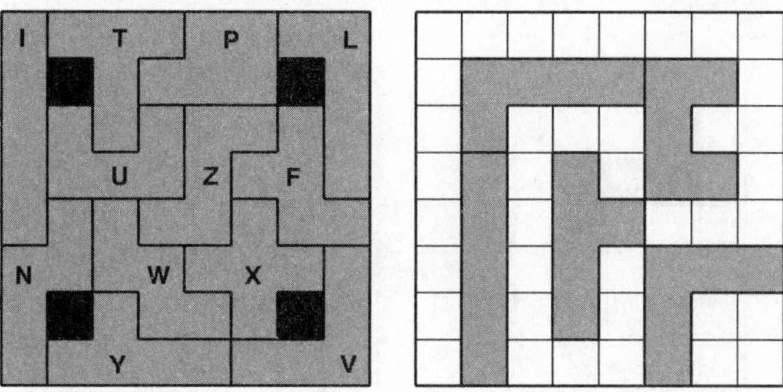

Fig. 10.4. Pentominoes forming a chessboard with symmetrically-placed gaps. Letters denote Golomb's identification of individual pieces. *Right*: End of game: no unused pentomino can now be placed.

of forward visualization. In Fig. 10.5, Odd (who moved first) played Z, as shown in black,

This practical example demonstrates a basic tactic of the game, which is to attempt to play in such a way as to leave a single area that will take exactly two of the remaining pieces, or two areas each of which will take exactly one each—or possibly two, though this is harder to guarantee. Golomb offered the further advice that runs 'If in doubt, complicate'. In other words, if the position is too hard to analyse, play a piece that will make it even harder for your opponent.

Enjoyable as the game is in its raw form, one has a natural tendency to introduce elaborations and restrictions for the sake of interest. In my version of the game, the winner scores 1 point per piece played. Either player may resign in order to reduce the prospective winner's score. However, the opponent of one who resigns may go for a higher score by swapping roles, playing the next piece, and continuing alternately from there. This doubles the winning score for whoever eventually wins. The same thing can happen again, thereby quadrupling the score; and so on. The game is then played up to an agreed target of, say, 25 or 50 points. In another variation, each in turn selects one of the pieces as his personal property, and the game is then played with each player permitted to play only from his own stock of six pieces. In a third, a player does not place a piece until the other has declared which piece he intends to play next. Several competitive games based on Pentominoes have been marketed from time to time, but none has made any significant improvement to the basic idea, which probably remains too abstract for general appeal.

Pentominoes can also be played on a 6×6 trellis, giving a total of sixty-one squares, but in that form is less flexible and ends sooner. Fig. 10.6

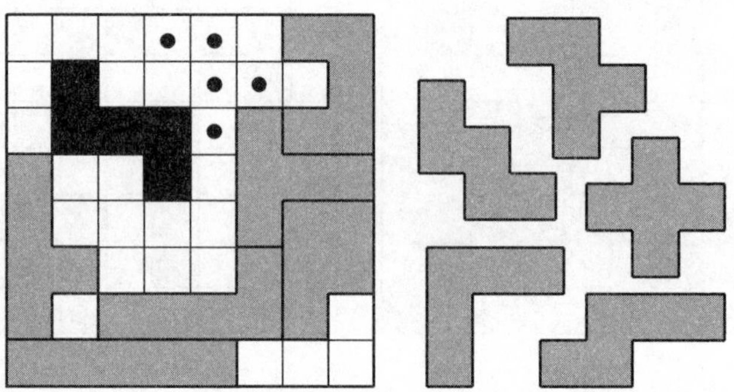

Fig. 10.5. Odd's Z loses to Even's F. He could have won with N.

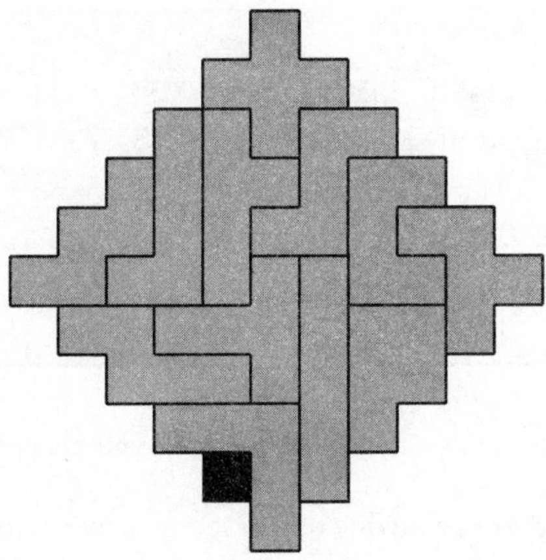

Fig. 10.6. Pentominoes on a 61-square trellis.

shows how all twelve pieces can be placed, though it is impossible to leave the odd square at the centre.

The game can be expanded by duplicating the six pieces which differ in reflection (F, L, N, P, Y, Z), starting with the two members of each reflective pair opposite ways round, and prohibiting a player from turning either of them over. This produces eighteen pieces occupying ninety constituent squares. The puzzle would be to use them all in the construction of a rectangle of size 9×10, and the competitive game would be played on a board of size 9×9 or 10×10. Endless variations on the basic theme can be devised, such as using hexominoes (of which there are thirty-six distinct varieties), or similar shapes consisting of conjoined hexagons rather than squares.

Of many easily derived variations on the Nim theme represented by Pentominoes it will suffice to mention two, one of movement and one of placement.[6] In Lewthwaite's Game (Fig. 10.7) White and Black start with twelve pieces each arranged alternately on a 25-square grid with the centre square vacant. Each in turn slides a piece of his own colour into the vacancy as it moves around the board, and the first player unable to move loses. This game demonstrates the close relationship between Nim games and sliding-block puzzles, none of which that I have ever seen makes a satisfactory game for two. The other, which has just occurred to me, is a linear version of Pentominoes played with Cuisenaire rods, which are used for teaching numbers and lengths to young children. The linear equivalent of Pentominoes would be a set of rods each consisting of a number of squares joined

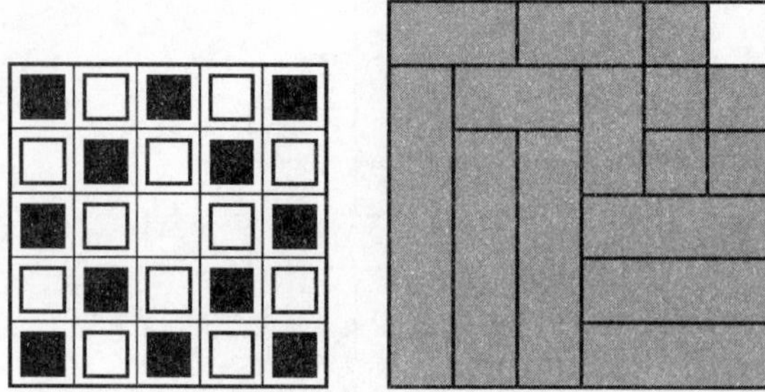

Fig. 10.7. *Left*: Lewthwaite's Game, *Right*: the Cuisenaire game.

in a straight line, there being one of five squares, two of four, three of three, four of two, and five of one. There being fifteen such pieces occupying between them thirty-five of the constitutent small squares, the game would be played on a 36-squared board. Each in turn places a piece on the board until one player loses throughout being unable to move. To make a playable game requires an additional constraint, namely, that all the single squares must be placed first, then the doubles, the triples, and so on, as far as possible. A variant would be to play on an 11-squared board with fifteeen pieces, the first one square long, the second two squares, and so on up to one of fifteen squares, thus accounting for 120 of the 121 squares.

NOTES

1. E. Berlekamp, J. H. Conway, and R. K. Guy, *Winning Ways* (London and New York, 1982).
2. Communicated to R. C. Bell by W. B. Gould of New Zealand and detailed in an addendum to *Board and Table Games*, ii. 148.
3. Elsdon Best, *The Maori*, iv, 1924 (Murray, *History of Board Games*, 93).
4. Edward de Bono, 'The L-Game', *Games & Puzzles*, 1st ser. 30 (Nov. 1974), 4–6.
5. David Parlett, 'Pentominoes' (series), *Games & Puzzles (1)*, 9–17 inclusive (Jan.–Sept. 1973).
6. For more, including Lewthwaite's Game, see Berlekamp, *et al.*, *Winning Ways*, ii, ch. 22, 667–96.

Space Control

Games of Territorial Occupation: Go, Reversi, Boxes

It is written in the *Wú Ts'ah Tsú* that among the playthings of ancient and modern times there is nothing more remote than Go. Next to wine and women, it leads men astray. If they think it difficult, even villagers and common people can play it very skilfully; but if it be thought very easy, even the wisest and most intelligent, though they investigate it through generations, may not acquire it correctly.

Stewart Culin, *Games of the Orient*, 98

'Just one more game, then,' they agreed, and started play.
– That was yesterday.

Yamaoka Genrin (Quoted in *The Go Player's Almanac*)

Go and Reversi (Othello) are the chief representatives of a small but distinctive family of games of placement only. Though sometimes described as war games, this is to employ a metaphor that tends to obscure rather than clarify the ludic concepts involved, for here the fundamental object is not to capture material but to occupy territory. They therefore properly belong with the class of space games, and indeed are not far removed from games of configuration and congregation as described in the previous chapter. The chief difference is that pieces here serve no other function than to indicate territorial ownership. In a computerized version there is no real need to simulate pieces at all, for the only essential requirement is to show, at any given time, whether a given point of territory belongs to Black, White, or neither. What counts towards the win is primarily the point of territory, not the piece used to mark it.

Go (Wei-qi)

Go, more formally *I-go*, is the Japanese name for a game of Chinese origin known in China as Wei-qi. Wei-qi may be interpreted as meaning 'surrounding pieces', the basic idea being that each in turn places a stone on the board with a view to ultimately enclosing the largest amount of territory. It is almost certainly the oldest board-game in the world, in the sense of having remained virtually unchanged over the longest time-span. It is also unusually well documented by comparison with ancient and medieval board games of the Occident. William Pinckard's masterly account in *The Go-player's Almanac*[1] is a model of historical writing on games, and the following summary is very largely based on it.

Legend credits its invention to the emperor Yao (2357–2256 BC) for strengthening the brain of his half-wit son Tan-Chu, though the same story sometimes features other emperors, and is as unlikely as the supposed invention of playing-cards for the amusement of the half-mad French king Charles VI. A more plausible origin may relate it to a divinatory practice of casting black and white stones on a board representing the heavens, or earth and heaven, and interpreting the resultant patterns. This is lent some weight by the astrological terminology by which various parts of the board are referred to even today, but one may well feel constrained to ask which in fact came first—the game or the divination. It is, however, generally accepted that Wei-qi dates back to the second millennium BC. A game mentioned in the *Analects* of Confucius (sixth century BC) almost certainly denotes it, while in the second century BC Mencius speaks of the game's antiquity and of the existence of masters and disciples in its practice and philosophy.

In the first century AD the historian Pan Ku wrote:

> The board has to be square, for it signifies the earth, and its right angles signify uprightness. The pieces (of the two sides) are yellow and black: this distinction signifies the Yin and the Yang—scattered in groups all over the board, they represent the heavenly bodies. These significances being manifest, it is up to the players themselves to make the moves, and this is connected with kingship. Following what the rules permit, both opponents are subject to them—this is the rigour of the Tao.

Wei-qi prospered particularly in the Tang dynasty (618–906), when Taoism held sway. Whereas Confucianists, the Puritanical materialists of their day, considered games useless because non-functional, the more spiritually-centred Taoists, and many Mahayana Buddhists too, practised Go as a voyage of self-discovery and enlightenment. This period saw the recognition of Wei-qi as one of the four accomplishments of the gentleman-scholar, a status it enjoyed well into modern times; and the poet Po Chü-i (772–846) asserts its Buddhist flavour:[2]

> Mountain monks sit at the Wei-qi board
> under the bamboo's semi-lucent shade.
> No one sees them through the glittering leaves –
> but now and then the click of a stone is heard.

The subsequent history of Wei-qi in China has been one of growing prestige. Important treatises on the game appeared in the eighteenth century, one by the great player Huang, whose style of play was much admired by the Japanese and widely adopted by them.[3]

When Korea became part of the Han Empire in the second century the game travelled thither with the advent of Chinese officials. Korea remains one of the nations most dedicated to the game, with (today) some 100 professional players of what is there called Baduk (or Badug; described by Culin under the older spelling Pa-tok).[4]

It is, however, to Japan that belongs the honour of having developed the game to a higher degree of sophistication than any other of the world's great board games, with the possible exception only of Chess, and from Japan that it began to gain converts and experts in the second half of the twentieth century. In this context it will now be more appropriate to speak of it as Go.

Go must have reached Japan in the fifth–sixth centuries AD through the constant stream of political, military, commercial, and private traffic between the two countries. Tradition credits its introduction to Kibi Daijin under the emperor Shomu in AD 735, its practice being at first deliberately restricted to the court of Kyoto; but this appears to be too late. As in China, it became popular in aristocratic and court circles, and in Buddhist monasteries. A monastic discipline dated 701 decrees 100 days hard labour for monks and nuns who indulge in music and 'gambling' (probably a Japanese variety of Tables), but exempts playing the *koto*—a sort of Japanese psaltery—and the practice of Go. *Kido*, or The Tao of Go, was developed as a route to enlightenment. 'Like Zen practice and the tea ceremony, it was officially encouraged as being especially suitable for the warrior classes, since it inculcated the virtues of modesty, patience, and courtesy as well as clear thought unclouded by the illusion of ego.' The play of Go by both men and women figures prominently in the novel *The Tale of Genji*, written by a lady of the court, Murasaki Shikibu, in about AD 1000. In 913 appeared the oldest known Japanese book on Go, the *Go Shiki*, written under royal commission by the monk Tichibana Kanren. (Kanren, according to ancient legend, 'once had the unforgettable experience of being asked to play by an attractive female ghost. What frightened him was not that she was a ghost but that her strength proved to be so formidable that she captured every one of his stones'.) The oldest game on record is said to date from 1253 and was supposedly played between the eponymous founder of the of Nichiren School of Buddhism and his 9-year-old disciple, Nis-shomaru.

The ascendancy of the warrior class over the aristocracy from the twelfth century onwards did nothing to lessen the cultivation of Go, the study of tactics and strategy being regarded as good moral and intellectual training.

Many great warlords kept a Go teacher-in-residence. The term *meijin*, literally 'illustrious name',[5] for a master of Go, is said to have been uttered in admiration by the late sixteenth-century warlord Nobunaga while watching the play of such a teacher called Nikkai. His successor Toyotomi Hideyoshi studied with Nikkai and in 1588 sponsored the first great national tournament. Nikkai won, and was rewarded with an annual state income, thus establishing Go-playing as a profession. Under Tokugawa Ieyasu, established as the first Shogun in 1603, government offices were created specifically for the regulation and development of Go and Shogi (Japanese Chess). Nikkai left retirement to become first principal of the Go academy (Godokoro), and took the name Honinbo Sansa. (It is a name that remains legendary in the annals of Go, the twenty-first and last of that line dying as recently as 1940.) His régime saw the development of a nationwide system of controls, and the establishment of the four main Go schools (Honinbo, Inoue, Yasui, Hayashi) which were to last, with government subsidy, until the collapse of the Shogunate in 1868. Thus arose the system of hereditary professionals, including both masters and disciples, which raised Go to unparalleled heights of skill and cultivation. Graduates of the academy became professional players. They could seek permanent employment at the court of the emperor or a local *daimyo*, or travel around like poets and swordsmen, giving demonstrations and instruction. The best players were appointed once a year to appear before the Shogun to demonstrate their skills, in later tradition by re-enacting games that had been played in advance. Oshiro-Go ('Castle Go'), as this procedure was called, lasted until the fall of the Shogunate. A feature still remarked upon by western writers is the patience and assiduousness with which the game is followed by spectators from all classes of society.

The fall of the Shogunate in 1868 led to the end of state-sponsored Go professionalism and the extinction of three of the four traditional houses. To prevent the collapse of the game itself, an organization of players called the Hoensha sought ways of expanding the game's popularity with a wider public with a view to encouraging other sources of patronage. The first decades of the twentieth century saw the rise of the Go column in newspapers and the beginnings of newspaper-sponsored tournaments, resulting in greater security for the professionals. In 1923 the Hoensha was disbanded, having split into factions and become riven with professional rivalries, and was replaced by the still-current Nihon Ki-in, whose directorial posts were statutorily reserved for non-players (or, at least, non-professionals). The twenty-first and last hereditary Honinbo became head of that house in 1908 and took the name of Shusai. His last match, played in 1938 shortly before his death against the vigorous young modernist Kitani, is immortalized in Yasunari Kawabata's Nobel prize-winning novel *The Master of Go.*[6] Today's professionals can earn a respectable living from tournaments sponsored by newspapers, television companies, and commercial organizations, especially as the stated emoluments are for playing and not just for winning. They must, however, be members of either the Nihon or the Kansai Ki-in, neither of which normally accepts apprentices beyond the age of 16. Becoming a professional is said to be harder than gaining a Ph.D., and most will have exhibited a particular aptitude while still at primary school.

In China, the status of Wei-qi has correspondingly improved under the auspices of the Chinese Wei-qi Association, with main centres in Beijing, Shanghai, and Sichuan. While there is no theoretical or graded distinction between amateurs and professionals, players whose local branches can afford to support them can become professionals in all but name. The game has enormously increased in popularity in recent years. Of the first ten World Amateur Go Championships organized by Japan Airlines, seven were won by Chinese, two by Japanese, and one by a Hong Kongese. As a further mark of distinction, the Republic of China has produced the world's greatest women players.

In South Korea, exactly 100 professional players are affiliated to the Hankuk Kiwon, founded in 1955 as the governing body for regulation of the game.

The latter half of the twentieth century has seen Go expanding its formerly oriental frontiers. The European Go Federation organizes an annual series of tournaments for the Grand Prix d'Europe, culminating in the European Go Championship. More than fifty annual tournaments are sponsored by the American Go Association. The New Zealand Go Society has produced a set of rules based on the Chinese area count, as opposed to the Japanese territory-plus-prisoners system. Its procedure may well be thought simpler and more logical than that of traditional Go, but is unlikely to prevail against the weight of tradition.

The following description of Go is intended to assist in the appreciation of the game, not to serve as a practical introduction for learners (such as myself). Beginners are advised to play first on the quarter-board of 9 × 9 points, to find their nearest Go club, and to study only books written by expert players recognized by the British Go Association, as a number of currently available English-language introductions are either out-of-date, erroneous, or both.[7]

The board. Go is played on the 361 points of a grid of 19 × 19 lines crossing at right angles. Nine are picked out as handicap points, and facilitate orientation (Fig. 11.1).

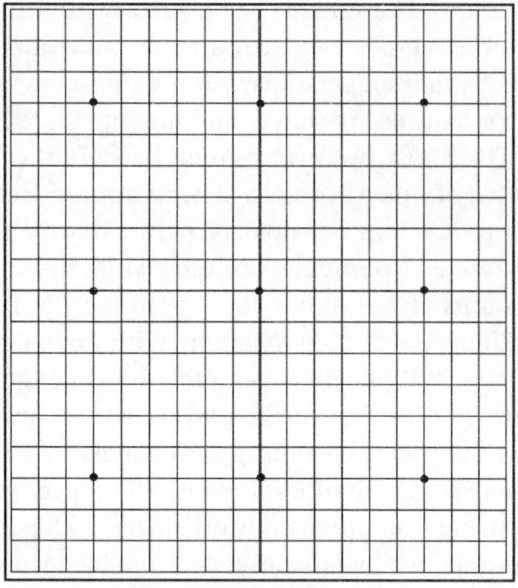

Fig. 11.1. The 361-point Go board is slightly but deliberately out of square, perhaps to counteract the foreshortening effect of perspective. Spots mark the nine handicap points.

The pieces. Black and White face each other from the opposing shorter ends of the initially empty board. Each starts with a bowl of pieces of his own colour called stones, Black with 181 and White with 180, though rarely will all be needed. Japanese stones, traditionally made of slate and cowries, are lentiform (biconvex) discs. Chinese are flat on the underside.
Object. The object is to so place stones as to enclose territory, thereby capturing any enemy stones it may contain. At end of play each player scores 1 point for each point of territory enclosed, and either 1 point per enemy piece captured (territory count, Japanese system), or 1 point for each stone played and point of territory enclosed (area score, the Chinese system). The difference between the two scores is the margin of victory, and is normally the same regardless of which system is used. The Japanese system tends to obscure the fact that Go is essentially an exercise in space control and not material capture.
Play. Each in turn, Black first, places a stone on any vacant point. A stone joined by a line to a vacant point is said to have a 'liberty'. It therefore has four liberties if placed on an empty board, or three on an edge, or two in a corner.
Capture. A stone deprived of all its liberties by enemy stones is thereby captured and removed from the board. In Fig. 11.2, a black stone played

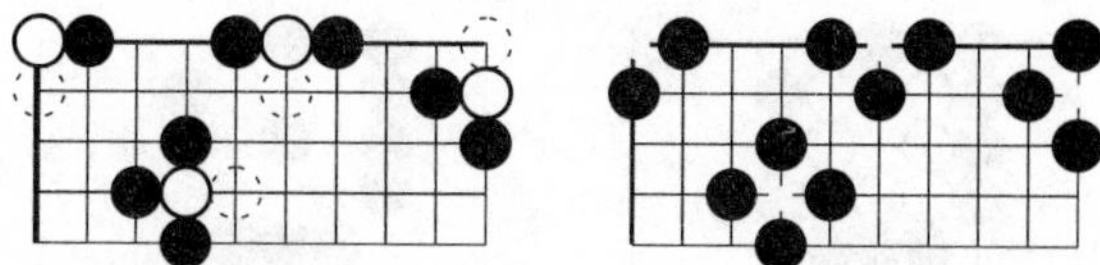

Figs. 11.2, 11.3. Singleton captures at corners, edges, and mid-board.

to the dotted point captures a white stone by removing its last remaining liberty. The resultant positions are shown in Fig. 11.3. In each case, Black has gained one point of territory. (I show captured territory by blanking out its constituent points. Though unconventional, it facilitates counting.)

Groups. Stones of the same colour constitute a group (or army) if they are all solidly connected, each being orthogonally adjacent to at least one friendly neighbour. Thus, in Fig. 11.4, playing a white stone to either of the dotted points would absorb the singleton into a group of eight.

Group capture. A group of two or more stones of the same colour is captured and removed from the board if all are deprived of their liberties. Thus, playing a black stone to the dotted point (Fig. 11.5) would complete the enclosure of the white army, thereby capturing it and gaining 11 points of territory (Fig. 11.6).

Suicide rule. Suicide is forbidden. Thus, in Fig. 11.7, White cannot play as indicated, since it would deprive the group of its only liberty. Black can play there, however, so killing the white group and gaining 10 points of territory (Fig. 11.8).

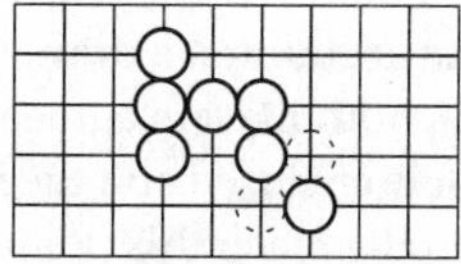

Fig. 11.4. Stones are only grouped if orthogonally connected.

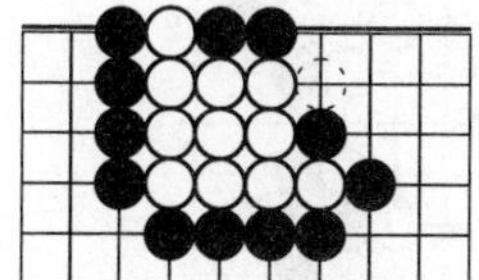

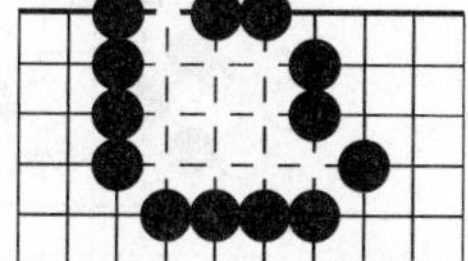

Figs. 11.5, 11.6. Capturing a group.

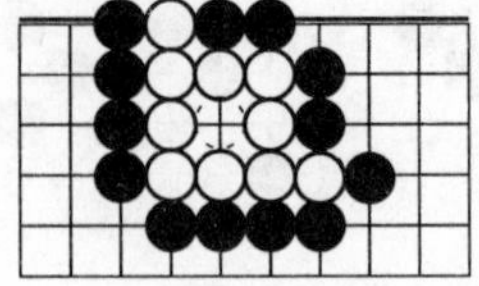

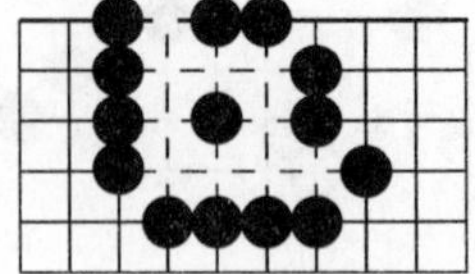

Figs. 11.7, 11.8.

Rule of Ko. Apparent suicide is permitted if it results in a capture. Thus, in Fig. 11.9 (*a*), Black can play to the centre of the white stones, thereby capturing one to produce the position (*b*). Theoretically, White could then play to the point just lost, thereby capturing the black stone and producing position (*c*), which is identical with (*a*), and so on. This would result in an endless game with no change of overall situation, were it not prevented by the 'ko' rule. This prohibits the second player, in such a case, from immediately recapturing, requiring him first to play elsewhere on the board. Thus if Black plays at (*a*) to produce (*b*), White may not immediately play at (*b*) to produce (*c*). If the same position still obtains on his next turn (that is, if Black does not immediately connect his stone by playing at (*b*) to produce (*d*)), White may now do so, since the two intervening moves will have altered the overall board situation. If he does then play at (*b*) to produce (*c*), then Black in turn may not immediately play at (*c*) to produce (*b*), but must play elsewhere first. The situation at (*a*) is called *ko*, the Japanese word for 'eternity', whence the name of the rule.

Drawn game. If precisely the same position occurs twice in a game, it is declared a 'no game' and should be replayed, although, under pressure of time, it may in practice be accounted a draw.

Scoring. Play ceases when both players agree that no more territory can be gained, most being safely enclosed and the rest too equally contested. Experienced players naturally reach this point sooner than beginners. A

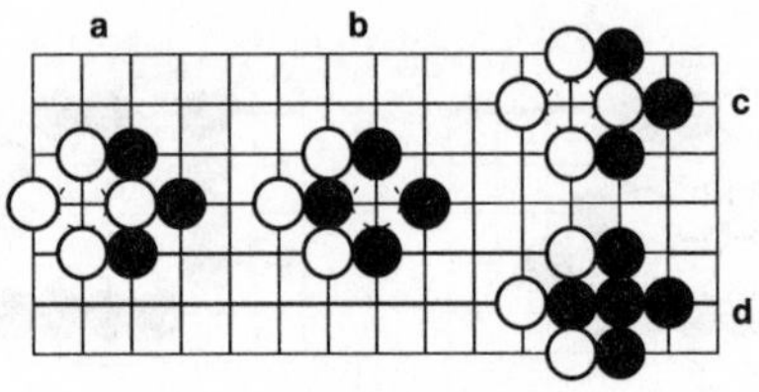

Fig. 11.9. The *ko* rule obviates repetition of captures.

player may pass his turn at any time. If both players pass in succession, the game ends. An end agreed, each player scores 1 point for each point of territory enclosed and 1 point per enemy piece captured, the difference being the margin of victory.

Fig. 11.10 shows a completed game to illustrate the scoring. Note, first, that there are three neutral points of territory belonging to neither player, which I have indicated by blanking the intersections out. Black captured eight white stones in course of play, and won territory as follows. Proceeding clockwise from top right, Black has 2 points in the corner and 5 to the left of the uppermost neutral point. He also controls most of the lower edge of the board, amounting to 24 on the left and 43, including 12 white stones, on the right. To the left of the board he has isolated points of 2, 1, and 1. This gives him a territorial total of 78 points, which, with eight prisoners, makes 86.

White captured seventeen black stones in course of play. His territory consists of 2 points at top right, 18 on the eastern border, and 10 on the western. At top left he has 32 points, after removing the seven enclosed black stones. Adding the odd point in the middle, White's total is thus 71, plus 17 prisoners captured in play, making 88 in all—a winning margin of 2 points.

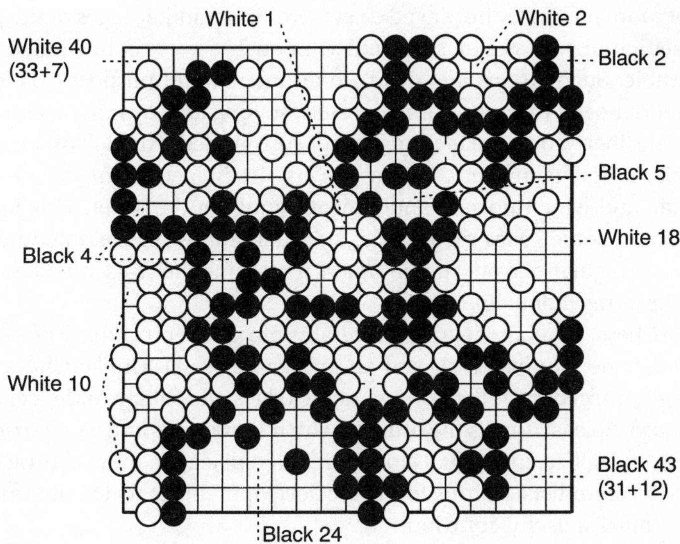

Fig. 11.10. Black counts 78 to White's 71, but took only 8 prisoners to White's 17. White therefore wins by 2 points (88 to 86).

In practice, players adopt a simplified counting procedure by so rearranging the stones as to straighten out the borders of individual territories, making the vacant points they enclose fall into easily countable lines or rectangles. Each then counts the vacancies he has enclosed, and the difference between these two totals will produce the same margin of victory as calculated by the method shown above. (Try it!)

The remarkable feature of such simple playing material is the seemingly infinite variety of positions to which it can give rise and the depth of mental complexity to which it gives scope. To the non-player, the opening moves of a game between experts appears baffling in its inconsequentiality, each in turn placing a stone on the board apparently at random and with no discernible pattern or logic. Gradually, out of the mists of formlessness, there begin to crystallize suggestions of small chains or groups of like pieces marking out local areas of the board on which secure areas of territory may eventually be established. As each player recognizes where either of them is most likely to prevail, he ceases either contesting or consolidating it and turns his attention to those still exhibiting a degree of uncertainty—or what should rather be called dynamic tension. Rarely will a solid group of stones be captured as shown in Fig. 11.5. Unless there were some chance of attacking part of Black's wall, White would have abandoned the group as lost in order not to lose so many stones which might more profitably be played elsewhere. The middle stages of the game will see groups of stones surrounded in such a way as to render them unsavable. Such stones are 'dead', to all intents and purposes. They are not yet removed from the game because, so long as they have access to at least one liberty, they are technically not surrounded. The skill of the game, to experts, and its mystery, to non-players, lies in recognizing which areas are safe and which unsafe, and concentrating on the latter. This in turn involves in some cases recognizing stock situations whose outcomes are known to regular players, and in others foreseeing the consequences of an obvious or inevitable line of play.

Like Chess, the play of Go falls naturally into an opening phase (*fuseki*), a middle game (*chuban sen*), and an end-game (*yose*). Unlike Chess, play tends to proceed from the corners to the edges and finally to the centre of the board. At least, that is the order in which formations and won territories tend to crystallize; individual stones are often placed in more central areas like fifth columnists, waiting for future developments to which they may be able to make a useful contribution.

Much of the subtlety and tension of the game derives from the fact that, while a number of stones must be solidly connected to form a coherent group, they need not be so in order to enclose space and effect a capture, for

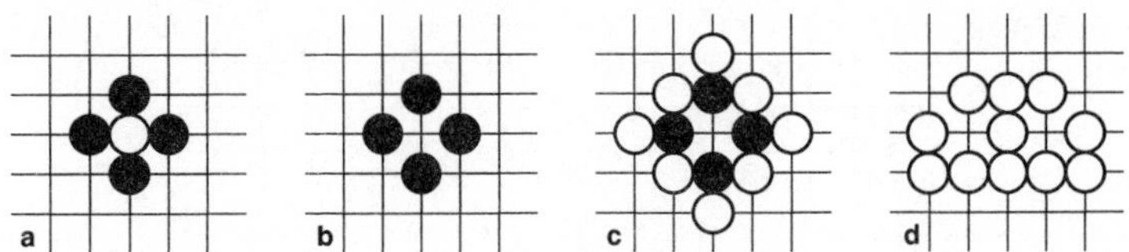

Fig. 11.11. Four blacks enclose and capture a white stone (*a*, *b*), but are not necessarily invulnerable to capture (*c*). A minimum safe group in mid-board is eleven stones (*d*).

which purpose a diagonal adjacency suffices. For example, in Fig. 11.11(*a*), the white stone is deprived of all its liberties by four black ones, and is therefore captured, leaving position (*b*).

The capturing stones, however, are not themselves invulnerable to capture, as demonstrated by the surrounding whites in (*c*). Here, Black cannot play to the centre (suicide rule), but White can so play, thereby capturing four black stones. White in turn could subsequently be captured, at least up to the point at which he makes a solidly connected group with at least two safe eyes. The minimum safe group requires eleven stones, as at (*d*), reducing to eight on an edge and six at a corner.

Grading and handicapping. The margin of victory between well-matched professionals rarely reaches double figures. Black is considered to have an advantage of about 5 points by virtue of moving first, so a loss by White of not more than 5 need not be considered degrading. Victories of one or two points are not unusual, and draws not unknown (unless obviated by the 5½-point deduction noted below). Between unmatched players it is customary for the stronger to give the weaker the advantage of anything from two to nine stones. The weaker player starts by taking the agreed number of black stones and placing them on the handicap points in a conventional pattern as shown in Fig. 11.12 (the player sitting south). The stronger player then starts the game proper by placing his first white stone. A 'one-stone' handicap amounts to ceding to the weaker player the right to be Black and play first. In this case it is a matter of courtesy for Black, if he chooses to open 3-4 (equivalent to e4 in Chess), to do so in the upper right quadrant and nearer the edge than the top of the board.

In expert and tournament play Black's opening advantage is acknowledged by subtracting a number of points—The *Kani* or handicap—from his final score. In Japan the *Kani* is 5½ points, a number which also, usefully, prevents draws.

The ranking system developed in Japan is used throughout the world. Professionals are ranked in nine grades called *dan*, from *sho-dan* (grade 1)

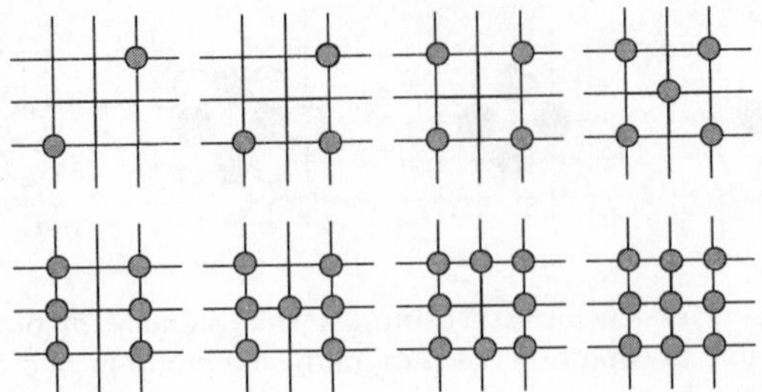

Fig. 11.12. Positions for handicaps of two to nine stones on the handicap points shown in Fig. 11.1.

up to *kyu-dan* (grade 9). Although the ranking system remains constant within itself, it varies according to place and circumstance. Japanese professionals do not handicap one another despite differences of degree, but a professional *sho-dan* would give an amateur of the same rank the advantage of five or six stones. For amateur players, seven grades of *dan* are recognized, while those with no pretensions to such grades are ranked in terms of *kyu*. These might be regarded as minus grades, since they count downwards from the lowest level. A beginner is counted as 35 *kyu*. After several weeks he may get down to 25 *kyu*. Thereafter progress is slower. The great event of the amateur's life is to pass from the level of one *kyu* to that of *sho-dan*. *Kyu*-rated players use a handicap system of one stone for each difference in level. In Britain, *kyu* gradings are controlled by local Go clubs, *dan* ranking by the British Go Association.[8]

Reversi (Othello)

Another product of the late nineteenth-century explosion of abstract game ideas, Reversi has enjoyed a more eventful history than its other great contemporary Halma. Though patented in 1888 by Lewis Waterman, one James Mollett later asserted that Reversi differed only from his own game of Annexation, published in 1870, in using a draughtboard instead of one of special design. Following an initial burst of popularity, it dropped out of favour after the First World War, but subsequently reappeared, with minor modifications, under such names as Exit and Chain Reaction. More startlingly, it was miraculously reinvented by Goro Hasegawa and published in Japan in 1968 under the name Othello. Despite misguided assertions to the contrary, Othello differs from Reversi only in requiring the first two pieces of each colour to be placed diagonally to one another on the four central squares, whereas Reversi merely requires the first four to be

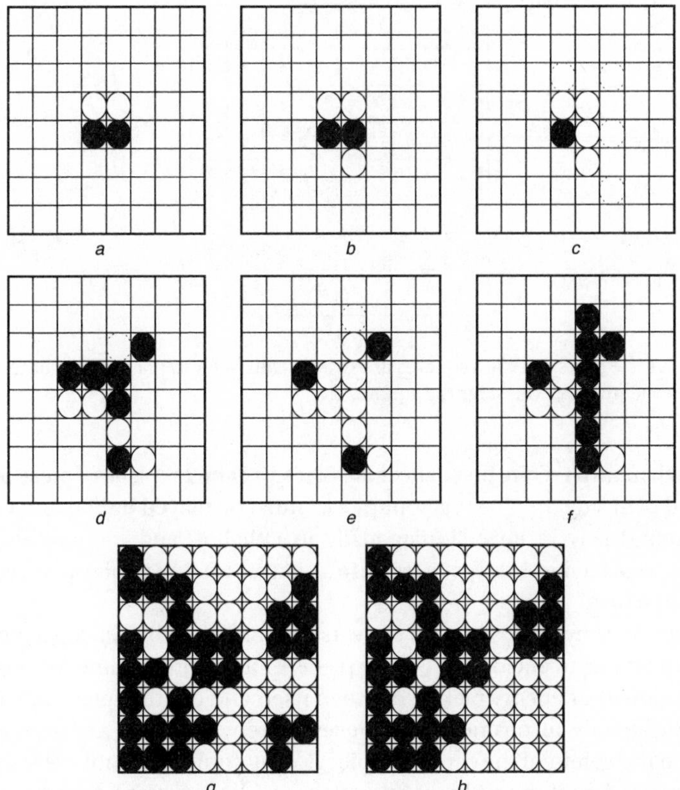

Fig. 11.13. Reversi: the first four pieces are played to the centre (not necessarily diagonally, as required in Othello). White's capture (*b*) produces position (*c*), giving Black a choice of four placements as shown by dotted circles. Later, (*d*), White makes the first multiple capture by playing to the dotted circle, producing (*e*). Here, Black plays to the dotted circle, producing (*f*). The game continues, captures being made at each turn. At (*g*), Black cannot play to the last vacant square because this would not effect a capture. White occupies it instead, producing (*h*) and winning by 37 to 27.

played to the centre. Furthermore, adds Dawson,[9] while the precise placing is optional, 'It is generally considered to be bad play on the part of the first player if he places his diagonally' (!)

Like Go, Reversi is a game of territorial occupation involving placement and capture but not movement. It is played by two on an 8 × 8 board, preferably unchequered, with sixty-four discs black on one side and white on the other. A set is easily constructed by sticking together sixty-four draughtsmen of each colour.

8	1	3	4	4	3	1	8
1	2	5	6	6	5	2	1
3	5	7	7	7	7	5	3
4	6	7			7	6	4
4	6	7			7	6	4
3	5	7	7	7	7	5	3
1	2	5	6	6	5	2	1
8	1	3	4	4	3	1	8

Fig. 11.14. Reversi. Certain squares are strategically safer to play to than others. The higher the number, the safer the square.

Each in turn (White first in Reversi, Black in Othello) places a piece on the board own side up. The first four pieces must be played on the four centre squares (freely in Reversi, diagonally in Othello), and each subsequent piece so placed as to effect a capture. A player unable to play and capture misses a turn.

Capture is by enclosure and conversion. It is made by placing a piece in such a way as to enclose an enemy piece, or an unbroken line (orthogonal or diagonal) of enemy pieces, between itself and another piece of its own colour already in position. The pieces thereby enclosed are reversed to match the colour of the capturing pieces. Play continues until every square is occupied, and the winner is the player with a majority of pieces of his own colour uppermost.

Mig Mang. This Tibetan game, described by R. C. Bell,[10] resembles Reversi sufficiently to suggest at least an inspirational connection, but differs in being a game of movement without placement.

Black and White each start with thirty-four pieces of their own colour, of which seventeen are placed on all the points of two contiguous sides of a reticular grid of size 17×18 and the remainder kept in store. Each in turn moves a piece along a line to any adjacent vacancy. A singleton, or an orthogonal line of pieces of the same colour lying next to an enemy piece, is captured by custodianship if another enemy piece moves on to the immediately adjacent point on the opposite side. Captives are removed and replaced by pieces of the capturing colour. A player wins by converting all enemy pieces, or all except from one to four occupying corner points from which they cannot move.

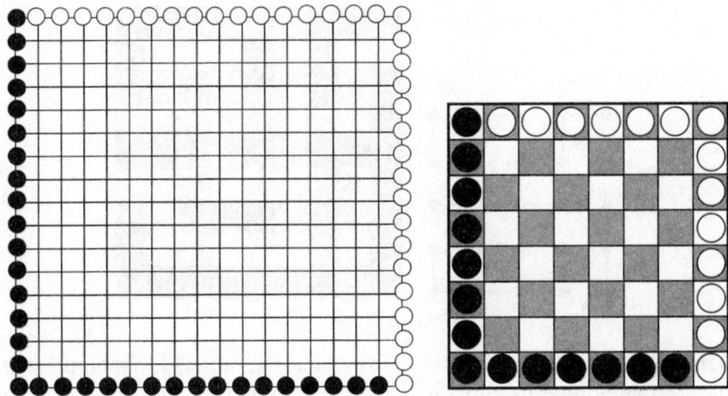

Fig. 11.15. Mig Mang: Tibetan game on 17×18 points. It can be adapted, smaller, as a chessboard game.

Guerilla, by David Wells (1976), is an interesting exercise in converting a space control game based on Go into one of placement, movement, and capture. Black and White play on the points of a triangular grid (equivalent to the cells of a hexagonal grid). Each in turn (1) places a piece on a point that is both vacant and not directly connected to an occupied point, (2) adds a piece to one of his groups, up to a maximum of five, and (3) moves each singleton and group bodily by a process of jumping elements of a group over one another to vacant points. A group consists of a number of pieces from two to five of which each is directly connected to at least one other member. Following a move, any member of a player's group attacks any member of an enemy group provided that it is directly connected to it and that it has more of its own pieces supporting it than the piece attacked has defending it. An attacked piece is removed from the board. Play ends by mutual agreement. The winner is the player commanding the greater amount of territory, counting for this purpose each point occupied by a piece of his own and each vacant point directly connected to a piece of his own, provided that it is not neutralised by being directly connected to an enemy piece. In addition to sixty pieces each of black and white, there are sixty red pieces. If the number of pieces successfully attacking an enemy piece is greater by two or more than the number of defenders, the point of attack is marked as a 'massacre' by the positioning of a red piece on it. Reds remain unmoved and belong to neither player. The game is slow and cumbersome, and it is easy to lose count of which pieces have been moved by the time a turn is half complete.

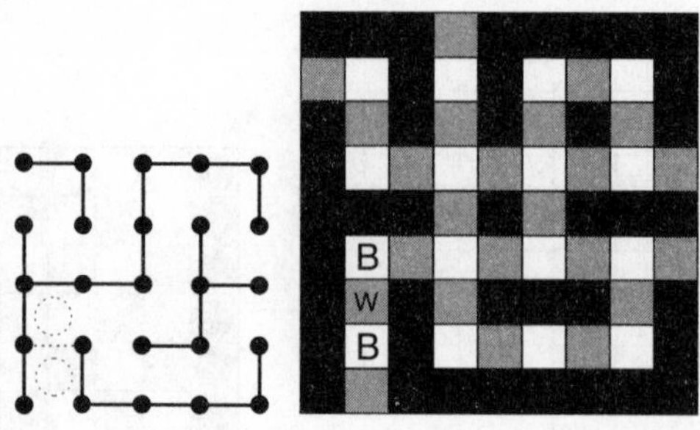

Fig. 11.16. Boxes converts (not well) into a board game, with dots represented by fixed black squares, lines by individual black squares placed on spaces coloured grey, and black and white counters for initials. White, to play, must lose, even though initially restricting Black to two boxes by playing bottom left as shown.

Boxes, or **Dots and Boxes,** is a long-popular children's game of territorial acquisition played with pencil and paper. Like many such games, it could (just about) be taken apart and reassembled as a board game, as shown in Fig. 11.16. A grid of 5 × 5 dots, making 4 × 4 boxes, is the smallest size for which no winning strategy is self-evident.[11]

NOTES

1. Richard Bozulich (ed.), *The Go Player's Almanac* (San Jose, London, and Tokyo, 1992).
2. I have taken the liberty of slightly rewording what is presumably Pinckard's translation in *The Go Player's Almanac.*
3. Daniele Pecorini and Tong Shu, *The Game of Wei-Chi* (Singapore, 1991, originally 1921), 5.
4. Culin, *Korean Games* (1895), republished as *Games of the Orient* (Tokyo, 1958), 91.
5. Sometimes translated *brilliant man*, but by confusing different words *mei.* The relevant Chinese characters literally mean 'name person'.
6. Y. Kawabata, *The Master of Go* (1951), translation by Edward G. Seidensticker (London, 1973). Warning: The first English-language edition contains faulty diagrams.
7. *The Go Player's Almanac* is essential for anyone intending to take the game seriously, though it does not contain anything specifically directed at beginners. The introduction by Francis Roads, President of the British Go Association, in *The Illustrated Book of Table Games* (London, 1975), 62–95, is ideal if you can find it. The book by Arthur Smith, first published in 1908 and still frequently reprinted, is notoriously incompetent.
8. Francis Roads, *Games & Puzzles*, 1st ser. 10 (Feb. 1973), 20.
9. Lawrence Dawson, *Hoyle's Games Modernised* (London, 1923), 446–9.
10. R. C. Bell, *Games to Play* (London, 1988). Chessboard variation in Stephen Addison, *100 Other Games to play on a Chessboard* (London, 1983), 60–1.
11. See E. Berlekamp, J. H. Conway, and R. K. Guy, *Winning Ways* (London and New York, 1982), ii. 507–17.

CHASE GAMES

Corner your Fauna

Fox & Geese, Tigers & Leopards, Tablut, and Hnefatafl

Can you play at no game, Master Harry?
– A little at Fox and Geese, madam.
Henry Brooke, *A Fool of Quality* (1765–70)

Fox & Geese is the best-known English representative of a group of games characterized by the unusual fact that they are contests between two unequal forces, both with different powers of action and winning objectives. Typically, one player operates a single piece of great mobility and powers of capture, the other a relatively large number of pieces with restricted mobility and no powers of capture. The aim of the large but weak force is to blockade the powerful singleton so that it cannot move, while that of the singleton is to capture so many of the weaker forces that not enough remain to hem it in. In some games the larger force can win by occupying an area of the board designated as a fortress, and in some the singleton can alternatively win by reaching a place of safety. All such games are traditionally played on the points of a reticular board with movement only along marked lines, though some have subsequently been adapted for play on the cells of a chequerboard. Since the European games are played on the same boards as those used for alignment games such as Merels/Mill/Morris, I will refer to them as mill-boards. (Murray calls them Alquerque boards, but this is too long-winded for constant repetition, and implies an Arabic connection which is confessedly speculative.)

I deliberately describe these as a group rather than a family of games, for although they are remarkable for their similarities, and all have much the same feel about them, no one has yet demonstrated an historical link between them. Several fairly distinctive clusters can be distinguished as follows:

1. Fox & Geese, and other faunal varieties of predator and prey, are played throughout Europe on the quadruple or quintuple mill, usually with diagonals. There is one predator and from twelve to seventeen prey, though sometimes the predator is itself the prey and the numerous force represents hunters or their hounds. This group

includes extensions and variations made by increasing the size and format of the mill to unorthodox dimensions, increasing the number of prey, doubling or tripling the number of predators, or any combination of these factors.

2. Asalto and its relatives appear to be Fox & Geese extensions with a doubled predator, and converted to a military theme featuring two officers and a larger number of rebel soldiers. In addition, one arm of the quintuple mill is delineated as a fortress, and the rebels can win by completely occupying it. These are evidently influenced by oriental 'rebel' games.
3. Similar Chinese and Japanese games involve a loyal general and sixteen or more rebel soldiers. They are typically played on a quadruple mill with a triangular extension representing a fortress. The general captures by intervention, but can himself be captured by custodianship. This feature is characteristic of equally balanced war games and may suggest a line of development therefrom.
4. Tiger games of south-east Asia involve from one to four tigers and anything up to twenty-four hunters, dogs, or cattle. The method of play and objectives closely resemble those of Fox & Geese, except that the pieces of the larger force are often placed on the board one by one in alternation with moves of the singleton, making them games of placement and movement instead of movement alone. Most of these also feature a triangular extension to the board, and a few are played on triangular boards alone.
5. Tafl* is the generic term for an ancient group of Scandinavian games that may be regarded as a hybrid, in that they combine the unbalanced forces and unequal objectives of Fox & Geese with the general principles of war games such as Chess and Draughts.

Murray classifies Tafl as a war game, and describes the other five under the general heading 'hunt-games'. Because 'hunt' strongly implies animals, whereas many of the games are military rather than pastoral, I prefer 'chase' games, which strikes me as being of broader applicability and equally descriptive of the sort of activity that goes on. This applies as well to Tafl, since the King (equivalent to the singleton of Fox & Geese) may be chased to the edge of the board, whence he can win by making good his escape.

This summary suggests why the games cannot easily be united into a genetic whole in default of far more information than at present available.

* Tafl is often said to be pronounced *tabl*; but this applies only in Icelandic, where, since the *b* is voiceless anyway, it sounds more like a *p*.

One would expect them to form a single family, since they have much in common, and are restricted in origin to the Eurasian landmass, being significantly absent from Africa except as a later import. But how to divide them? A geographical distinction may be drawn between European and Oriental games, a thematic one between game-hunting and military rebellion, a procedural one between those capturing by leaps and those by custodianship, and a formal one between those played on mill-boards and those played on triangular boards; but none of these overlaps intelligibly with any other, and the formal link is complicated by the hybrids played on mill-boards with triangular extensions.

Hares, Hounds, Fox, Geese, and their Relatives

An early European chase game is recorded in the Alfonso MS of 1283 as *Cercar la Liebre*, or Catch the Hare. Murray believes the Spaniards acquired it from the Moors together with the Alquerque board on which it is played, in turn implying a cultural diffusion from the Orient via Arabia, but admits that its absence from any known Arabic source does nothing to support this view.

Catch the Hare was played on the quadruple mill, with one hare and twelve hunters, or their hounds, positioned as shown in Fig. 12.1, and following the rules and objectives of Fox & Geese. In course of time the diagonals were gradually lost, as indicated by intermediate forms described by Culin as found among various Amerindian tribes in the Spanish New World. Both the full board and that with only two diagonals was used for the Mexican game of Coyote & Chickens—the former represented by a red bean and the latter by grains of corn—while the purely orthogonal board was used by the Tigua of New Mexico for Indian and Jackrabbits, in which pebbles represented rabbits and the Indian's position was shown by pointing with a stick.

Of equal antiquity with the Spanish manuscript is the record of an Icelandic game called Hala-Tafl, or the Fox Game, which is mentioned in the Grettis Saga, and may (as Fiske suggests) relate to the game of Freystafl mentioned in the later sagas.

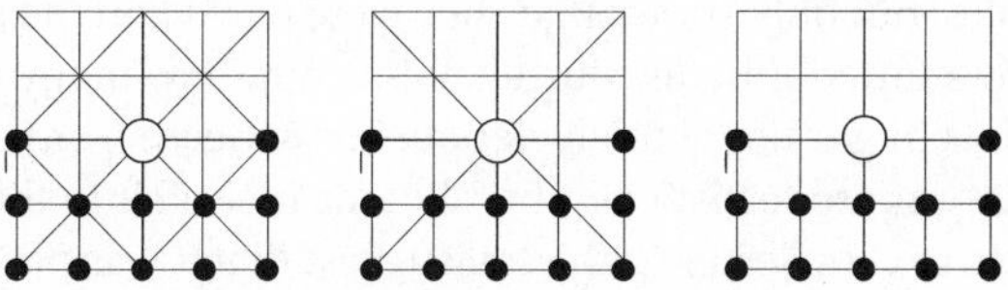

Fig. 12.1. Cercar la Liebre, with progressive loss of diagonals.

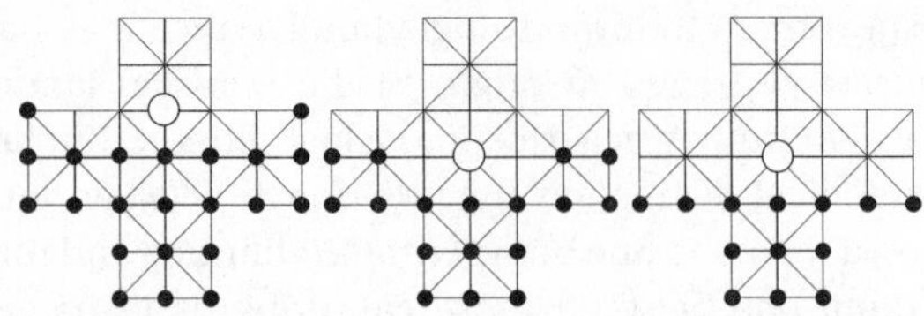

Fig. 12.2. Fox & Geese, with various numbers and arrangements of geese (13, 17, 22).

English Fox & Geese is played on the board shown in Fig. 12.2. The geese are thirteen black pieces on the points of the lower half of the board, and the fox the larger white piece, which starts from any ungoosed point the player chooses. Geese move first and aim to immobilize the fox, who seeks to prevent this by capturing so many geese that not enough remain to surround him. Any piece may move from its present point to the nearest unoccupied point, but only along a line. Geese cannot jump or capture, but the fox can do so by leaping over a goose, along a line only, to land on the necessarily vacant point beyond, and may enchain as many captures as possible in one turn.

The game is also known as Fox & Geese in Germany, though sometimes there as Fox & Hens, as it is in France (*Fuchs und Gänse, Fuchs und Hühne, Renard et les Poules*). An English dialectal alternative is recorded by Murray as Tod & Lambs, where tod = fox, as in the surname Todhunter. It is Wolf & Sheep in Dutch, Swedish, Italian, Russian (*Schaap en Wolf, Vargen och Fåren, Lupo e Pecore, Volki Ovtsy*). Fox recurs in other Scandinavian contexts, such as Icelandic *Refskak* or *Halatafl*, Swedish *Rävspelet* ('the Fox Game'). This refers to the original form, whereas *Vargen och Fåren* now denotes the version played on a chequerboard. The fauna naturally changes when the game is carried into other countries. To the Piman Indians of Mexico it was Coyote & Chickens.

That Fox & Geese was known in England from at least the fifteenth century is witnessed by an entry in the accounts of the Royal Household (Edward IV) for the purchase of two foxes and twenty-six hounds of gilded silver, thus making two sets of equipment. The fact that these games are called 'Marelles' not only shows that they were played on the same boards but also throws into doubt, as Murray points out, how many earlier references to Merels might not actually denote Fox & Geese—or Fox & Hounds as the case may, more realistically, be.[1] Boards incised into the stone seats in the cloisters of Gloucester Cathedral suggest that it was played at least a century earlier. Murray traces the game through seventeenth-century literary references to notices of its survival as a folk game in Lincolnshire and

Shropshire up to 1939. From 1600 on it has been subject to many variations, all designed in some way to counter the fact that, with proper play, the geese should win. The fact that no variant has established itself as standard suggests lack of higher strategic potential and so confirms its status as a folk game.

The geese were first weakened by denying them diagonal and backward movement. When this proved excessive, some power was restored by introducing additional geese to produce such varying totals as 15, 17, and 22. In some cases the fox was also prohibited from moving (but not from capturing) diagonally. In others there was a 'huffing' rule whereby the fox's failure to capture when possible resulted in the spontaneous creation of an extra goose.

Further expansions of the game were made by extending the arms of the cruciform board to varying degrees, producing thereby such games as the Double and Treble Fox & Geese described by Randle Holme (in *The Academy of Armory*, 1681), and the Venetian Lupo e Pecore described in a sixteenth-century Italian games manual in the Victoria & Albert Museum.

Chequerboard variants. Traditional European games were played on three main types of board: the 'pointed' board of Tables and Backgammon, the reticular boards of Alquerque, Merels, and Fox & Geese, and the chequerboard of Chess and Draughts. It is perhaps partly because reticular boards were more varied and less stable that neither Merels nor chase games have retained the status still enjoyed by Backgammon and Chess. Many reticular games have therefore been adapted to the chequerboard, on which they are equally playable, albeit with variations necessitated by the absence of directional lines.

An early example occurs in a sixteenth-century Latin manuscript from Perugia,[2] containing three diagrams, unfortunately without rules of play, of what is presumably the starting position of a game called *Ludus Rebellionis*, or Rebels. All are alike in being played on the squares of one colour, one player having sixteen pawns or pieces presumably representing the rebels, the other a Chess King and Queen presumably equivalent to commanders (or foxes, in the rustic game). The commanders start at opposite ends of one back row (b8, h8, for example), the rebels on alternate squares of the four rows furthest away (Fig. 12.3). One would guess this to be an adaptation of Fox & Geese if the fox equivalents were equal in power, but this is countered by the fact that different pieces are used, and that the two squares nearest the King, one in each direction, bear a mark of unexplained significance. Similar to these is Le Jeu de Renard in Mallet's *Le Jeu des Dames* (Paris 1668). This is played with one fox and twelve hens starting

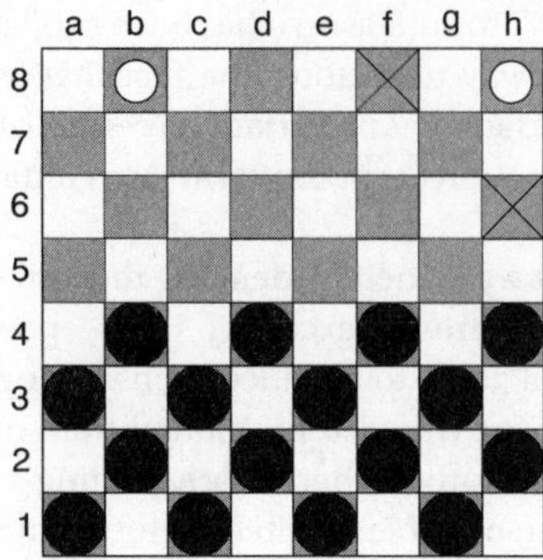

Fig. 12.3. Sixteenth-century Perugian game, with unexplained markings.

on the white cells of the first three rows. Variants include one with two foxes, which must move alternately, and from thirteen to sixteen hens. The latter approaches the first of the Perugian games, and the requirement of alternate moves for the foxes might account simply for its differentiating the two commanders as King and Queen, though still leaving the marked squares unexplained. Murray relates to this group the Indian game of Shatranj shir bakri, 'Lions and Goats Chess', with two lions opposing thirty-two goats initially placed on all cells of the first four rows.

The modern version of chequer-board Fox & Geese pits one fox against only as many geese as occupy the furthest back row—that is, four on the 8×8 board, five on the 10×10, and six on the 12×12 Sri Lankan board used for the native game of Leopard & Dogs (or Cattle). On a chequerboard all pieces move diagonally, the geese forwards only and the fox in any direction. The fox cannot capture, but wins by reaching the opposite side of the board; the geese win by hemming the fox in, or, more improbably, by themselves all reaching the furthest rank before the fox gets home.

Fox & Geese has also been played on Solitaire boards, but not before the geese were restricted to orthogonal movement only. This hardly counts as a significant variation, however, since the pattern of holes on the 33-hole Solitaire board replicates the arrangement of points on the Alquerque board on which Fox & Geese was originally played.

Asalto is the usual name for what may be regarded as an extension of Fox & Geese made by doubling the number of foxes. Randle Holme (1681) already refers to double and treble Fox & Geese played on enlarged boards with,

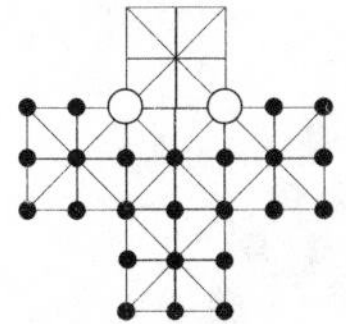

Fig. 12.4. Dogs & Bears.

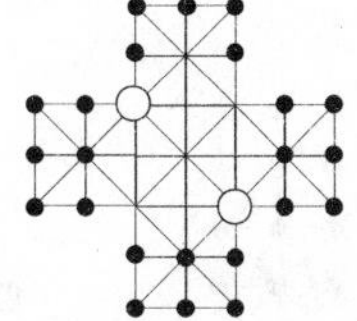

Fig. 12.5. Ritterspiel (The Knight's Game).

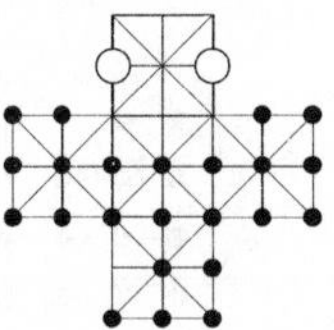

Fig. 12.6. Asalto.

respectively, two foxes and thirty geese, and three or four foxes and fifty geese.[3] Strutt, in 1810, says 'The fox must inevitably be blocked if the geese are played by a clever hand; for which reason, I am told, of late some players have added another fox; but this I have not seen.' Glonnegger implies a nineteenth-century dating for the German games illustrated here as Dogs & Bears and the Knight's Game. Asalto can be safely taken back to late eighteenth-century Germany,[4] and represents a shift of theme from field sports to the military. The game was also played in France as Assaut. The top squares are marked out as a fortress in which White positions two commanders or officers ad lib. Black posts twenty-four soldiers outside the fortress as illustrated. Soldiers move one step along any marked line, but only towards the fortress, and they cannot capture. Officers move one step in any direction and capture by a short leap as in Fox & Geese. Both officers may capture in the same turn of play, and an officer who fails to do so when possible is huffed and removed from the board. Black wins by occupying all the points of the fortress, or by immobilizing or huffing both officers. White wins by dispatching enough soldiers to render occupation impossible.

Similar games were known in Germany and Scandinavia as 'Beleaguering' games (German *Belagerungsspiel*, Danish *Belejringsspel*, Swedish *Fästningsspel*, Icelandic *Beleiringsspel*, etc.). Two variations described by Glonnegger are illustrated in Figs. 12.7 and 12.8. The first is merely a gigantic enlargement of the standard game. The second, Pyramid Siege, transfers Asalto to a triangular board, though the game is still played by two. The defender places three officers on any three points of the central fortress shown here by thick lines. Moves and captures are as in all the standard games. Black's aim is to occupy all six points of the triangular fortress. A piece once in position there cannot be moved, but may be captured by an officer.

Asalto—which is the equivalent Spanish word, but why Spanish was chosen I do not know—was published in Britain as a proprietary game

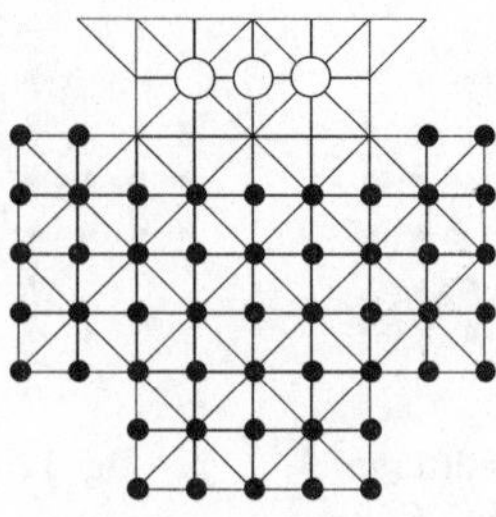

Fig. 12.7. Siege.

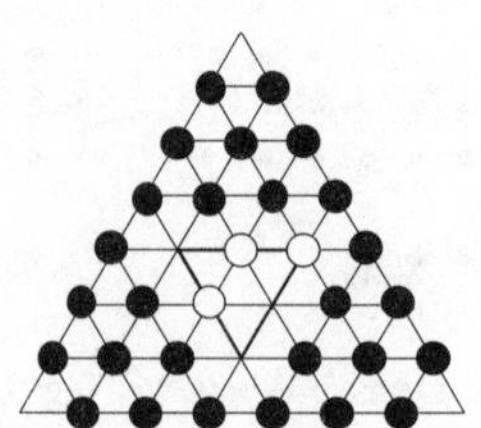

Fig. 12.8. Pyramid.

called 'The Officers and the Sepoys' following the sieges of the Kanpur and Lucknow garrisons in the Indian Mutiny (1857).

Maharajah, an extraordinary hybrid of Chess with the Fox & Geese family, originated at about the same time, and was also known as The Maharajah and the Sepoys. One player starts with the full complement of Chess pieces, while the other places on any unattacked square a King or Queen known as the Maharajah, which moves and captures like a Queen or Knight ad lib. Play as at Chess, except that pawns do not promote. The Maharajah wins by mating the King, the King's forces by capturing the Maharajah. Royalty should always win. A winning line of play, regardless of the singleton's move, is a4, a5, a6, a7, e3, Nh3, Nf4, Bd3, 0-0, Qh5, Nc3, Ncd5, Ra6, b4, h3 (if M on g7), Bb2, Rfa1, Re6, Rae6, Re7, Rae6, and mate next move.[5]

General and Soldiers. A group of Oriental games formally related to Fox & Geese are typified by Figs. 12.9 to 12.11. The board is a quadruple mill with a triangular extension representing a refuge. The singleton represents a general, initially surrounded by sixteen rebel soldiers, or twenty-six in one extension of the game. The general's aim is to capture all the rebels, the rebels to immobilize the general or confine him to the refuge, which he alone may enter, or, in the Chinese games, to capture him. All pieces move one step along a line to a neighbouring vacancy. In the Japanese game only the general may capture, which he does by a short leap as in Fox & Geese. In the Chinese games, two soldiers may capture the general by custodianship, i.e. one of them moves to a point adjacent to the general at a time when another soldier stands on the point further away from him in a straight line, so making a line of three with the general in the middle. If, however, such a line is formed by the general's moving into that central position, then he captures the two soldiers by intervention. Murray remarks 'Since the

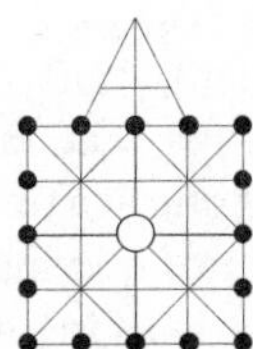

Fig. 12.9. Sixteen Soldiers (China).

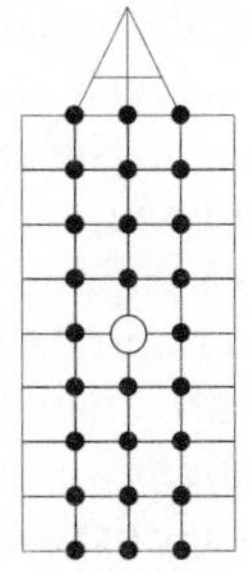

Fig. 12.10. Twenty-six Rebels (China).

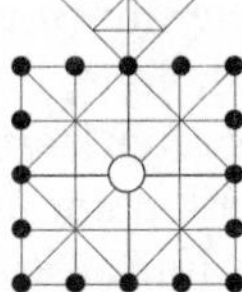

Fig. 12.11. Sixteen Soldiers (Japan).

custodian capture is more primitive than the leap capture in war-games, this may be an older type of hunt-game than the others . . .'[6]

The origin of the triangular extension is problematical. It may derive, by compounding, from the tiger games of India played only on a triangular board. Or it can be regarded as a logical extension of the enlargement of quadrilateral mill-boards. For example, the quadruple mill can be analysed in terms of a single mill with a triangle based on each of its four sides:

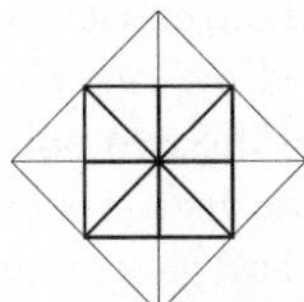

Similar boards with more complex triangular extensions are used for war-games related to Alquerque. This raises the possibility that hunt-games were developed, at least in one part of the world, by altering a war-game from one of equal forces to one of a powerful singleton versus a numerous but weaker adversary.

Asian Tiger Games

Murray lists some two dozen games of south-east Asia, ranging from India, through Indo-China, to Malaysia and Indonesia, played on the quadruple mill of Fig. 12.12, sometimes with the peripheral triangular extensions of Figs. 12.13 and 12.14, and variously with or without diagonal markings. In Malaysia, the triangles are designated *gunung*, 'mountain', and they are usually curved, i.e. fan-shaped, though Murray does not show this. The smaller force consists of at least one and up to four tigers, the larger from twelve to twenty-four pieces variously described as men, goats, sheep, calves, oxen, and cattle in general. The weaker pieces always move one step along a line from point to point, and never capture. Tigers start on predetermined points and always capture by leaping, usually short, occasionally long, but then only over an odd number of victims. The cattle-player often starts with some or all of them in hand, placing one at a time on a vacant point in alternation with moves of the tiger, and not moving any cattle until all are in position. In one or two games the cattle start in piles of five to a point. Such a pile is depleted by the movement of individuals off it on successive turns of play, or by capture, only one of a pile being removed when leapt over by a tiger.

Games played on Fig. 12.12 include the Malaysian *Main tapal empat*, described by Murray as follows. Two tigers are placed on the central point. The opponent, with twenty-four goats in hand, starts the game by entering them one at a time on vacant points in alternation with tiger moves. A tiger can move any distance along a marked line provided that all the points are vacant, but captures only by a short leap. Goats cannot move until all have been entered, then move but one step at a time. The goats win by immobilizing the tigers, and lose by being too depleted for this purpose. Heger in 1976 described much the same game as current in Nepal under the name *Bagh Chal*.[7] This has twenty goats, which can leap over the tiger but not capture it. The Indian *Bagh guti* is played on Fig. 12.12 with or without diagonals, starting with a tiger on each of the two points shown in the diagram, and twenty goats in four piles of five, also as shown. Only the topmost goat of a pile can move or be captured, and goats move only to vacant points—they cannot be re-piled. In the Assamese version, a tiger is placed on each corner, and each of twenty goats is entered on any vacant point in alternation with a tiger move. Tigers must always move in the same rotation until the goats are on board, when any one of them may be moved on any turn.

Games played on Fig. 12.13, with two 'mountains', are typified by the Malaysian game of Tigers. The tiger starts at the apex of either triangle, and nine of the twenty-four 'men' on the central points as illustrated. The tiger-player begins by removing any three men and placing the tiger on any vacant point. The other then enters fifteen men one at a time in alternation with a tiger move. Men cannot move until all have been entered, and move only one step at a time. The tiger also moves one step at a time, and captures by leaping one, three, five, or (theoretically) seven men in a straight line, provided that the line is uninterrupted by vacancies and the the furthest point is vacant. Capturing is optional. The hunters will usually resign when reduced to ten or fewer. A close relative played in Sumatra has

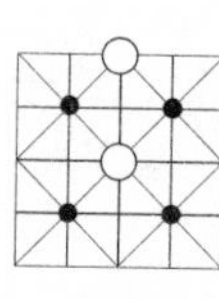

Fig. 12.12. Bagh-guti (India).

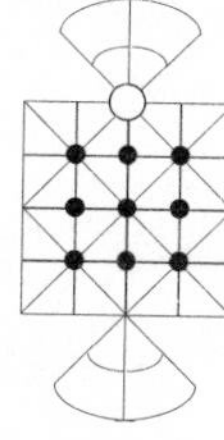

Fig. 12.13 Tigers (Malaysia).

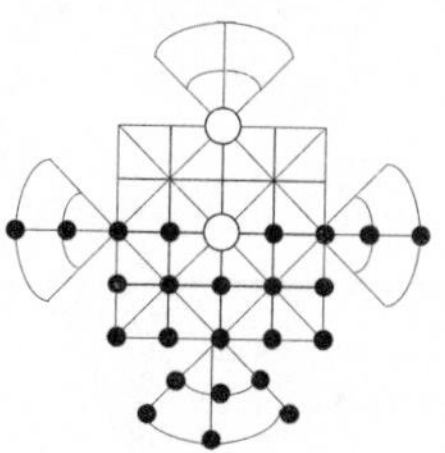

Fig. 12.14. Leopards & Cows (Sri Lanka).

two tigers, one on each apex point, and twenty-four goats, of which eight occupy the positions shown in the diagram apart from the centre point. This game lacks the elaborate opening sequence of the previous game, and, when played with one tiger, the tiger cannot capture more than one goat at a time.

The Sri Lankan game of Leopards and Cows[8] is played on Fig. 12.14, with four mountains. One player has two leopards and the other twenty-four cows. All start off the board and need not be entered in the positions shown in the diagram, which I have marked only for the sake of appearance and symmetry. Each in turn, starting with the leopard player, enters one of his beasts on any vacant point. The first leopard may not move until the second is in place, and no cow until all twenty-four have been entered. All moves are short, and only one cow may be captured at a time.

Murray also mentions three oddities in this section. The Siberian game of Boar-Chess, recorded in the Upper Yenisei valley, features two boars and twenty-four calves, but the board is not specified. Kaooa, from the Central Provinces of India, is played on a pentagram, with one tiger and seven *kaooas*. An unnamed game from Sikkim and Assam is played on a board consisting of seven concentric circles and six diameters, with one tiger and an unspecified number of goats.

Triangular Variants. Some south-east Asian Tiger games are played on triangular boards. Fig. 12.15 is used for the Thai game of Len Choa, with a smaller force numbering six, and the Sri Lankan game of Hat Diviyan Keliya, 'the Seven Leopards', in which the tiger usually starts from the apex while the seven leopards, or 'dogs', are entered ad lib on vacant points. Fig. 12.16 is for the Indian game of Pulijudam, which starts with three tigers in the positions shown and involves the placement of fifteen leopards, sometimes called lambs, or, in the Sumatran version, sheep. The enlarged board of Fig. 12.17 has the same number of pieces. Placement once

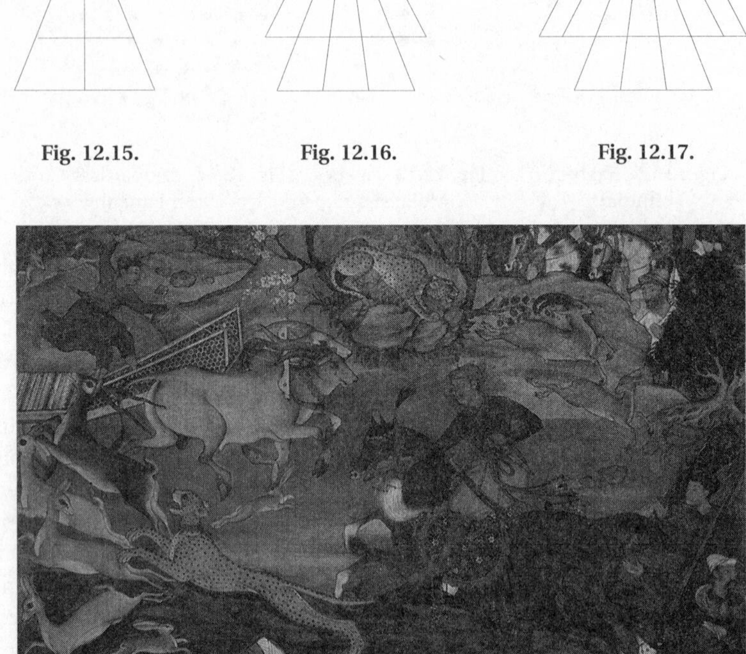

Fig. 12.15. Fig. 12.16. Fig. 12.17.

Fig. 12.18. Hunting with cheetahs, detail from a sixteenth-century Persian manuscript of the *Akbar Nama*.

completed, the remaining rules of play are as for Fox & Geese, in that only tigers can capture, which they do by the short leap. The games in this section are all taken from Murray,[9] who designates them 'Leopard' games from the most usual referend of the smaller force. We may see in this the Asian equivalent of European hounds, reflecting the fact that trained cheetahs, or hunting-leopards, assisted the tiger-hunters in their quest.

Tafl Games

Murray's introduction[10] to this branch of the family is concise enough to bear repetition:

Tafl...was the older, and *hnefatafl* the later name of a board-game which was already played by the Scandinavian peoples before A.D. 400. It was carried by the Norsemen to Iceland, Britain, and Ireland, and spread to Wales. It was the only board-game played by the Saxons. After the introduction of chess into England in the eleventh, and Scandinavia in the twelfth century, *hnefatafl* fell out of use except in remote and isolated districts: the last mentions of the game as still played are from Wales, 1587, and Lapland 1732.

This distinctive series of ancient northern European games looks like a hybrid of war games, such as Chess, and chase games, such as Fox & Geese. They share with war games the feature of two opposing armies whose members capture one another by custodianship. Furthermore, one of the armies is headed by a King, whose capture results in loss of the game. With chase games, however, they share the fact that the two armies are of unequal size, that they are arranged radially rather than bilaterally, and that their objectives are also unequal, in that the royal side wins by getting its King to a place of safety. It is therefore more logical to regard Tafl games as extensions of the Fox & Geese principle, with the singleton converted to a King and assisted by a small army, and the introduction of custodian capture already prefigured in some of the chase games described above, than as the conversion of a wargame into one of radial symmetry and unequal forces.

Information on the play of Tafl games is widespread but disparate. Remains and fragments of the gaming equipment tells us the size and patterning of various boards and the design of the individual pieces, but nothing of their initial arrangement and powers of action. Some written records imply the initial arrangement or powers of action, but rarely both, or without eliciting unanswerable questions. On the other hand, such rules as can be inferred from all known sources are so consistent with one another that it is possible to reconstruct an archetypal Tafl game from which no individual game is likely to have deviated in any significant respect. The greatest degree of difference lies in the size of the boards found and hence the number of pieces involved. The essence of the game is as follows.

The board is an odd-numbered square array. Known sizes include 7, 9, 11, 13, and 19 (Fig. 12.19). Some games were played with peg-shaped pieces fitted into holes, others with flat-bottomed pieces on the points of intersection of a board with an even number of squares, and others, especially after the influence of Chess, on the cells of an odd-squared board. The centre square bears a distinctive design, sometimes also the corner squares, and other forms of patterning or shading may be introduced, as much for ease of orientation and a guide to initial placement as for

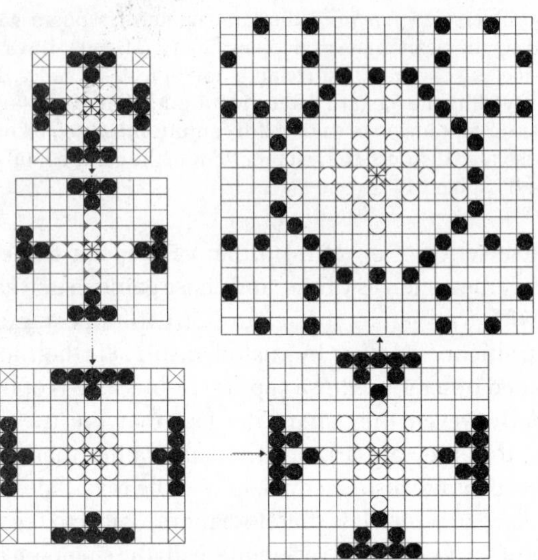

Fig. 12.19. Tafl boards of various sizes: 7 × 7: Ballinderry game-board, Ireland, tenth century. (Actually 7 × 7 holes for pegs. Arrangement conjectural.) 9 × 9: Tablut, Lapland, eighteenth century. 11 × 11 Tawlbwrdd, Wales, sixteenth century (number correct, arrangement conjectural). 13 × 13: Hnefatafl, Gokstad ship, tenth century (number and arrangement conjectural). 19 × 19: Alea Evangelii, Britain tenth century (actually played on points of 18 × 18 board).

decorative effect. The mostly wooden boards are often carved of a piece with an integral handle on two opposite sides, enabling the players to dispense with a table by holding the board between them using one hand each, leaving the other free for moving the pegs. Tables, in fact, are rarely mentioned in this connection: rather, players are described as resting the games on their laps, thus rendering more lifelike the frequent references to hot-headed heroes violently upsetting their game-boards and hurling the pieces in the air.

The royal army consists of a King placed initially on the centre square and surrounded by a number of guards or defenders in a radially symmetrical pattern. The number of defenders is invariably half that of the number of enemy pieces, or attackers, and usually about one tenth of the total number of squares or points of the field of play. The attackers are initially placed in a symmetrical pattern around the four sides of the board.

In the diagram, the number and arrangement of pieces on boards of order 9 and 19 are known, as is the number on the 11-board, their conjectured arrangement being derived from that of the 9-board. The number and arrangement of pieces on the 13-board are both conjectural, but based on all the same principles. The attackers' aim is to capture the King, that of the royal force to get the King to any peripheral square, from which he is presumed to make his escape. Either occurrence ends the game and wins for the side achieving it. The royal player calls the equivalent of 'Check' if the King has a single clear path to one of the edges, enabling his adversary to block it, and the equivalent of 'Mate' if he has two clear paths to different edges, which cannot be blocked in a single move. This feature may be a borrowing from Chess.

In some games the defenders move first, in some the attackers. All pieces move any distance orthogonally, provided that all squares passed over are vacant. An attacker cannot land on the centre-point, even when it is vacant, but may pass over it.

All pieces capture by custodianship—that is, by trapping an enemy piece between two of their own, as any one of three black pieces can do in the position illustrated in Fig. 12.20. An attacker can be captured by a single defender if the square on its opposite side is the centre-point. Some boards exhibit special marking on the corner squares, suggesting similar capturing powers. A piece can, however, occupy or traverse a square sandwiched between enemy pieces without being captured; furthermore, it is not thereby prevented from making a capture itself if the resultant position so warrants. Captured pieces are removed from the board and do not re-enter.

The King can only be captured by double custodianship—that is, by a move that results in his being flanked by an enemy piece on all four sides, or on three sides and the central square.

An interesting strategic point applicable to all versions of the game is that the King, in its initial position, is blocked from reaching an edge square by three or four pieces. The royal player's aim, therefore, is to do everything in his power to clear a pathway. The enemy, however, is in something of a double bind. While wishing to capture royal guards in order to render the King vulnerable, he may equally prefer to leave them be, since their continued presence, in the hands of an inexpert player, can restrict the King's

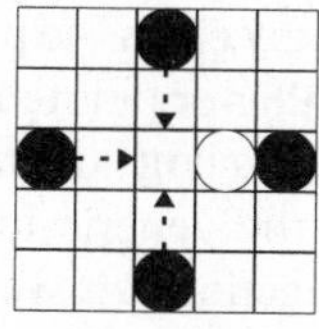

Fig. 12.20. Custodian capture between two pieces, or one piece and central square.

field of movement and block his passage to the edge. Between equally matched players, the royal force should normally win.[11] For a balanced match, the two players might alternate between sides, and the first to lose for the royal side loses the match.

The early existence of Tafl is demonstrated by fragmentary finds of boards and gaming pieces consistent with what we know of the game in Scandinavian graves and burial mounds of the Roman Iron Age. A wooden board found in a grave at Wimose, Fünen, is about 45 cm. square and marked with an unchequered pattern of 18 × 18 square cells, evidently for play on the 19 × 19 points.[12] Another, from the late ninth-century Viking burial ship found at Gokstad, near Oslo, has 13 × 13 squares, some of them shaded, showing that the game was played on the cells. It may be of interest that the reverse of this board is marked with a triple mill-board (twenty points, no diagonals, as for Nine Men's Morris). A wooden game-board about 25 cm. square found in the remains of a lake dwelling at Ballinderry, near Meath, Ireland, contains holes for pegged pieces arranged in the form of a 7 × 7 square. The centre-point is distinguished by a surrounding circle and each corner marked off by a quadrant. In the Tafl diagram I have translated this into a squared board for ease of comparison, and suggested an initial arrangement of pieces for a form of Tafl that could be played on it. Another 7 × 7 board, with the centre-point encircled but the corners undistinguished, was found scratched on a flagstone from the ninth-century Norse homestead at Buckquoy, Orkney. Plausible but inconclusive attempts have been made[13] to associate the 7 × 7 board with the game of Brandubh ('black raven') frequently mentioned in *Táin Bó Cuilgné* (The Cattle Raid on Cooley), the central story of the Ulster Cycle of Irish myth and legend of which the earliest known manuscript is the twelfth-century *Book of Leinster*. Four fragments of a late ninth- or early tenth-century slate gaming board from the remains of a Viking settlement at Jarlshof, in the Shetlands (Fig. 12.21), imply a grid of at least 9 × 9 squares, of which the five forming a central quincunx are cross-cut as if to suggest the placement of a king and either eight or twelve guards.[14] Such boards are more descriptive of the nature of the game than the numerous playing-pieces often found in conjunction with them. These are variously made of wood, bone, glass, amber, occasionally clay. In many cases the pieces of one side are rounded or hemispherical, the others taller or pointed, or shaped into the heads of men or hounds, and with an extra large or crowned piece evidently representing a King, thus putting the generic identity of the various games beyond question. In this connection it is worth reminding ourselves that our concept of 'standard' games with 'official' rules is a peculiarly modern one, and inconsistent with the inherent variability of folk games, especially

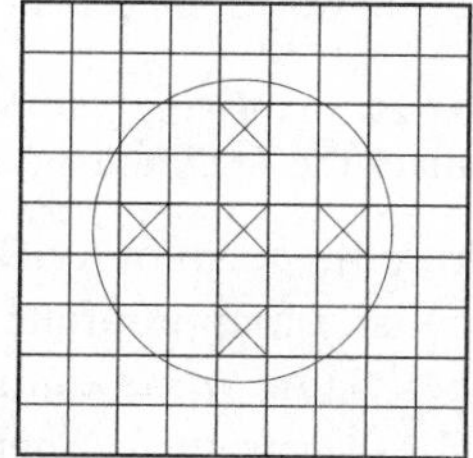

Fig. 12.21. Design of the slate gameboard of Jarlshof, Shetland.

those of wanderers and explorers. It may therefore be misleading to think in terms of a specifically Irish or Icelandic or Norse version of Tafl, but rather be the case that any given version of the game was specific only to a purely local community. It is even conceivable that individual Tafl players might make a board of any size from 7 × 7 upwards according to the size and shape of the materials to hand, and then fit an appropriate number of pieces on it—ensuring only that there should be exactly twice as many attackers as defenders—in accordance with a general pattern of play with which everyone was generally acquainted.

Tafl is also well documented in literature, especially in the Icelandic sagas from the eleventh century on, though many such references have been disguised in translation by being referred to as Chess, the true nature of Hnefatafl having only become apparent in the twentieth century. Paradoxically, some light is cast on the play by two riddles in the *Herverar Saga* forming part of a battle of wits between King Heidrek and Odin in disguise:

Q. Who are the maids that fight weaponless around their lord, the brown ever sheltering, and the fair ever attacking him?
A. The pieces in Hnefatafl.
Q. What is the beast all girdled with iron which kills the flocks? It has eight horns but no head.
A. The *hnefi* in Hnefatafl.

This suggests that the sides were distinguished as light and dark, as at Chess, and that the dark ones were royalists. *Hnefi* ('fist') is the usual word for the king, and 'eight horns' evidently refers to the distinctive way in which it was carved, perhaps to resemble a crown. (Might not *hnefi* originally have designated the centre-point, and subsequently become transferred to the piece occupying it?)

In *Frithiof's Saga*, Frithiof advises Hilding on military procedure by reference to the game of Hnefatafl he is playing with Björn:

Frithiof: A bare place in your board which you cannot cover, and I shall beset your red pieces there.
Björr: A double game, and two ways of meeting your play!
Frithiof: Your game is first to attack the *hnefi*, and the double game is assured.

An English manuscript from the reign of Athelstan (924–40) describes a form of Hnefatafl in a peculiarly inappropriate allegorical guise, stating 'Here beginneth the Gospel Game (*alea euangelii*) which Duibhinnsi, bishop of Beinchair, brought over from... Athelstan, king of the Angles.' More interesting than the allegory is the fact that rectifying the obvious errors enables the reconstruction of the board and arrangement of pieces for the tenth-century Saxon game. An illustration shows a king or *hnefi* and twenty-four guards pitted against forty-eight attackers arranged on the 19 × 19 points of a board of 18 × 18 squares, which in the accompanying diagram I have changed to the cells of a 19 × 19 board for ease of comparison.

Welsh literature from about the tenth century on includes references to a form of Hnefatafl called Tawlbwrdd, or Dalwbwrdd. The fact that both names mean 'throw-board' might suggest a dice-game of the Tables family—a point of confusion reinforced by the fact that Welsh *taflu*, 'to throw', is pronounced almost the same as Greek *tavli*, meaning the game of Tables. Perhaps the choice of *tawl* as the name of the game was influenced by the Scandinavian name *tafl*, itself derived from *tabula* (Tables) by another route. Its identity with Hnefatafl, however, is proved by a passage in the Laws of Hywel Dda making quite explicit that it was played by two sides, one consisting of a king and eight pieces, the other of sixteen pieces. A manuscript of 1587 in the Welsh National Library contains an unambiguous description by Robert ap Ifan of a form of *tawlbwrdd* played on a board of 11 × 11 squares with a king and twelve men against twenty-four attackers. Ap Ifan illustrates the board and describes the opening position as 'The king in the centre of the board and twelve men in the places next to him, and twenty-four lie in wait to capture him. These are placed, six in the centre of every end of the board and in the six central spaces.' The position as reconstructed in the diagram given here forces the conclusion that the last phrase should refer to four central spaces, rather than six. (Bell[15] arranges the six on each side in an arrowhead formation like that of the central six of each peripheral group in my suggested reconstruction of the Gokstad 13 × 13 board.)

Welsh legends and romances earlier in date than the tenth century, such as some portions of the *Mabinogion*, portray Arthurian heroes playing at a game called Gwyddbwyll, traditionally rendered as Chess in translation, but assuredly not so, since Chess did not reach Europe until after the first millennium. The fact that Gwyddbwyll gives way to Tawlbwrdd in similar contexts suggests that it was not a form of Tafl either. Murray conjectures it to represent the continuation of a Roman war game of the Latrunculi type. The first syllable of Gwyddbwyll can be related to several semantic clusters, including 'wise/wisdom/knowledge/science/wizardry' and 'Irish man/language'. The likeliest, however, is 'wood/wooden', in which respect the whole word is cognate with that denoting the Irish game of Fidhcheall mentioned, for example, in *Cormac's Glossary* of the tenth century (though incorporating later additions). Fidhcheall literally means a wooden board, or plank, thus bringing us back to our opening comments on the meaning of 'board-game'. The glossary expounds it thus: 'In the first place the Fidhcheall is four-cornered, its squares are right-angled and black and white men are on it, and moreover it is different people that in turn win the game.'

In modern Irish, Ficheall (as it is now spelt) is generic for any kind of wooden board game, such as Draughts, Chess, and Backgammon. A chess piece is *fidhchillin,* which may relate to *fiothal,* 'dwarf'.[16] Bell unhesitatingly equates 'Fithcheall' with Tafl. This derives plausibility from the comment about 'different people in turn winning the game', surely a reference to the procedure of alternating sides to compensate for its inherent inequality. If Gwyddbwyll is cognate with Fidhcheall, does this make it a Welsh form of Tafl? Not necessarily, in view of the notorious tendency of names to attach themselves to different games as each in turn becomes obsolete. Murray cites the fifteenth-century *Book of Lismore* as describing the gift of a Fidhcheall to Pope Boniface in the seventh century, 'and says that it had nine lines and half of the pieces were men and half women, but by the time this work was written Fidchell [*sic*] had long been obsolete and had generally been equated with Chess'.[17]

The last game of the series is the one that clarified the whole family in a way that eluded Willard Fiske in his quest for a definition of *tafl* that formed the substance of his misleadingly titled *Chess in Iceland* (1910). For this we are indebted to the indefatigable Murray and his confessedly 'chance discovery' of an account of the Lapp game of Tablut, played as late as the eighteenth century. The account in question was originally made by the Swedish botanist Linnaeus, 'the father of taxonomy', who noted details of the play in his journal of travels through Lapland, specifically in the entry for 20 July 1732.[18]

Tablut is played on a 9×9 squared board. The nine forming the central cross are shaded, and four peripheral groups of four cross-cut, thereby marking the positions of the Swedish king and eight blond guards, and sixteen swarthy attackers designated Muscovites (see diagram Fig. 12.19).

The King's centre-point, which he alone can enter, is called the *konakis*, 'throne' – a word tantalizingly reminiscent of the second element of the Hindi *char koni*, 'all square', designating the central home square of Pachisi. The rules of play are as given at the start of this section, and, as Murray remarks, consistent with all that we know from other sources. The King is not actually captured, but loses the game when surrounded on all four sides. If the royal player clears a passage for his King to one edge of the board, he warns his opponent by calling '*Raichi!*'; if two, he claims '*Tuichu!*', thereby winning the game.

NOTES

1. Murray, *History of Board Games*, 102, citing V. B. Redstone, 'England among the Wars of the Roses', in *Trans. RHS*, NS 21 (1902), 195 ff. (with 26 misprinted as 46).
2. In the Communal Library. See Murray, *History of Board Games*, 105.
3. Randle Holme, *The Academy of Armory*, cited by Murray, 104.
4. An Asalto board of this date is illustrated in UNICEF *Games of the World* (Zurich, 1982), 94.
5. By William Rudge, here taken from David Pritchard, *The Encyclopedia of Chess Variants* (Godalming, 1994).
6. Murray, *History of Board Games*, 101.
7. Ferdinand Heger, 'Himalayan Games', *Games & Puzzles*, 1st ser. 52 (Sept. 1976), 4.
8. H. Parker, *Ancient Ceylon* (London, 1909).
9. Murray, *History of Board Games*, 106–7.
10. Ibid. 56.
11. For a brief but sound strategic analysis, see David Pritchard on 'Tablut' in *Brain Games* (Harmondsworth, 1982), 176–80.
12. R. C. Bell refers the description to du Chaillu, *The Viking Age*, i. 216 (Bell, *Board and Table Games*, i. 79).
13. e.g. by Michael O'Shea, in 'Forum', the correspondence column of *Games & Puzzles*, 1st ser. 41 (Oct. 1975), 36.
14. R. C. Bell, 'Tafl Games', in *Games & Puzzles*, 1st ser. 38 (July 1975), 11.
15. Bell, *Board and Table Games of Many Civilisations*, ii. 43.
16. As usual, I have my brother Graham to thank for researches into Irish and Icelandic terminology.
17. Murray, *History of Board Games*, 35.
18. See the account in J. E. Smith, (ed.), *Lachesis Lapponica* (London, 1811), and, for a further discussion of Tafl in general and Tablut in particular, Murray, *History of Chess*, 445–6.

DISPLACE GAMES

Bean and Gone

Mancala Games

I was beginning to wonder where all the men were when I suddenly came round a corner and found a crowd of them. Two were seated on stools on either side of a long board with two rows of holes cut into it, and the rest were excitedly shouting advice. One black arm after another appeared from nowhere and what seemed to be little pebbles were rapidly scooped up and transferred from one hole to another with great skill and dexterity. All the movements seemed random and arbitrary, but I knew by the groans and cheers that some sort of game was being played and that everyone was having fun and enjoying it.

Ian Lenox-Smith, 'Mancala' (*Games & Puzzles*, July 1974)

Mancala—variously spelt,[1] and deriving from Arabic *naqala*, 'to move'—denotes a large but highly distinctive family of games with the following peculiarities:

1. The pieces are totally undifferentiated not only as to function but also as to player, all being common to both parties. They are represented by naturally fungible objects such as pebbles, seeds, or beans; I will refer to them generically as beans. The aim of the game is to capture beans and (normally) remove them from the playing area. This puts it with the category of 'displace' games.
2. The board is a double track of holes, cups, or other containers each capable of holding a dozen or more beans at a time. The track is essentially one-dimensional (linear), but looped, like a Backgammon board. In most varieties, each side of the board 'belongs' to one player.
3. The game is one of pure skill based on counting and calculation, and involves absolutely no external element of chance. Nevertheless, Mancala is typically played at great speed, sloth being felt to contradict the spirit of the game. Despite the skill, it is often played as a gambling game, or ritually, and with its outcome regarded as at least partly fate-determined. In some communities, the urge to win is subordinated to a desire to keep the game going as long as possible.
4. Mancala is probably of Black African origin, and Culin rightly characterizes it as Africa's national board game. There is, however, no universally accepted 'official' or 'standard' version. On the contrary,

> it is a typical folk game—the ludic equivalent of a series of mutually intelligible dialects each of which is standard only for its own locality. Any given variety may have several different names within a single gaming community; conversely, the same name, or variants of it, will often denote a number of different but similar games. Playing Mancala is as generic an activity as playing cards.

Mancala is played throughout Africa and by Black African descendants in the New World, notably in the Caribbean and down the eastern coast of South America, though in the USA its survival was prevented by slave-owners' deliberate suppression of Black culture. It is played throughout the Arab world and northwards into Syria, Turkey, and the Kazakh and Kirgiz Republics. Its eastward expansion embraces Iran, the Indian subcontinent, including Pakistan and Sri Lanka, Malaysia, Indonesia, the Philippines, Thailand, Vietnam, and southern China. Remarkably, it seems not to have spread any further westwards into Europe than some of the Greek islands of the Aegean—at least, not as a naturalized activity, though in recent years it has attracted considerable attention from games researchers and (as its nature would suggest) computer programmers. Commercially produced sets do now appear sporadically in the western world, but are generally inferior to what anyone with a little imagination can produce at home from materials readily to hand.

Hitherto, Europeans encountering Mancala for the first time in its native habitats tended to regard it as a baffling but trivial local pastime, often remaining unaware of its vast history and oblivious of its depth and subtlety. A reference by Richard Jobson in 1623 describes the social activity rather than the game as such. In 1665 the French traveller Thévenot described a game he encountered in the Levant some 30 years earlier: 'They play Mancala very frequently, which is made in the shape of a box, about two feet long and half a foot wide, with six small holes in the box itself and six in the lid which is hinged to the box (for it opens like a chessboard). Each player has 36 shells, six of which are placed in each hole at the beginning of the game.'[2] In 1694, Hyde[3] gave a detailed description of two forms of Mancala as played in Mesopotamia and Jerusalem from information given him by native players, but too sketchily to be of much practical help. Bell[4] reproduces a late eighteenth-century woodcut by Thomas Bewick showing two Africans with 2×6 board. The earliest sensible appreciation of the game by a westerner occurs in Lane's book[5] on 'modern Egyptians', written in the 1830s. Murray (1952) describes, or at least lists, some 200 varieties of Mancala, but lacked sufficient playing information to classify them satisfactorily. The history, taxonomy, and continued discovery of new varieties are the subject of intense activity at time of writing, making it impractical here to do more than offer a brief survey of characteristic games.

The general principles are best introduced by describing the two forms most widespread in the English-speaking countries of West Africa.

Wari is recorded under the following names by the peoples indicated: *Wari*, sometimes *Woro*, in Senegal (Wolof), Gambia (Mandingo), Guinea (Fulani), Ghana (Ashanti), Gabon, Guyana, Grenada, Barbados, St Lucia, Martinique, Dominica, Antigua, St Kitts, Surinam; *Awèlé* in Guinea (Fulani), Ivory Coast (Kru); *Kboo, Kbo* in Liberia (Gola); *Ayo* or *Ayoayo* in Nigeria (Yoruba); *Kale* in Cameroon (Fang); *Aghi* in Surinam (Aucaner). The following description is from Russ,[6] with additions from Lenox-Smith.[7]

North and South face each other across the shorter axis of a game-board consisting of twelve holes in two rows of six. Each hole is about 5 cm. in diameter and 2.5 cm. deep. The larger hole at each end is a store for captured beans and not part of the playing area. The board is initially dressed with four beans per hole to produce the opening position of Fig. 13.1. I designate this set-up $2 \times 6 \times 4$ (= rows, times holes per row, times beans per hole).

The aim is to win most beans. South starts by lifting all the beans from any hole on his side of the board and 'sowing' them one by one in each successive hole in an anti-clockwise direction. Starting from C, for example, he would sow one each in (D-E-F) on his own side of the board, and (a) on North's side, to produce the position shown in Fig. 13.2. I refer to the last hole of a sowing (in this case (a)) as the drop hole.

North then plays by lifting all the beans from any hole on his own side of the board and sowing them in an anti-clockwise direction as South did. For example, playing from (a) in Fig. 13.2 would produce the position of Fig. 13.3. Each in turn continues sowing all the beans from any hole on his side of the board anti-clockwise one by one in successive holes.

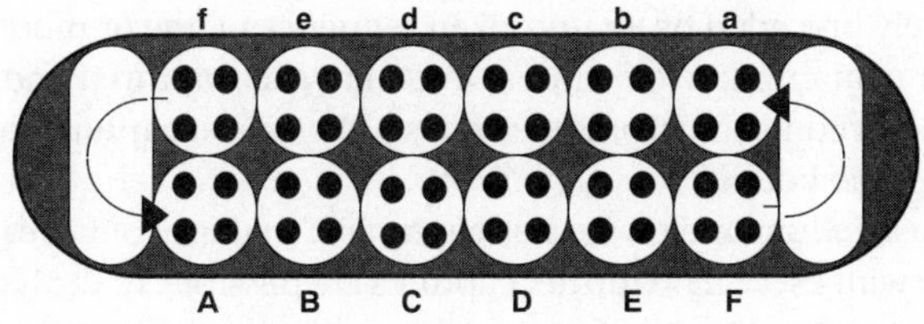

Fig. 13.1. Wari ($2 \times 6 \times 4$): opening position and direction of travel. Each player stores won beans in the large hole at his right.

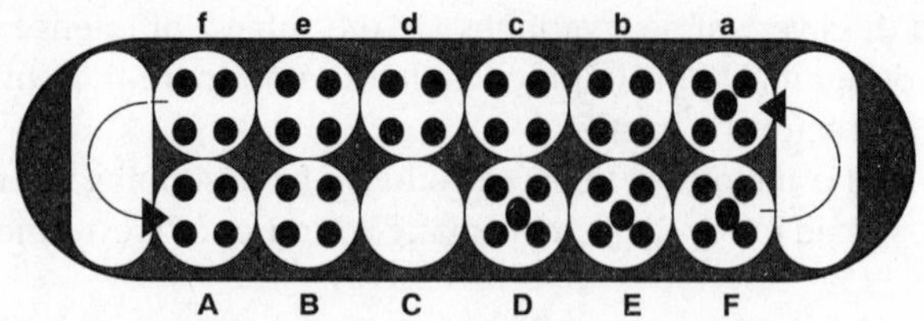

Fig. 13.2. Wari: position after initial sowing from C.

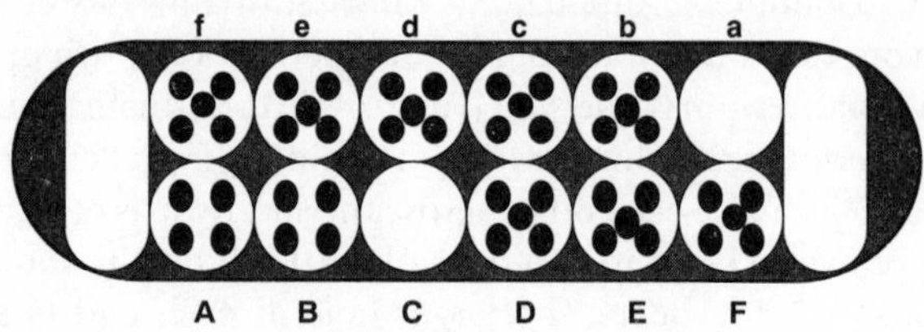

Fig. 13.3. Wari after one sowing each by South and North.

If the lift hole contains twelve or more beans, it is skipped in the sowing, and remains empty throughout that turn of play.

The player may not lift from a hole which would leave no beans in the opponent's sector, thus immobilizing him. If this is impossible, he wins all the uncaptured beans and the game ends. (This is known as 'cutting off the head'.) *Variation*: in some communities, the uncaptured beans are credited to the opponent, or divided equally between them.

Either player may, when about to move, remove the beans from any of his own loaded holes (but not his opponent's) in order to count them. He need not then move from that particular hole.

If the last bean of a sowing drops in a hole on the opponent's side of the board that previously contained one or two beans, the sower captures the two or three resultant beans and adds them to his store. If the drop hole is immediately preceded by an unbroken sequence of one or more opposing holes also containing two or three, these are also captured and placed in store. In no circumstance, however, does a player ever capture beans on his own side of the board.

Play ceases when one player has captured a majority of beans (25 +), or both draw with 24, or if no further captures are possible. In the latter case, if neither player has 25, either the game is drawn, or the uncaptured beans are divided equally among the players, with the odd one going to the player whose sector it is in.

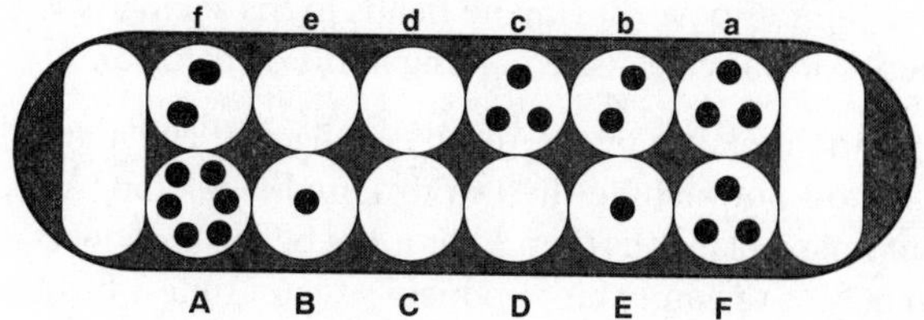

Fig. 13.4. South has sown five beans from (D) and dropped in (c), which previously contained two. He now captures the contents of (c), (b), and (a), but not those in (F), because they are on his own side of the board. He thereby wins eight beans. This leaves North with only one possible move, namely (f) to (A,B), winning two from (B). If then South plays (F) to (c), he will leave singletons in three successive holes, threatening then to play the seven from (A) to (b), thereby winning two each from the last two holes. North might counter this by playing the singleton from (b) to (c), so that South's turn would end with a singleton in (b).

Endodoi is played by the Masai of Kenya and Tanzania. The basic set-up is $2 \times 6 \times 4$ as for Wari, though larger versions also occur (up to $2 \times 10 \times 4$). As above, the aim is to win most beans. See Fig. 13.5.

Each in turn lifts all the beans from any hole in his sector and sows them one at a time in successive holes in an anti-clockwise direction. This constitutes a lap. If the drop hole is already occupied, the player treats it as the lift-hole for another lap of sowing, taking all its contents including the last bean dropped from the previous lap. Play continues in laps until the last bean drops in an empty hole. Now:

If the drop hole lies in the opponent's sector, or if it lies in the player's sector opposite an empty opponent's hole, the turn ends without capture.

If, however, it lies in the player's sector, and the opposite hole on the opponent's sector is not empty, then the player wins the contents of the opposite hole *plus* the capturing singleton from his own sector.

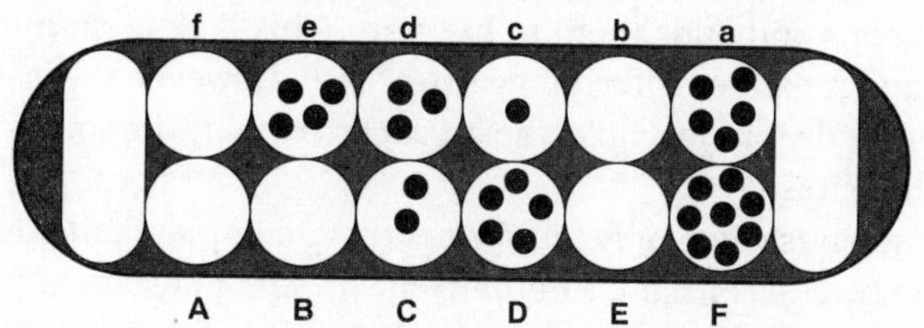

Fig. 13.5. Endodoi. South sows eight from (F), ending in (B), and capturing five from (e) plus the one in (B). If there were only seven in (F), he would win one each from (A) and (f). If he played from (C) or (D), his turn would end without capture.

If a player cannot move, having no beans in his sector, play ceases, and the opponent wins any beans remaining in his own sector.

Ayoayo is a variant played by the Yoruba of Nigeria. The main difference is that captures do not include the last dropped singleton. Also, and as in Wari, the lift hole is skipped when 12 or more beans are sown, and a player may not so play as to empty his opponent's sector unless he has no choice.

Nam-nam (Oware, Adi). The national game of the former Ashanti Kingdom centred on Kumasi, Ghana, has several names, and is also played in Sierra Leone and Nigeria. Lenox-Smith[8] writes:

> The game of Oware, or Nam-nam, is a 'long' one in both senses of the word. The board is 'long', and, if the players are well matched, the game can also be a long one. Indeed, one version of the origin of the name is that a man and a woman once started playing and they eventually decided that they had better get married so that they could continue for as long as they wished. The word Oware is Akan for 'he marries'. How's that for a tip on how to snare your mate?

Distinctive features of this game, which is substantially similar to Adi described by Larry Russ, are the capturing of beans by fours, the winning of holes, and the fact that a whole game usually consists of a series of part-games, of which the initial dressing of the second and subsequent games vary according to the result of the previous one.

The initial set-up is $2 \times 6 \times 4$ and the aim is to win a majority of beans in one game, or over a series.

Each in turn lifts four beans from any hole on his own side of the board and sows them anti-clockwise one at a time in successive holes. If the last bean drops in an empty hole, the lap and the turn end. If not, another lap begins with the two or more beans of the drop-hole, regardless of whose sector it is in. Further laps are played in the same way, ending only when the last bean drops in an empty hole, leaving a singleton.

If, during the course of a lap, a bean is sown in a hole already containing three, the owner of that hole immediately captures and removes the four resultant beans and adds them to his store. This is done in mid-lap, as it happens, and regardless of who the sower is. If, however, the last bean of a lap leaves exactly four in a hole, those four are won by the sower, regardless of whose hole it is.

The round ends when only four beans remain in play, and these are won by the last sower as of right. Alternatively, players may agree to end when eight beans remain but neither has any discernible advantage. In this case, each player adds four of them to his store. The winner is the player who has captured most beans. Alternatively, further rounds may be played as follows.

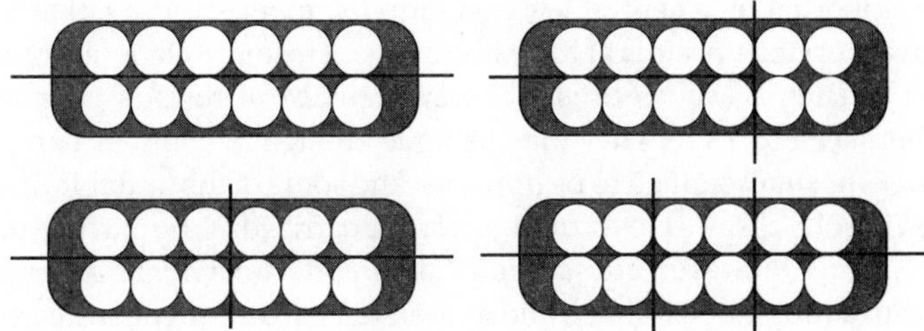

Fig. 13.6. Division of the 2 × 6 board into sections for (respectively) two, three, four, and six players.

If both have the same number of beans (24), the board is dressed and another round played as described above, but starting with the other player. If not, the player with more beans dresses the board with four beans per hole, starting with the leftmost hole on his own side of the board and continuing in an anticlockwise direction. The other player similarly fills the remaining holes with the beans he has won. In the ensuing round each player 'owns' all the holes he was initially able to fill, so that the winner's 'side' of the board may include one or more holes originally belonging to his opponent. With this proviso, another round is played as described above, starting with the opponent of the player who went first before. Play continues until one player owns all the holes on the board, or the other concedes defeat.

Three, four, or six may play, each on their own account. The twelve holes are divided into the appropriate number of sections as shown in Fig. 13.6. Each player 'owns' one of the sections, and must always start a move from a hole in that section. Play is always anti-clockwise.

Theme and variations

Mancala games are extremely numerous, varied, and fecund in gaming ideas. Before describing further examples, it may help to survey the range of variability and propose a convenient terminology.

Boards. Physically, the simplest and most ephemeral boards are made by scooping holes in the ground, or even chalking them on a hard surface. The most permanent are made by carving or incising in fixed natural features. Murray[9] refers to boards cut in projecting tree-roots in Nigeria, and into rocks by the roadside in Ethiopia and Angola. Portable boards are typically carved from wood, often from a single piece. Many take the form of a small table supported by a central leg or plinth, its upper surface either flat or concave (curving upwards at the extremities). The more elaborate ones are carved in such a way as to give the appearance of rows of cups joined together (see Fig. 13.7). They may be large enough to count as part of the furniture, or small enough to be portable, and some of the portable ones are hinged in such a way as to form a box for the carriage of the playing-pieces. Bush Negroes, however, are said to disdain perfect carving: they prefer to start with a rough-hewn shape and allow it to be worn smooth by caressing hands in the due course of time. In the West Indies there is or was a superstition to the effect that making boards was a spiritually dangerous activity, and its practice was restricted to elderly widowers—who are, however, in the nature of things, likely to have been not only the best craftsmen, but also very adept at maintaining the restrictive powers of superstition.[10]

In most games each half of the board is regarded as belonging to the player sitting on that side. He must begin sowing from his own sector, loses beans by capture from it, and, in some versions, loses the game if his sector is emptied, or reduced to one bean per hole. For convenience, the holes in South's sector are designated by upper-case letters (A, B, C...) from left to right, and in North's by minuscules (a, b, c...) from North's left to right. I use the terms lift-hole and drop-hole for the first and last holes of a sowing, and 'vulnerable' for a hole whose contents can thereby be captured, or the contents themselves.

The 2×6 board is the commonest format throughout the Mancala-playing world, but other games vary from 2×3 for the simplest to as many as 50 for team play. Two-row boards normally incorporate recep-

Fig. 13.7. Mancala boards (from Murray). *Above*: Wari board, West Africa. *Below*: Ayo board, Nigeria.

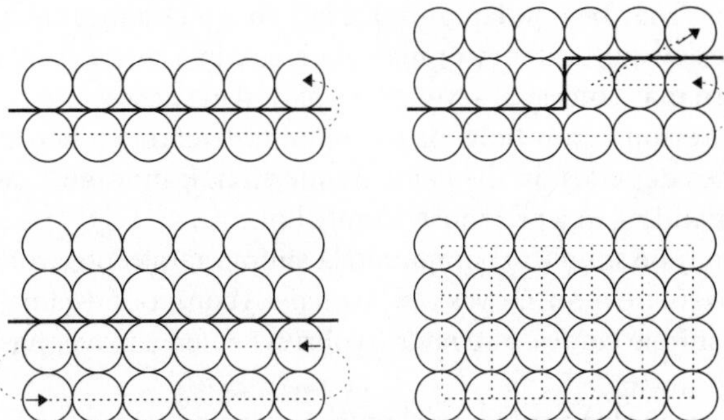

Fig. 13.8. Mancala boards of two, three, and four rows. Stores are not shown. The number of holes per row varies from four to twelve or more. The thick line separates South's sector from North's, the broken line shows South's direction of sowing (assuming anti-clockwise play). In the three-row board, sowing jumps from centre to top right. In the double four-row (African), each sows only in his own sector. In four-player Dongjintian, there are no personal sectors and sowing is virtually unconstrained.

tacles for storing the beans won in play, and these have sometimes been drafted in as part of the playing area, notably in some games of Malaysia, Indonesia, and the Philippines. Some boards have three or four rows. Those with three are essentially two-row games with half of each row doubled over into the middle. Those with four fall into two quite distinct classes. In simple four-row games each player sows over the whole board, whereas in double four-row games each sows only in his own sector. (See Fig. 13.8.) In both, however, the two rows on each player's side constitute his sector for the purposes of lifting and vulnerability.

Pieces. The playing-pieces may consist of any objects of suitable shape and size and reasonable uniformity—nuts, beans, shards, sticks, pebbles, cowries, goat dung, whatever may be to hand. A common object in western Africa is the Mulacca Bean or Nicker Nut (*Caesalpinia bondue*). Commercial products tend to provide wooden marbles or suchlike—a great mistake, as they are too easily dropped and lost. I have one such game made of highly polished wood, but the board is too small, the holes too shallow, and the beans too small and too perfectly spherical. As Lenox-Smith observes, 'It is not sufficiently realised that much of the pleasure of the game lies in the skill of handling the playing pieces; this is not a factor in Chess or Draughts, for instance, and is not something which is usually considered.'

Play. Games may be one-lap or multi-lap. In a one-lap game, a turn consists of one sowing, and may or may not result in a capture. In a multi-lap game, a turn may consist of several laps played in succession, each starting from the previous drop-hole, or the one immediately following it. What ends a series depends on the game in question: it may, for example, be a capture, or ending in a previously empty hole.

Games may be simple or compound. A simple game ends when all beans are captured or no more moves can be made. A compound game consists of a series of simple games, and ends (typically) when a player has reached a given score.

The object of play may be to capture a simple majority of beans, or to reach a target total of captures over as many games as it takes, or to leave one's opponent with no beans in his sector or otherwise immobilized. In some games not only beans but also holes can be won. Won holes become part of their winner's sector, and a player wins by leaving his opponent no territory to play from.

Constraint may be attached to the choice of lift-hole. Some require lifting from a specified hole. Some forbid sowing a singleton, or sowing in such a way as to leave no beans in the opponent's sector; others account this a win.

The direction of play is typically to the right (anti-clockwise). But some require play to the left; some allow sowing in either direction ad lib; and some require play to the right from right-hand holes and to the left from left-hand, with a free choice for the central hole if there is an odd number.

Methods of capture are equally varied. Vulnerability may attach to the drop-hole, to all holes immediately preceding it, to the one following it, to holes opposite the drop hole on the other side of the board, to holes containing exactly four beans, and so on.[11]

Most boards contain two larger holes, one at each end, and designated stores. Each player stores his won beans in one store, usually the one on his right. In most games the stores are not included in the sowing, but in some games they are, and in some of these (but not all) they can be rendered vulnerable.

In short, practically every variation one can think of playing on the basic rules has already been thought of, and is quite customary in a particular locality. Yet other variations may remain to be discovered.

Origins and Nature of the Game

Rows of holes suggesting Mancala games are of great antiquity. Many have been found carved on slabs in ancient Egyptian structures, including the temple of Kurna, the Ptolemaic great Pylon at Karnak, at Luxor and

Memphis, and in the pyramid of Cheops. Some in Sri Lanka date from the second to fourth centuries BC, though doubt has been cast on their actual function. Some 2 × 13 boards found in Kenya were declared by Richard Leakey to be Neolithic. Fragments of stone boards for what looks like the game of Hus have been found in excavations of Zimbabwe civilization of 1450–1800.[12] Remains of Mancala-like gaming surfaces have been found in the Sahara dating from about 3000 BC, when that area was fertile plain.[13] The conceptual (as opposed to geographical) origins of Mancala offer a subject for speculation yet to be crystallized into hypothesis. Murray, who classifies games by reference to their 'real life' basis, ignores, rather surprisingly, the literal process of sowing beans or seeds in holes in the ground. Indeed, he goes so far as to say that 'they form a special class of board-games, and . . . do not exemplify any of the more ordinary activities of early man'. The only other parallel that has been hinted arises from the suggestion that some of the apparent boards carved in stone on ancient sites may in fact have been forms of abacus, or aids to counting or making payments. From the purely gaming viewpoint, no one has (to my knowledge) commented on the remarkable similarity of Mancala to Backgammon, or Tables in general. Either can be played, after a fashion, with the equipment of the other. Mancala could almost be characterized as an extension of Backgammon without dice, or Backgammon as an extension of Mancala *with* dice.

Mancala is a game of perfect information, perfect equality, much freedom of significant choice, and hence great skill. Westerners will assume at first sight that one player, probably the first to move, has a certain win or at least a draw, and that the play will be slow and drawn-out as each in turn considers every possible move and as many branches down the resultant strategy tree as the human brain can manage. It is obviously ideal for computer analysis, and researches along this line suggest that a complete solution is imminent.[14] Some might eschew Mancala on the ground that it lacks, on one hand, the random elements of Bridge and Backgammon which render them amenable to intuitive play, and, on the other, the two-dimensional structure of Chess which poses more of a challenge to intellectual analysis. The complexity of Chess lies in its depth, that of Mancala in its length. What the westerner tends to ignore, however, is the value of games as a form of social bonding and mental recreation. In fact, native practitioners of Mancala play at surprising speed, and experts with deadly accuracy. Even without counting the contents of the most heavily loaded holes, many have a knack of unerringly selecting the best line of play from what appears to be the benefit of intuition derived from experience. To play at the sloth of Chess is to miss the point of the game. As our epigraph shows, the play of Mancala, at least in Africa, is a social activity, to which bystanders contribute so substantially that it is sometimes impossible to distinguish players from kibitzers. Some of the larger and more elaborate games are indeed played by two teams commanding either side of a particularly long board. Against this background, however, Lenox-Smith regretfully notes that 'cultured' West Africans nowadays tend to regard Mancala as a game for children and peasants, and that some of the boards commercially available in large towns are of the wrong size or feel, suggesting that their producers have lost touch with their cultural roots. This will be recognized as a well-known social phenomenon in any country dominated by one (in this case 'The West') whose culture is perceived as more advantageous and hence more worthy of emulation.

In Syria, Egypt, and West Africa generally, Mancala is played by men, women, and children. Men usually play only with men, and women with women. Among the Tamils of south India, in Sri Lanka, Malaysia, Indonesia, and the Philippines, Mancala is predominantly a women's game and only played by men in less civilized or more remote regions. In central, east, and southern Africa, four-row Mancala is almost entirely a man's game. As Driberg says: 'women very rarely play and then only among themselves, and they play it not with much skill or enjoyment, but apparently in more trivial moods, inconsequentially, in the interval of gossip.'[15] In a study of Wari in the New World, Herskovits[16] asserts that the game is played mostly by men, but that there are also strong women players, whom the men will not take on for fear of losing the game and thereby losing face. They play for amusement and prestige, not for money; but there is also a religious dimension to the game. It is played in Houses of Mourning to amuse the spirit of the dead awaiting burial—but only by daylight, for nightfall brings with it the danger that Yorkas (spirits of dead) might carry the players off.

Further Examples

Pallanguli (Bell[17]), **Pallam Kuzhi, Pallamkurie** (Russ[18]) is played by the Tamil women of Southern India and Sri Lanka, sometimes also by men as a gambling game. The set-up is $2 \times 7 \times 6$ or $2 \times 7 \times 4$ and the game is multi-lap and multi-round. Captures are made by fours, as in Nam-Nam, but the method of sowing is characteristically Asian, in that the lift-hole for each succeeding lap is that following the last drop-hole (drop + 1) and not the drop-hole itself. Specifically:

- If drop + 1 is not empty, sowing continues therefrom.

- If it is empty, the sower captures all the beans in drop + 2, and continues play from the first loaded hole lying beyond that, regardless of its position.
- If drop + 1 and drop + 2 are both empty, the turn ends without capture.
- If any hole is raised from three to four beans in course of sowing, its owner immediately captures those four. Four in a hole constitute a 'cow'.

At the end of the first round, each player takes her captured beans and fills the holes on her side of the board, six in each, as before. If any remain after seven holes are filled, they are returned to her store of winnings. Any holes the loser cannot fill to six are designated 'rubbish holes' and flagged with a piece of stick. In succeeding rounds of play, rubbish holes are ignored. Further rounds ensue, and the game ends when one player has five rubbish holes and cannot even fill the sixth. It is possible, however, for a player with one or more rubbish holes to win so great an excess of beans as to be able to open them up and eventually turn the tables. This can make for a very long game.

Gabata (Russ[19]) is a three-row game played in Ethiopia, Tigre province. The format is $3 \times 6 \times 3$, and each in turn sows from his own sector as shown in Fig. 13.9.

- If the last bean drops in an empty hole the turn ends without capture.
- If it drops in an opponent's hole containing three beans, making four, the sower acquires ownership of that hole, marks it in some way, and ends his turn without capture. Such a hole is called a *wegue*. The first player may not make a *wegue* on his opening move. On subsequent turns, a player may not start sowing from a *wegue* belonging to either player.

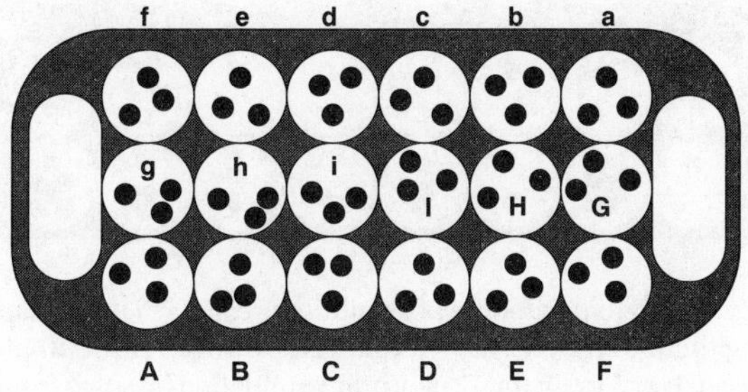

Fig. 13.9. Gabata. South plays (A–I), (a–i), (A–I), and so on.

- If the last bean drops in a *wegue* belonging to the sower (on the opponent's side of the board), the turn ends without capture.
- If it drops into a *wegue* belonging to the opponent (on the sower's side), the sower captures the dropped bean and one other from it (if any remain), and sows again from any non-*wegue* hole on his own side.
- A player who cannot make a legal move must pass.

Play continues until both pass, whereupon each wins all the beans remaining in his own *wegue* (plural). Further rounds may be played. In this case the player with a majority of beans fills his own holes with three each and continues with three each in his opponent's holes from (a/A) on. If fewer than three remain for the last hole, one or two are contributed by the opponent. All those to which he contributed three or two beans now count as part of his sector for the ensuing round. The opening move alternates from round to round. The game ends when one player, at the end of a round, has fewer than three beans left.

Hus. This four-row Hottentot game is played in Zaire. Bell's account[20] followed here differs slightly from Russ's description of Namibian Hus.[21]

Format 4 × 8 × 2. The aim is to immobilize one's opponent. A match is best of seven (first to four). The first to move is always decided by lot. Each player plays only within his own sector—the two rows on his own side of the board—and all play is clockwise. Thus, in the diagram (Fig. 13.10) South plays from (A) to (P) and North from (a) to (p). Captured beans are not

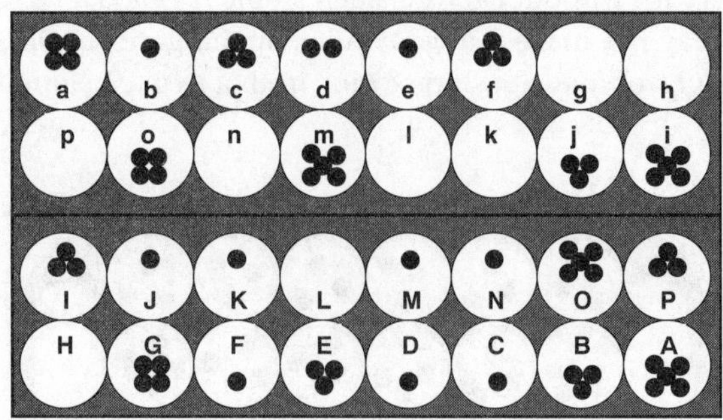

Fig. 13.10. Hus. South to play. Some possibilities are: (A) = 5 to (F), capturing 3 from (c) and playing them to (I), etc.; (B) = 3 to (E), capturing 2 from (d) plus 5 from (m) plus any other, such as 5 in (i); the 12 captures would then be sown from (F), leaving a singleton in (B) and so ending the turn; (E) = 3 to (H), ending the turn. (G) = 4 to (K), 2 to (M), 2 to (O), 7 to (F) capturing 3 in (c) and sowing 3 to (I), etc.

removed from the board but transferred from the opponent's to one's own side of the board for continued play by the capturer.

- Each in turn sows from any hole in his sector containing at least two beans.
- If the last bean falls in an empty hole, leaving a singleton, the turn ends.
- If it falls in a loaded hole, its contents are lifted and sown in the same way. But:
- If it falls in a loaded hole in the outer row (A–H, a–h), and the diametrically opposite hole in the opponent's outer row is loaded, the sower captures all those in the opponent's equivalent hole and continues sowing on his own side of the board with them instead of with the contents of the last hole he sowed to. A single turn may yield several such captures. Furthermore:
- If the opponent's corresponding hole on his inner row (I–P, i–p) is also loaded, the sower takes not only those of that outer hole but also those of the inner hole and those of any hole he chooses in the opponent's sector. He then continues sowing in his own sector with them instead of with the contents of the preceding drop hole.

Play ends when one player has only singletons, or no beans at all, in which case he loses double.

Dongjintian is one of several games from Yunnan Province described by Vernon Eagle.[22] A distinctive feature of these Chinese games is that laps continue from the post-ultimate hole (drop + 1) in the direction of play. If it is empty, the sower captures the contents of drop + 2 together with those of consecutive loaded holes ahead of it. If drop + 2 also is empty, he captures the contents of drop+ 3 and all consecutively alternating holes ahead of it (+ 5, + 7 etc). Only if the drop is followed by two empty holes does the turn end. Games of this type, which Eagle designates Pussa Kanawa from its proposed genotype, are known from Vietnam, Thailand, India, Pakistan, Sri Lanka, Somalia, and Ethiopia. Dongjintian is played by two in a 2 × 5 × 5 format, but its four-hand version uses a 4 × 5 × 5 format with extraordinary fluidity of play, in that each in turn may play from any hole on the board, without restriction. As to the direction of sowing, Eagle's instructions are:

> The first stone may be sown in any hole horizontally or vertically neighbouring the hole being played; subsequently stones are sown forward, left or right, but may not double back. Thus if a corner hole is lifted it may be sown in two directions; if one of the ten holes on the edges of the board which are not corners are [*sic*] played there are

three possible directions, and if one of the middle six holes is lifted, there are four possible directions. If a stone has been sown in a corner, edge, or middle hole and there remain stones to be sown, there are respectively one, two, or three possible choices for the hole in which to sow the next stone. This results in a huge number of possible moves. For example, if four stones are lifted from one of the holes diagonally neighboring a corner, there are 52 different ways in which they can be sown.

It will be seen that this virtually converts the game from a one-dimensional linear to a two-dimensional reticular format.

NOTES

1. Also Mankala, Manqala, Mangala. Manqala is technically the best transliteration from Arabic, but Mancala, used by Hyde in his (Latin) study of 1694, is too well established to justify rejection. Murray says it is accented on the first syllable in Syria, the second in Egypt.
2. Jean de Thévenot, *Voyages* (Paris, 1665), cited by Murray, *History of Board Games.*
3. Hyde, *De Ludis Orientalibus* (1694).
4. Bell, *Board and Table Games*, ii. 71.
5. Edward William Lane, *An Account of the Manners and Customs of the Modern Egyptians* (London, 1836), 344–52.
6. From Larry Russ, *Mancala Games* (Hoboken, 1995), 14–15, who also includes authorities.
7. In *Games & Puzzles*, 26 (July 1974), Lenox-Smith describes Wari under the name Ayo, and vice versa. Ayo, however, means 'game' or 'play', and implies any variety of Mancala.
8. Ian Lenox-Smith, 'Mancala' (Part 2), *Games & Puzzles*, 1st ser. 27 (Aug. 1974), 16–17.
9. Murray, *History of Board Games*, 160.
10. Bell, *Board and Table Games from Many Civilisations*, i. 122.
11. These are detailed in Philip Townshend, *Games in Culture: A Contextual Analysis of the Swahili Board Games and its Relevance to Variation in African Mankala* (Ph.D. thesis, University of Cambridge, Department of Social Anthropology, 1986). I regret that I was unable to consult this in time.
12. Grunfeld, *Games of the World* (UNICEF, Zurich, 1982), 20.
13. Found by Henri Lhôte; see Lhôte, 100.
14. Awari ranks a little lower in terms of game-tree complexity, and a little higher in terms of state-space complexity, than Nine Men's Morris, putting it on a par with Draughts and somewhat lower than Othello. See L. V. Allis, 'Beating the World Champion: the State of the Art in Computer Game Playing', in *New Approaches to Board Game Research* (IIAS, Leiden, 1995), 155–75.
15. This paragraph is from Murray *History of Board Games*, 159, and J. H. Driberg is the author of 'The Game of Choro or Pereaüni', in *Man*, 27 (1921). Grunfeld, *Games of the World*, illustrates the four-row game of Hus with a photograph of women at play.
16. Herskovits, 'Wari in the New World', *Journal of the Royal Anthropological Institute*, 42 (1923), 23–37.
17. Bell, *Board and Table Games from Many Civilisations*, i. 115, citing H. G. Durai, 'Pallanguli', *Man* (Nov. 1928), 185, and a personal communication of 1957.
18. Russ, *Mancala Games*, 58–60.

19. Ibid. 68–9.
20. Bell, *Board and Table Games from Many Civilisations*, ii. 75–7, itself based on P. A. Wagner, 'A Contribution to our Knowledge of the National Game and Skill of Africa', *Trans. Royal Society of South Africa*, (1917–18), 47–68, and plates xiii–xvii. Also in Grunfeld, *Games of the World*, 24, probably based on Bell. Bell describes another four-row game, Mangola, also played in Zaire (but not indigenous to it), in *Games & Puzzles*, 1st ser. no. 46 (March 1976), 4–5.
21. Russ, 87.
22. Vernon A. Eagle, 'On some newly discovered Mancala games from Yunnan . . .', *New Approaches to Board Game Research* (IIAS, Leiden, 1995), 48–62; the quotation is from p. 57.

War and Pieces

Games of Material Capture

A war game is one in which two players direct a conflict between two armies of equal strength upon a field of battle, circumscribed in extent and offering no advantage of ground to either army.

H. J. R. Murray

'Tis all a Chequer-board of Nights and Days
Where Destiny with Men for Pieces plays:
  Hither and thither moves, and mates, and slays,
And one by one back in the Closet lays.

Edward Fitzgerald (*The Rubáiyát of Omar Khayyam*)

'War games' is the well-established term for those in which the primary object is to capture material. The winner is he who captures and removes from the board all his opponent's forces, or so many of them as to render even an equalizing recovery impossible, as at Draughts; or who, as at Chess, succeeds in capturing a principal piece of game-determining value. In some respects, however, the term is unsatisfactory. For one thing, it is ambiguous, being used also for thematic board games which purport to simulate actual wars and historical battles in a deliberately realistic way. For another, it is a label based on cultural analogy rather than one that accurately indicates the formal mechanism of play. Hence, for a third, it fails to embrace Mancala games, which are also won by capturing the greater amount of material. I would prefer to categorize games of material capture as 'displace games', which both expresses the defining activity and chimes in with my other proposed super-family headings of race games and space games (and chase games, which are a hybrid of space and displace games).

Nevertheless, now that Mancala has been dealt with, there is no point in not referring to the residue of displace games as war games, provided that a distinction is borne in mind between the traditional abstract and symbolic games considered in these chapters and the historically recent class of military theme games to be considered later.

In symbolic war games, then, each of two players (rarely more) directs a force of equal strength and composition to that of his opponent; each army is disposed in a fixed opening position on a bilaterally symmetrical board; the play involves movement and capture but rarely placement; the two make alternate moves, neither side enjoying any advantage other than that of moving first; and the game is one of perfect information throughout. Individual variants may deviate from one or more of these features without falling out of the classification. It would be unreasonable, for example, to exclude from the Chess group such fundamental variations as Kriegspiel (Blind Chess) or four-player dice-chess.

Murray classifies war games primarily by the method of capture and secondarily by the method of movement, and then adds some families of games not well included in either of the foregoing, producing the following arrangement:

Custodian capture, orthogonal moves (Latrunculi, etc.)
Custodian capture, diagonal moves (some New World games)
Leaping capture, move on the lines, i.e. reticular (Alquerque, etc.)
Leaping capture, diagonal moves (Draughts etc.)
Leaping capture, orthogonal moves (Dama, Siga, etc.)
Replacement capture (Chess, Rithmomachy)
Withdrawal capture (Fanorona)
Territorial games (Go, Reversi, etc.)
Blockade games (Do-guti, etc.)
Clearance games (Solitaire)
Lot games (Tab)

Bell implicitly follows much the same pattern, but simplifies them into the Latrunculi, Alquerque, Draughts, Tafl, and Chess groups, rejecting others from the war-game category, but adding a class of 'running fight' games such as Tablan and Puluc.

For the purpose of this survey I exclude from the war-game category territorial, blockade, and clearance games, having already classified them as 'space' games, and also Tafl, whose characteristic asymmetry classes it as a 'chase' game. As to the remainder, classification by mode of capture is not without merit, but the distinction between orthogonal and diagonal movement is hardly definitive, since either can be translated into the other by changing the design of the board, and many games include both. In any case, different classifications can be made according to the relative importance attached to different gaming features. Displace games may, for example, be classified by:

pieces — neutral (completely undifferentiated), e.g. Mancala
undifferentiated (except by ownership), e.g. Siga
differentiated (by function/power/value):
  by promotion, e.g. Draughts
  by definition, e.g. Chess

movement orthogonal, diagonal, compound ('hippogonal')
capture custodianship, jumping, replacement, etc.; single or multiple; immediate or delayed
determination capture all opposing pieces; capture most of them; capture figurehead

A fully worked out structural classification would thus need to be multi-dimensional, and hence unwieldy for the present survey. For this purpose it must suffice to allot Draughts and Chess a chapter each, and to divide this one between linear and basic two-dimensional games.

Linear War Games

It is tempting to perceive primitive linear war games as representing a stage in the conceptual evolution of areal war games from linear race games. Murray, in fact, classifies Boolik as a race game, but the object is clearly to capture pieces rather than to get home, and Bell more accurately characterizes it as a running-fight game.

Boolik (Murray, from Culin), and **Puluc** (Bell,[1] from Sapper), are substantially similar games, or varying descriptions of the same game, played by the Kekchi of North Guatemala, a tribe descended from the Maya.

Culin's correspondent T. J. Collins said it was common in the outlying districts, and was usually played at night 'by the light of the fire', a feature which one hopes will be incorporated as a requirement into the official laws of the World Boolik Federation, should such a body ever see the light of day (or fire).

The track is a line of fourteen spaces marked by setting fifteen corn cobs in a row. Two players or teams each start with five distinctive pieces in hand. Movement is governed by four binary lots consisting of ears of corn blackened on one side and plain on the other. The values are:

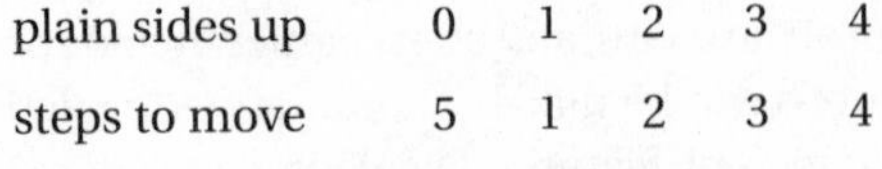

plain sides up	0	1	2	3	4
steps to move	5	1	2	3	4

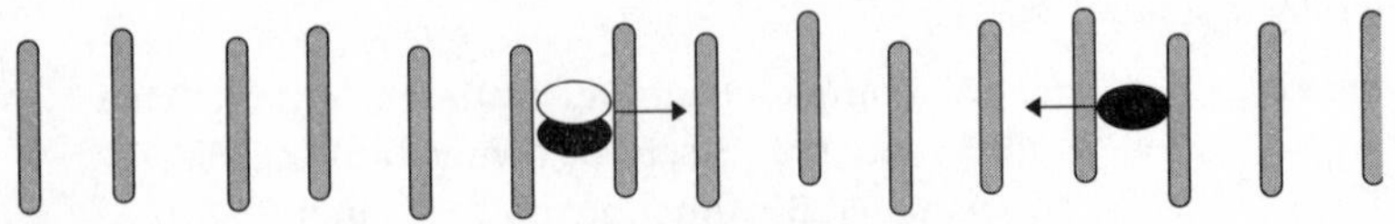

Fig. 14.1. Boolik (Puluc). White has made a temporary capture, entitling Black to enter another piece.

Whoever throws higher moves first. Each in turn throws the lots twice, adds the totals, and either enters a piece that distance from his start, or moves it that distance if it is already in play. One player starts from the right and moves leftwards, the other vice versa. If a piece lands in a space occupied by an enemy piece, it captures it, but must then reverse direction and carry it back home before removing it from the board and setting out again. The opponent, meanwhile, may then enter another piece.

A capturer carrying a captive forms a compound piece belonging to the former's owner. If a piece lands on a space occupied by a compound belonging to the opponent, it captures that compound and starts moving it back again. A compound may therefore keep increasing and changing direction, until its current owner gets it home and unloads the enemy captives. If a piece reaches the further end without capturing or being captured, it is returned to hand and may be entered again. A piece may not land on a space occupied by a piece or compound of its own side.

'The game lasts from one to three hours [says Collins, unsurprisingly] and is ended when one side has no more counters to enter (*laex chixgunil xa guak*, you have eaten all).'

Tab, an Egyptian game described by Hyde in 1694, Lane in 1890, and (more lucidly) by Bell[2] in 1979, amounts to a more elaborate version of the same thing. Murray ascribes it also to Arabia, Turkey, and Iran, and describes related games played in various African countries. The board consists of four rows of square cells and almost any odd number of columns.

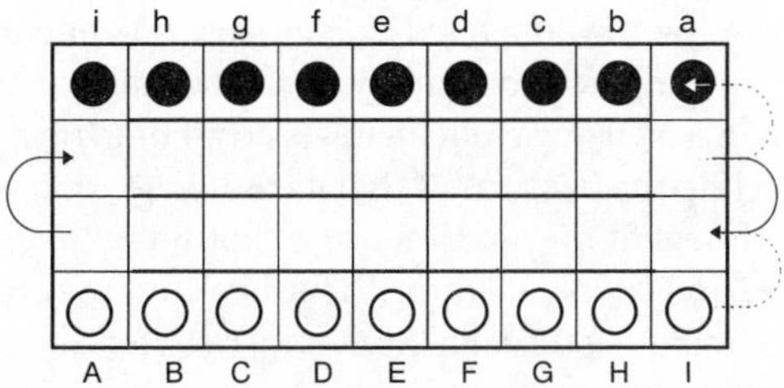

Fig. 14.2. Tab. South enters his dogs in order from (I) to (A) into the central rows, where they continue to circulate clockwise. On one occasion only, White may enter a dog or team into Black's home row as shown by the upper dotted arrow. Having once passed through this row it must return to the central rows and there circulate for the rest of the game. Corresponding rules apply to North.

Black and White each start with nine pieces ('dogs') on the upper and lower rows of a board of four rows of nine. Each in turn throws four binary lots, consisting of split sticks about 12 cm. long, against a wall or an upright stick in the ground, and moves one of his dogs forwards according to this schedule:

flat sides up	0	1	2	3	4
score	6+	1+	2	3	4+

A throw of 1 is a *tab*. Each in turn casts the lots until one throws a tab. That player starts and the tab counts as part of his first turn. He, and each in turn thereafter, makes a series of throws so long as the result is a 1, 4, or 6, but stops as soon as a 2 or a 3 turns up. The overall total specifies the distance to move in that turn. On his first turn he must move the dog at the extreme right of his home line. In subsequent turns, throwing a tab entitles him to move the next dog along to the left, and so on. So long as dogs remain in their home row they are called Christians; once they have entered the central rows they are converted to Muslims.

A dog makes a distinct move for each of the numbers thrown, but (as in Backgammon) may take them in any order. For example, a player throwing 1-4-2 may move 1-4-2, 1-2-4, 2-1-4, 2-4-1, 4-1-2 or 4-2-1 ad lib. Such choice enables him to make captures, since any step of the move that brings his dog to a square occupied by an enemy dog entitles him to capture and remove it from the board. (It also enables him to make, or avoid, 'harnessing' moves—see below.) Moves may be split between several dogs. Tabs need not be used when thrown but may be noted for future reference and cashed at a more profitable time.

Muslims continue circulating clockwise in the two central rows. However, at the end of the second row a Muslim may turn anti-clockwise into the opponent's home row, provided that at least one enemy dog remains there. A player who enters a dog into the back row must leave it in position so long as any of his own dogs remain in his own home row. The advantage of moving a dog into the back row is that it cannot be captured so long as it remains there, though it may itself make a capture in that row. A dog that has once entered and circulated through the back row may not re-enter, but must continue circulating through the central rows for the rest of the game. In no circumstance may a dog re-enter its own home row. (Apostasy is forbidden. A Muslim may not reconvert to a Christian.)

When a dog lands on a square occupied by a friendly dog, the two are automatically harnessed together and move thereafter as a team. The same occurs when a team lands on a single friendly dog, or vice versa. A team of two or more dogs must move as a singleton, but a team can be unharnessed in two ways. First, throwing a tab (1) entitles a player to move the top dog of a team, thereby unharnessing it and converting it to a singleton. Second, if a team passes into a row through which it or any of its members have already circulated, it is automatically unharnessed and the pieces played off it separately, though they may be reharnessed on a subsequent occasion.

Play continues in the central rows until one player wins by capturing his opponent's last remaining dog.

Tablan, evidently related to Tab, is described by Bell[3] as a traditional game still played in certain villages of Mysore.

Black and White start with twelve pieces arranged in a line on their own home row of a board of twelve columns and four rows. The aim is to be the first to transfer all one's own pieces to the opponent's home row, not necessarily in order, though it may be agreed that occupation should take place in order (a–l). Since captures are involved, the winner is the player who achieves this with the larger number of pieces, or, if equal, who does so first. Pieces are not moved forwards; instead, each moves his pieces from his own left to right (a–l) in the first and third rows and from right to left in the second and fourth (boustrophedon movement). Pieces of opposite colour therefore find themselves meeting head-on in course of play. A capture is made by landing on an enemy piece by an exact move and removing it from the board, but neither player may capture on his own back row.

Movement is governed by four dicing sticks blank on one side and painted on the other. A player keeps throwing and moving until he throws two or three plain sides up, which ends his turn. A throw of one plain side is required to start. This confers a move of two steps, which may be made by one piece or split between two. Subsequent throws may similarly be taken whole or piecemeal. Two pieces may not occupy the same square. Once a piece has reached the back row it may not be moved further. Every throw must be taken if possible.

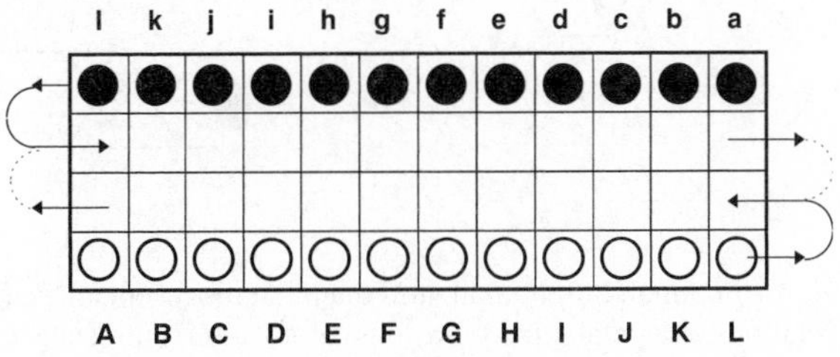

Fig. 14.3. Tablan.

plain sides up	0	1	2	3	4
steps to move	12+	2+	0	0	8+

Tablan is both a war game and a game of traversal, but the former predominates, in that a completed traversal merely ends the game, while the win is determined by the amount of material captured.

Movement in Two Dimensions

Before exploring two-dimensional war games it is desirable to establish a terminology of movement and capture, as a surprising amount of confusion, ambiguity, and inconsistency is exhibited in the existing literature of games. Even Murray falls into the trap of relating orthogonal and diagonal to the orientation of the board on the page rather than the cells on the board.[4]

On a reticular board, such as that of Alquerque, movement takes place along marked lines, rendering directional terminology unnecessary. On a cellular board, however, where pieces move from cell to cell:

Orthogonal describes a move in which a piece, travelling in straight line through the centres of two or more connected cells, crosses each successive border at right angles to it. (The word derives from roots meaning 'right angle'.)

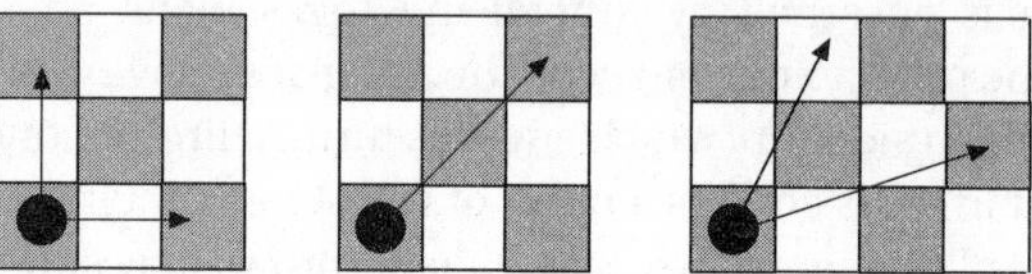

Fig. 14.4. Orthogonal, diagonal, and two types of hippogonal move (m = 1/2, m = 1/3) on a squared board.

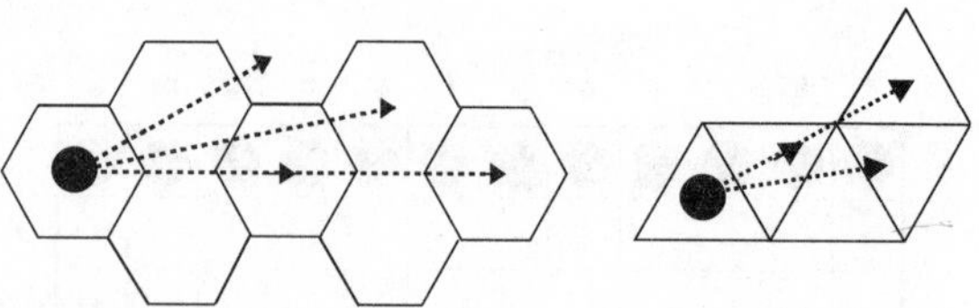

Fig. 14.5. *Left*: Orthogonal, hippogonal, and diagonal moves on a hexagonal board. On such tesselations, diagonal moves may pass along intervening edges. *Right*: On a triangular board, a straight line passing through centre-points only (upper line) is alternately orthogonal and diagonal. The lower line is a hippogonal equivalent.

Diagonal describes a move in which a piece, travelling in straight line through the centres of two or more connected cells, exits and enters each successive cell through a corner, thereby bisecting it. (The word derives from roots meaning 'through [the] angle'.)

Hippogonal is a term I propose (no other being current) for a compound move such as that of the Chess knight. (The first element is from *hippos*, 'horse'.)

Many varieties of Chess feature pieces with moves differing from those of International Chess. For example, the Japanese Chu-Shogi includes a piece called the horned falcon, whose move is described as 'any distance in all directions except vertically forwards and backwards; a leap to second square vertically forwards'. To avoid such circumlocutions, I propose an algebraic notation of the form m = {*expression*}, where 'm' is 'move' and the expression is composed of the following elements:

1 a distance of one (i.e. to the adjacent square or point)
2 a distance of two (squares or points in the same direction)
n any distance in a given direction
✱ orthogonally or diagonally (any of eight directions)
+ orthogonally (any of four directions)
> orthogonally forwards
< orthogonally backwards
÷ orthogonally sideways
<> orthogonally forwards or backwards (but not sideways)
>÷ orthogonally forwards or sideways (but not backwards)
<÷ orthogonally backwards or sideways (but not forwards)
× diagonally (any of four directions)
×> diagonally forwards (not backwards)
×< diagonally backwards (not forwards)

On this basis, the orthodox Chess king moves (1(✱), queen (n(✱), bishop (n×), rook (n+), pawn (1>) with the option of (2>) initially, and horned falcon (n÷x, 2>). The last could be expanded to (n ÷x, 2>, 0<) to make quite clear that one direction of travel— orthogonally backwards—is forbidden.

Hippogonal moves are expressed as two orthogonal moves connected by a slash or solidus. The knight's move, for example, is m = 1/2. A move consisting of a series of such steps concludes with an ampersand—thus the move of the nightrider in Fairy Chess is m = (1/2&). In Shogi, the *kei-ma*, or honourable horse, moves like a knight but must end on a square in advance of its starting-point. Obviously, this is expressed as m = (1/2>). In some games, a hippogonal piece cannot move if the intermediate space is occupied. This may be expressed by doubling the solidus. Thus a piece with the move of a Chess knight but constrained in this way would be expressed 1//2.

Methods of Capture

The following terms are customary for methods of capture.

Replacement (or *displacement*). A piece captures by moving on to a square occupied by an enemy piece and removing it from the board, as in Chess.

Leap (or *jump*). A piece captures an adjacent enemy piece by passing over it in a straight line and landing on the immediately following square in line of travel, which must be vacant. This is the *short leap* characteristic of Draughts or Checkers. Only three squares are involved: the point of departure, the occupied square leapt over, and the point of arrival on the other side. The *line leap* is the same, but captures two or more enemy pieces in an unbroken line between the points of departure and arrival, as in Reversi. In the *long leap*, any number of vacant squares may lie on either side of the piece captured, as in Dama (Turkish Draughts).

Custodianship (or *interception*). A piece captures an enemy piece flanked by a friendly piece by occupying a vacant square adjacent to it and on the opposite flank, so forming a line of three with the enemy captive sandwiched in the middle. Custodianship characterizes the classical Roman game of Latrunculi, and occurs in certain games of Africa and the Middle East.

Enclosure. An extension of the above. A piece captures an enemy piece by moving into such a position as to complete the captive's encirclement, thereby depriving it of any escape move. It is the capturing procedure of Go and of the King in Hnefatafl.

Intervention. A piece captures two enemy pieces by occupying the single square by which they are separated, so forming a line of three with the capturing piece sandwiched in the middle.

Approach. A piece captures an enemy piece by moving towards it in a straight line and stopping on the square immediately before it, thereby capturing both it and any further enemy pieces in unbroken succession behind.

Withdrawal. The reverse of approach: a piece captures an adjacent enemy piece by moving away from it in a straight line. This is peculiar to the Madagascan game of Fanorona, though it has since been borrowed by modern games inventors.

Conversion, which may be combined with any of the foregoing, is less a mode than a result of capture, namely, that a piece equivalent to the one captured is added to the forces of the capturing player.

Any given method of capture may be *immediate*, meaning that the capture takes place on the move, as in Chess, or *delayed*, meaning that the removal is effected on the following move provided that the position has not been materially changed. Immediate captures may be either *single*, as in Chess, or *multiple*, as in Draughts. (Delayed multiple captures are barely conceivable.)

Other forms of capture—co-ordination, reflection, immobilization, etc.—are relative novelties and will be described as they occur. Finally, there remain traditional forms of quasi-capture that do not result from direct interaction between opposing pieces. These include:

Huffing. If a player makes a non-capturing move when a capture was available, the opponent may 'huff' (confiscate) a piece that could have captured.

Suicide. Some games permit a player to remove one of his own pieces.

Telekinesis. This is presumably the word for a capture effected by a move or configuration made elsewhere on the board. Aligning three of one's own pieces entitles the removal of any desired enemy piece in Merels, but I know of no war game that employs it.

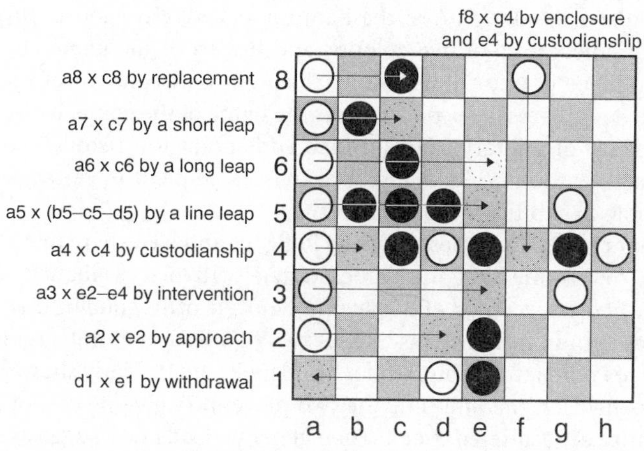

Fig. 14.6. Methods of capture, assuming orthogonal moves (m = n +).

Primitive War Games

Petteia. In his well-known study of Greek board games,[5] R. G. Austin notes with regret the absence from classical literature of conclusive evidence as to what games were played and how. Literary references abound from Homer down, but no Greek Hoyle emerges to enlighten us further. Two games often mentioned from the fifth century BC onwards are Petteia and Kuboi, both apparently generic terms and, in Plato's belief, of Egyptian origin. While the latter means dice, or games played with them, the former is regarded as strategic. Petteia derives from *pessos, pessoi,* 'pebble(s)', denoting the pieces with which the game is played—compare Latin *calculus* and the modern use of 'stone(s)' for the game of Go. Its strategic character is brought out by Plato, who in the *Republic* suggests that mastery of the game demands long and continuous practice, and by Philostratus in *Heroica,* 2.2, who characterizes a game assumed to be Petteia as 'no idle sport, but one full of shrewdness and needing great attention'.

French scholars, following Becq de Fouquières, equate Petteia with Pente Grammai. We have already encountered this as a possible race game, but it could also be interpreted as a 5×5 reticular game similar to Merels if a space game, or Siga if a war game. Murray, noting Plato's comment (*Republic* 422e) to the effect that *poleis* are a feature of Petteia, considers it ancestral to or identical with a game designated Polis, or Poleis ('city, cities'), by Pollux[6] in the second century AD. In Murray's translation, it is 'a game played with many pieces . . . [on] a board (*plinthion*) with spaces disposed along lines; the board is called 'city' and each piece a 'dog'. The pieces are of two colours, and the art of the game consists in taking a piece of one colour and enclosing it between two of the other.' Becq de Fouquières takes *plinthion* as the name of the game. It also means a solid body of military troops, which adds point to Aristotle's comment that 'a man without a city-state is like an isolated piece in Petteia'—that is, vulnerable to capture by custodianship.

Similar custodian games surviving in Egypt and elsewhere in Africa lead Murray to assume that the game started with pieces aligned on each player's two back ranks and that they moved orthogonally ($m = n+$). A terracotta group from Athens[7] shows two figures apparently arguing over a game of Petteia (probably) while a third looks on. It clearly shows how the board is held on the knees by the two players. Twelve pieces, of notable uniformity, are scattered over it. Their general disposition suggests an areal rather than reticular game, and those on the left may be thought to be occupying their initial positions.

Ludus Latrunculorum or **Latrunculi** was the Roman equivalent of Petteia, if not a variety of it. *Latrunculus* is the diminutive of *latro*, denoting a hired mercenary ('freelance', in its most literal sense), and hence, by subsequent extension, a freebooter or highwayman, cf. Spanish *ladrón*, 'thief'. The term may also imply custodian capture, the idea of two against one being appropriate this more disreputable profession. Although no single description of the game enables its certain reconstruction, Roman literature contains many more explicit references to it. The earliest useful comment is by Varro (first century BC), who describes a board marked with lines and spaces, and pieces of variously coloured glass or precious stones. Black, white, and red are mentioned; blue, white, and yellow have been found. Ovid confirms the custodian capture, adds that pieces can move backwards as well as forwards, and has the player capturing the most pieces declared *imperator*. A first-century poem in praise of Piso eulogizes his skill at a game which can hardly be other than Latrunculi, though not mentioning it by name:

The pieces are strategically drawn up on the open board, and battles fought between glass militia, with White now trapping Black, and Black now White. Every foe yields to you, Piso— but does any of your own men, once you have marshalled them, ever surrender? Which of them has not felled an enemy though himself upon the brink of death? Your battle tactics are legion. One man, fleeing from an attacker, turns and overpowers him; another, hitherto standing guard, advances from a distant corner; another rushes stoutly into the fray to cheat the foe that creeps upon his prey; another invites blockade on either flank, and, pretending to be trapped, himself traps two others; another more ambitiously tears through the massed phalanx, swoops into the lines, and razes the enemy's rampart to wreak havoc in the walled stronghold. Meanwhile, though the fight still rages fiercely, the enemy ranks are split, and you victoriously emerge with ranks unbroken, or with the loss of but one or two men, and both your hands rattle with the horde of captives.[8]

Martial applies to the game the rare technical term *mandra*, which derives from the Greek for a stall or pen and in other contexts means a drove of cattle. Perhaps here it denotes a massed formation, and hence is equivalent to the term *plinthion* in Petteia. The size of the board is nowhere stated, but physical remains of the game widespread over the former Roman Empire suggest that there was no universal standard, even within the same regions. Boards of 7 × 8, 8 × 8 and 9 × 10 have been found at Cilernum, on the Roman Wall. On the smaller side, Chester Museum houses a specimen of 7 × 7; on the larger, Colchester has yielded one of 12 × 10, and Richborough of 10 × 13. Not surprisingly, 8×8 is common, being easy to construct by a process of successive halving, and producing a game large enough for strategic interest but small enough to balance on the knees without discomfort.

Latrunculi remains a popular target for reconstructions by games historians, and at least one version has been marketed commercially. Such reconstructions are summarized in a recent study by Ulrich Schädler,[9] who notes that most depend on elements borrowed from various different games to fill the gaps and create a sense of purpose—Chess by Becq de Fouquières, a presumed ancient Egyptian game by Falkener, Siga by Bell, Draughts by Schmitt, Go by Haarsch. Schädler offers a reconstruction based on a critical review of all such predecessors and modified in over-the-board conditions in a workshop exercise conducted in 1992 at the Deutsches Spiele-Archiv in Marburg.

Schädler accepts that the game was played on variously sized boards, and supposes, reasonably enough, that Black and White each started with a number of pieces equivalent to about one quarter the number of cells in the grid. Presumably these pieces were functionally undifferentiated. Some inventors have read into the variable terms *latrones* and *latrunculi* a difference in function, and others have assumed the existence of a king or chieftain as at Chess or Tafl, but neither conclusion is supported either by the physical evidence of surviving gaming pieces or by literary references such as the *Laus Pisonis*.

More radically, Schädler believes (with Bell alone) the game to have been one of placement and movement, starting with an empty board rather than with pieces arranged on each player's two or three home ranks. Support for this view might be suggested by the reference to *tabula variatur aperta calculus* in the *Laus Pisonis*, where *tabula aperta* suggests an empty board (but may it not merely imply an open position, or the initial array?). Bell's reconstruction[10] has pieces placed two at a time, and prohibits captures during the placement phase. This suggestion is convincingly negated by the Colchester find of 1996, where a 12×8 board was found in a tomb set up in a position suggesting that either two or three moves have been made from the initial array (Fig. 14.7)

As to movement, previous opinion divided between (m = n +) 'rook', (m = 1✱) 'king', or (m = 1 +). Schädler favours (1 +), but adds the unusual idea that a piece could jump over an adjacent friendly piece to land on the (necessarily) vacant space beyond (Fig. 14.8). Some have assumed (m = n +) from the line *Longo venit ille recessu qui stetit in speculis,* 'he who was standing on watch comes up from a distance'. Schädler considers this inconsistent with the praise accorded by Ovid and the author of the *Laus Pisonis* to the skill required to withdraw a piece stuck firmly in the enemy lines, which would be relatively simple with (m = n +). Movement by jumping speeds up the otherwise cumbersome process of single-step movement, and justifies frequent contemporary references to the need for pieces to work in pairs.

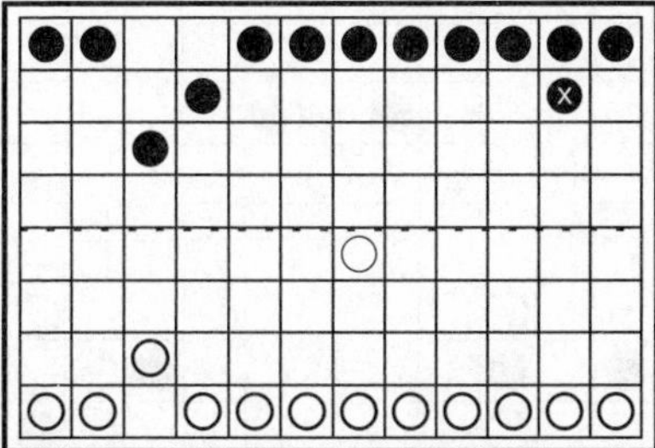

Fig. 14.7. Roman board game, probably Latrunculi, found in a tomb at Colchester in 1996, with blue and white pieces arranged as if early in play. The wooden board could be folded longitudinally (dotted line). The blue piece marked 'x' was positioned upside down, and the central white piece was smaller than the others. (Of several revised reconstructions, this is the latest at time of going to press.)

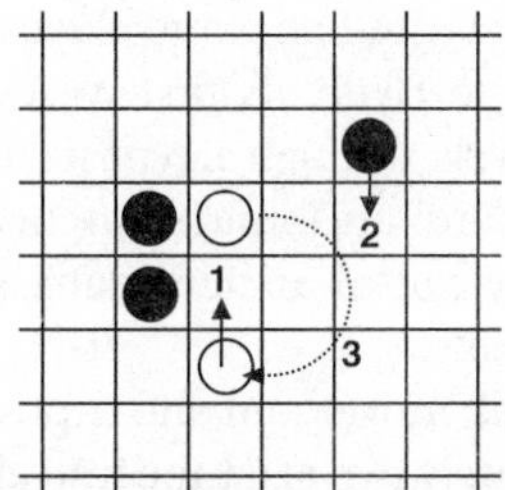

Fig. 14.8. White moves forwards in anticipation of escape (1). Black's (2) threatens a left move to trap White's upper piece. White's (3), a jump, brings both out of immediate danger. (After Schädler.)

They also work in pairs to capture by custodianship, a process to which Schädler adds further refinements. The first is that a trapped piece cannot move, and therefore cannot escape. The second is that capture is delayed to the next move, with that removal counting as a move in itself. The consequent delay enables the owner of the trapped piece to pose a counterthreat that may force the attacking player to withdraw rather than complete the capture, as in Fig. 14.9.

Schädler believes delayed capture to be implied in a letter by Seneca: 'No one in a hurry to [rescue things from] his burning house is going to examine a Latrunculi-board to discover how to extricate a trapped piece.'[11] Another possibility is that a trapped piece cannot be removed if either of the two custodians itself becomes trapped.

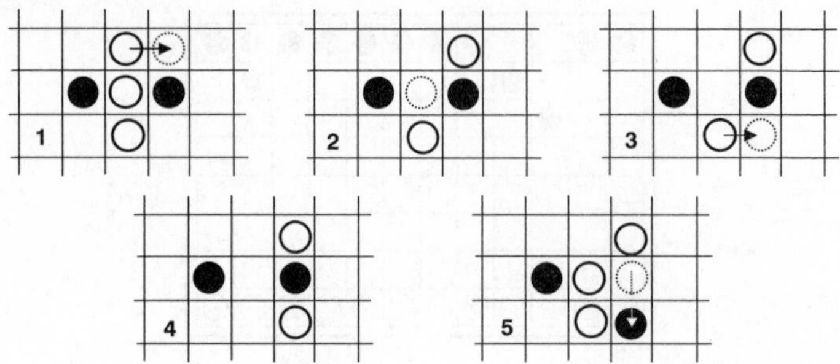

Fig. 14.9. Latrunculi tactics suggested by Schädler. Black (1) has trapped a white piece. White moves right, and Black completes the capture (2). Now White moves right again (3), and equalizes the loss, since Black cannot escape (4). Better for Black would have been to eschew the capture and move downwards (5), allowing him to attack with impunity whichever of the two aligned white pieces does not move next.

Siga (Seega, Kharbga) is a custodian game played in parts of Africa. One of the few games unknown to Hyde, its first western description occurs in Lane's account of his travels through Egypt in the first third of the nineteenth century.[12] Seega boards are found scratched on the Great Pyramid of Cheops, though evidently not of ancient date, and in many places it is played with *ad hoc* materials.

It is a game of placement, movement and capture. Black and White enter their twelve pieces alternately two at a time into all but the centre square of a grid of $5 \times 5 = 25$. Then each in turn, starting with the player who last entered a pair, moves a piece to an adjacent vacancy. If it thereby traps an enemy piece by custodianship, the captive is removed from the board, and the capturing piece may make any further consecutive captures that may be possible. If a player has no legal move, his opponent must make a move that gives him one—or, in some versions, remove one of his own pieces from the board to the same end. Similar games played in Somalia (Shantarad, Dub) and Sudan (Sija, Syredgé) afford immunity from capture to a piece occupying the centre. The game is also played on boards of 7×7, with twenty-four pieces each, and 9×9, with forty each.

Theoretically, a player wins by reducing his opponent's forces to one. Bell, noting that the game is too easily drawn, suggests that if a position is reached in which each player's pieces are secure behind a 'barrier' that his opponent cannot penetrate, the player with the greater number of pieces should win, a draw being declared only if both have the same number.[13] A variant described by Parker[14] replaces custodian capture with captures by the short leap, as in Turkish Draughts.

Gala, an Indonesian game recorded by B. F. Matthes in 1859,[15] may be related, but is an asymmetric game and hence more reminiscent of Tafl. The board is 7 × 7, with crosscuts on the centre and four middle-edge squares. Black has ten pieces to White's thirteen. Black starts by placing a piece on the centre square, then each in turn (White next) places a piece on any vacant square in his own half of the board. A piece moves one step orthogonally, and captures by custodianship. The object is unclear, but appears to be one of blockade.

Nard. Murray (*History of Board Games*, 54) quotes another version of the story of the introduction of Chess into Persia. In this one, from Firdawasi's *Shahnama*, each player moves a king and eight men of his own colour on a board of 8 × 8. The kings were invulnerable, but the men capturable by custodianship, as implied by the line *When two on one side have surprised a man by himself, he was lost to his side.* Murray surmises this to be a modification of Latrunculi, perhaps introduced by Roman legionaries guarding the Empire's Asian border.

Mak-yek, is or was, a Thai equivalent in which each player started with eight pieces on the first and third rows of his side of an 8 × 8 board. They move orthogonally (m = n +), and capture both by custodianship and by intervention (the reverse of custodianship: one takes two). A Malaysian version is given as Apit-sodok.[16]

Hasami-shogi, or 'intercepting Chess', is the Japanese equivalent, played on the 9 × 9 Shogi board with nine pieces arranged on each player's home rank. The pieces move (m = n+) and capture by custodianship.

Awithlaknakwe, 'Stone Warriors', is or was played by the Zuñi Indians of New Mexico. Culin[17] reproduces a description by Frank Hamilton, indicating that two players start with six pieces each arranged on their respective home ranks, move them forwards from point to point along the marked diagonals only, and capture by diagonal custodianship. The first piece lost by each side is replaced by a more elaborate piece called the Priest of the Bow, which is entered in its owner's home row and can also move orthogonally, but not backwards. Four can play, with West partnering North and East South. All start with six pieces of their own colour on their respective base lines, but only one Priest of the Bow is established for each partnership. 'The object of the game', says Hamilton, 'is to cross over and take the opponent's place, capturing as many men as possible on the way.' Presumably, this means the game is won on the number of captures made rather

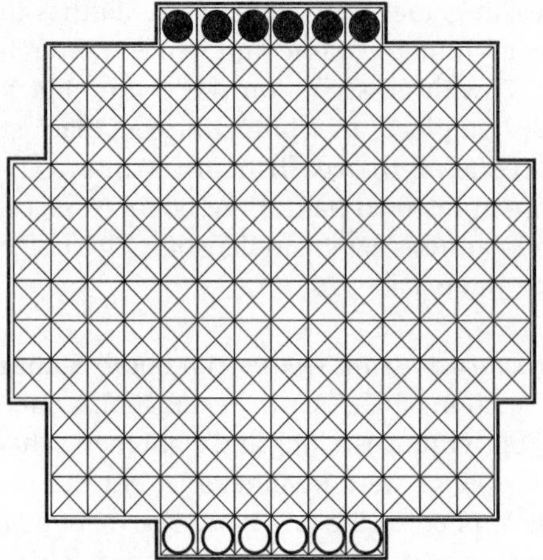

Fig. 14.10. Awithlaknakwe (Stone Warriors), Zuñi Indians, New Mexico.

than by being the first to cross over, making it a war game rather than a mere game of traversal.

Although the pieces used were often prehistoric discs, Culin says there is no evidence to suggest that Awithlaknakwe was played before the coming of the Whites, and was probably introduced by them. It could be interpreted as an enlarged and elaborated version of Tab or Tablan.

NOTES

1. Murray, *History of Board Games*, 149; Bell, *Board and Table Games*, i. 89–90, from the German of von Karl Sapper (*sic*), *Boas Anniversary Volume*, article 190, 238.
2. Hyde, *De Ludis Orientalibus* (1694); E. W. Lane, *An Account of the Manners and Customs of the Modern Egyptians* (London, 1836), 317–20; Murray, *History of Board Games*, 95; Bell, *Board and Table Games from Many Civilisations*, ii. 49–51.
3. Bell, *Board and Table Games Murray, History of Board Games* i. 87–9.
4. On p. 83 of *History of Board Games*, for example, fig. 34 clearly demands orthogonal moves, contradicting 'diagonal' in the text.
5. R. G. Austin, 'Greek Board Games', *Antiquity*, 14 (Sept. 1940), 257–78.
6. In *Onomasticon*, 2nd cent. AD. In the previous century, Suetonius wrote a work on Greek games which is now lost apart from some excerpts from it made by Eustathius in the 12th cent. AD.
7. Illustrated in Richter, *Spiele der Griechen und Römer* (1887), reproduced by Murray and others.
8. See also R. G. Austin, 'Roman Board Games', *Greece & Rome*, 4: 10 (1934), 24–34; 11 (1935), 76–82.

9. Ulrich Schädler,'Latrunculi—ein verlorenes strategisches Spiel der Römer', *Homo Ludens*, 4 (1994), 46–67.
10. Bell, *Board and Table Games from Many Civilisations*, 84–7.
11. Seneca, *Epistulae morales* 117: '*Nemo, qui ad incendium domus suae currit, tabulam latruncularium perspicit, quomodo alligatus exeat calculus.*'
12. Lane, *Modern Egyptians*, 320.
13. Bell, *Board and Table Games from Many Civilisations*, i. 83.
14. H. Parker, *Ancient Ceylon* (London, 1909); cited by Murray, *History of Board Games*, 82.
15. In his *Makassarsch-Hollandsch Woordenboek* and *Ethnographische Atlas*, thence via Kaudern to Murray, p. 55.
16. Murray, *History of Board Games*, 54, from sources dated respectively 1836 and 1915.
17. Culin, *Games of the North American Indians* (Nebraska, 1992; orig. Washington, 1907), ii. 799–800.

Take That!

15

Games with leaping capture: Alquerque, Draughts, Lasca, Fanorona, et al.

The game of Draughts is played by a maximum of persons with a minimum of intelligence. I am one of those who have always played but never understood.

W. G. Grace (1896)[1]

Whether it may claim descent from the Greeks or Scandinavians is a point that may be left to the antiquarian without any great social loss should he never succeed in settling it.

Bohn's Handbook of Games (1850)

Draughts would be universally recognized as one of the world's great games were it not eclipsed by the social hegemony of Chess. 'There is a collective inferiority complex amongst Draughts players with regard to Chess,' says Tom Landry, 'which usually ends up with a potential recruit to Draughts thinking "There must be something about this game Chess", and he ends up instead as another Chess addict'.[2] Edgar Allan Poe, in *The Murders in the Rue Morgue*, was more forthright:

The higher powers of the reflective intellect are more decidedly and more usefully tasked by the unostentatious game of Draughts than by all the elaborate frivolity of Chess. In this latter, where the pieces have different and bizarre motions, with various and variable values, what is only complex . . . is mistaken for what is profound . . .[In Draughts], what advantages are obtained by either party are obtained by superior acumen.

As it is, the game is usually learnt in childhood because it is easily picked up, abandoned in adolescence because youth has more urgent calls on its attention, and thereafter classified in most people's subconscious as a childish activity.

In essence, Draughts is a game of material capture distinguished by the fact that pieces are taken by jumping, or leaping, as opposed to the more primitive custodian capture of Latrunculi and the replacement capture of Chess. There are several reasons why jumping games have largely displaced custodian games in the western world. One is that they involve capture by singletons, making it less vital to keep pieces together in pairs.

Another is that the leap itself constitutes a move, or change of position, and so speeds the game up. It does not necessarily shorten it, however, as the constantly shifting positions now call for more advanced forward thought and strategic planning. There is also a pleasing logic to the short leap, in that it may be regarded as an extension of custodian capture: instead of requiring the assistance of a friendly piece on the opposite side of the captive, the capturer merely moves to the place where the friendly piece would otherwise be, and so plays both roles in one turn. A possible derivation of one from the other is suggested by the two varieties of Siga distinguished only by their method of capture.

Draughts is further distinguished from more primitive games by the promotion of otherwise undifferentiated ordinary pieces to pieces of a more powerful type, so imparting a two-act structure to the play. This feature is paralleled in Chess, but here it is incidental and may not happen at all, whereas it is the very essence of Draughts, which cannot be won without it. The play upon a chessboard, the promotion of pieces, and a sharing of terminology, inevitably invite speculation as to the derivation of one game from the other. The popular assumption is that Chess represents an elaboration of Draughts; the more subtle, that Draughts represents a simplification of Chess; the most sophisticated, as espoused by Murray and Kruijswijk, that Draughts represents a hybrid of Chess and the medieval game of Alquerque; the most revolutionary, as developed by Arie van der Stoep, that Draughts *is* Alquerque, transferred to a chessboard, and contributing more to Chess than it ever derived from it.

Alquerque

The Alfonso manuscript of 1283 describes three games of Alquerque, distinguished as *de tres* (by three), *de nueve* (by nine), and *de doze* (by twelve). The first two are varieties of Merels, respectively three- and nine-men's Morris. The last is said to resemble Chess in that it is 'played with the mind', and there is a delightful illustration of a game between two bearded sages, each accompanied by an armed adviser. The game runs as follows.

Black and White each start with twelve pieces arranged on all but the centre point of a 5 × 5 reticular grid (Fig. 15.1*a*). Each in turn moves a piece along a line to the nearest vacant point, the first move being necessarily to the centre. If the nearest line-connected point is occupied by an enemy piece, and the further point beyond it in the same direction of travel is vacant, it captures and removes the enemy piece by jumping over it to the further vacancy. If it can make a further capture from this point, not necessarily in the same direction, it does so, so that a turn may consist of a series of consecutive jumps. Alfonso does not say whether capture is compulsory, nor is a win defined, but 'he who is the worse at saving his pieces and soon loses most of them is vanquished' implies that the winner is the player with more pieces remaining when no more captures can be made.

The first to play is determined by lot (dice), as he is held to be at a disadvantage—partly because he has no choice of opening, and partly because when he does have a choice he necessarily is the first to reveal his strategy, enabling the second, if clever enough, to counter every move. *Et si amos los iogadores lo sapieren iogar, comunalmientre puede se mannar*—if both players are equally skilled, it will [usually] end in a draw. This obviously occurs when both have made the same number of captures and neither can make any more, but the author does not define a draw, nor says what happens if one player is immobilized. To fill this and other obvious gaps, Bell proposes additional rules.[3]

1. A piece cannot move backwards or to a point it has previously occupied.
2. Capture is compulsory under penalty of the huff.
3. A piece that has reached the back rank cannot move, except to capture. (Sideways, certainly, and presumably backwards also; but Bell does not say.)
4. A player who cannot move loses, even if he has more pieces remaining.

Krujswijk's reconstruction[4] allows backward moves and makes captures optional, but neither researcher admits promotion, assuming that it would have been mentioned had it existed.

The game was known in Catalonia (as Marro), Italy (Marelli), Sicily (Riga), and France ('jeu de mereles qui se fait par douze mereles' in a fifteenth-century translation of *Vetula*). Its distinctive board also appears on a late sixteenth-century Swiss game-box now in the Victoria & Albert Museum, in a manuscript in Trinity College, Cambridge, on a sixteenth-century tomb in Suffolk, and in the cloisters of Norwich Cathedral.[5] It was evidently not widely played in Europe, and was soon ousted by its descendant Draughts. Alquerque may be the referend of an unspecified game called Qirkat in *Kitab-al Aghani*, whose author died 976; but the word is not authentically Semitic, and may be of Spanish Moorish origin, with *qirq* < *querque* < *calculus* 'stone, playing-piece'.[6] We have already noted (in the chapter on Merels) that it also denotes part of an olive-oil mill with channels or grooves to collect the oil. The game itself is one of dozens, if not hundreds, of variants involving different designs and numbers of pieces and played

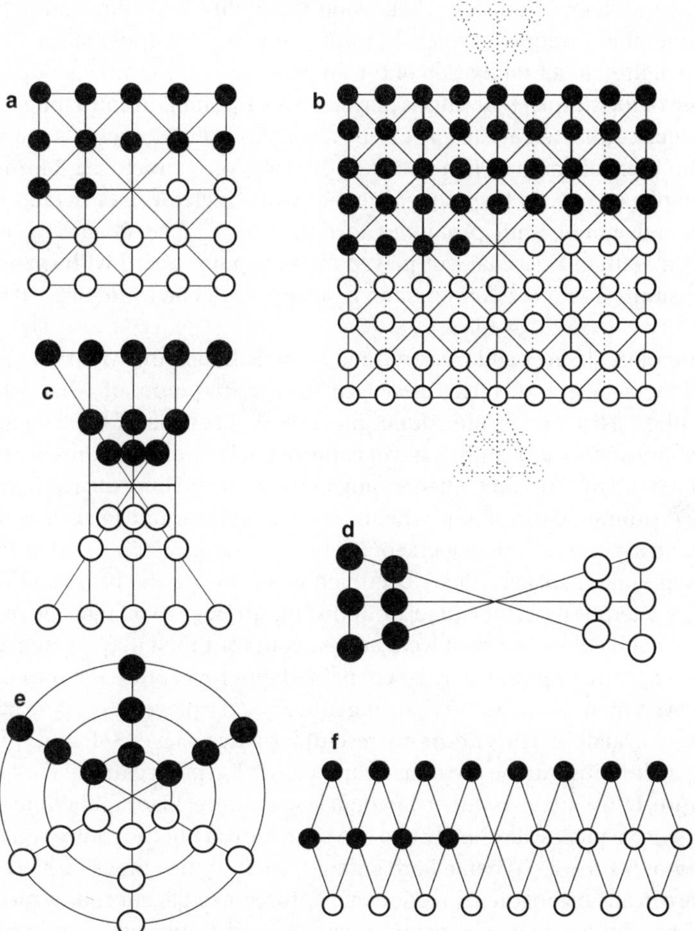

Fig. 15.1. (*a*) Alquerque; (*b*) Quadruple (81-point) board found in India, Indonesia, Sahara (with omission of horizontals and verticals here shown in broken outline), ancient Egypt (Kurna), and (with two triangular extensions) in Simalur, off the coast of Sumatra; (*c*) Egara guti, Central Provinces, India; (*d*) Felli, Morocco; (*e*) Pretwa, Bihar; (*f*) Awithlaknannai, 'Stones Kill', Zuñi Indians, New Mexico, but not native.

throughout northern Africa, the Middle East, India, and south-east Asia as far as Indonesia. Many are still being discovered. Murray describes about three dozen in varying degrees of detail, and Lhôte another dozen or so. Most are reticular games with ortho-diagonal moves and short-leap, multiple capture. Some involve promotion, but so few as to suggest a later borrowing from Draughts. Their wide variability and diffusion suggest considerable antiquity, which is underlined by the appearance of Fig. 15.1*b* incised in a roofing slab of the ancient Egyptian Temple at Kurna.

One of the simplest variants is played on a 13-point grid consisting of two triangles connected at the apex. Felli, a version from Morocco, is matched by the Bengali game of Lau kata kati.[7] Fetach, or Quirach, is a Moroccan game played exactly like Alquerque, but with singletons restricted to forward movement until promoted to doubletons.[8] The Bengali game of Mughal Pathan is similar but played on a 25-point board with triangular extensions.[9] Karat is a Tuareg game typically played on a grid of 8×8 holes by women, or 6×7 by men.[10]

One of the largest and most refined is the Saharan and Mauritian game of Zamma or Srand.[11] This is played on the 81 points of what Murray describes as a quadruple Alquerque board. Each has forty singletons which move forwards only but can capture backwards. Captures are compulsory and may be enchained. A singleton upon reaching the furthermost edge is promoted to a sultan, which can move and capture in all directions. By contrast, the Hawaiian game of Ko-na-ne[12] is played on a grid of 100 or more points or spaces. All are occupied to start with, the black and white pieces alternating rather than in opposing armies. Two adjacent pieces, one of each colour, are removed, and each in turn then plays by making a jump capture. Captures may be enchained, but no capture is compulsory. However, there are no non-capturing moves, and a player loses if he has no capture available. Thus Ko-na-ne resembles a two-player Solitaire.

Siga, described in the previous chapter as an Egyptian game of custodian capture, is also played with orthogonal leap capture. Black and White enter their twelve pieces alternately two at a time into all but the centre square of a grid of $5 \times 5 = 25$. When all are entered, each in turn moves a piece one square in any orthogonal direction, or captures an adjacent enemy piece by landing on the necessarily vacant square beyond. Captures are compulsory and multiple. The Somalian games of Koruböddo ('High Leap') and Lorkaböd ('Jump Over') are substantially similar.

Choko, played by tribes in the Gambia Valley, differs from Siga as follows. The pieces, of long sticks for one player and short for the other, are entered one at a time, and if either player moves a piece instead of entering one before all are entered (which is legal), the other must also move instead of entering. Only one short leap capture may be made in one turn, but this entitles the capturing player to conclude his turn by removing a second enemy piece from any position on the board. Helga, from the Libyan Desert, is probably the same, except in so far as the two side's pieces consist respectively of onions and camel dung. The fascinating feature of these

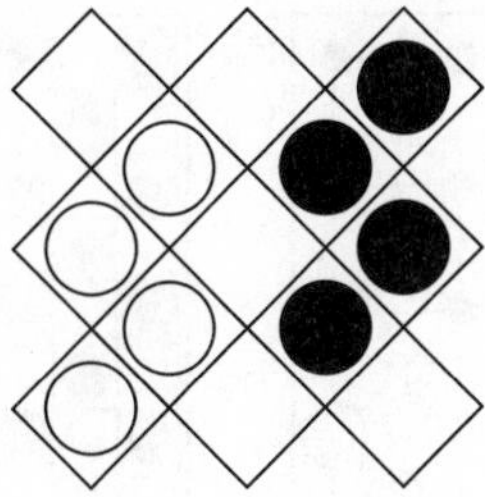

Fig. 15.2. Queah game from Liberia (after Murray).

games is the fact that they seem to combine all the basic elements of Alquerque, Draughts, and Merels in the simplest possible format, suggesting a possible common origin for all.

Murray records an unnamed game played by the Queah tribe of Liberia as follows. Two play on a 13-squares trellis made of interwoven twigs. Each has ten sticks, one with tops cut aslant and representing men, the other with tops cut straight and representing women. Each places four pieces as illustrated (Fig. 15.2). Each in turn then moves a piece one space orthogonally—that is, across an edge into an adjacent cell (Murray calls this 'diagonally', misled by the orientation of the board)—and may take one enemy piece per turn by a short leap. When a piece is captured, its owner replaces it by entering another anywhere on the board to restore his total to four, so long as any remain.

Tobi-Shogi, 'Jumping Chess',[13] is a Japanese leap-and-capture game played by children. Each starts with ten pieces on the points of the two back rows of a 9 × 9 celled board. Pieces move forwards (only) one square at a time and capture by the short leap.

Kolowis Awithlaknannai (Fighting Snakes) is one of several related Mexican Indian games described by Stewart Culin,[14] including Stone Warriors mentioned in the previous chapter. A jump-capture equivalent was also played on a board of twenty-five points called *awithlaknan mosona*, or on a 49-point expansion of it called *kolowis awithlaknannai*, the first word meaning 'snakes'. The rules of play, so far as they are known, are identical with those of Alquerque.

Dablot Prejjesne. This obscure and fascinating Lapp game from Frostviken, Sweden, was first described in English by R. C. Bell.[15] It appears to be a hybrid of Alquerque and Tablut. *Dablot* is evidently related to *tablut* (ultimately from *tabula*), and *prejjesne* is given as 'board', making the name a tautology.

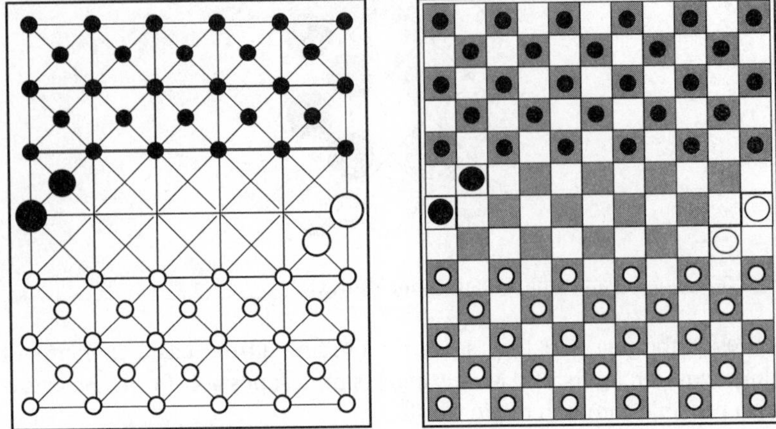

Fig. 15.3. Dablot Prejjesne (*left*), and its notional chequered equivalent (*right*).

The board is a linear grid of seventy-two points (Fig. 15.3). The two players represent Lapp warriors and tenant farmers. Each starts with thirty pieces arranged as shown. The Lapps have 28 uniform warriors, a (slightly larger) prince, and a (much larger) king. The twenty-eight uniform farmers are correspondingly headed by a landlord's son and a landlord. Each in turn moves a piece along a line to an unoccupied vacancy in any direction, or may capture an enemy piece occupying a connected point by jumping over it to the necessarily vacant point beyond. No piece may capture above its station—king and landlord can therefore capture any opponent, but prince and son cannot capture landlord or king, and warriors and farmers capture only each other. Captures may be enchained, but no capture is compulsory, nor need a potential series of captures be completed. There is no promotion. The game ends when one player is defenceless and resigns.

Fanorona, native to the Malagasy Republic, is unique in exhibiting the complementary methods of capture described as 'approach and withdrawal'. It first appeared about 1680 and is self-evidently derived from Alquerque. One of Murray's informants assured him that during the storming of the capital by the French in 1895 the Queen and her people founded their hopes for victory less on their armed forces than on the outcome of the official game being played to that end by the ritual professionals.

Black and White each start with twenty-two pieces arranged on all but the centre point of a double Alquerque board, as illustrated. The aim is to capture or immobilize all the enemy pieces. Each in turn moves a piece

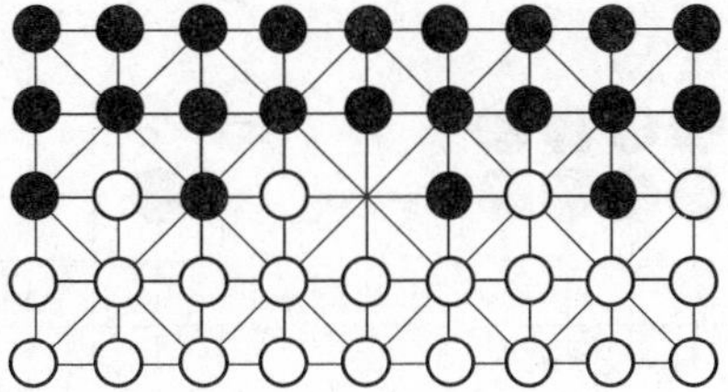

Fig. 15.4. Fanorona. White may play upwards or rightwards to the centre. If the latter, he may capture the adjacent black piece by approach, or the initially adjacent black piece by withdrawal.

along a marked line to any adjacent vacancy. If the next point in the same direction of movement is occupied by an enemy piece, it is captured and removed from the board, together with any and all enemy pieces forming a straight line in the same direction behind it. This effects a capture by approach.

Capture by withdrawal is its reverse. If a piece occupies a point connected by a line to an adjacent enemy piece, it captures that enemy piece by moving away from it to an adjacent vacancy. Also captured are any and all enemy pieces forming an unbroken straight line behind it along the line of movement.

Capture is compulsory, but if a given move offers both types simultaneously only one of them may be taken. ('Don't eat at both ends like a leech', runs a Malagasy proverb.) The first time a player makes a capture, his turn ends. Thereafter, a capturing piece is entitled to make additional successive captures in the same turn, provided only that each successive capture involves moving along a different marked line from those of preceding captures in the same turn of play.

'When one player is defeated, the next game is played differently, the new form of play being known as *vela*. The defeated player begins and the winner proceeds to sacrifice man after man until he has parted with seventeen men. During this play the winner refrains from making any capture and his opponent may only take one man each move.' Thus Murray, who also gives specimen games under both methods of play.[16]

Surakarta, first described in English by R. C. Bell, is peculiar to the island of Java and named after one of its towns, though prior to the arrival of the Dutch in the sixteenth century AD it was called Solo, from the river on which Surakarta lies. The diagram (Fig. 15.5), often drawn in the sand, consists of a 5 × 5 squared grid with circular extensions as illustrated.

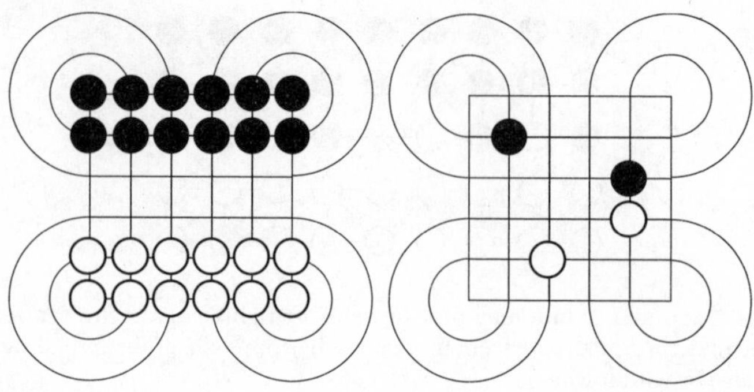

Fig. 15.5. Surakarta—an aberrant Alquerque relative?

Black places twelve stones on the points of his two home ranks, and White twelve cowries on his. Each in turn moves a piece one step forwards, backwards, sideways, or diagonally to the nearest point, provided that it is unoccupied. It may not land on or jump over an occupied point, nor capture the occupant, except as described below. To effect a capture, a piece must travel along a line of unoccupied points in such a way as to enter a circular track, follow it round, and continue along the resultant path until it meets an enemy piece, which it thereupon captures by replacement.

For example, in Fig. 15.5 *right*, the left-hand white piece may travel north, around the north-west corner, then east until it captures the right-hand black piece. If it starts by travelling west, it goes round the south-west corner, proceeds north, and captures the left-hand black piece. It cannot, however, travel east or south, as its route is blocked by the right-hand white piece. The latter cannot travel north, as it is blocked by the black piece; but it can capture this by travelling east and completing two circuits. Pieces are always mutually *en prise*. Thus, if it is Black's move, he can make the equivalent captures by following the reverse paths. Although capture is by replacement rather than by leaping, Surakarta looks and feels like an extension of Alquerque, especially in view of the diagonal moves.

Draughts

At some unknown time and place in medieval Europe Alquerque developed into Draughts. The new game was distinguished by two features: first, in being played on the cells of an 8 × 8 chessboard rather than the points of a 5 × 5 network; second, in that a piece upon reaching the furthermost edge of the board was promoted to a new piece with greater powers of movement and capture. In English, the basic piece is called a *man* and the promoted piece a *king*; in most other countries, the equivalent terms are *pawn* (French *pion*, Spanish *peon*, Italian *pedina*, Greek *pioni*, etc.), and what appears to be *queen* (Spanish *dama*, French *dame*, German *dame*, Greek *dama*, Dutch and Scottish *dam*, etc.). For uniformity, I will refer to them respectively as singleton and doubleton. The latter is appropriate, in that the promoted piece is universally indicated by being 'crowned' with a second piece of the same colour. Originally, 'queens' denoted singletons, doubletons being referred to as 'queened queens' or 'doubled pieces' (German *doppelstein*, Dutch *dubbele dam*, etc.). This yields the commonest name of the game, i.e. Dama, Damas, Jeu de Dames, Damenspiel, and so on.

I should add that the easy association of *dame* with 'queen', which implies both an etymological identity with *dame* < *domina* and a ludic identity with the queen of Chess, and which underpins Murray's account of the game's origin, is under heavy attack at time of writing. An alternative proposal argues that *dam(e)* was originally one of several words for a gaming-piece (like *table*[*man*] and *merel*), bearing neither any linguistic relation to *domina* nor any notional connotation of rank or femininity.[17] It is only on the understanding that such connotations have naturally developed with the passage of time that I render the modern French terms *pion* and *dame* (and their cognates) as 'pawn' and 'queen' where it seems contextually appropriate to do so.

The name of the game in English-speaking countries was originally Checkers, primarily meaning the chequered squares of the board, and subsequently Draughts, primarily meaning 'moves'. As Hyde put it in 1694, *Hic ludus Anglicè dicitur Draughts, à trahendo calculos*: 'This game is called Draughts in English, from the fact that pieces are drawn [dragged] along.' American English, as so often, preserves the older term. As Fiske explains:

> In New England chess was almost entirely unpractised until a century and a half (or more) after the country's settlement. To the colonists, therefore, the chess-board (or 'checker-board', as it was oftenest styled) was only known as a board used in playing the game of draughts, and draughts was accordingly looked upon as preëminently the game of the *chekyr* [Old English term], with little thought or knowledge of chess. 'Checkers' continues to be the household game of the country district in very many sections of the United States—especially in the winter evenings of the villagers and farmers. It may therefore be appropriately styled 'rural chess'.[18]

Like most great games, including Chess, Draughts is not a single game but a family of closely related games exhibiting national and historical variations. Unlike Chess, it is a game of purely European origin and development, though it has naturally spread over the globe in consequence of

European expansion and colonization. Also unlike Chess, no single form of Draughts has established itself as a world standard for international tournaments, there being no rapprochement between the Anglo-American and the Continental game. Major national varieties of Draughts may be classified, on formal grounds, as follows (see also Table 15.1):

Short Draughts, played on the diagonals of an 8 × 8 chequered board, the doubleton moving one step at a time (Anglo-American and Italian Draughts).
Long Draughts, played on the diagonals of an 8 × 8 chequered board, the doubleton moving any distance (Spanish, German).
Great Draughts, the same, but played on the diagonals of a 10 × 10 (or 12 × 12) chequered board (so-called 'Polish' or 'French', actually Dutch).
Straight Draughts, also Long, but played on an 8 × 8 unchequered board, all pieces moving orthogonally (Graeco-Turkish Draughts).

Table 15.1. Varieties of Draughts.

Type	Designation	*bd*	*pc*	*or*	*singleton*	*cap*	*prom*	*dbltn*	*m*	*p'col*
Short	English[a] *Draughts*	8^2	12	R	*man*	fo	stop	*king*	S	free
	American *Checkers*	8^2	12	R	*man*	fo	stop	*king*	S	free
	Italian *Dama*	8^2	12	L	*pedina*	fo[d]	stop	*dama*	S	più
Long	Spanish *Dama*	8^2	12	L	*peon*	fo	stop	*dama*	L	most
	German *Damenspiel*	8^2	12	R	*stein*	fo	stop	*dame*	L	free
	Swedish[b] *Damspel*	8^2	12	R	*bricka*	fb	back	*dam*	L	free
	Russian *Shashki*	8^2	12	R	*shashka*	fb	forth[e]	*dam*	L	free
Great	European ('Polish')[c]	10^2	20	R	*pion*	fb	back	*dame*	L	most
	Canadian	12^2	30	R	*man*	fb	back	*king*	L	most
	Indian	12^2	30	R	*man*	fb	back	*king*	L	most
Straight	Gk-Turkish *Dama*	8^2	16	O	*pioni*	fs	stop	*dama*	L[f]	most

Notes: *bd* = board, *pc* = pieces (each), *or* = orientation (see Fig. 15.6), *cap fo* = singleton captures forwards only, *fb* = forwards and backwards, *fs* = forwards and sideways, *prom* = promotion, whether stop on crownhead and promote, or capture backwards (if possible) without promoting, *dbltn* = name of doubleton, *m* = move (short or long), *p'col* = capturing protocol (most = longest possible series of captures must be made, *più* = special Italian rule explained in the appropriate section).

[a] English Draughts also current in Denmark, formerly in Germany to 17th cent., France and Poland to 18th cent.

[b] Swedish includes Norwegian.

[c] International, also called Continental or (misleadingly) Polish Draughts, is of Dutch origin, and is naturalized in France and Switzerland. Originally played on 8 × 8 board.

[d] Italian: singleton may not capture doubleton.

[e] Russian: singleton on promoting may immediately continue capturing as king.

[f] Graeco-Turkish: in multiple capture, pieces are removed as captured, so do not block. (In all others, a king may land on the same vacant square, but not pass over the same enemy piece, more than once. Captured pieces are not removed from the board until the end of the multiple capture.)

The ultimate aim of the game is to capture or immobilize all the enemy pieces. Singletons advance one square at a time towards the opposite end of the board, and capture enemy pieces by jumping over them to land on the necessarily vacant space beyond. If a capturing piece lands on a square from which it can capture again, it does so, and keeps doing so in the same turn of play so long as any further captures continue to present themselves. Multiple capture is common to all forms of Draughts and hence one of the defining features of the family.

A singleton upon reaching the far end of the board is 'crowned' with a spare piece of the same colour and thereby promoted to a doubleton. Doubletons have the increased power of moving in any direction, backwards or forwards ad lib, and, in many forms of the game, can move any distance instead of only one square at a time.

Promotion may be reminiscent of Chess, but its role in Draughts is considerably more significant. In Chess, pawn promotion is never an initial strategic objective; it often remains more of a threat than a reality; rarely does either player promote more than one pawn; and many a game is won without it. A game of Draughts, however, cannot be won with singletons alone, except by co-operation or incompetence on the part of the loser. Each player's primary objective is therefore to promote as many pieces as possible and as soon as possible. The game consequently falls into two distinct parts, the second inaugurated by the first promotion.

Most forms of Draughts hold capture compulsory. Having made an initial capture, a player must continue capturing with the same piece so long as captures are possible. Given a choice of initial capture, some games allow the player to choose freely, others may require the longest series to be made, or doubletons to be captured in preference to singletons. The penalty for failing to capture when able to do so varies. Traditionally, the opponent may, before making his own move, capture any opposing piece (but not more than one) that could have captured but didn't. This is known as 'huffing', as it is traditional to indicate the fact by taking up the defaulting piece and blowing on it (French *souffler*, German *blasen*, Spanish *soplar*, Italian *soffiare*, etc.) before laying it aside. In most countries, huffing has been abolished from modern tournament play, and a move made instead of a capture must be rescinded and replaced by the capture. In some versions, the opponent may either insist on the capture or accept the non-capturing move as valid. Rarely, players agree to waive compulsory capture. This obtains chiefly when playing with children or beginners or triflers, since the purpose of enforcement is to enable players to lay traps for each other by forcing an unfavourable exchange for a favourable one or a better position, thereby increasing the scope for forward planning and favouring the more skilful player.

A player wins outright by capturing all his opponent's pieces or by blocking them so that he has no legal move. Draws are frequent between well-matched players. A draw is declared when both agree that neither can win outright. In tournament play, a player with a material advantage may be required to win within a certain number of moves in order to avoid a declared draw.

Playing on the diagonals of a chessboard gives Draughts a peculiarly asymmetrical property lacking from original Alquerque. The fact that one of the long diagonals of occupied squares is a single line of eight, while the other is a double line of seven (French *trictrac,* Dutch *triktraklijnen*) significantly affects the strategy of the game, and to reverse the custom of play by either giving the board a quarter-turn, or setting the pieces out on the 'wrong' colour, has a naturally (and literally!) disorientating effect on regular players. While it is therefore technically correct to say that it makes no essential difference which way round the board goes, or which squares are played on—as evidenced by the fact that all four possibilities are or have been regularly used (see Fig. 15.6)—, it is nevertheless not surprising to find

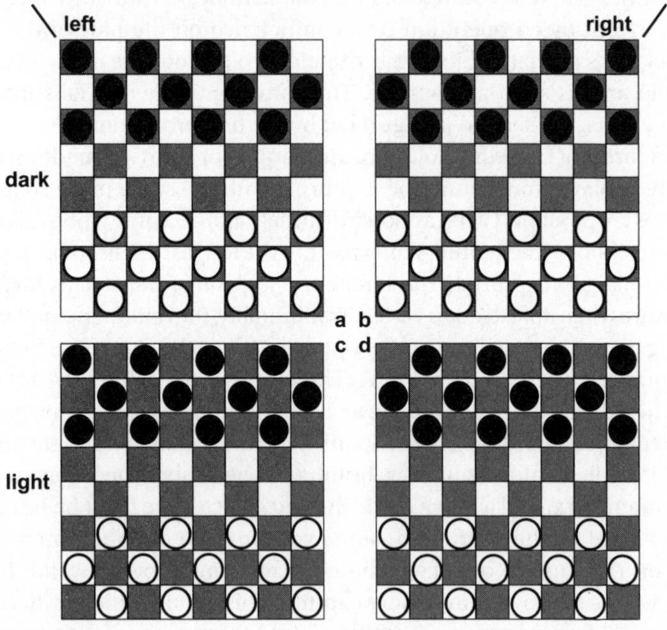

Fig. 15.6. Diagonal Draughts may be played on dark or light squares, and with the long diagonal oriented upwards to the left or the right: (*a*) Italy, (*b*) Modern international, (*c*) Spain (Italy to eighteenth cent.), (*d*) France (and England to eighteenth cent.).

each Draughts-playing community quite adamant about the 'correct' way of setting the game up. Attempts to trace and compare varying customs from place to place and time to time are complicated by the fact that printed illustrations in books and pamphlets often show pieces on light squares, regardless of the actual colour used, partly for ease of printing and partly because they 'read' better that way on white paper. To add to the confusion, when colours are reversed for graphic reasons, authors may or may not compensate by rotating the board to ensure that the arrangement of the pieces conforms with the appropriate left–right orientation. The actual colours vary considerably. Everyday boards are usually black and white, and the pieces white(-ish) and either black or dark red. For club and tournament play, the English Draughts Association favours green and buff squares, and red and white pieces.

Original Draughts. Murray[19] believed Draughts originated in twelfth-century Provence and was played up to 1400 under various forms of a name based on *fers*, the name of the medieval Chess queen. He offered three circumstantial references in support.

1. An anthology by ibn Dihya of Valencia (d. 1235) mentions a lost Arabic work on games (by ibn Sharif) including *farisia*, 'which means the player's queen (*malika*), wherewith one plays as with the Chess'. Murray derives this from a Provençal game-name *fersa*, which is nevertheless unattested.

2. In 1243, a panegyric on King Philippe Auguste by Philippe Mousket includes the couplet *Cie n'estoit mie rois de gas / Ne roi de fierges, ne d'escas*... This implies that pieces called 'kings' were common to three games, of which *gas* is unidentifiable, *escas* is Chess, and *fierges* the hypothetical Ferses. Murray takes this to imply promotion. If so, it is the only known example of *roi* = doubleton in the whole history of French Draughts.

3. Chaucer, in *The Book of the Duchess* (*c.*1369), recounts a dream in which a knight bemoans the loss of his lady allegorized as a queen at Chess: *With hir false draughtes dyvers / She staale on me and tok my fers*. Chaucer's persona returns a Job-comforting response including the lines *Thogh ye had lost the ferses twelve / And ye for sorwe mordred yourselve / You should be dampned*... (Had you lost the twelve ferses, and killed yourself for sorrow, you would still be damned). Murray takes 'twelve' as supporting Ferses = Draughts, arguing the change of game as made with humorous intent to show the poet's ignorance of such a high-class game as Chess. Van der Stoep observes that 'twelve' may be suggested by the exigencies of

rhyme, that in Christian tradition it denotes infinity (completeness, more like), and that some editors interpret it as 'lost twelve games of Chess'.[20]

Murray's theory is based on the assumption that the later French term *jeu de dames* means 'game of [long-moving, Chess-type] queens', and was modelled on an earlier 'game of *ferses*', which, as in medieval Chess, move only one square diagonally. In fact, French *dames* means flat, circular gameboard pieces in general—it still denotes pieces at Backgammon and Merels—and (as Murray himself acknowledges) did not specifically denote doubletons at Draughts until about 1750. All of which weakens the case for identifying original Draughts with a hypothetical Provençal *fersa*.

Firmer references to Draughts, however, are of English provenance. A case may be argued for it in lines from *Sir Ferumbras*, a romance of about 1380:

> Tho that willieth to leue at hame
> pleyeþ to the eschekkere,
> & summe of hem to iew-de-dame:
> and summe to tablere...

which seems to list in order Chess, Draughts, and Tables. Disconcertingly, however, *iew-de-dame* here antedates by at least 120 years the first occurrence of French *jeu de dames,* which always has *dames* plural rather than singular. Also it is a translator's interpolation, being absent from the French original. Could it, perhaps, be the Anglo-Norman equivalent, and, as such, absent from the *langue d'oïl* (mainland French)?

An English version of the French *Destruction of Troy*, *c.*1400, includes the lines:

> Mony gaumes were begonnen the grete for to solas.
> The chekker was choisly there chosen the first,
> The draghtes, the dyse, and other dregh gaumes...

Here, too, the apparent reference to Draughts is a translator's interpolation.

Note that *checkers* (variously spelt), though subsequently meaning *draughtsmen,* originally meant the individual squares of a chequered board; hence 'playing at [the] checkers' cannot be automatically taken for Draughts without additional evidence. In the two previous examples it means Chess. In others, including a judicial record of 1376, it self-evidently denotes Quek, a gambling game played on a chequerboard with dice rather than moving pieces. A better example is that of an early fifteenth-century moral treatise entitled *Jacob's Well,* in which the line *Pleyin at the tablys, at the chesse & the chekyr, at the hasard*... clearly distinguishes *chekyr* from Chess on the one hand and a dice game on the other. From John Lydgate's

The pilgrimage of the life of man of 1426 comes 'And for to makë lordys cher / Both at ches and the cheker, / The drawthes ther-off, ful wel I kan...' Here, too, Quek seems excluded by *drawthes* (= draughts, i.e. 'moves').

These examples lead van der Stoep to conclude that Draughts—i.e. chequerboard Alquerque—first appeared in England, and under the name Checkers, though it is possible that some early references to Merels or Morris may in fact have denoted the same game. Unambiguous references to Draughts are few and far between prior to 1500, after which it suddenly achieves widespread popularity and analytical attention throughout Europe. Murray ascribes this to the adoption, in France, of the rule of compulsory capture under penalty of the huff, which greatly increases the strategic potential of the game. Before outlining its expansion, however, perhaps we may speculate on the earliest form of the game.

It is my belief that Alquerque was the low-level game it appears to have been from Alfonso's description. Sketchy as some of Alfonso's game descriptions are, I cannot believe that the manuscript would have failed to mention promotion had it existed. I therefore see the game as played with uniform pieces throughout, capable of moving in all linear directions, and so resulting—as Alfonso critically notes—in frequent draws. Capture may have been compulsory, perhaps as a variation rather than as universal practice, but it hardly seems a necessity in view of the fact that the initial array forces immediate engagement and capture between the two sides. Transfer this game to the diagonals of a chessboard, however, and a new situation arises. There are now two empty rows between the forces, and the opening moves do not necessarily entail immediate capture. If pieces can move backwards and forwards as in the reticular game, a hesitant or easily intimidated player can simply jam the game up by a defensive and escapist repetition of moves. There are two obvious ways of overcoming this. One is to introduce compulsory capture, the other to prohibit backward moves. Of these, the latter produces the more immediately engaging effect. I assume forward movement to have been the first consequence of transferring Alquerque to the diagonals of a chessboard. A second consequence is that of promotion, since without it a piece attaining the far end of the board cannot move. By imposing forward movement on ordinary pieces, players automatically necessitated the invention of secondary pieces, thereby transforming Alquerque into one virtually identical with Short Draughts. The process is not so much one of imparting additional powers to the basic piece as restoring to it those full and natural powers of which it was temporarily deprived in the opening phase of statutory forward movement. Promotion, in any event, proves upon examination to be so natural an outcome of prohibiting backward moves that there is no need to insist upon it as a borrowing from Chess. Van der Stoep, indeed, goes so far as to suggest not only that promotion did exist in reticular Alquerque, either inherently or as a variant, but also, in view of the apparently ancestral grid on the ancient Egyptian temple of Kurna, may even have predated Chess—in which case, who borrowed what from whom?

Thus derived, Short or Anglo-French Draughts differs little, if at all, from the modern Anglo-American game. All it lacks besides the refinement of modern tournament rules is a demonstrable rule of compulsory capture, which I believe was originally absent or sporadic. Murray asserts that what led to the expansion of interest in Draughts in the sixteenth century was the invention, in France, of the rule of compulsory capture under penalty of the huff, which 'raised Draughts to a parity with Chess'. The resultant game was known as Forcé, short for *le jeu des dames forcé,* later as Forçat—i.e. Draughts with forced capture, as opposed to *le jeu plaisant des dames,* meaning 'Draughts with capture at pleasure'. Rabelais gives both *dames* and *forcé* in his list of Gargantuan games (1535), and in a later book uses the verb *damer,* 'to crown a man', in the sense of 'to cap a story'. That Cotgrave's French–English Dictionary of 1611 defines *forçat* as 'a game of draughts, wherin one must take his aduersarie when he may, or else he himselfe is taken',[21] and Urquhart's translation of Rabelais' *dames* and *forcé* as, respectively, Dames and Draughts, might suggest that compulsory capture was original to Draughts. It may, however, merely mean that the term Draughts became transferred from the original to the game generally regarded as superior and therefore definitive.

The earliest probable equation of French *dames* with Draughts occurs in Eloy d'Amerval's *Livre de diablerie* (1508), with *jeu d'echecz ou des dames / que sont beaulx jeux, non infames.* The first French book on Draughts—Pierre Mallet's *Le Ieu des Dames* (Paris, 1668)—deals primarily with an advanced version of the game invented in Paris around 1650. Called Grand Forçat, this introduced the restrictive capturing protocol later known as *il più col più* in Italy. The new game does not seem to have spread beyond the confines of the capital, where it became obsolete by 1700. In Mallet, too, occurs the last reference to Plaisant, the free-capture game, which in England also failed to outlive the seventeenth century.

Spanish Draughts. The basic form of the game in which the doubleton moves long is known as Spanish Draughts. Spain plays an important role in the early history of Draughts. Her players were renowned for their prowess in the sixteenth century, from which period also date the first books specifically devoted to the game. In 1547 appeared *El ingenio a juego de marro de punta o damas,* by Antonio de Torquemada, and in 1591 *Libro del iuego de* *las damas, vulgarmente nombrado el marro,* by Pedro Luiz Montero. Marro, a Catalan word perhaps derived from Iberian (pre-Latin) *marr,* a gaming-piece (compare *calculus* > *alquerque*), originally denoted a game identical with or similar to Alquerque. Its earliest mentions emanate from Menorca in 1370 and 1437, the latter referring to a gaming board 'suitable for Chess on one side and Marro on the other' (Van der Stoep, *History of Draughts,* 81). Marro de Punta, in Torquemada's title, means 'Marro played on the squares of a chequerboard', thus reconfirming the relationship between Draughts and Alquerque. According to Govert Westerveld—in an article arguing that the origination of Draughts by transferring Alquerque to the chessboard occurred in fifteenth-century Spain[22]—the reason why the chessboard prevailed over the lined board from about 1500 onwards is cultural rather than technical. The primary meaning of *marro* is 'deviant' or 'unorthodox' (cf. French *marron,* 'quack [doctor]'). This would explain not only why the 'vulgar' name Marro was dropped in favour of the more refined-sounding Damas, but also why the practice of playing it on a chequerboard prevailed over that of a lined grid, since the latter was associated with such heterodox members of Spanish society as Jews and Moriscos.

In deriving Damas (Marro de la Punta) from Alquerque (Marro), Westerveld brings into play a game called Andarraya. First mentioned in a poem of 1434, it is glossed in a Spanish–Latin dictionary of 1495 as *calculorum ludus,* as is Alquerque, but with a note to the effect that it is a new entry. Westerveld sees Andarraya as played on a linear grid equivalent to the topology of the diagonals of a chequerboard, like that of Draughts as still played in the Philippines, a former Spanish colony (Fig. 15.7). Perhaps Andarraya was Alquerque extended by the principle of promotion to a long-moving doubleton, like the newly empowered Chess queen. At this point we may agree with Westerveld in placing the invention of the long

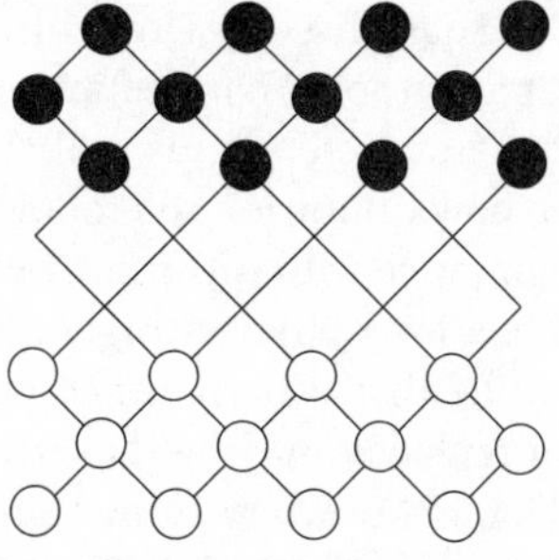

Fig. 15.7. Philippine Draughts, perhaps also Andarraya.

queen at both Draughts and Chess in fifteenth-century Spain, rather than with Murray in crediting it to Italy, which is unlikely in view of the fact that Italy is one of the few countries not to have adopted the long queen into its national form of Draughts. Adopting the theory of a Spanish origin *in toto*, however, leads to the incredible assumption that Draughts was originally played with a long queen, but in Italy and northern Europe the doubleton was subsequently reduced in power to that of the short king.

Just as the idea of promotion can be shown to have arisen independently in Draughts without being a borrowing of Chess, so we can agree with Westerveld that the long queen in both games arose from the fever of experimentation that was taking place in all games throughout the fifteenth century, and not necessarily as a borrowing by Draughts from Chess (Murray *et al.*) or vice versa (van der Stoep). The long queen is better regarded as the invention of a gaming community rather than of a particular game, as was invariably the case before the growth of printing and consequent concept of 'official rules'. Westerveld identifies this with the Jewish community of Valencia. It was here that the two earliest Draughts treatises were published, and both Torquemada and Montero appear to have been Jewish. Montero declares it fitting that he should publish his own book on Draughts in that kingdom, where the most skilful players are to be found. It may have been by the dispersion of the Sephardic Jews, shortly after the birth of a game to which they had significantly contributed, that long Draughts spread throughout Europe, to the Levant and into North Africa. This might explain the variety of forms in which it occurs—including orthogonal Draughts—as partly due to the fact that experiments were still going on with long queen moves on a chessboard, and that different versions of the game were carried by emigrants from different points of departure.

The subsequent history of Draughts in Europe is dominated by a tussle between original Anglo-French Short Draughts and the more exciting and skill-demanding game of Spanish Long Draughts. Long Draughts spread northwards along the 'Spanish road' connecting all the Habsburg possessions of Charles V, reaching the Netherlands probably before the stationing of Spanish troops on the Low Countries' soil following the Dutch Revolt of 1566. To this early acquaintance with the improved game may be ascribed the fact that Draughts has long enjoyed higher status and is still more popular in the Netherlands than in any other European country.[23] The Short Draughts which it replaced may be that depicted in an illustration in a fifteenth-century Flemish breviary from Tournai reproduced by van der Stoep.[24] Tournai was French, but the illustration shows play on the dark squares, which follows Dutch rather than French tradition.

'Polish' Draughts. The eventual success of Long over Short Draughts in most of Europe occurred not in its original Spanish form but in a variety mistakenly designated 'Polish' Draughts. The distinguishing features of this game are, first, that the singleton can capture (but not otherwise move) backwards as well as forwards, and, secondly, that it is typically played on an enlarged board of 10 × 10 squares and consequently with twenty pieces rather than twenty-four.

The legendary origin of 'Polish' Draughts goes back to an enquiry made by one Charles de la Condamine in the *Mercure de France* of July 1770, and a subsequent study published by M. Manoury in 1787. Manoury concluded that it was invented jointly by an officer at the court of the Regent, Philippe II of Orleans (1713–23), and a Pole known as the Polonese. The latter thought backward captures for the singleton would improve the game, and the former suggested that a larger board would enhance the improvement. De la Condamine had himself heard from ex-King Stanislas Leczinski that the game was known in Poland as *le jeu de Dames françoises,* thus apparently confirming a French origin.

Far from being invented in Paris in the 1720s, 10 × 10 draughtboards are evidenced in the Netherlands as early as the first half of the seventeenth century, one being depicted in a painting of 1635 and another in an engraving by an artist who died in 1636 (van der Stoep, *History of Draughts,* 105). Writing in 1617, Daniel de Souter[25] describes as 'the common game in Holland' a form of Draughts with 15 pieces per player, implying a 10 × 10 board, upon which an extension to 20 a side would be a natural development. As to the ability to capture backwards, such a rule is implied in a four-player Draughts variation by C. D. M. Zeel, published in The Hague in 1681, perhaps also in some lines of a Dutch play of 1671 (van der Stoep, *History of Draughts,* 102). A French–Dutch dictionary of 1710 renders *Sçavez-vous damer à la Polonaise?* as *Kend gy op zyn Pools dammen?* In this connection, van der Stoep points out that while Dutch *Pools* primarily means 'Polish', it carries the figurative sense of exotic or bizarre—rather like the 'Chinese' in Chinese snooker, Chinese finesse, etc. Perhaps it implied 'muddled' or 'confusing' and was originally coined for the expansion to 20 pieces a side.

Italian Draughts. Draughts is recorded in Italy under the name *Dame* from 1611, *Dama* from 1750, and as *Ludus dominarum* in a Latin text of the late sixteenth century. Murray's 1527 reference to *donne* actually denotes playing-card queens.[26] Draughts has never been called *donne,* nor even *guioco de dama,* but always plain *dama.* It originally denoted the singleton, which, when promoted, became *damata.* This game, first described by Mallet in 1668, is distinguished by its unusual capturing protocol known as *il più col più*, whereby a player confronted with alternative captures must choose that which

- takes the greatest number of pieces
- if equal, captures with a queen rather than a pawn
- if two or more queens can capture, takes more queens than pawns
- if still equal, takes a queen first, or as many as possible before taking a pawn.

The first books devoted to Italian Draughts were a collection of games and problems by Cesare Mancini, *Il giuoco della Dama all'uso italiano* (Florence, 1830), and a more substantial treatise by Michelangelo Lanci, *Il Trattato teorico-pratico del gioco di Dama* (Rome, 1837). The *Federazione Italiana Dama* was founded in 1924 and the first championship title contested at Milan the following year. Its affiliation to the World Draughts Federation in 1964 has resulted in an increase in the practice of Continental Long Draughts.

German Draughts. The earliest German mention occurs in Selenus, *Das Schach- oder König-Spiel* (Leipzig, 1616), where it is called Dammen-Spiel; but a German board and twenty-four pieces preserved at Nürnberg certainly date from the previous century. The traditional German game is virtually identical with Spanish Draughts, with capture obligatory but no requirement to make the longest series (*Mehrschlagzwang*).[27] When this replaced original Short Draughts is unclear, as Selenus does not specify the doubleton's move. 'Polish' Draughts reached Germany in the early eighteenth century, but was often played on the 8 × 8 board. Rules subsequently published in German books often combine (or confuse) one form of Draughts with another, though the term 'Polish' consistently implies backward capturing for the singleton.

Scandinavian and Baltic Draughts. Apart from Iceland, a latecomer to the Draughts scene, Short Draughts was current in Scandinavia and the Baltic countries until the early seventeenth century, when it was overtaken by Long and subsequently 'Polish' Draughts—except in Denmark, where the Short game still flourishes. This group includes the Swedish and Norwegian Dam, Polish Dama or Warcaby, and the Ukrainian Damki. In the Russian Shashki a singleton promotes immediately upon reaching the crownhead, and may, if possible, continue capturing as such in the same turn of play. In Finnish Draughts, the doubleton is obliged to end its series of captures (or single capture) by landing on the square immediately beyond the last piece captured. Interaction between different varieties produced a game called Makvær (Danish) or Marquere (Swedish). It is basically Long Draughts except that the singleton, upon capturing a necessarily appointant piece, need not land on the square immediately beyond but may pass over any number of successively vacant squares in the same direction—a quasi 'long' capture. It first appeared in a Danish manual of 1802, while the first Icelandic Draughts book, of 1858, describes Makvær and 8 × 8 'Polish'.

Frisian Draughts, still played in the northern Netherlands, was formerly more widespread. In the 1730s it became popular in Paris under the name Babylonian Draughts (*dame à la babilonienne*), threatening for a while to become established as the standard game in place of 'Polish'. This it resembles in being played with twenty pieces per player on a 10 × 10 board; but its distinction is the fact that they can move orthogonally as well as diagonally. Orthogonal Draughts is mentioned in Poland, and Munich is home to an 8 × 8 board of apparently Russian provenance accompanied by sixteen pieces of one colour (only seven remain of the other), again suggesting an orthogonal variety. Eighteenth- and nineteenth-century German literature mentions a variety designated *englisch* (possibly in mistake for Frisian), in which the doubleton may move diagonally or orthogonally.[28] Hyde in 1689 describes an 8 × 8 German game in which each player starts with sixteen pieces on his two back ranks. They move and capture either forwards or sideways, and, upon promotion, move and capture long in any of eight directions—like a Chess queen, but remaining always on squares of one colour.

Frisian and its relatives at first sight recall Graeco-Turkish Draughts, but, whereas these are played on unchequered boards and with orthogonal movement only, those of northern Europe use chequered boards and combine both types, thus reinforcing the symbiotic relationship of chequering and diagonal movement. Lacking historical records, we might suspect that Frisian represents an early transference of Alquerque to the chequerboard, retaining the sideways movement of the parent game before it was abandoned in favour of diagonal movement only.

It remains to add that forms of ortho-diagonal Draughts are also reported from Armenia and Thailand.[29]

Graeco-Turkish Draughts. The form of Draughts played in Eastern Europe, Israel, and Egypt (Greek and Turkish Dama, Turkish also Atlanbaj), characterized by its play with orthogonal moves on an unchequered board, awaits historical research to establish its relationship with western Draughts. The fact that it has a long-moving doubleton suggests an

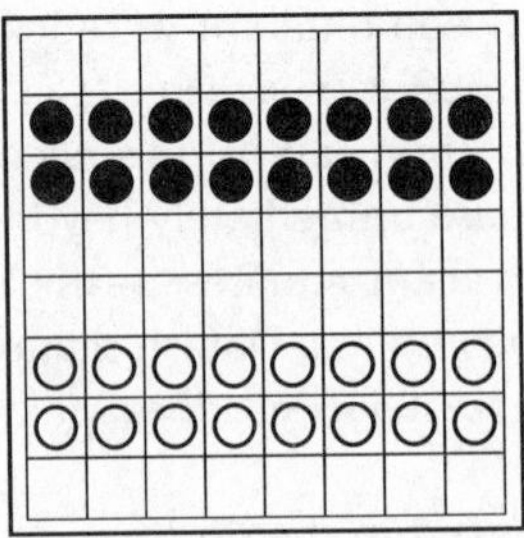

Fig. 15.8. Graeco-Turkish (orthogonal) Draughts: initial array.

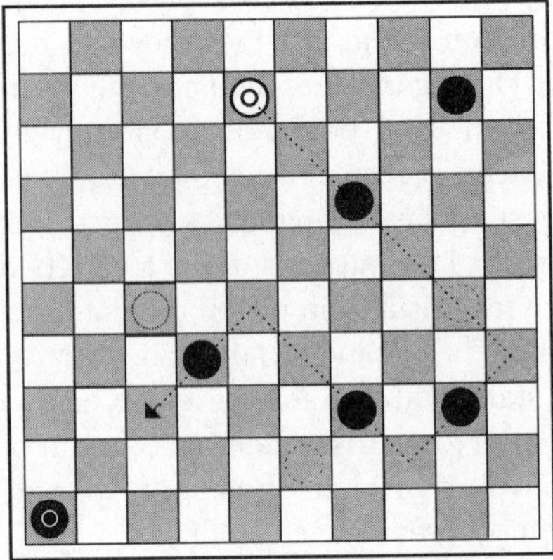

Fig. 15.9. Implications of the long queen at Continental ('Polish') Draughts. This white queen must make four captures, finishing on either of two squares of the long diagonal, whereupon it will be captured by the black queen. It cannot evade capture by making only three (dotted circles), as it is obliged by law to make the longest possible series. Nor, after the first three, can it capture the black piece at top right, so evading capture itself, because its route is blocked by the body of its first victim.

historical relationship with Spanish Draughts, which Westerveld ascribes to the expulsion of Jews from Spain. The unchequered board is, of course, also characteristic of eastern Chess. It renders diagonal patterns less evident, but the perfectly logical orthogonal equivalents strengthen the theory of an ultimate derivation from Alquerque.

International Draughts. Following the Second World War a need was felt for a variety of Draughts capable of being embraced by all countries, with their differing traditions, as a standard tournament game. In 1946 the Dutch player Hermann Hoogland proposed a game with the following features: board 8 × 8; singletons move forwards only but can capture backwards; they promote only upon reaching the crownhead and having no further captures to make; queens move and capture long; capture is compulsory and a longer series must be taken in preference to a shorter; no huffing. A few matches were played under these rules, but in 1947 a World Draughts Federation was founded, with the active participation of French, Belgian, Dutch, and Swiss Associations, which favoured a game with substantially similar rules but played on the 10 × 10 board. The Federation has been officially known as the Fédération Mondiale du Jeu de Dames since 1956 and has affiliated to it the national Federations of over twenty European countries.

Board: 10 × 10 = 100. Play on dark squares to the right.

Each places twenty singletons on four home ranks. White starts.

Singletons are pawns, doubletons queens.

The pawn moves diagonally forwards one square only.

A pawn may capture either forwards or backwards (like a king in Short Draughts), and a multiple capture may consist of any number of captures in either or both directions.

Upon reaching the crownhead it must continue capturing if possible, in which case it remains a pawn. It becomes a queen only upon reaching the crownhead and remaining there.

A queen moves any distance in any diagonal direction (like a Chess bishop), but not over a piece of its own colour nor over more than one enemy piece.

It captures by jumping an enemy piece and landing on any further vacant square beyond, provided that all intervening squares are vacant.

In a multiple capture, a queen may pass over the same vacant square more than once, but not over the same enemy piece more than once. Captured pieces are not removed from the board until the end of the series, and may therefore block subsequent moves in the same turn.

Capture is compulsory. Given a choice of initial captures, a player must take that which will capture the greatest number of pieces in the same turn. If equal, the choice is free.

If a player fails to capture when able to do so, his opponent may either accept the move, or insist that the position be restored and the capture made. Huffing has been abolished in tournament play.

The game is drawn if both players agree that neither can force a win, or if the same position occurs three times in three moves (by each player).

A game ending with three queens against one is deemed drawn if the advantaged player does not win within fifteen moves, or five moves if the lone queen is on the single long diagonal.

An expansion of Draughts to an even larger board became well established in Canada in the second half of the nineteenth century, though 12×12 boards are said to have been on sale in London in 1805. Play takes place on the dark squares, oriented to the right, each player starting with thirty singletons on his first five ranks. The rules of play are identical with those described above. Indian Draughts (Dam) is the same.

Anglo-American Draughts (UK), Checkers (US), Dams (Scotland)

Board: $8 \times 8 = 64$. Play on dark squares to the right.
Each places twelve singletons on three home ranks. Black starts.
Singletons are *men*, doubletons *kings*.
The man moves diagonally forwards one square only.
Upon reaching the crownhead it promotes to a king and stops.
The king moves in any diagonal direction, one square only.
In a multiple capture, a king may land on the same vacant square, but not pass over the same enemy piece, more than once. Captured pieces are not removed from the board until the end of the multiple capture.
Capture is compulsory. Huffing has been abolished in tournament play.
If more than one capture is possible, the choice is free.
The game is drawn if both players agree that neither can force a win, or if in a period of fifty consecutive moves (by each player) neither has made a king or a capture, or if the same position has been reached four times in four moves (by each player).

Draughts seems not to have been taken seriously in England before the late eighteenth century. It rates but brief descriptions in Holme (1688) and Hyde (1694), though the former does place it second after Chess and before 'Miracle', i.e. Merels. But not a word of it appears in Cotton's *Compleat Gamester* of 1674, or in Cotgrave's *Wit's Interpreter* (1652) on which he drew, nor yet in any of the subsequent editions and spin-offs of Cotton's work, including the various editions of Seymour's early eighteenth-century *Court Gamester*. Seymour was superseded by Edmond Hoyle, who also found nothing to say about it—a fact so remarkable as to suggest that he evidently did not regard it as a game played by those persons of leisure and refinement to whom he habitually addressed himself. In fact, it had been favoured by sharps and gamblers of the Restoration period, such as

Jonathan Laud of Lincoln, of whom Theophilus Lucas writes in *Lives of the Gamesters* (1714):

At length he became an excellent player at Draughts, at which he had ruin'd several tradesmen in and about London; and won many hundreds of pounds by a decoy of giving such as play'd with him 4 Kings to only 1 King and 3 Men; which were so plac'd, that 2 of the men must be lost move how he would, but nevertheless he won the game, by reason his 1 King at last takes the other's 4 Kings all at one moving. He was such a great artist at this game, that he would give any man a guinea that would bring a person to play with him for three guineas, till at last he was so noted for his ingenuity at Draughts, that none would play with him.

(Unusually for one of Lucas's subjects, who typically paid their debts at Tyburn, Jonathan Laud made a fortune at dice, bought an estate in Oxfordshire, married well, and lived happily ever after.)

A taste for Draughts at this time may have been imported from the Low Countries, where it always has been more popular and where the English court spent much of its time before Charles II was invited home. Murray believed it was through Scottish soldiers serving in Dutch wars that Scotland derived an interest in the game that has always exceeded that of England; but it does not follow that the game itself reached Scotland from Holland. For one thing, Dams is Short Draughts and Dutch is Long: for another, the word Dams more probably derives from French *dames* than from Dutch *damspel*, reflecting the long cultural association between France and Scotland prior to the Treaty of Union of 1707. Possibly a Dutch influence on the Scottish game is reflected in the different arrangement of the board from that of England, and in its terminology—*Dams* for the doubletons and hence the name of the game, and *dambrod* for the board.

It must have been as a student at Edinburgh University that Dr Johnson's biographer James Boswell became a Draughts enthusiast. Referring to 1756, he wrote:

This year Mr. William Payne, brother of the respectable bookseller of that name, published 'An Introduction to the Game of Draughts', to which Johnson contributed a Dedication to the Earl of Rochford, and a Preface, both of which are admirably adapted to the treatise to which they are prefixed. Johnson, I believe, did not play at Draughts after leaving College, by which he suffered; for it would have afforded him an innocent, soothing relief from the melancholy which distressed him so often. I have heard him regret that he had not learned to play at cards; and the game of Draughts we know is peculiarly calculated to fix the attention without straining it. There is a composure and gravity in Draughts which insensibly tranquillises the mind, and accordingly the Dutch are fond of it . . .

That Johnson had played as a student suggests a reasonable degree of respect for the game at Oxford around 1730. It was evidently at this time that Draughts, like Whist, began to attract more socially acceptable attention. Payne himself refers to 'the Multitudes that practise', and to a famed player, possibly his own mentor, 'the Great Randell, of whom it may with probability be asserted, that what he could not attain will never be discovered'. Even so, his own introduction appears modest to the point of apologetic:

It is not for a Man to think ill of the Art which he professes to teach, and I may therefore be expected to have some Esteem for the Play of DRAUGHTS. I would not, however, be thought to over-rate it. Every Art is valued in a just Proportion to its Difficulty and Usefulness. The use of DRAUGHTS is the same with that of any other Game of Skill, that it may amuse those Hours for which more laudable Employment is not at Hand...

The rest of the book is devoted to fifty sample games, starting with one later to be classed as a variant of the Single Corner opening (11–15, 22–18: 15–22, 25–18: 8–11, 29–25: 4–8, 25–22, etc.), and followed by a number of positions with an accompanying commentary. (The playing squares are numbered 1–4 from right to left along the bottom row, followed by 5–8 in the same direction, and so on.)

Payne's work shows that Draughts had come of age by the mid-eighteenth century, despite some remarkable absences in contemporary literature. Hoyle survived to 1769 without having turned his pen to Draughts, and not until 1791 did it eventually appear in an edition (by Charles Jones) of the title that continues to perpetuate his name. By the end of the century Strutt writes 'The pastime of draughts is well known in the present day (1800), and I believe there are now in London as excellent draught-players as ever existed.' That same year saw the publication in London of *The Guide to the Game of Draughts, containing 500 select games* by Joshua Sturges. Dedicated to the Prince of Wales, it boasted a list of notable subscriptions, including two on the part of Lady Hamilton ('His and Hers?', as Derek Oldbury[30] pertinently—or perhaps impertinently—enquires). It incorporated almost all of Payne's work, albeit revised and vastly expanded, and remained a classic for at least 100 years.

Oldbury characterizes the nineteenth century as an 'Age of Giants', with 'professionals stalking the land, closely guarded by their patrons and backers', their epic encounters reported blow-by-blow in *Bell's Life,* better known under its later title *Sporting Life.* Newspapers throughout the English-speaking world, including the UK, US, Australia, and Canada, carried regular features on the theory, practice, and current news about the game. By the end of the century Draughts was the subject of hundreds of handbooks and pamphlets, and of no fewer than four periodicals in Britain alone. It was an age brought to an end, avers Oldbury, 'by the rise of amateurism and the forming of National Organisations for the promoting of the game'.

Both the English and the Scottish Draughts Associations were formed in the 1890s, some twenty years after an international match between the two countries, which resulted in a resounding win for Scotland. One outcome of the Scottish pre-eminence at Draughts is the picturesque, if technically irrelevant, range of titles for standard openings and their variations, amongst which may be noted *Ayrshire Lassie, Laird and Lady, Flora Temple, Maid o' the Mill,* and the more pedestrian *Glasgow, Kelso, Dundee, Paisley,* etc. Another may have been the final adoption by English players of the practice of playing on the dark squares rather than the light. Payne had long since directed that 'The Draught Table must be placed with White at top right', and Sturges in 1800 observed:

> The rule (almost universal with English Draughts) is to play on the white squares. The exception (limited we believe to Scotland) is to play on the *black*. When, therefore, players are pledged to a match without any previous agreement as to which squares are to be played upon, white must be taken as the law.

These early tournaments—the first was at Glasgow in 1893—were soon tightened up by the introduction of the so-called 'two-move restriction'. Without restrictions, a player whose sole intention is not to lose can specialise in one or two openings and can expect to draw over 95 per cent of his games, with obvious loss of interest.[31] Under the two-move restriction, the players started not from the standard opening position but from one of 43 positions attainable after Black and White have each made one move. In fact there are 49 possibilities, but two were rejected out of hand because they led to the immediate loss of material for White, and four less obviously unbalanced positions were identified later.

It was with the two-move restriction that a combined British (Anglo-Scottish) team took on the American Draughts Association at Boston in 1905 and beat them by 73 to 34 games, with 284 drawn. At the Second International, held at New York in 1927, the Americans got their own back with 96 wins to 20, and 364 draws, and went on to consolidate their position at the third, held in 1973 at Bournemouth, with 79 wins to 21, and 200 drawn.

In the 1930s, the American Checkers Association introduced a three-move restriction, whereby Black and White's first and Black's second move were predetermined. The number of possible openings thereby increased to 144, of which some 80 favour White (if only marginally) and about a dozen Black. This was obviously motivated by the fact that, as Checkers increased in popularity (especially during the Depression, which also favoured the explosive expansion of Contract Bridge and the invention of Monopoly), so players explored and discovered standard continuations for the original 43 opening positions, resulting in yet more drawn games. Some, less charitably, have voiced the opinion that at least part of the motivation was to nullify the title of World Champion which a Scot, Robert Stewart, had held from 1922 to 1937 without having been obliged to defend it, the argument being that the title had been gained under 'obsolete' rules.

Variations on a Theme

Bashnya, reportedly an old Russian game,[32] differs from Lasca (see below) only in that it is played on an 8×8 board with twelve pieces on each player's three home ranks.

Black and White (Parlett) is an ortho-diagonal variant. Play like Anglo-American Short Draughts, but with this difference: Black places his pieces on the black squares of his three home ranks, while White places his on the corresponding white squares (or vice versa). Singletons move forwards one square diagonally, but capture orthogonally, either forwards or sideways. Kings follow the same principle, but can move and capture backwards as well as forwards.[33]

Contract Checkers (L. S. Stricker, Chicago, 1934). Play as Anglo-American Draughts, but with twelve pieces (each) on the board and an agreed additional number in hand. As soon as a player moves a piece from his single corner, or any other agreed home square, he immediately enters an additional piece on the vacated square.

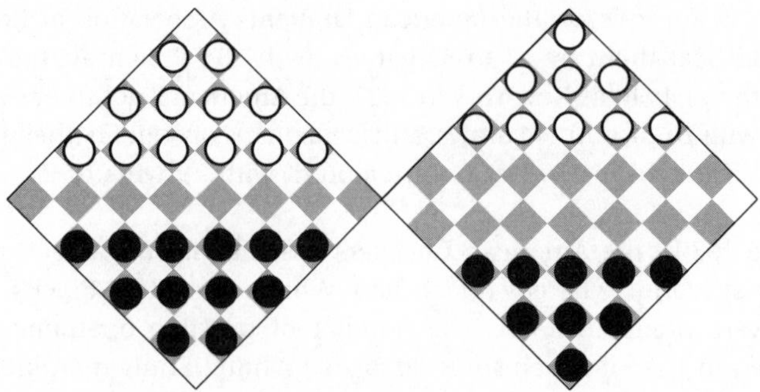

Fig. 15.10. Two varieties of Diagonal Draughts.

Diagonal Draughts (traditional) is merely Anglo-American Draughts with each player's twelve pieces so placed initially as to leave clear the long diagonal of dark squares. A piece is crowned upon reaching a diagonally opposite edge of the board, but players may agree to restrict the crownhead to the diagonals of five and seven squares only.

Digital Draughts (Sackson). Each player's twelve men are numbered 1 to 6, two of each number. One player arranges his men ad lib on his first three rows, and the other reflects this initial arrangement on his own side. When a man is crowned, the 'crown' is placed beneath it, leaving the king with the number it had as a man. No piece may capture a man or a king of a higher number than itself. A player wins by immobilizing all the enemy pieces, or by capturing both enemy sixes. If neither can force victory in this way, the winner is the player whose remaining pieces have the higher total value. *Variant*: Upon reaching the crownhead, a man is removed from the board (so there are no kings). The winner is the first player to reach a total of 30 or more by counting together the values of pieces so removed and of enemy pieces captured.

Double-back Draughts (Addison).[34] Standard Anglo-American, but a player wins by being the first to return a king to his own back rank.

Double-Cross (Parlett) is a combination of Short and Long Draughts. It starts as Anglo-American Draughts, but when a king reaches its own home rank it is re-crowned with a third piece and becomes a queen, with the power of moving and capturing long.

Indians and Trappers. A nineteenth-century variant also called Smugglers and Customs Officers, this game is really a hybrid of Draughts and Halma. Set the 8×8 board up as for Anglo-American Draughts. The aim is immobilize the enemy entirely, or to get all one's pieces across the board in such a way as to occupy all the cells initially occupied by enemy pieces. There are no captures and no promotions. Pieces move diagonally backwards or forwards to the next available unoccupied point, which, if not adjacent, may involve jumping over an unbroken succession of one or more enemy pieces.

Lasca, also called **Laska** and **Laskers,** is a classic game deserving a wider audience.[35] It was first described by Emanuel Lasker in a booklet of 1911 published in Germany, where it is still played. Lasker obviously derived the game from Bashnya, which he may have encountered on one of his visits to Russia in his capacity as World Chess Champion. (Compare Pasta, Chapter 8.)

Lasca is played on a board of 7×7 cells, using only those cells of the majority colour, or on the interior points of an 8×8 draughtboard. The twenty-two draughtmen are plain on one side and marked on the other. A piece with its plain side up is a 'soldier', with its marked side up an 'officer'. Each player starts with eleven soldiers on the points of his three home rows $(4 + 3 + 4)$.

The aim is to gain total control by immobilizing all enemy pieces. Captured pieces are not removed from the board but are held (and moved) in custody, and may regain their freedom.

Each in turn moves a soldier one point diagonally forwards, or captures (short) by jumping. The jumpee is not removed from the board, but placed beneath its capturer to form a pile of two. The top piece of a pile is its 'guide', and the pile counts as a compound piece belonging to the player whose guide is on top. If a single or compound piece jumps a singleton, the latter is added to the bottom of the pile to form a larger compound piece. If it jumps a compound piece, however, only the latter's guide is captured and added to the bottom of the capturing pile. The top piece of the reduced pile thereby becomes its new guide, and its colour determines who owns it and in which direction it moves. In this way, piles may grow to a maximum of twelve pieces.

When a piece or pile reaches the opposite side of the board, relative to the colour of its guide, its guide is turned upside down and is thereby promoted from a soldier to an officer. An officer, or any pile headed by an officer, moves one point diagonally in any direction, and jumps enemy pieces or piles in the same way as before. Officers retain their rank for the rest of the game: they are never turned over or decommissioned.

A player who fails to capture when able to do so loses the game. Captures are enchained, but it is not obligatory to make the longest series possible.

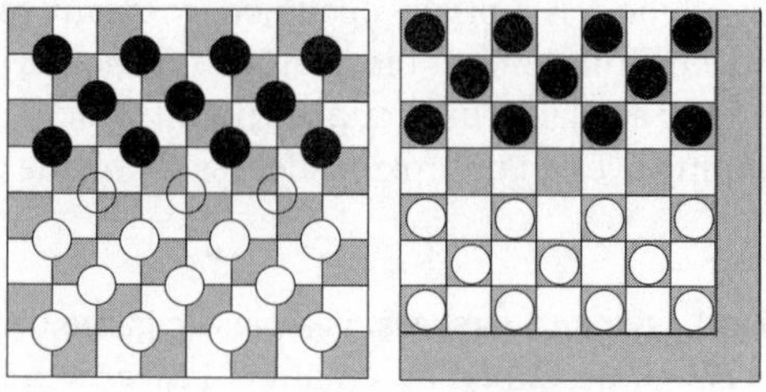

Fig. 15.11. Lasca, on the points (*left*), on the cells (*right*).

Losing Draughts (Traditional). Any form of Draughts can be played negatively, the aim being to be the first to lose all one's pieces, or to have lost more than the other at end of play. Failing to capture when able to do so results in immediate loss. The losing variant of Long Draughts is usually played in an asymmetrical form reminiscent of Fox and Geese. One player starts with his usual complement of twenty pieces on the two back ranks, the other with a single queen that cannot be captured. Losing Draughts is recorded in Germany as *das verkehrtes Damenspiel* ('Draughts in Reverse') from 1744. The French game was described by Mallet in 1668 under the name Coc-Imbert (*sic*). The Gargantuan game of Coquimbert (*qui gagne perd,* 'who wins, loses') listed by Rabelais is undoubtedly the card-game ancestral to Hearts, and not Losing Draughts as Murray suggests.

Redrafting Draughts (Addison). There are no kings. Upon reaching the crownhead, a man is removed from the board and re-entered on any square of its home rank on the first subsequent turn on which this is possible. Re-entry precedes but does not count as a normal move on the same turn.

Stack (Focus). Sid Sackson's[36] relative of Lasca is played on a draughtboard under the name Stack, or on a special board as published under the name Focus. The Focus board is equivalent to the fifty-two squares of an 8×8 board from which are omitted each corner square and each of the two adjoining it on either side. It is not strictly a Draughts game, since capture is by replacement rather than jumping.

Each player starts with eighteen pieces of his own colour arranged in adjacent pairs on the central thirty-six squares (see Fig. 15.12). All moves are orthogonal. Each in turn moves a piece one space. If it lands on a piece of either colour, it forms a stack. A stack belongs to the player whose colour is on top, and it moves as many spaces as it contains pieces. A player need not move an entire stack belonging to himself: he may instead break it at any point and move just the top section. Such a 'sub-stack' moves as many

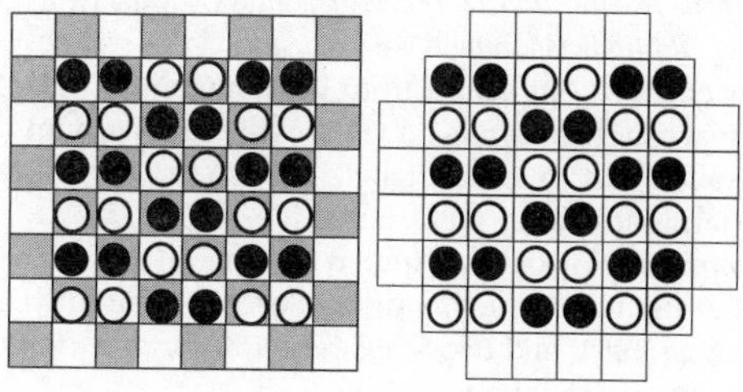

Fig. 15.12. Sid Sackson's game of Stack (*left*), Focus (*right*).

spaces as it contains pieces, and the portion left in place belongs to whoever controls the uppermost piece.

If a piece or stack, by landing on another, thereby creates a stack of five or more, the pieces below the fifth piece from the top are removed from the board. Those belonging to the enemy are captured, and never return. Those belonging to the capturing player return to hand. On any turn, a player may, instead of moving a stack, enter a piece from hand to any vacant space or stack on the board, but may not move it in the same turn.

The winner is the last player able to move.

Transportation Draughts (Addison). Each player's twelve pieces move like kings. An opposing king may be jumped in the usual way, but is not removed from the board. The winner is the first to either immobilize all the enemy kings, or to get all his own kings on to the twelve squares initially occupied by them at the opposite end of the board.

NOTES

1. Cited by F. W. Lewis in his preface to an otherwise worthless paper, namely G. Limbrey, *The Ancient History of the Game of Draughts* (London, 1913).
2. Tom Landry, 'The Third International Draughts Match', *Games & Puzzles*, 22 (Feb. 1974), 6.
3. Bell, *Board and Table Games*, i. 48.
4. K. W. Kruijswijk, *Algemene historie en bibliografie van het damspel* (The Hague, 1966).
5. Murray, *History of Board Games*, 66, gives details.
6. Alberto Zamboni, 'Etimologie Friulane e Venete', in *Studie linguistice Friulane*, cited by A. van der Stoep, *A History of Draughts* (Rockanje, 1984).
7. Lhôte, 481 and 521, the latter also in Bell and Murray.
8. Lhôte, 482, from A. Bouhajbane, *Jeux Morocains* (University of Paris, 1989).
9. Lhôte, 559, from Bell and Murray.
10. Lhôte, 514, from Capt. Bissuel, *Les Touareg de l'Ouest* (Algiers, 1888).
11. Lhôte, 614, from *Jeux et Stratégie* (June/July 1984); also Murray.
12. Lhôte, 518.
13. Murray, *History of Board Games*, 82.
14. Culin, *Games of the North American Indians*; cited by Murray.
15. Bell, *Discovering Old Board Games*, 42–5.
16. Murray, *History of Board Games*, 89, from W. Montgomery, 'The Malagasy Game of Fanorona', in *Antananarivo Annual*, 3 (1896). All other accounts I have seen derive from the same source, but for some original notes on strategy see also David Pritchard, *Brain Games* (Harmondsworth, 1982), 60–85.
17. The *dame* < *domina* etymology is disputed by Arie van der Stoep in a doctoral thesis not completed at the time of (my) writing. See, however, this author's *A History of Draughts* (Rockanje, 1984) and *Een Schaakloze Damhistorie* (Rockanje, 1994), in two parts, i, *Bouwstoffen*, ii, *Geschiedenis*.
18. Fiske, *Chess in Iceland*, 93 n.

19. Murray, *History of Board Games*, 73–6.
20. Van der Stoep, *History of Draughts*; *Een Schaakloze Damhistorie*, i and ii.
21. Murray, verbatim, 76.
22. Govert Westerveld, 'Historia de la nueva dama poderosa en el juego de ajedrez y Damas', *Homo Ludens*, 4 (1994), 103–24.
23. Van der Stoep, *History of Draughts*, 112.
24. Ibid. 65.
25. Souterius, *Palamedes* (Leiden 1617), p. xx.
26. Murray's reference (*History of Board Games*, 72), has been examined and negated by Franco Pratesi, so I am informed by van der Stoep.
27. Claus D. Grupp, *Dame—das Brettspiel in allen Variationen* (Leinfelden, 1979), 99.
28. The earliest occurs in the *Deutsche Encyclopädie* (Frankfurt, 1782), vi. 699.
29. Armenian is recorded in an article by Willi Schmidt in *La Revue française du jeu de dames* (1934), 393–4. For Thailand, van der Stoep writes: 'In Thailand, Draughts on 64 squares is said to be extremely popular. A Dutch Draughtsplayer who visited Thailand some years ago swears that the Thai are playing Frisian Draughts (and still another variety). The Thai call it MAK-YAEK (< MAKVAER?)'. (Personal communication.)
30. Derek Oldbury: *The Complete Encyclopaedia of Draughts*, i (Torquay, 1978), 120.
31. Tom Landry, 'The Third International Draughts Match', *Games & Puzzles*, 1st ser. 22 (Feb. 1974), 6 (verbatim).
32. Glonnegger, *Das Spiele-Buch*, 160.
33. Since reading this, van der Stoep has sent me part of an illustration made at Versailles in 1690 which distinctly shows a form of 10 × 10 Draughts, also attested elsewhere, in which the white pieces play on black squares, and *vice versa*.
34. Stephen Addison, *100 Other Games to play on a Chessboard* (London, 1983).
35. See D. B. Johnson-David, 'Laska', *Games & Puzzles*, no. 44 (Jan. 1976), 6–9, and an annotated game by the same author (but now spelling it 'Lasca') in no. 59 (April, 1977), 8–9; also David Pritchard, 'Lasca', in *Brain Games* (Harmondsworth, 1982), 102–5.
36. Sid, Sackson, *A Gamut of Games* (London, 1974), 125–34. Draughtboard variant taken from Addison, *100 Other Games*, 73–4.

Conquering Kings

The Royal Family of Chess Games

Chess is a Royal Game and more difficult to be understood than any other Game whatever, and will take up sometimes in the playing so long a time that I have known two play a fortnight at times before the Game hath been ended: and indeed I believe the tediousness of the Game hath caus'd the practice thereof to be so little used; however since this pastime is so highly ingenious that there is none can parallel it, I shall here lay down some brief instructions tending to the knowledg thereof.

Charles Cotton, *The Compleat Gamester* (1674)

Strange that I, who rule the world from the Indus in the east to Andalusia in the west, cannot manage 32 chessmen.

Caliph al-Mamun

I once read a review of a television quiz programme hosted by a popular entertainer of the day, now long deceased. The answer to one of the questions was 'Chess', to which the host had added, with a smile ingratiating to the point of obsequiousness, 'And what a grand game that is!' It was a comment to which the reviewer took quite justifiable exception. With this in mind, we will take as read the cultural equivalence of Chess with Beethoven's Ninth, and, pausing only to wonder why so many of its greatest exponents have been social misfits, proceed to treat it like any other game in the collection.

Western culture regards Chess as a particular game with a particular set of rules governed by an international authority (FIDE—the Fédération Internationale des Echecs). Variously known as International Chess, World Chess, Orthochess, and so on, it is, in this capacity, far too well documented to justify repetitious elaboration here. For the purposes of the present survey Chess is not 'a game' (and certainly not '*the* game'), but a large family of related games, none of which is inherently superior to any other. They chiefly cover varieties of Chess which in the course of centuries have become the national games of individual countries and cultures, such as Chaturanga (Indian Chess), Xiang-qi (Chinese), Shogi (Japanese), and so on. From this viewpoint, International Chess is merely the 'national' game of Europe, and may be designated Modern European Chess to distinguish it from (for example) the medieval European game, which more closely resembled Chaturanga. Other family members are historical varieties that were once the standard game of particular countries and cultures but are now no longer played—whether because they evolved into later forms, or developed non-viable and ephemeral aberrations, or were ousted by socially superior forms of the game introduced by immigrants or invaders, or simply passed away with the death of the community that played them.

All these varieties can be traced back to a few primitive games that undoubtedly derive from a common ancestor. The nature of this common ancestor remains the basis for all its descendants, and so adopts into the fold of Chess any game based on the following pattern:

A game of movement and capture, rarely of placement.
Bilateral symmetry and equality of material.
Functionally differentiated pieces.
Capture by replacement.
Win by capturing a definitive singleton (commander, king, etc.).

Any game exhibiting this combination of features, whether traditional or invented, is a variety of Chess. Also classifiable as Chess are deliberately invented variants and perversions, which are legion in number. As David Pritchard remarks in the introduction to his invaluable *Encyclopedia of Chess Variants*, 'Anyone can invent a new C[hess] V[ariant] within ten seconds (try it), and unfortunately some people do.'[1]

Archetypal Chess may be outlined as follows:

Two players, nominally Black and White, play on the cells or points of a board of at least $8 \times 8 = 64$ squares.

In the initial array, each starts with a row of differentiated pieces on his back rank and of undifferentiated pieces (pawns, originally representing foot soldiers) on the next or next-but-one rank. Pawns move forwards only. Upon reaching the furthermost rank they promote to more powerful pieces.

Of the differentiated pieces, the most important (but least powerful) is the commander or king, which is initially positioned on one of the centre squares, and whose capture defines the end and loss of the game.

The principal piece is attended by a companion piece (viceroy, minister, counsellor, etc.) initially positioned on the other central square of the first rank. Originally a weak piece, its promotion to the queen of modern European Chess has rendered it the most powerful piece on the board.

The remaining pieces are normally paired, the pairs occupying corresponding positions on the left and right of the board. They typically comprise two pieces that move orthogonally (chariots, ships, or castles known as 'rooks'), two that move diagonally (with a variety of designations from elephants to bishops), and two that move hippogonally (fairly consistently represented as horses, or mounted knights).

Pieces capture one another by replacement, and captured pieces are removed from the board.

The aim of the game is to capture the opposing commander or king—or, in practice, to threaten it in such a way that it cannot escape capture on the next move. A threat of capture is a *check*, an inescapable threat is [*check*] *mate*.

Other possible outcomes are variously treated in different traditions. They are:

Resignation. A player may resign, thus losing the game.

Stalemate. A player cannot move any of his pieces, but his principal is not in check. In International Chess, it draws; in other traditions it wins for the stalemated player; in some, it must by law be avoided.

Bare king. This is the situation in which one player loses all his pieces except the king, which is not in checkmate. In International Chess, play continues. In other traditions, it variously counts as a win or a loss.

Draw by repetition of moves. In International Chess, it is a draw if the same position is reached three times in succession.

Origins

The earliest reference claimed for Chess occurs in Subhandu's *Vasavadatta*, an Indian romantic fantasy about a princess of Ujjayini and dating from not before AD 600. The lines at issue translate: 'The rainy season played its game with frogs for chessmen: green and yellow, as though mottled with lac, they leapt up on the black field squares.' It is not a strong claim. No game is mentioned by name, and the word translated 'chessmen' (*nayadûtair*) is not specific to Chess but can mean gaming pieces in general. The reference to green and yellow frogs does not really imply some of each, like opposing pieces in a board game, but clearly characterizes each one of them as piebald. 'Black squares', which some prefer to translate as 'fields of grain', cannot be taken to imply a chequered board, as chequering is a much later European invention and has never been indigenous to Asia.

A more positive Indian reference dates from about 625. This occurs in Bana's *Harshacharita*, an account of the reign of King Sriharsha of Kanyakubja (606–47), who was renowned for the peacefulness of his character and reign. Light in tone and full of puns, it includes the following lines: 'Under this monarch ... the only quarrels occur among bees in collecting their dews; the only feet cut off are those of metres [in verse]; only from the ashtapada [gaming-board] can one learn how to draw up a chaturanga [army].' The context clearly implies a war-game, and an *ashtapada* is an 8×8-squared gaming board.

Also from the seventh century, and, again, from perhaps as early as 600, comes the first Persian (Iranian) mention of Chess. This occurs in the *Karnamak-i-Artakhshatr,* a Pahlawi romance based on the life of the national hero, Ardashir. Ardashir ruled Persia from 226 to 241 and was the founder of the Sasanian dynasty, which lasted until the Arabian conquest of 641. In a list of complimentary attributes, Ardashir is said to have been 'doughtier and more skilled than all in ball-play, in horsemanship, in *chatrang,* in hunting, and in other accomplishments'. While it is beyond credibility that the game existed as early as the hero's reign, what this extract shows is that Chess was regarded as a royal and intellectual game in seventh century Persia, and certainly the sort of thing at which prowess is right and proper to a national hero. It also supports an Indian origin of the Persian game, as the name *chatrang* is not sufficiently Persian in form to be other than a loan-word, but can clearly be derived from *chaturanga.*

The firmest of ancient documentary evidence for the basics of Chess, including the 8×8 board and the names of the pieces, occurs in the *Chatrang-namak,* 'the invention of Chess', a seventh-century Persian story purporting to explain how the game reached Persia from India. Dewasaram, a great (but fictional, or at least unidentified) Indian raj, sends his vizier Takhtaritus to Nushirwan, the so-called Shahanshah or 'king of kings' of Persia (531–78), together with many riches including an ornate Chess set with emerald and ruby pieces. These are all for Nushirwan, provided that he can explain the nature and use of the Chess set. If not, Nushirwan hardly merits the greatness he claims for himself, should return the riches with interest, and pay tribute into the bargain. Chess being then unknown to the Persians, Nushirwan is, to say the least, embarrassed. Fortunately, the problem is solved by the sage Wajurgmitr, who not only realizes that this *chatrang* thing is a war game, but also deduces the aim of the game and the movement of the pieces, and demonstrates his skill by beating Takhtaritus twelve times in a row. As if this were not enough, he devises a completely new game—Nard, the equivalent of Backgammon—and on behalf of Nushirwan takes it to the court of Dewasarm with the same challenge. Needless to say, no one in the Indian kingdom could deduce its rules. Accordingly, 'Wajurgmitr received from Dewasarm twice the tribute and revenue, and he returned in good health and with great ceremony to Iran.'[2]

This story—later repeated with minor variations in Firdausi's *Shāhnāma* (Book of Kings) of 1011—is of interest for two reasons. First, it specifically describes *chatrang* as a two-player war game involving 'two supreme rulers after the likeness of kings (*shāh*), with the essentials of rooks (*rukh*) to right and to left, with a counsellor (*farzīn*) in the likeness of a commander of the champions, with the elephant (*pīl*) in the likeness of a commander of the rearguard, with the horse (*asp*) in the likeness of the commander of the cavalry, and with the foot-soldier (*piyādak*) in the likeness of so many infantry in the vanguard of the battle'.[3] Second, and more amusingly, it reinforces the authenticity of an Indian origin for Chess by the very fact of disclaiming Persian credit for its invention in favour of Backgammon, as if the latter were intellectually superior.

A third point of interest is its dating of the introduction of Chess to the reign of Nushirwan (531–78). Murray calls this a persistent Persian tradition, and cites another example in an account of the reign of Nushirwan in al-Masudi's *Muraj adhdhabad,* dating from 947: 'He had sent from India the book *Kalila was Dimna,* the game of *chatrang,* and a dye called hindi . . .'. An important description of Indian Chess, with further confirmation of its transmission into Persia, may date from the mid-ninth century, although the two manuscripts in which it appears—both versions of *The Book of Chess: extracts from the works of al-'Adli, as-Suli, and others*—date only from the twelfth century. The Arabic Chess master al-'Adli flourished around the year 840 and wrote a now lost treatise on the game from which the following passage, quoted in the twelfth century, may well have come:

> [This is] the form of Chess which the Persians took from the Indians, and which we took from the Persians. The Persians altered some of the rules, as is agreed. It is universally acknowledged that three things were produced from India, in which no other country anticipated it, and the like of which existed nowhere else: the book Kalila wa Dimna, the nine cyphers with which one can count to infinity, and Chess.

We subsequently learn some details of the Indian game as played in al-'Adli's time, represented as points of difference with the then current Arabic game. For instance, the Indians start with elephants on the corner squares, and ascribe a win to a stalemated player, or to the first to bare the other's king even if his own king is supported by only one man, and that *en prise.*

By the end of the first millennium a substantial Chess literature was flourishing in the Islamic world of Arabia and Persia (modern Iraq and Iran). Ironically, little is recorded of it in its country of origin, for only two other indisputable Indian references are earlier in date than 1000. Ratnakara's *Victory of Siva, c.*850, positively equates the four branches of the army with those of the Chess set, while Rudrata, writing in the last decade of the nineth century, elaborates a series of verse puzzles that involve writing successive syllables on the sequence of squares obtained by the chessboard tours of individual pieces. His examples of knight's, rook's, and more complicated elephant's tours confirm the powers of the movement of these particular pieces.

A final millennial reference to the Indian origin of Chess comes from the *Shahnama*, 'Book of Kings', the national epic of Persia begun by Daqiqi in 975 and completed by Firdausi in 1011. The material is based on older writings, many since lost, but has proved sound where checkable. It includes a different version of the *Chatrang-namak* story about an Indian king's challenge to Nushirwan to deduce the game of Chess from the equipment alone. Again, the problem is solved for him by the sage Buzurj-mihr (cf. Wajurgmitr), who goes on to return the compliment by inventing the game of Nard. In this version, however, Nard is not Backgammon but apparently a Chess variant.

Mention of variants makes this a suitable point at which to issue a warning against the discredited but oft-repeated theory deriving two-handed Chess from Indian four-handed dice-Chess, in which a die is thrown to determine which piece to move. This theory, launched by Hiram Cox in 1802 and subsequently elaborated by Duncan Forbes,[4] draws on a claimed reference to it in the Sanskrit text *Bhavishya Purana*, then thought to be some 5,000 years old. In fact the text is now ascribed to 550–500 BC and all copies of the passage in question go back to Raghunandana's *Tithitattva*, which dates from the fifteenth century AD. The first recorded description of the game itself—still played at the time of Murray's *History of Chess* (1913), and perhaps surviving today—comes from the pen of al-Biruni, an Arab geographer and scientist who travelled in the Punjab in about 1030. He does not say that this is the only or even the commonest form of Chess he encountered in India; rather, the tenor of his introduction suggests that he describes it because it struck him as unusual, if not bizarre. It is also briefly mentioned as a Chess variant in an early twelfth-century Sanskrit manuscript entitled *Manasollasa*, 'Joy of the Mind'.[5]

All these references suggest that Chess originated in north-west India some time prior to AD 600, that it was called Chaturanga, and that it spread thence to Persia under the name Chatrang, and from Persia to Arabia as Shatranj. As we shall see further, the game reached Christendom from Islam around the turn of the millennium, and Medieval Chess forms a fourth branch of this series of substantially similar games. The problem it raises is how then to relate this branch to the only other form of Chess mentioned earlier than 1000, which is that of China, and differs substantially from the 'Indo-Aryan' game.

The earliest Chinese description of an activity indisputably classifiable as Chess dates from around AD 800. It appears in a story, in the *Yu Hüan Kuai Lu* ('Book of Marvels') of Niu Seng-Ju, of a man who dreams the circumstances of a forthcoming battle in such gaming terms as 'The celestial horse springs aslant over three, the commanders go sideways and attack on all four sides, the baggage-waggons go straight forwards and never backwards, the six men in armour go in file but not backwards . . .'. This takes place in the first year of Pao Ying, i.e. 762. There are earlier mentions of the word for Chess, namely Xiang-qi, but what game they actually denote is in dispute. The second element, *qi*, means a playing board—cf. Wei-qi, the Chinese equivalent of Go.[6] The first means primarily *elephant*, and by various extensions *ivory, celestial figure*, and *figure* in the sense of image or figurine—so, according to Murray, Xiang-qi is 'the game of figures', just as *chess* itself derives from *scacchi*, meaning the pieces played with. The emperor Wu-Ti, founder of the Chou dynasty, is reported to have written a book on Xiang-qi which he expounded at a meeting in 569, but it is clear from several accounts that the game in question was astronomical, with figures representing the sun, moon, and planets, and could indeed have been not so much a game as a divinatory ritual. That the same name applied to other games is implied by the title *Manual of the three Xiang-qi's* subsequently (618–97) attached to Wu-Ti's book.

The similarities between Xiang-qi and Chaturanga are too great to deny the derivation of one from the other or both from a common ancestor. Nineteenth-century theories supporting Chinese priority were based on misunderstandings as to the age of key Chinese references, and two centuries' worth of credit has subsequently been added to the Indian side of the ledger. Also favouring India is the fact that China has never claimed the invention of Chess for itself, but has acknowledged India as the source of Chaupur (its equivalent of Backgammon) in the third century BC, thus establishing a cultural precedent. On the other hand, differences between the Indian and Chinese games are too great to believe that they could have arisen naturally in the space of two centuries, and the possibility must remain open of a common ancestor of greater antiquity than has so far been demonstrated by documentary evidence.

We saw above that the earliest known form of Chess was a game called Chaturanga and that it was played on a board called *ashtapada*. The roots of this word are identical with those of *octo-pod*, i.e. 'eight-footed', and we know from an Indian dictionary of as early as the second century AD[7] that it means a board of 8×8 squares used for gaming, along with a similar 10×10 board, the *dasapada*. Indian literature throughout the first millennium is full of references to the use of this board for dice games, to such an extent that Ashtapada itself becomes a generic and undefined game name. A game played with dice on a board marked with squares is more likely to be a race game than one of positional strategy, and the example of Pachisi suggests that such a board may have evolved by a process of folding a linear track in upon itself. In support of Ashtapada as a race game, Murray draws attention to the fact that Indian and other Asiatic squared gaming boards feature distinctive cross-cut markings on certain symmetrically placed squares. These may indicate squares upon which a piece progressed from one orbit to another, or upon which it was invulnerable to capture, or both. On an even-squared board, the four central squares would be the exit or 'home' squares equivalent to those in the centre of a Pachisi board, or of modern Ludo.

'The game of chess was invented when some Hindu devised a game of war, and, finding the ashtapada board convenient for his purpose, adopted it as his field of battle.' The words are Murray's, and he evidently came to regret expressing himself in so simplistic a fashion, since in his later *A Short History of Chess* he seems at pains to cover its nakedness with a veil of more becoming vagueness. I don't believe he ever intended his metaphorical expression to be taken literally, and he certainly never intended to imply, as some have uncharitably supposed, that the mechanics of the supremely strategic game derived from those of a dice-bound race game. The point he is making amounts to no more than that the war game of Chaturanga developed or settled down into one played on an 8×8 board which was already in existence and that it is first recorded in India. This reasonable assumption has yet to be disproved.

Chaturanga means 'army'; specifically, the classical Indian army of four branches—infantry, cavalry, elephantry, chariotry—that would, for example, have confronted Alexander the Great at the battle of Hydaspes in 326 BC. The word itself means 'four-limbed', being composed of two elements cognate with those of our word *quadrangle*, or, even more precisely, a hypothetical but etymologically possible *quater-ankle* (*quater* as in *ace, deuce, trey, quater*). Chaturanga was therefore the 'four-limbed army game', and came, naturally enough, to be played on the 'eight-footed gaming board'. As such, it was the only way of learning how to draw up an army in the halcyon reign of King Harsha of Kanyakubja.

Just as we need not take literally Murray's hypothetical 'some Hindu' as unique inventor of such a game, so should we not insult his memory by imagining him to believe that the game was invented as a representation of warfare—as if someone had said 'You know the four-limbed army? Well, how about turning it into a board game?', and someone else replied 'Brilliant! Let's make the chariots move orthogonally, because they don't turn corners very well, and give the horses a sort of prancing move...' and so on. A gratuitous Aunt Sally of this kind is set up and knocked down with Teutonic thoroughness, but little wit, by Hans Holländer in an article in *Homo Ludens.*[8] As Holländer rightly but redundantly argues, the origins of Chess probably lie in the elaboration of an essentially abstract game of material capture to which representational elements would subsequently have gravitated—just as the game of Merels came to be known as 'Mill' in some countries from some fancied resemblance to the process of milling, or the pieces moved round the circuit of a simple race game came to be known as 'horses' in so many cultures.

There is a view that a game of pure strategy can hardly be credited to a culture in which human fate depends less on rational thought than on the capricious will of the gods, or the random workings of chance, and in which dice-play is exalted to the level of a religious activity. This being characteristic of Hinduism, its proponents believe that Chaturanga may have arisen, through contact with the Greeks, from the influence of a game of the Petteia variety on a previously existing army game played with dice. This may be so, but does nothing to account for that differentiation of pieces which is not attested in Petteia but is one of the defining features of Chess.

A diametrically opposed view of Indian culture is implied by the mathematical theory espoused by Russian researchers such as Bidev and Rudin, and conveniently summarized by Ricardo Calvo.[9] This derives from the observation that the moves of the various Chess pieces can be executed in a regular order or 'tour' in such a way as to yield the same total. In the case of an 8×8 magic square, of which many can be composed, the total of every row, column and long diagonal will necessarily be $4 \times (8^2 + 1)$, or 260. More remarkable instances of the same total appear on such a square named from its earliest known description by the Arabic mathematician as-Safadi (d. 1363). For example, a horse (knight) placed on square 1 and traversing the linear route 47-35-13-60 (assuming the bottom of the board to be contiguous with the top)-22-26-56 will notch up a total of 260, as it will if it performs the same feat from any other given square of the board. Again: a complete knight's tour of the board, such as that illustrated in Murray (*History of Chess*, 335), consists of eight sequences of eight steps, each of which totals 260. Again: the eight squares initially occupied by each rook and its accompanying pawn (1-9-8-16-56-64-49-57) total 260, as do those of knight, bishop, and the royal pair.

Calvo draws attention to further points of interest arising from the Safadi board. One is that it lends weight to a theory advanced by Johannes Kohtz around 1910, but firmly rejected by Murray, to the effect that the original rook move was an orthogonal leap over two squares to the third beyond

1	2	3	4	5	6	7	8
9	10	11	12	13	14	15	16
17	18	19	20	21	22	23	24
25	26	27	28	29	30	31	32
33	34	35	36	37	38	39	40
41	42	43	44	45	46	47	48
49	50	51	52	53	54	55	56
57	58	59	60	61	62	63	64

1	63	62	4	5	59	58	8
56	10	11	53	52	14	15	49
48	18	19	45	44	22	23	41
25	39	38	28	29	35	34	32
33	31	30	36	37	27	26	40
24	42	43	21	20	46	47	17
16	50	51	13	12	54	55	9
57	7	6	60	61	3	2	64

1	2	62	61	60	59	7	8
9	10	54	53	52	51	15	16
48	47	19	20	21	22	42	41
40	39	27	28	29	30	34	33
32	31	35	36	37	38	26	25
24	23	43	44	45	46	18	17
49	50	14	13	12	11	55	56
57	58	6	5	4	3	63	64

Fig. 16.1. *Centre*: The magic square designated 'Mercury' by Cornelius Agrippa (1486–1535) derives from the serially numbered 8 × 8 square (*left*) by rotating those blocks of squares left unshaded. Rows, columns, and long diagonals all total 260. The more elegant Safadi board (*right*) yields 260 by starting at any point and travelling eight equidistant steps in the manner of any medieval Chess piece, e.g. 1-47-35-13-60-22-26-56. At least one knight's tour consists of eight consecutive series each totalling 260, such as that beginning 59-16-34-21-61-19-40-10. Kohtz hypothesized from the Safadi square an original rook move of (m = 3 +), e.g. 1-61-7-34-55-13-49-40. But he could equally well have deduced a fairy hippogonal piece moving (m = 3/4), e.g. 1-36-7-31-60-25-62-38, and seems not to have observed that the attested rook move of (m = 2 +) is inherent in the Mercury square, e.g. 1-62-19-48-33-30-51-16.

(m = 3+)*. The 'leaping rook' tour, starting from its original position on a corner square, also covers squares totalling 260—for example, 1-61-7-34-55-13-49-40. (Kohtz himself seems to have been on the point of making this connection shortly before his death in 1917.) Another is that the pattern of cross-cut cells on Indian and other Asiatic chessboards—which Calvo describes as 'otherwise unexplained', despite Murray's references to the 'safe' squares of an *ashtapada* race game—may have served as a guide or mnemonic to the conversion of a serially-numbered 8 × 8 board into one exhibiting 'magic' properties. Yet another is that it renders plausible the possibility asserted in Persian legend of deducing the nature, pieces, moves and initial positions of the game from a (mathematical) study of the board itself. His overall conclusion is that 'Proto-chess was originally a game of numbers, and was introduced into Persia as such.' It may be argued against this that Calvo is too easily impressed by the properties of magic squares, which become less startling as one explores their internal logic. For example, given that one way of creating a magic square is to start in a corner and number off in accordance with a simple rule based on following the path of a knight, or nightrider, it is hardly surprising that the resultant square will exhibit knightly properties. All magic squares of order eight

(m) = move, (+) orthogonal, (×) diagonal, (✱) both, (>) forwards, (<) backwards, (÷) sideways, (1/2) knight move. For all, see p. 231.

will yield coincidences revolving around the number 260. The fact that some of these relate to chesspiece moves is not a strong enough argument for positing Chess as the logical outcome of playing with magic squares. It would, for example, be quite easy to infer from the Safadi square alone the existence of a hippogonal piece with ($m = 3/4$).

A more promising line of enquiry into the origins of Chess takes as its starting-point the defining characteristic of check-mate—that is to say, the determination of the game by the capture of a principal piece rather than of a majority of undifferentiated pieces. This feature bears an obvious relationship with that of asymmetrical chase, hunt and siege games such as Fox & Geese, in which one player has a full complement of undifferentiated pieces and the other a powerful singleton, whose aim is to capture so many of the former as to prevent them from cornering and beating him. In default of convincing proof as to the anteriority of either category, we may be justified in believing that an evenly-matched war game of the Chess variety could have arisen from playing a sort of double chase game, whereby each player had both to defend a singleton and to wield a battery of pieces against an opposing singleton. As to the differentiation of pieces, it is sufficient to note that two move diagonally, two orthogonally, and two a combination of the two, and to ask what could be more natural or logical once the basic idea of differentiation had occurred to some imaginative player. If further speculation is invited, one possibility is that a differentiation of moves applied originally not to particular pieces but to particular positions, whether cells or points, and only later became attached to the pieces initially occupying them.

National Varieties

Chaturanga (Indian Chess). The oldest known ancestor of European Chess can be placed in north-west India (the Punjab) in the seventh century AD, and is presumably much older. From there it spread gradually southwards throughout the subcontinent in the latter half of the first millennium, contemporaneously with its spread westwards into Persia and Arabia, and eastwards into Indo-China, China, and Japan.

The earliest known description occurs in the early twelfth century Sanskrit manuscript *Manasollasa*, 'Joy of the Mind'. It indicates a game played on an 8×8 board, unchequered, but bearing a pattern of cross-cuts as shown in the diagram. Comparison with the immediately derivative Persian and Arabian games suggests the array illustrated in Fig. 16.2. A pawn promotes at the eighth square to the master piece of its file, but may not move there before the original master piece has been captured.

raja, m = 1✱
minister (*mantri*) m = 1x
elephant (*hasty*) m = 2x (leap)
horse (*ashwa*) m = 1/2 (leap)
chariot (*ratha*), m = n+
pawns (*padati*), m = 1> (never 2>)

Fig. 16.2. Chaturanga.

So far as can be established on such a notoriously ill-documented subject, many different varieties of Chess are currently played in India, all of them influenced by the International game, but none of them still passing under the name Chaturanga, though still exhibiting in varying degrees some features of that presumed original. Murray identified several forms of Indian Chess still played in the early twentieth century, and quoted Indian commentators as distinguishing three groups: the Hindustani (northern), Parsi (southern), and the Rumi. The last, as suggested by its name Shitranj, is a form reintroduced by the Muslim conquerors of northern India. The others now bear names based on the word *buddhi*, 'intellect', following the transfer of the name Chaturanga from Chess to a race-game played on the same board. Pritchard[10] doubts that the threefold division is as sharp as Murray implies, and lists a number of features common to modern Indian 'mainstream' games. On this basis one might construct, as follows, a typical or generic form of modern Indian Chess without guaranteeing its specific authenticity. Note that the old, weak moves of minister, elephant, and chariot have been replaced, probably everywhere by now, by those of the modern queen, bishop, and rook.

1 king (*raja, shah*) on e1-e8, m = 1✱
1 minister (*wazir, farzīn, mantri*) m = n✱
2 elephant (*gaja, fil, pīl*) or camel (*ushtra, unt*) m = n×
2 horse (*asp, ghora*) m = 1/2
2 chariot (*ratha, rukh*) m = n+
8 pawns (*padati, pīyada*) m = 1>.

White starts by making an agreed number of moves, typically four or eight, occasionally three, and Black does likewise. In this phase no piece may be moved more than once or entered into the enemy half of the board.

A pawn on file a-d-e-h may initially move 2> provided that its master is still in its starting position, but may not capture *en passant.* Upon reaching the eighth square a pawn promotes to the master piece of its file, provided that it or its partner has been lost (except for elephants, where that of the opposite 'colour' diagonal does not count, and kings, whose pawns promote to ministers). A pawn promoting to a horse may immediately make a knight move in the same turn, unless the promotion square is under attack. Although there is no castling, a king can, on one occasion only, make a knight move—but not to capture, and not if it has been checked. It is illegal to make a move resulting in stalemate or perpetual check. Baring the enemy king counts as a minor win, mating with a pawn as a superior win. 'To list the recorded variations on all the rules given would be both tedious and unhelpful', Pritchard considerately adds.

Xiang-qi (Chinese Chess) is probably the most widely played of all national Chess varieties, its estimated two million players including those of China itself, parts of Indo-China and the Malayan archipelago, and the world-wide Chinese diaspora. First accounts of it were brought to Europe

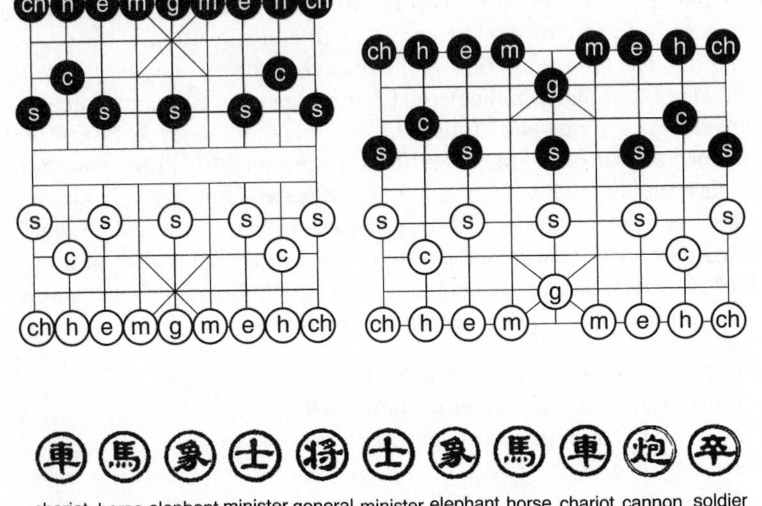

Fig. 16.3. *Above left*: Xiang-qi (Chinese Chess). *Above right* Changgi, its Korean equivalent. *Below*: Chinese chessmen.

by sixteenth-century Jesuit missionaries, enabling Hyde to devote a substantial but not very enlightening portion of his *Mandragorias* to it in 1694. W. H. Wilkinson's *Manual of Chinese Chess* (1893), for long the only English-language account of the game, was based on a classic Ming Dynasty work of 1632 by Jin-zhen-Zhu entitled *The Secret Inside the Orange*—reportedly referring to a legend about a mysterious giant orange which, when peeled, was found to contain two old men playing Chess against each other. The games and end-games illustrated in this work are still of value, as are those of Zai-yue Wang's *The Plum-Blossom Meter* of about 1690.[11]

Throughout its long history Xiang-qi has been a game of *hoi polloi*—the upper classes preferring Wei-qi—and it is only in the latter part of the twentieth century that it has attracted serious attention in its own country. Nowadays it has the support of a World Xiang-qi Federation and an Asian Xiang-qi Federation, and there are both European and American championships.

Xiang-qi is played on the 9 × 10 points of an 8 × 9 nominally squared board. The board is divided laterally by a row of blank or patterned squares representing a river, variously known as *Hwang-Ho* (the Yellow River), *Kyai-ho* (Central River), *T'ien-ho* (Celestial River, i.e. the Milky Way), and no doubt by other names. The 3 × 3 central points at each end of the board are connected by crossing diagonal lines and represent a fortress or royal palace. The pieces are circular discs with identifying characters painted on them. The nominal colours are Red, representing the forces south of the river, and Blue, representing those north, though actual colours vary with the materials used. Some pieces on opposite sides of the river bear different names or characters from those of their transfluvine counterparts, though enjoying exactly the same powers. With reference to Fig. 16.3:

G = General (red *jiang*, blue *shuai*). This is the king equivalent, whose loss determines the game. It moves m = 1 +, but it may not leave the confines of the palace. The two generals may not occupy the same file unless separated by at least one piece of either colour.

M = Mandarin, minister, counsellor, or officer of the guard (*shi*). It moves m = 1 ×, and, like the General, it may not leave the palace. It is equivalent in status and power to the medieval Chess queen.

E = Elephant (blue), Assistant or Minister (red) (both *xiang*). It moves m = 2 ×, and the intervening diagonal point must be vacant. It may not cross the river, and so is restricted to seven points on its own side.

H = Horse (*ma*). It moves m = 1/2 in that order, the first point being necessarily vacant.

R = Chariot (*ju*). It moves m = n+ and approximates to a rook.

C = Cannon (blue), catapult (red) (both *piao*). It also moves m = n+, but can only capture a piece by jumping over exactly one intervening piece of either colour (the 'screen') and capturing on the other side. Any number of points may separate the screen from the cannon on one side and its target on the other, but they must all be vacant.

S = Soldier (blue *zu*, red *bing*). Pawn equivalents, the foot-soldiers move m = 1> (never diagonally). Once over the river, however, they can move and capture one point orthogonally sideways (m = 1> ÷). They do not promote, but upon reaching the further edge of the board can continue to move and capture sideways.

Any piece not restricted to its own side of the board can enter the opposing palace to deliver check or mate. Stalemate wins for the player giving it. Perpetual check is not permitted: the first player must vary his move. If an unprotected piece moves from A to B to escape attack, and the attacker repeats the attack by moving from C to D, and the former returns to A, the attacker may not immediately return from D to C. (This rule seems to have been borrowed from Go.)

To the western Chess-player, Xiang-qi has a pleasantly representational feel to it, especially in the capturing move of the cannon and catapult. Unlike International Chess, it has no long-range diagonal mover and pawns do not capture sideways, so the thrust tends to be orthogonally forwards, favouring especially the chariots and the cannons. Because there is no promotion, the game tends to an inexorable diminishment of material, thus placing considerable strategic importance on the management of the end-game. The fact that generals may not oppose each other on an open file can lead to the interesting by-product of trapping an intervening piece on its file by moving one general behind it. The fact that the first point of a horse move must be vacant makes it possible to block a check from one of them. As Murray notes, 'The greater possibilities permitted by the varieties of checks that can be covered or discovered lead to such complicat[ions]... as triple and quadruple check.'

Changgi (Korean Chess), evidently derived from Xiang-qi, seems never to have been taken very seriously until 1956, when the first Changgi Association was formed. '[It] is regarded, in spite of its unusual diffusion, as a somewhat frivolous pastime, suitable for young persons and rustics', wrote W. H. Wilkinson in 1895.[12] 'The educated Korean, deeply imbued as he is with Chinese sympathies, prefers to play Patok [= Wei-qi].' The board, though elongated into a horizontal rectangle, is topologically identical with that of Xiang-qi except for the absence of a central river. The pieces are usually green and red, and octagonal in shape. The piece marked M in the diagram is a guard or counsellor. The rules are substantially similar, though disagreeing in a number of details, of which the most interesting is a player's entitlement to pass his turn to play.[13]

Shogi (Japanese Chess). Japanese tradition credits Shogi to China. The name may derive from Chinese Xiang-qi, but the characters representing it give it the meaning 'the Game of Generals', which is certainly more appropriate than either the Elephant Game or the Images Game, and the Chinese connection is now under attack. Tradition also associates it especially with the Ohashi family, of whom the first known, Ohashi Sokei, was appointed Chief Shogi-Player of the Empire by the Mikado Go-yo-zei (r. 1587–1611). 'The Japanese government', says Murray, 'would seem to have been excellent patrons of Shogi, for [in 1768 it was said] that the Government allowed the best player of each generation to build a house called *Shogi Tokoro*, "Chess Place", where the principles of the game were taught, and the player received an official salary for his services. And in 1860 there were seven State teachers of Chess in Yeddo alone.' Since the Meiji restoration of 1868 Shogi has increased in popularity and is now the most widely played game in the country. A grading system similar to that of Go is governed by the Japan Shogi Federation (founded 1927), and major events, of which the Meijin title is the most prestigious, are lavishly funded and get wide press coverage.[14]

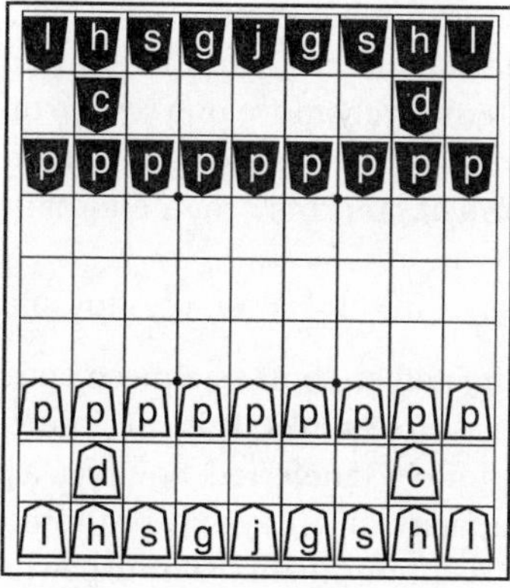

Fig. 16.4. Shogi—Japanese Chess.

Shogi is played on the cells of a 9×9 board slightly elongated in the direction of the players. The 'squares' are therefore slightly rectangular (typically 22×25 mm), the better to accommodate the shape of the pieces. Markings on the board show it to be divided into three horizontal areas of three ranks each, of which the central three are neutral and those at either end considered part of the appropriate player's territory.

The pieces are irregular pentagons variously described as shield-, wedge-, or punt-shaped, tapering in width and reducing in thickness towards the point, and placed on the board in such a way as to point forwards towards the opposing army. Each piece bears a black character on the upper surface showing its identity before promotion, and may (but need not) bear a red character on its underside to indicate, by reversal, its identity after promotion. Colour is not used to distinguish one army from another, as captured pieces are held by the capturer and may subsequently be returned to the board as part of his own army. The allegiance of every piece is shown solely by its orientation, in that it always points towards the enemy. The initial array, as shown in Fig. 16.4 consists of:

1 Jewelled General (*o-sho*, m = 1✱). Equivalent to the king, its capture determines the game.
2 Gold Generals (*kin-sho*, m = 1 + or 1 × >). A royal bodyguard.
2 Silver Generals (*gin-sho*, m = 1 × or 1 + >). A royal bodyguard. Promotes to Gold.
2 Honourable horses (*kei-ma*, m = 1/2>) Like a knight but moving forwards only. Promotes to Gold.
2 Lances (*yari*) or fragrant chariot (*kyo-sha*, m = n>, i.e. any distance orthogonally forwards only). Promotes to Gold.
1 Flying chariot (*hi-sha*, m = n +). Promotes to a dragon horse (*ryo-ma*), and may then alternatively move one square diagonally (m = n + 1×)
1 Diagon (*kaku-ko, kakko* = 'diagonal-mover', m = n×). Promotes to a dragon king (*ryo-wo*), and may then alternatively move one square orthogonally (m = 1 + n×).
9 Footsoldiers (*fu-hyo*, m = 1>). Promotes to Gold.

Promotion may be effected as soon as a piece enters enemy territory, i.e. any of the furthermost three ranks. It is not immediately obligatory, but may be deferred indefinitely. If deferred, however, a piece must continue to move in its original capacity, and may only be promoted upon the termination of such a move. Exceptions to this rule are pawns, which must promote upon crossing the promotion line, horses upon reaching the eighth or ninth rank, and lances upon reaching the ninth.

Capture is invariably by replacement. Captured pieces are retained 'in hand', but must be shown on request, and are usually left in view. On any subsequent turn, a player may enter one captured piece in its original (unpromoted) capacity, such entry counting as a move. It may be entered on any vacant square subject to the following restrictions:

A piece may not be entered and promoted in the same turn.

A piece must be entered only on a square from which it has (at time of entry) at least one legal move available to it in its unpromoted capacity. (Hence it is illegal to enter a pawn or lance on the ninth rank, or a horse on the eighth or ninth).

A pawn may not be entered on a file already occupied by a pawn of the same army, under penalty of being huffed.

A pawn may not be so entered as to deliver immediate checkmate (but check is permissible, as is mate by entry of a piece other than a pawn).

Though not illegal, it is bad form to enter a piece that does not actively contribute to an attack—a waiting move is considered cowardly. Perpetual check is forbidden: the checking player must vary his move. It is not illegal to move the jewelled general into check, which amounts (in effect) to a resignation. In the rare event of an impasse, each player counts 5 points per chariot and diagonal mover (rook and bishop equivalents), and 1 for each other piece other than the jewelled general. If one player (only) has 24+ points, he wins, otherwise it is a draw.

Whereas Go and the equivalent of Backgammon are recorded in Japan from the seventh century, Shogi is not mentioned before the late eleventh century. Thereafter it is often referred to in the journals of noble families and Buddhist monks. Unlike Chinese Chess, which was always a game of the people, Shogi could appeal only to those literate enough to be able to read identifying characters. Its first description appears in an early thirteenth-century encyclopaedia,[15] which refers both to the basic variety (*sho-shogi*) and a larger one of 13 × 13 (*dai-shogi*), but the compiler appears inexpert and treats of it only briefly. The larger game differs from that recorded in the *Zogei Sosho* of 1443. The game of intermediate size, Chu-Shogi, with 12 × 12 squares and ninety-two pieces of twenty-two different types, first appears in the fourteenth century and was played until the nineteenth. The standard 9 × 9 game is recognizable from a position illustrated in 1587.

Archaeological excavations carried out in 1992 in connection with restorations at the old temple of Kofuku-ji yielded, from a well, many Shogi pieces, pieces of sandalwood and other raw materials for making them, and sketches for the characters. One item is dated from year six of

Tenki's rule, i.e. 1058. Some pieces are unknown from later games, including one labelled *sui-zou*, 'lively' or 'sprightly' person.

Sho-shogi and Dai-shogi are also partly described in a Buddhist manuscript of 1297–1302.[16] The latter is played on a 15 × 15 board with 130 pieces of twenty-nine different types, including the lance-bearer (*kyo-sha*), the reversing chariot (*hen-sha*), the flying chariot (*hi-sha*), the messenger or negotiator (*chu-nin*), the raging wild boar (*shin-i*), and the honourable knight (*kei-ma*). From this it seems that the small game appeared first, to be followed by two varieties of a large game (13 × 13 then 15 × 15). The intermediate game, Chu-Shogi, size 12 × 12 with forty-six pieces per side, then appeared in the mid-fourteenth century. By the mid-fifteenth there was a wide range of variants of many different sizes.

Koichi Masukawa[17] doubts the received opinion deriving Shogi from Xiang-qi, asserting that their differences are greater than what the western observer sees as their similarities. The ancestor of Shogi more probably emanated from the Indus delta region and travelled round the South China coast via the *Kuro-shio*, or Silk Sea Straits, perhaps as early as the eighth century. There is a notable resemblance between the Indian game and the Japanese arrangement of chariot, horse, silver general (with its elephantine fivefold move), general (minister), king. Also notable is the practice in Thai Chess of using cowries for pawns, and turning them concave-side up to show promotion. The affinities of Shogi seem to relate more to south-east Asiatic Chess than to that of China.

Sittuyin (Burmese Chess) was still played in Mandalay in the 1950s—'Old men play it with passion and arguments are commonplace. It is usually played for money, except at funeral parties, where games are played to pass the time' (Pritchard),[18]—but is now largely confined to tea-houses in the north-west, particularly round Bhamo and Katha. It differs from most national varieties of Chess in being partly a game of placement. Red and Black start with pawns on the eight squares so marked in Fig. 16.5. Red arranges his remaining pieces ad lib in the area behind his pawns, and may, if desired, substitute a piece for a pawn and replace the latter. Black then does likewise, subject to certain restrictions, such as not placing a rook on the same file as Red's king if Red objects. A favoured opening position is illustrated. The queen moves $m = 1\times$, the elephant $m = 1 > \times$ (fivefold move), other pieces as in International Chess, excluding the pawn's opening two-step. A pawn promotes only to a queen when standing on a square on either long diagonal on the enemy side of the board. It does not promote upon reaching such a square, but may do so on any subsequent turn, provided that its original queen has been captured (and subject to further

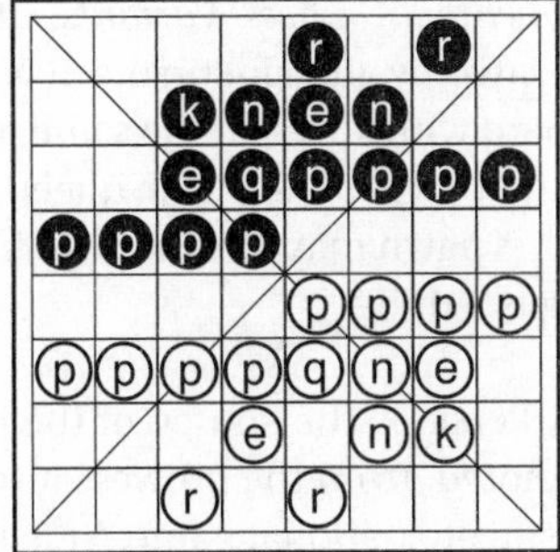

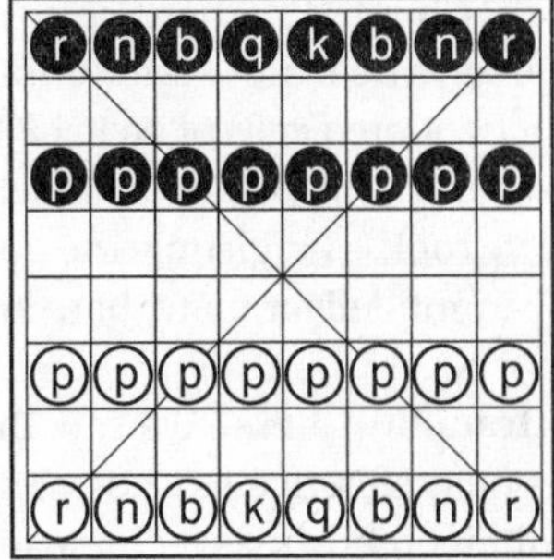

Fig. 16.5. *Left*: Sittuyin (Burmese Chess): a typical array. Only pawns occupy statutory positions. *Right*: Makruk (Thai Chess).

qualifications). A pawn may not promote once it passes its promotion square.

Sittuyin, pronounced *sitturin*, may derive from *chaturanga*. The game was first described in English in 1800, but it and subsequent European accounts tend to be garbled, contradictory, or otherwise suspect. A more reliable source is the 'Burmese Chess Guide' (*Myan-ma sit bayin lan-nyunt sa-ok gyi*), published in about 1924.

Makruk (Thai Chess) is still widely played in Thailand, sometimes in open-air performances with people dancing the parts of pieces and engaging in mock duels upon being captured. The array (Fig. 16.5) recalls Shogi, especially in that pawns promote upon reaching the rank initially occupied by those of the enemy. The queen, or *met* (fruit-stone), moves $m = 1\times$, the bishop-equivalent, or *thon* (nobleman?), moves $m = 1 +> \times >$ (one forward orthogonally or diagonally).

Main Chator (Malay Chess), known to have reached the peninsula prior to the fifteenth century, is probably extinct, but the Bataks of Sumatra continue to play a substantially similar game. The array is as International Chess but with king and queen reversed.

Cambodian Chess is played on the 9×9 points of an 8×8 board with nine 'fish' (pawns) and pieces each. Each king is flanked by two each of elephant (m = 1✱ but cannot capture backwards), boat (rook), horse (knight), official ($m = 1\times$ but cannot capture backwards). Fish move and capture (1>) only, but upon crossing the centre line are reversed and move like kings (m = 1✱).[19]

Mongolian Chess (Pritchard, *Encyclopedia of Chess Variants*, 1994) is thought to have been not entirely eradicated by alien incursors. It is played on the unchequered cells of an 8×8 board with kings on the same file. The rook is a chariot, the bishop a camel, the pawn a child. The queen moves $m = n + 1 \times$ (rook + king); only the queen's pawn may advance two initially; a knight cannot deliver mate; bare king is a draw.

Persian (Iranian) Chess. We saw that Persia is the source of the earliest unambiguous reference to Chess, and noted, from the prowess attributed to Ardashir, its renown as a characteristically national game. 'It is not too much to say', as Murray does, 'that European chess owes more to its Persian predecessor Chatrang than to its more remote and shadowy ancestor, the Indian Chaturanga.'[20]

The name Chatrang, now obsolete, clearly derives from Chaturanga and is itself the source of Arabic *Shatranj* (which has come to replace it in Iranian) and Greek *Zatríki*, thus demonstrating a key link in the western transmission of the game. One might add also the supposed origin of the word 'rook' in Persian *rukh*, 'chariot'; but this is disputed,[21] and in the *Shāhnāma* it is occasionally also called *mubariz*, 'champion'. The other pieces are traditionally *shāh* king, *farzīn* sage or counsellor, *pīl* elephant, *asp* horse, *piyadah* foot-soldier. As to *māt*, 'mate', this is not now thought to derive from Arabic *mat* 'dead', but rather from *manad* 'at a loss, helpless', from the verb *mandan*, 'to remain' (cf. Latin *maneo, -ere*).

The Persian game has remained fairly constant over the centuries, though the *Shāhnāma* contains a legend about the (Indian) invention of Chess in which, unprecedentedly, the game described is played on a 10×10 board with the addition of a camel (*shutur*) positioned between the equivalent of elephant (bishop) and horse (knight). Its move ($m = 2 +$) neatly complemented that of the elephant ($m = 2\times$). Otherwise Persian Chess has remained virtually identical with the Muslim Shatranj and its medieval European counterpart. According to some Persian noblemen interviewed in Paris in 1845–6, kings were placed crosswise on d1-e8, a king that had not been checked could move once like a knight, or could castle king's side,[22] pawns never opened $m = 2 >$, neither player could have more than one queen on board at a time, and a bared king was lost. Castling took place on the king's side as in European Chess, on the queen's side with a knight move from d1-e3 while the rook moved to f1.[23]

Shatranj (Islamic Chess). The death of Mahomet in 632 was followed by the expansion of Islam and the Arab world culminating in the golden age of Arabic civilization under the Abbisid caliphate in the eighth–tenth centuries. It was a civilization that had both time and talent for the cultivation of Chess to a hitherto unparalleled degree. That the game reached Arabia from conquered Persia as part of the cultural booty of the 640s is both accepted by Arabic historians of the time and demonstrated by the name of the game, Shatranj being an Arabicization of the Persian Chatrang. Shatranj retained a coherent fixity of rules and structure over many centuries. Thanks to the superior playing and analytical skills of Arabic Chess masters, and especially to their voluminous writings, it could be regarded as the first truly 'international' form of Chess from 800 to the development and expansion of the modern European game from 1500 on.

The board was a grid of 8 × 8 squares usually ruled on a cloth or other material capable of being rolled up and easily transported. Squares were not differentiated either by cross-cuts as in the Indian game, or by chequering as in the subsequent European game, but were often decorated for artistic rather than functional purposes.

With reference to the array shown in Fig. 16.6, and comments from as-Suli, each army comprises:

1 *shāh*, m = 1✱. The king.

1 *firzān*, m = 1×. Equivalent to the medieval European queen. 'The firzan is the vizier, because he protects and covers the king, and is placed next to him, advancing before him in the battle.'

2 *fīl* m = 2×, leaping any intervening piece. The etymological sense of 'elephant' was lost. 'How beautiful is the function of the fīl in Chess! He resembles the secretary who reveals and plans. His use in war is slight, except when he does a deed of renown...'

2 *faras*, m = 1/2. Equivalent to a knight, 'The faras... is a bold horseman, and this is his function in Chess.'

2 *rukh*, m = n+. The original sense of 'chariot' is also lost. 'The rukh, it is said, is like a commander and a general of an army: like the faras he is a horseman, and the command is his.'

8 *baidaq*, m = 1 > (never 2 >), capturing 1× >. Pawns 'are like the foot-soldiers who move in advance and hinder the horses and rukhs; but when the rukh gets behind them and attacks them from the rear, he destroys them just as horsemen in war destroy the foot-soldiers'.

Pawns promote only to firzan. There is no castling. A player wins by checkmating, stalemating, or baring the adverse king.

The game seems slow and cumbersome by modern standards, given the lack of castling, of the pawn's opening two-step, and its enforced promotion to a firzan, which cannot deliver mate without assistance. An unavoidable feature of the opening, due to the time it took for the opposing armies

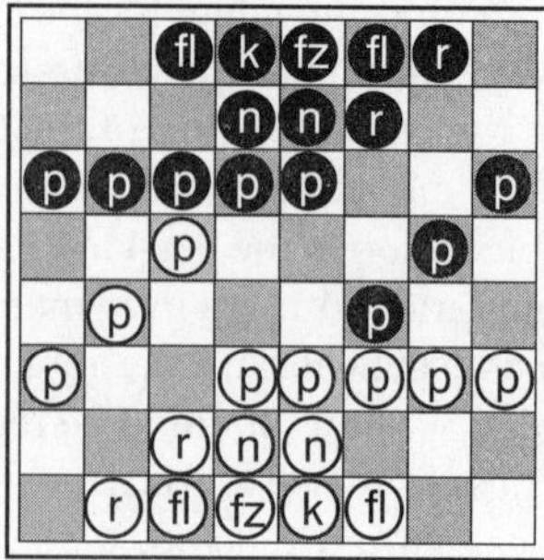

Fig. 16.6. Shatranj (Arabic Chess; fz = firzān, fl = fīl, other initials modern). *Left*: A ninth-century *ta'bīya* designated *watad al-'anz*, 'the goat peg' (after Murray, p. 237). *Right*: White's *firzān* controls all white squares, Black's all black squares, and each *fīl* eight mutually exclusive squares of one colour.

to engage with one another, was the tendency for players to start by developing their pieces into a favourite or recommended position on their own side of the board virtually regardless of what their opponents were doing. Standard opening positions, or *ta'bīyāt*, were well documented. Unlike the contents of *Modern Chess Openings*, which amount to a forest of branches deriving from all the dynamic consequences of alternating moves, each *ta'bīya* was essentially static, a target position for one side only. The middle game was relatively impoverished by the weakness of some of the pieces. Apart from the king, only rooks and knights can cover every square of the board. Initial firzans occupy opposite diagonals, enabling each to cover only thirty-two squares and preventing either from engaging the other. Each fil covers only eight squares, enabling neither to support its partner or engage either of its adverse counterparts. Skilled players must have developed a mental image of the board such as that of Fig. 16.6 (right), showing which squares were commanded by which diagonally-moving pieces of either side. With checkmate inevitably rare between well-matched players, play was often directed towards the alternative objective of a bared king.

The development of Shatranj prior to the founding of the Abbisid dynasty in 750 is ill recorded. One of the earliest contemporary Arabic references occurs in a verse containing the term *baidaq*, which cannot mean other than a Chess pawn, from the poet al-Farazdaq, who died in 728.[24] The great Harun-al-Rashid (r. 786–809) is claimed by later writers as an enthusiast for the game—plausibly, perhaps, but without hard evidence. Caliph al-Ma'mun is said to have watched Rabrab play Jabir while on an expedition in 819. Jabir, Rabrab, and Abu'n-Na'am are cited by as-Suli (see below) as ninth-century Chess masters. The first master whose writings on the game survive is the pseudonymous al-Adli, who is reported to have played ar-Razi before the caliph al-Mutawakkil (847–61). Al-Adli was succeeded and eclipsed by the great as-Suli (d. 946), a member of a Turkish princely family who came to prominence at the court of al-Myktafi (r. 902–8). As-Suli and his pupil al-Lajlaj ('the stammerer'; all wrote under pen-names or nicknames, and not all can be further identified) continued the tradition of earlier masters by writing treatises on the game. A typical treatise started with legendary accounts of the game's invention, considered its lawfulness for Muslims, then proceeded to the classification of players, the relative value of pieces, symbolism, notation, *ta'bīyāt*, and typical end-game positions. Considerable space is devoted to the illustration and solution of *manṣūbāt*, 'problems'—that is, end-game studies arising from actual play, rather than in the modern sense of unlikely positions seeking miraculous mates in *n* moves.

The burst of creative intellectual activity characterizing the Abbisid dynasty petered out with the latter's demise, leaving the works of its Chess masters unrivalled, and the names of such as al-Adli, as-Suli and al-Lajlaj immortalized as semi-legendary figures. The subsequent history of Shatranj is less eventful than that of its European descendant.

European Chess. Chess entered western Europe from Islam in the tenth century—perhaps earlier, but sporadically and unrecorded. The oldest literary reference is that of the *Versus de schachis*, a 98-line poem giving dramatic expression to the role and powers of the various pieces. It occurs in two manuscripts of the Swiss monastery of Einsiedeln, and has been dated to the 990s.[25]

Two eleventh-century references occur in wills bequeathing (amongst other things) valuable chess pieces to the monastery of St Gilles, near Nîmes. That of Count Ermengaud I of Urgel in 1008[26] specifies *ipsos meos schacos*; that of his sister-in-law Countess Ermessind of Barcelona dated 1058 speaks of *eschacos christalinos*, 'crystal chessmen'. In 1061 Cardinal Damiani wrote to pope-elect Alexander II complaining about the gaming propensities of the clergy in general and specifically of an indulgence in Chess by the Bishop of Florence, arguing:

Schachum, inquam, Scriptura non ponit, sed utriusque ludi genus alee nomine comprehendit.

Chess, I declare, is not named in Scripture, but belongs to the same class of games as alea *[sc. dice games, which are forbidden].*

The knightly hero Ruodlieb, in an epic poem of that title probably written around 1050 by a monk at Tegernsee, acts as emissary to a foreign court, and there is made the (not unwitting) victim of a species of Chess hustling:

> Schachorum ludo temptat me vincere crebro,
> Nec potuit, ludo ni sponte dato sibi solo.

He keeps trying to beat me at the game of chessmen, but cannot, [unless I give him the game deliberately/or else deliberately spoils his own game]

These scattered fragments yield many points of interest to the introduction of Chess into Europe, a process presumably occupying much of the tenth century. The fact that they cover Spain, France, Italy, and Germany, suggests first that, exactly like playing-cards some four centuries later, Chess reached Europe from the world of Islam via both Spain and Italy. Most of the Iberian peninsula lay in Islamic hands from the eighth century onwards, so the game may have been played technically 'in Europe' before being played 'by Europeans'. Italy probably received it through Venice, the tradesmen's entrance to medieval Europe, and it may be from here that it spread northwards.

Next, there is the name of the game. All early references are in medieval Latin, and in the line from the *Ruodlieb* I have deliberately retained the literal translation '*game of chessmen*', because to its first European players this is exactly what it was. Unlike most recipients, Europe did not take in the name of the game, Shatranj, with the game itself. Rather, it followed the (as yet unexplained) step of generalizing the name of the chief piece, *shah*, to embrace all pieces used in the game, and hence the game itself. From *schachi* (variously spelt) derives *chess* itself and nearly all its western European congeners: French *échecs*, Italian *scacchi*, Romanian *şah*, German *Schach*, Dutch *schaak*, Swedish *schack*, Polish *szachy*, Czech *šachy*, Hungarian *sakk*, and so on. The few exceptions include Spanish *ajedrez*, Portuguese *xadrez*, which derive from *shatranj*, and Welsh *seccyr* from Latin *scaccarium*. The Greek *zatríki* comes direct from Persian Chatrang, showing that Byzantium did not obtain its game from the Arabs, and undermining any alternative theory deriving western European Chess from eastern Europe. As a matter of complication, and a warning to game historians, the terms *scacchi* and *échecs* also came to be applied to gaming-pieces in general; so, unless the context is quite specific, it is unwise to ascribe to Chess a reference which could equally well apply to Draughts, Tables, or Merels.[27]

The bequests of chessmen to churches says something about the social status of Chess players (rich) and raises questions about the Church's attitude to them. Ecclesiastics railed continuously against gaming, ostensibly because it filled time trivially instead of usefully, encouraged greed, promoted fatal arguments, and led to destitution. Even those who could distinguish between games of pure chance like dice, chance and skill like Tables, and pure skill like Chess, remained influenced by the fact that all games were customarily played for money regardless of these theoretical niceties. Such bequests were partly motivated by a desire to atone posthumously for indulgence in an activity frowned on by the Church. But the situation is more complicated than that, and probably varied with the circumstances. Countess Ermessind's *eschacos christalinos* would have been objects of value in their own right, and may have provided a source of that same rock-crystal that was used in church ornamentation, often worked by the same artisans as those who produced the original gaming-pieces. (By a pleasing coincidence, such crystal pieces have been found in the same region and from about the same period as those of the Countess.) The richer the nobility, the more bejewelled the bequests, and the Church may have found itself in an embarrassing position if (*pace* Cardinal Damiani) it condemned Chess as whole-heartedly as it did dice and tables. A further potential embarrassment was that the appeal of Chess to those with time on their hands and a modicum of brain-power increasingly drew monks and higher clerics into its orbit.

Eales questions Murray's assertion that Chess, 'especially from the thirteenth to the fifteenth century... attained to a popularity in Western Europe which has never been excelled, and probably never equalled at any later date',[28] maintaining instead that Chess players inhabited only that very narrow stratum of society, the literate, leisured, and noble classes. That it may, in fact, have been socially more widespread than previously believed is suggested by recent archaeological finds of 'more and more objects of wood and stone that were part of the paraphernalia of all kinds of games in the eleventh and twelfth centuries... In particular, 'scacchis' (chess), and 'tabulae', played an important role in the daily lives of many people....'[29] In this connection it is worth remembering that history based on written records is largely the history of people who can write, and that Chess in China during the same medieval period was a game of the lower orders, the élite preferring Wei-qi. Be this as it may, it is from written records and the cultivated literature of the 'Twelfth Century Renaissance' that we gain a vivid picture of the role of Chess at a particular level of society, a role well documented by Murray and more coherently expounded by Eales. In these circles the play of Chess connoted cultivation and social status rather than the intellectual prowess it connotes today. Like horsemanship, archery, dancing, and so on, its practice was proper to the sons of nobles and could not be acquired without instruction. Jongleurs or 'wandering minstrels', those peripatetic purveyors of recreational requisites, would no more travel without a bag of chessmen than without a lute. Nor was it restricted to the male sex. That privacy whose accessibility we take for granted today was a rare luxury in the Middle Ages, and the intimacy of the chessboard was valued by many a pair of lovers. Chess, indeed, was often recognized as a valid reason, or pretext, for a woman to entertain a man alone in her chamber.

As to the game itself, medieval European Chess was, to all intents and purposes, virtually identical with the Islamic Shatranj from which it derived. Opposing kings were placed on the same file, but variably on (d) or (e). The queen and bishop equivalents moved respectively one and two squares diagonally. Pawns moved initially one forwards only, and promoted only to queens. The game was won by mating or baring the opposing king, but the original treatment of stalemate is uncertain. The greatest and perhaps most surprising departure from known Islamic practice is that European chessboards were, or at least could be, chequered—a practice recommended for its clarity as early as the Einsiedeln verses, which include the couplet

> Sunt quibus has placuit duplici fucare colore,
> Grata sit ut species et magis apta duplex.

There are those who like to colour the board two ways, so as to give it a pleasing and more appropriate appearance.[30]

Red and white are often mentioned, but, in the words of a similar piece in the *Carmina Burana*:

> Albescit primus, rubet atque colore secundus,
> Aut niger aut glaucus pingitur aut rubeus
>
> *White is the usual colour of one, and red of the other –*
> *If not red, black or blue or any old colour will do.*[31]

The new European players also had to find suitable equivalents for the names of the pieces. Some were more or less transliterated, some translated, and some accorded more meaningful replacements. The overall result, which increased with the passage of time, was to remove the game further from its roots in a representation of warfare and closer to that of the medieval feudal social hierarchy.

King. (Arabic < Persian *shah*). There being no doubt as to the identity and significance of this piece, it naturally became *rex* in Latin and the equivalent in every other language.

Queen. (Arabic *firz[an]* = vizier, sage or counsellor.) The 'vizier', even if understood, had no effective counterpart in European court hierarchy. Thus from an early date the word was simply transliterated into, for example, Old Spanish *alfferza*, medieval Latin *ferzia*, Provençal *fersa*, O.French *fierge*, M.Eng. *fers*, Elsewhere, its conversion into a queen—Latin *regina* and national language equivalents—was virtually inevitable, it being the only unduplicated figure besides the king, and so forming a natural pair with it. (In English, *queen* is actually attested earlier than *fers*.) The inherent singularity of the queen may have been responsible for the alternatives *femina* and *domina* (whence *dame*) being applied to promoted pawns, and subsequently to the major piece itself when the latter acquired its more powerful move (m = n✱ as opposed to 1×) in the late fifteenth century.

Bishop. (Arabic *[al-]fil)*. Elephants had no more place in the European consciousness than in the Arabic, for which it had become merely the name of a chesspiece. As such, it was treated simply as a name, appearing in medieval Latin as *Alphilus* or *Alfinus* (sometimes converted into the more meaningful *alphicus* 'leper', *alfiere* 'standard-bearer') French *Aufin*, Welsh *Elphyn*, etc., though modern Spanish still retains the ancestral form *alfil*. It also adopted other identities, such as sage or counsellor (*calvus*, *senex* etc.), bishop (*cornutus*, *episcopus*, Czech *póp*, English from 1500), a count (*comes*) in early German sources, and, mainly in France, a fool or jester (*stultus*, French *fol*, modern *fou*). Germany, always a law unto itself in gaming nomenclature, eventually substituted a name more descriptive of its move in *Läufer*, 'runner'.

Knight. This piece has always been a horse (*faras*, in Arabic), itself a metonymy for horseman or mounted warrior, and unsurprisingly entered European consciousness as *eques*, *caballarius* (whence *chevalier*), or *miles*, all meaning 'knight'. Italy, however, has reverted to horse (*cavallo*), and some other countries have followed Germany's substitution of a title more descriptive of its move, namely *Springer* = jumper, leaper.

Rook. Arabic *rukh* came via Persian from the Indian for chariot. In its roll westwards it was almost invariably retained rather than translated, partly because chariots went out of date with the invention of the stirrup and consequent rise of the knight, and perhaps partly because it is easily pronounceable in any language, its fierce sound curiously appropriate to its tremendous power. Medieval Chess therefore retained the Latin approximation *rochus* and equivalents in all other European languages, including French *roc*, German *Roch*, Italian *rocco*. In the seventeenth century it began to be replaced by castle (French *tour*, German *Thurm* > *Turm*). Murray ascribes this change largely to the extraordinarily popular success of the much translated poem *Scacchia ludus*, by Marco Girolamo

Vida (*c.*1485–1566, Bishop of Alba from 1533). In attempting a thoroughgoing overhaul of current nomenclature along classical lines, Vida first transformed rooks into Cyclopes (1510), and in a second edition (1537) re-envisaged them as 'warring towers borne upon the backs of elephants'—the latter by courtesy of Livy.

Pawn. Arabic *baidaq*, foot-soldier, found its natural equivalent in Latin *pedes*. The role is so obvious that the word can hardly be called a translation. Germany later transformed it into a *Bauer*, meaning farmer, peasant, or knave (at cards), a change matched by Swedish and Danish *bonde*, farmer.

Reckoning from the *Einsiedeln Verses* of *c.*990, medieval European Chess lasted half a millennium, and was ousted by modern European Chess in *c.*1490. Such precision is exaggerated, of course, but not much. The principal features of the new game were such as to make it faster of engagement, grander in sweep, and bristling with pitfalls—such as the hitherto impossible fool's mate—for the unwary or inexperienced. They were:

- the queen's move extended from 1× to n✱
- the bishop's from 2× to n×
- the pawn's optional opening 2>, resulting in possible capture *en passant*
- possibly a primitive form of castling (Murray, *History of Chess*, 812, 830)

These features were, in themselves, not entirely new. From the outset, Europeans seem to have been dissatisfied with the slow opening of the Arabic game they inherited, and had indulged in all kinds of experimentation to make it more exciting. This inevitably produced variations in the detailed rules of play from region to region, and since medieval Europe was a teeming mass of travellers—of scholars and minstrels wandering, freelance knights roaming, messengers scurrying, pilgrims visiting, outlaws fleeing, and bandits preying on them all—it became desirable for any two players from different traditions to agree on which set of rules to follow. Such codes, known as assizes, were drawn up and circulated by interested parties, and it is in the surviving records of such assizes that many lines of experimentation can be traced, though it is hard to fit them into a coherent framework. Experiments followed several trains of thought: using dice to determine which piece to move, enlarging the board to accommodate new pieces, rearranging existing pieces, starting from advanced positions, and varying the powers of existing pieces. Of these, the last proved most effective.

The pawn's initial two-step, an obvious way of advancing engagement, appears in the Alfonso manuscript of 1283 and in the Spanish, Lombard, German and Anglo-French assizes, though with variations. In some cases the privilege was restricted to rook, queen, and king pawns, in others it ceased once a capture had been made. Capture *en passant* can be inferred from problems composed in accordance with the Anglo-French assize, which goes back to 1150.

The queen was sometimes permitted a comparable privileged opening, that of the bishop's normal m = 2×. This enabled her move initially to d3 or f3, over a pawn if necessary, but only to a vacant square (no capturing). The same privilege might also apply to a promoted pawn, so that, on promotion, it could move from (n)8 to (n)6. Similarly, the king was accorded an opening 2✱, even occasionally 3✱, provided that it had not been in check. The thirteenth-century Lombard assize allows a joint opening move of king and queen simultaneously. More eccentrically, the so-called 'short' Anglo-French assize ('long' was the orthodox game) started with all pawns on the third rank and the queen sharing d3 with her pawn, though the two then moved independently. Such a position is illustrated in two 15th-century works, leaving no doubt as to its validity.[32]

There is no record of the bishop's enhancement from 2× to n× before 1490, but a new piece with just such a move, the courier, had been invented for an enlarged form of Chess recorded in Germany from about 1200, so the idea had been in the air for some time.

How and why these threads suddenly drew together in a relatively coherent whole awaits adequate explanation, and some question remains as to where; but the 'when' is fairly certain. The new game is described as such, and distinguished from 'that which used to be played', in *Repeticion de amores e arte de axedrez,* by Luis de Lucena, who declares himself a student at Salamanca. The book's dedicatee certainly died in 1497, and typographical evidence shows that its printers worked there only in 1496–7.[33] Some of the openings it describes are matched in a manuscript at Göttingen, whose style of Latin suggests French or Spanish authorship, and which does not even mention an 'old' game. Undated, it is generally accepted as pre-1500, and some have placed it as early as 1471–5. It is a pity that Francesc Vicén's Catalan work *Jochs partits del scachs en nombre de 100,* printed at Valencia in 1495, does not survive: the last known copy perished by fire in 1834 before anyone recorded whether it dealt with the old or new game, though the new seems likelier. The new game certainly underlies *Scachs d'Amor,* a Catalan poem on the courtship of Venus and Mars, and a French manuscript entitled *Jeu des ésches de la dame moralisé,* but neither can be dated more precisely than 'about 1500'. As to the old game, a late positive reference to the old bishop's move ($m = 2\times$) occurs in a book on Rithmomachy dated 1476.

As to where the revolution was originally fomented, there are conflicting claims for Spain and Italy. Murray favoured Italy, largely because 'the main centre of Chess activity in the fifteenth century was neither Spain nor France, but Italy'. A case for Spain, reflecting the influence on cultural life of the powerful Queen Isabella, has recently been argued by Govert Westerveld.[34] Arie van der Stoep also favours Spain, and argues further that the queen's long move was imported from Draughts into Chess rather than vice versa.[35]

That players were well aware of the revolution they had witnessed is shown by the distinctions they drew between the old and the new game: in Italy between *scacchi al antica* and *scacchi della donna*, or *alla rabiosa*, France *le vieil jeu des ésches* and *ésches de la dame* [*enragée*], Spain *axedrez del viejo* and *axedrez de la dama*. The new game took a while to reach Germany, where in 1536 it is designated *current* or *welsches Schachspiel*—the former meaning 'rapid', the latter 'Italian', or perhaps merely 'foreign'. Italian and French descriptions of the queen as 'mad' pinpoint the focus of the revolution. So completely did it take hold that the old game was forgotten within a generation, except perhaps to problemists and to players in isolated corners of Europe. It was still played at Ströbeck when Selenus wrote in 1616. This is not to say that the new game was completely uniform and invariant: it took several hundred years of further development to achieve the degree of international uniformity which now justifies the motto of the FIDE *Gens una sumus*, 'We are one people'. Spain, for example, continued to recognize bare king and stalemate as half-wins rather than draws, Italy did not admit of capture *en passant*, France and Spain permitted the king an extended initial move, France alone allowed a pawn to promote to a piece other than a queen, but only to replace one that had been captured. There were various methods or equivalents of castling, of which the modern form is first attested in France and England in the 1620s.

The sixteenth and seventeenth centuries saw the movement towards uniformity accelerated by the appearance of itinerant champions and of a substantial literature dealing with the game in its own right rather than exploiting its material for literary effect. In this period Spain's mastery of the game declined, leaving the development of technique in the hands of French and Italian players. Britain did not come into its own until the eighteenth century. The earliest English book on the game (discounting such notable translations as Caxton's *The game and playe of the chesse*, 1474) was Arthur Saul's *Famous Game of Chesse-play* (1614), which Eales characterizes as 'easy to regard... as merely comic, so little does it conform to the modern idea of a chess book, but it actually provides valuable evidence for the way in which the game was played by the majority of gentlemen amateurs all over Europe in the seventeenth century. Men who learnt how to play chess from books like this were not seeking something that was mentally challenging, so much as adopting a pastime that was traditional, dignified, and long established as appropriate to their rank.'[36] The threat of intellectualism colours the introduction to the game in Cotton's *Compleat Gamester* of 1674 quoted in the epigraph to this chapter.

Cotton's 'Brief instructions', and the scores of specific games, were about all that was on offer until the appearance of Philidor's *L'analyze des échecs*, first published in London in 1749, in English in 1750, and in German in 1754.

The subsequent history of orthodox Chess ceases to be that of its internal evolution and becomes that of its players and styles, tournaments and champions, and principles and theory, all of which are too well documented to require repetition here.

NOTES

1. D. B. Pritchard, *Encyclopedia of Chess Variants* (Godalming, 1994). Limited edition.
2. Based on Murray's translation of Salemann's German translation.
3. The more usual terms for *shah* and *asp* actually appear in manuscript as their Huzvarish equivalents, respectively *malka* and *susya*.
4. H. Cox, 'On the Burmha Game of Chess', *Asiatic Researches* (London, 1801), vii. 486–511; D. Forbes, *Observations on the Origins and Progress of Chess* (London, 1855), *History of Chess* (London, 1860). See also Murray, *History of Chess*, 48.
5. Andreas Bock-Raming, 'The Literary Sources of Indian Chess and Related Board Games', in *New Approaches to Board Games Research* (IAAS, Leiden, 1995), 112–24.
6. But their ideographs differ. That of Xiang-qi is built on the radical for *wood*, that of Wei-qi on the radical for *stone*. (Murray, *History of Chess*, 121.)
7. From Patañjali's commentary on Pāninin's grammar, the *Mahābhāshya* (Murray, 33).
8. H. Holländer, 'Thesen zur Früh- und Vorgeschichte des Schachspiels', *Homo Ludens*, 4 (1995), 17–28.
9. Ricardo Calvo: 'Die Hypothese von Johannes Kohtz', *Homo Ludens*, 4 (1995), 29–45.
10. Pritchard, *Encyclopedia of Chess Variants*, 151.
11. H. T. Lau, *Chinese Chess* (Tokyo, 1985), 10. This work includes the games recorded in the two Chinese classics referred to.
12. W. H. Wilkinson, 'Tyang-keui—Chess', a chapter contributed to Culin, *Korean Games* republished as *Games of the Orient* (1958), 82–91.
13. For rules and sample games, see Murray, *History of Chess*, 134–7; J. Gollon, *Chess Variations* (Japan, 1974), 155–62; Pritchard, *Encyclopedia of Chess Variants*, 164–5.
14. Pritchard, *Encyclopedia*, 269 (verbatim).
15. The *Ni-Chureki*, published 1210–21.
16. The *Futsu-Shodo-Shu* (1297–1302), an anthology of prayers.

17. Koichi Masukawa, 'Der Ursprung des japanesischen Schachs', *Homo Ludens*, 4 (1994), 91–101.
18. Pritchard, *Encyclopedia of Chess Variants*, 31.
19. Details obtained in 1969 by P. A. Hill, cited in Pritchard, *Encyclopedia*.
20. Murray, *History of Chess*,158.
21. *Rukh* does mean chariot, but has never been the ordinary word for it. It also means 'cheek' and 'roc' (the fabulous bird), but neither has any apparent bearing on the game. That it denoted in the original Persian an elephant bearing a castle on its back, or the castle itself, or a camel, has been long discredited (Murray, *History of Chess*, 159). A supposed derivation from Italian *rocco*, 'castle tower', is plausible phonetically but not historically.
22. Murray's account of castling queen's side reads: '1 R~, 2 Ke2, 3 Kg1, using the Kt's leap.'
23. Murray, *History of Chess*, 358.
24. Richard Eales, *Chess: The History of a Game* (London, 1985).
25. Helena M Gamer, 'The Earliest Evidence of Chess in Western Literature', *Speculum* (1954), 740–4 (cited by Eales, *Chess: The History of a Game*).
26. Murray (*History of Chess*, 405–6) argues for 1010.
27. Arie van der, Stoep, *A History of Draughts, with a diachronic study of words for Draughts, Chess, Backgammon and Morris* (Rockanje, 1984).
28. Eales, *Chess: the History of a Game*, 57; Murray, *History of Chess*, 428.
29. Antje Kluge-Pinsker, 'Brettspiele, insbesondere "tabulae" (Backgammon) und "scacchis" (Scach) im Alltag der Gesellschaft des 11. und 12. Jahrhunderts', *Homo Ludens*, 4 (1994), 70–8, summary in English p. 79.
30. Murray reproduces the whole poem, *History of Chess*, 512–14.
31. David Parlett (trans.), *Selections from the Carmina Burana* (Harmondsworth, 1986), *CB* 210, pp. 169–70.
32. See Murray, *History of Chess*, 476.
33. Eales, *Chess: The History of a Game*, 73. Govert Westerveld ('Historia de la nueva dama ponderosa', *Homo Ludens*, 4 (1994)), dates it 1494–5 in his references, but in the text says it was written in 1496.
34. See above (specifically p. 259) and the chapter on Draughts.
35. Arie van der Stoep, *Een schaakloze damhistorie* (Rockanje, 1994).
36. Eales, *Chess: The History of a Game*, 88.

Diversions and Deviations

Other Things to Do on a Chessboard

Either at the commencement or in the course of the game, the players may mutually agree upon any deviation from the laws they think proper.

Code of Chess Laws, 1860 revision[1]

Fig. 17.1. Pacifist Chess, from *El Ajertivo: La Revista de los Juegos de Ingenio* (Buenos Aires), 23 (Nov. 1996), 12.

Puzzles and Problems

Mathematical puzzles involving a chessboard, such as the knight's tour, probably originated in India, but problems as such were first explored by the classical players of Islam, whose *manṣūbāt*, 'positions, arrangements', resembled what we should now call end-game studies.

Medieval European players adopted and adapted from their predecessors. Most of the 103 problems in the Alfonso manuscript of 1283 are of Islamic character, but a few introduce novel elements that would eventually come to dominate the world of European problemism, notably 'White to move and mate in *n* moves', and self-mates. The relatively low standard of European play is indicated by the fact that specifications were often devised to avoid cooks (alternative solutions not intended by the composer), and the fact that the number of specified moves is mostly two, sometimes three, compared with the four or five typical of Arabic problems. A typical European development was the 'impossible' problem. Medieval gaming being inseparable from gambling, a hustler, by collecting problems he knew to be unsound, could tempt the unwary to wager on a win for whichever colour he chose to play, himself knowing the traps and pitfalls to avoid in either case.

Medieval Chess problems flourished in Italy just before the invention of modern Chess. Collections continued to be published in the sixteenth century, but solvers soon lost interest in those involving old queens and effete bishops, or omitting them entirely, and even problems adapted to feature their more powerful counterparts failed to attract. Problems did not regain popularity until the publication, in 1737, of Stamma's *Essai sur le Jeu des Échecs*, containing 100 problematical mid-game positions of which many found resolution only in startling sacrificial combinations. These re-aroused the interest of Italian composers, who preferred to subordinate supposed over-the-board reality to the more intellectually attractive properties of elegance and economy.

Problemism subsequently became a field of activity in its own right, with particular centres of interest in England, Germany, and Bohemia. The word 'problem' first occurs in its modern sense in William Lewis's book *Chess Problems* (1827). Staunton started a problem column in the *Illustrated London News* from 1847, and the first composer tournament took place in 1850. By now completely divorced from the requirements of verisimilitude, the problem came to be regarded as an art form, with its own canons of merit and beauty. Desirable features included themes and variations, a multiplicity of defences, avoidance of checks prior to mate, economy of force (giving rise to the Meredith, featuring not more than twelve pieces in all, and the miniature, with not more than seven), pure mates (no adjacent king square covered twice, no double checks, no unattacked self-blocks), model mate (the same, plus every one of White's pieces contributing to the mate), and so on.

The American Sam Loyd (1841–1911) followed more amusing flights of fancy based on startling ideas requiring what we should now call 'lateral thinking'. Under the subsequent influence of T. R. Dawson (1889–1951), the problemist's fancy extended to the invention of unorthodox settings, and, in particular, unorthodox pieces.

Fairy Chess. The term 'fairy problem', proposed in 1914 by Henry Tate of Melbourne, has happily resisted all attempts to displace it, despite Dawson's own misgivings. It connotes all forms of heterodoxy, but chiefly those of pieces with unorthodox moves. Dawson himself invented the grasshopper, which moves like a rook but, like the Chinese cannon, must jump over a single intervening piece of either colour. A relatively sensible and logical piece, it has featured in so many problems as to have acquired the paradoxical status of an 'orthodox' fairy, represented by initial G or, graphically, by an upturned queen. Equally orthodox is his nightrider, represented by an upturned knight, which makes a succession of knight-moves in a straight line (m = 1/2&). The vast menagerie of pieces that have been devised over the years can be broadly grouped into three classes, which of course also embrace orthodox pieces. *Riders* move in straight lines (queen, rook, bishop); *leapers* move directly from one square to another, regardless of intervening pieces (knight = 1/2, camel = 1/3, zebra = 2/3); *hoppers* cannot move except by leaping over other pieces (cannon, grasshopper). There are also the inevitable composites, such as the amazon, which can move like a queen or a knight, as preferred.

Even with orthodox pieces, the conditions may vary. The solver may be required to seek stalemate, or helpmate (White to mate, with Black's co-operation), or self-mate (White to move and force Black to mate unwillingly). The shape or topology of the board may be altered, such as to a cylinder or a cube. Or the problem may be one of retrograde analysis, the object being to logically deduce the last move, or the forgotten position of a piece that has fallen off the board, or whether promotion has occurred, or whether castling or capture *en passant* is possible so that White may deliver mate, or Black evade it.

Chess Variants

Deliberate Chess variants, as opposed to regional variants produced by natural selection, became commonplace in the eighteenth century as a reaction against the tendency of the orthodox game to become more bookish and intellectually demanding.[2] One reason for innovating is that a novelty tends to reduce the disparity between good and bad players. Another common motivation is to speed the game up, and another that, since Chess is too deep to be exhausted by exploration, variants are an enjoyable way of exploring. Furthermore, as David Pritchard remarks,[3] 'Orthochess as a game is far from perfect, its present form the result of a series of changes that are part of the natural development of any enduring game. Theoretically at least, there are several good C[hess] V[ariants]s that are as good as, and possibly better than, orthochess.'

How many are there? Figures of 30,000–40,000 have been bandied about, but by a process of précis and rigorous selection Pritchard manages to concentrate on a mere 1,450. Of these, about half date from between 700 and 1970 (1,200 years!), half from the last quarter of the twentieth century. Some are one-off inventions for Chess club celebrations, and may find their way into Chess magazines. Some magazines include them, others are devoted to them. Of the hundreds of proprietary board games published each year some are obviously based on Chess, some are based on Chess but are so heavily disguised as to pretend to an undeserved originality, and some have no connection with Chess but mention it on the box in quest of a spurious respectability. Most of the great games inventors (Abbott, Freeling, Knizia, Randolph, Sackson, Solomon, *et al.*) have produced Chess variants; others are the work of specialists such as Tony Paletta and Vernon Parton (1897–1974). Many have been published only in the form of patent specifications. Yet others have appeared in fiction. The classic example is Edgar Rice Burroughs's perfectly playable game of Jetan in *The Chessmen of Mars* (1922), but the list extends also to such as Akers, Asimov, Klein, and H. G. Wells.

Major sources are Cohen's 'Olla Podrida' pages in *Nost-algia*, magazine of NOST ([k]Nights of the Square Table), and *Eteroscacco*, official organ of the Associazione Italiana Scacchi Eterodossi (AISE). This body, formed in 1975, is rooted in an interest in 'heterochess' evinced by the Florence Chess Circle in the late 1940s, and encouraged by such masters as Castaldi, Porreca, and Scafarelli. It organized the first Heterochess Olympiad 1988 by correspondence, with teams representing Italy, Canada, New Zealand, UK, and the USA. Italy took the first three places (Britain taking the fourth), thus confirming its position as the leading nation in this field.

Enthusiasts have classified Chess variants in a number of ways. Michael Keller, editor/publisher of *World Games Review*, distinguishes twenty-five basic categories and further subdivides almost every one of them. Disregarding his 'historical–regional' heading, the remainder can be broadly summarized as follows:

Board: dimension, shape, tessellation, dynamic variability, etc.
Pieces: movement, capture, promotion, etc.
Objective: checkmate, stalemate, bare king, suicide, etc.
Players: number, partnerships, teams, etc.
Procedures: advance placement, multi-move, multi-occupation, blind, etc.

These are not mutually exclusive, of course. Games played on larger boards usually include new pieces and may be played by three or four. Of Pritchard's 1,450 listings, roughly 150 are enlarged games, 100 are for four players, 50 three-dimensional, 50 feature randomization, 40 are hybrids (mostly with Draughts, but even Football and Pinochle are roped in!), 40 involve multi-moves, 30 have captives re-entered, 30 are miniaturized, 30 are for three players, 25 have an element of chance such as dice or cards.

Enlargements. Al-Masudi described an eighth-century game played on a 10 × 10 board, the additional pieces being a camel on each corner square (m = 2 +). In a later variant they are *dababas*[4] on files [d, g] (m = 1✱). A 10 × 10 game of presumably Moorish origin appears in the Alfonso manuscript of 1283. The extra pieces are judges, their moves unexplained. Alfonso also describes a 12 × 12 *Grande Acedrex* with the following pieces, two of which anticipate the courier of Courier Chess and the modern bishop:

1 king, m = 1✱, optionally 2✱ on its first move, leaping if necessary.
1 gryphon, m = 1 × followed by n +, not leaping
2 crocodiles, m = n × (bishop)
2 giraffes, m = 1/4, leaping
2 unicorns, m = 1/2 initially, but not capturing; thereafter m = n×
2 lions, m = 3 +, leaping
2 rooks, m = n +
12 pawns, m = 1> (never 2>). A pawn promotes to the master piece of its file

It was optionally played with an eight-faced die, each specifying which piece to move. Gollon describes the game as 'playable and entertaining', but with reservations.

Shatranj Kamil ('Perfect' Chess), a variant favoured and allegedly invented by Timur 'the Lame' of Persia (1336–1405), is well but inconsistently documented.[5] Several Turkish enlargements of the Islamic game are recorded in the nineteenth century, mostly on 10 × 10 boards, some larger.

Courier Chess. Courier is one of the most celebrated Chess variants in the historical canon, largely because of its mysterious origin, its association with a single village, and its extraordinary longevity. It is first mentioned in the *Wigalois*, a German poem dating from 1202–5, somewhat freely translated from a French original (which has *eschecs* in place of the key word):

> Da lagen vor der frouwen fier
> wurfzabel unde kurrier
> gewohrt von helfenbeine.
> *There before the ladies four*
> *were set backgammon and courier*
> *y-wrought of ivory.*

In another German poem, of 1337, Kunrat von Ammenhausen describes Courier as played in Constance, saying that he has never seen it anywhere in France, Provence, or Kurwahlen. The game is central to a painting of 1520 attributed to Lucas von Leyden. Its most detailed description occurs in Selenus, *Das Schach- oder König-Spiel* (Leipzig 1616), who says that it is played in neighbouring states but is particularly associated with the village of Ströbeck, now a suburb of Halberstadt, about half-way between Leipzig and Hannover. According to Selenus, the inhabitants of Ströbeck were famed Chess-players, cleaving still to the medieval form of the game and to Courier. When William Lewis went to see for himself in 1831, he found only modern Chess played. He contributed to this peculiar episode of Chess history the discovery that in 1561 the Elector of Brandenburg had given the inhabitants a combined Chess/Courier board and two sets of pieces, one of ivory and one of silver and gold. The latter had been borrowed by the dean and chapter at Halberstadt and never returned. According to Hooper and Whyld, 'A 20th-century visitor could find no-one who was able to play Chess, and noted that the villagers were fed up with being pestered about the subject.'[6]

The board is 12 wide by 8 deep, with a white square at bottom right. The first four pieces, one of each, are placed at either end of files (f-g-e-h) respectively:

1 king, m = 1✷
1 queen, m = 1 × (medieval queen)
1 counsellor, m = 1✷
1 sneak, spy, or jester (*Schleich*), m = 1 +
2 couriers, m = n × (modern bishop)
2 bishops, m = 2 × (leaping)
2 knights, m = 1/2
2 rooks, m = n +
12 pawns, m = 1>

White starts with four statutory moves, namely, rook pawns and queen pawn two forwards, queen g1–g3, after which Black responds equivalently and real play begins. No rules are recorded as to castling, pawn promotion, or the status of stalemate and bare king. Gollon's experience of play leads him to favour the normal rules of Shatranj. Efforts have been made to update and popularize the game, notably by Albers (1821) and Byway (1971).[7]

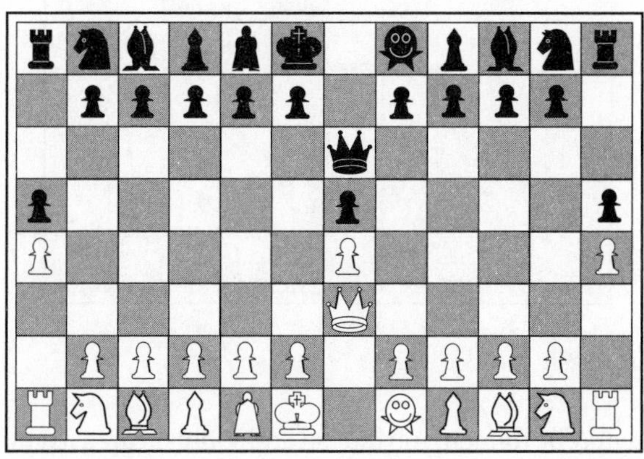

Fig. 17.2. Courier Chess: R, N, B, courier, counsellor, K, Q, sneak, courier, B, N, R. Position after statutory opening moves.

Enlargements proliferated from the end of the seventeenth century, possibly encouraged by the availability of the decimal board used for 'Polish' Draughts. A 10 × 10 game called Arch is said to have been played by Piacenza (1683), another appears in a Dutch edition of Greco of 1696, and one of 10 × 8 was said, in 1739, to be 'currently practised in Spain'. In the 1740s Philidor often beat Stamma at a variant played on a 14 × 8 board. Attributed to the Duke of Rutland, it included several new pieces, such as the crowned rook and the concubine—'a familiar figure of the Hanoverian court' (Eales). The fact that she was sometimes bowdlerized into a princess can hardly have alleviated the implications of such a move as 'bishop takes concubine'.

A more mysterious variant is one recorded by R. C. Bell[8] under the name Gala, or Peasants' Chess, apparently played until recently in Dithmarschen, Schleswig-Holstein, where the special 10 × 10 board may still be encountered in 'remote farmhouses'. It is distinguished by a two-square cruciform separation into four quarters of sixteen each, into which the pieces are initially arrayed (Fig. 17.3). A medieval origin is mooted, but the game's

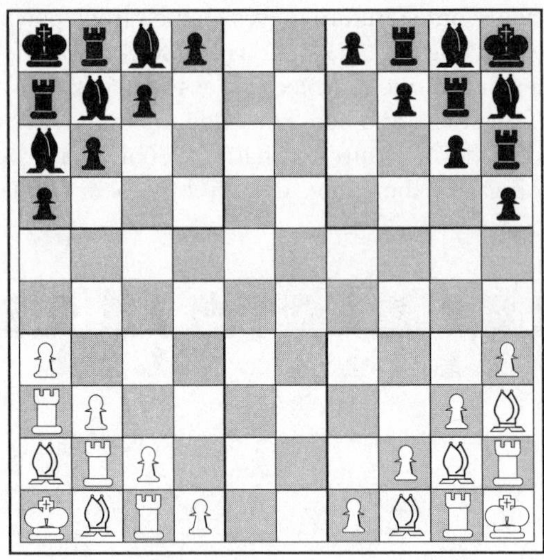

Fig. 17.3. Gala Chess.

peculiarities may be thought too radical and sophisticated to antedate even the nineteenth century.

Dimensional Variants. True three-dimensional Chess is played in cubes rather than on squares, though in order to render the game practical it is of necessity played on two or more vertical layers of two-dimensional chequered boards. Evidence for the earliest 3-D Chess, that reportedly demonstrated by Kieseritzky to Andersen in London, 1851, is anecdotal and unconfirmed. The classic game is that of Maack, developed in 1907 after experimentation with various sizes of board, though that of Kogbetliantz in 1918 has also acquired followers and inspired variants. Pritchard's survey of 3-D Chess games shows that the number of them has increased, is increasing, and ought to be diminished. Easier than all, but deceptively so, is Alice Chess (Parton, 1953). One of two adjacent boards is initially blank, the other orthodoxly arrayed. Each player's first move is made 'through the looking-glass' on to the appropriate square of the blank board. Thereafter, each player may move a piece on either board, but only to the appropriate square on the other board.

Topological Variants include Billiards Chess, wherein a piece reaching an edge of the board may 'bounce' off it at the correctly reflected angle. In Cylinder Chess, files (a) and (h) are considered contiguous; if this also applies to ranks (1) and (8), the result is Toroidal Chess. Hoppe's game of Es involves six chessboards arranged into a cube. Möbius Chess exists, but must be left to speak for itself.

Miniaturization is as modern a development as multi-dimensionality. It chiefly stems from a desire to save time, but the Victorian inventor of 'Diana' purported to simplify play for 'the fair sex', while the virtually identical l'Hermitte's Game of 100 years later was supposedly to help introduce children to the real thing (or vice versa). More recent experiments serve to make it easier for computers—or, more accurately, programmers. Mathematicians like Martin Gardner and Dave Silverman have sought to see how small Chess can become without losing interest.

Various miniature Chess forms are illustrated in descending order of size (Fig. 17.4; source Pritchard). Unless otherwise stated, pawns never advance two squares initially. In Dekle's 7 × 7 bishops may move either (n×) or (1 +), pawns may promote to queens, of which none appear in the array, and kings may castle. In Diana ('Huntress of the Chase'—a nice pun) kings castle unorthodoxly by changing places with a rook. Lilliputian merges bishop and knight into a new piece, the archbishop, which moves like either, and can therefore cover the whole board. Castling is permitted either side. L'Hermitte's and Dean-Smith's 6 × 6 both feature unorthodox rules. So does Chi-Chi Hackenberg's 8 × 4, which in any case is cooked (White mates in 11 or less). The 5 × 5 games are the smallest in which all legal moves are possible, including castling and the pawn's initial two-step (and therefore capture *en passant*). That favoured by AISE has been extensively played and analysed in Italy and may be regarded as the classic miniature game. It does not permit castling.

Smaller games have been suggested but mainly in order to set problems and puzzles—most, when played, give White an easy win. Of more theoretical than practical interest are ingenious attempts at devising a one-dimensional game. The most realistic of these, by Dan Glimne, is played on a line of 18 cells (Fig. 17.5). Pawns may advance two squares initially. Knights move either two or three squares ad lib, jumping if necessary. Bishops move only on squares of their own colour, completely ignoring those of the other. Kings move one or two squares. Castling is permitted, under normal restrictions, by simply changing places. Glimne believes White has a forced win, and awaits proof.[9]

Geometrical Variants. Circular Chess first appears in tenth-century Arabic manuscripts under various names, of which 'Byzantine Chess' raises questions as to its area of origin. It adopts the natural form of sixty-four

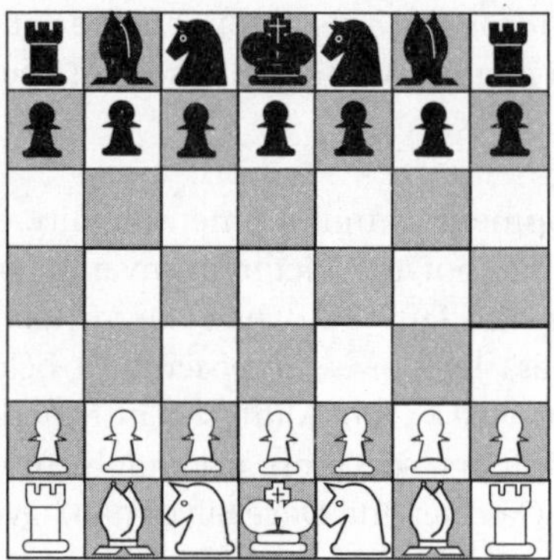

7x7 *Microchess-49* (Paletta, 1980)

7x7 *Microchess* (Dekle, 1987)

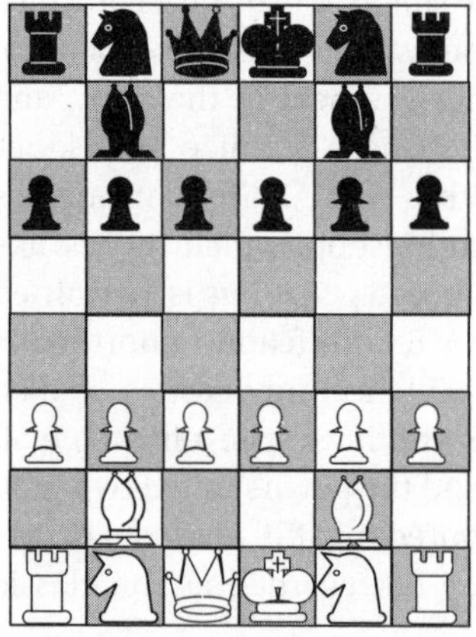

6x8 *Microchess-48* (Paletta, 1980)

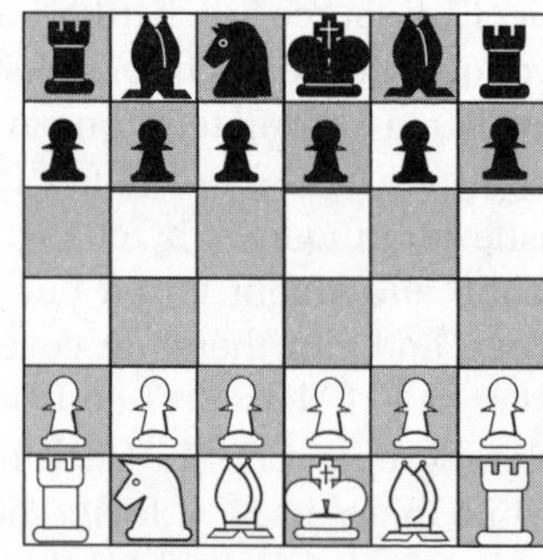

6x6 *Diana* (Hopwood, 1870); also (but with chequering reversed) *l'Hermitte's Game* (1969)

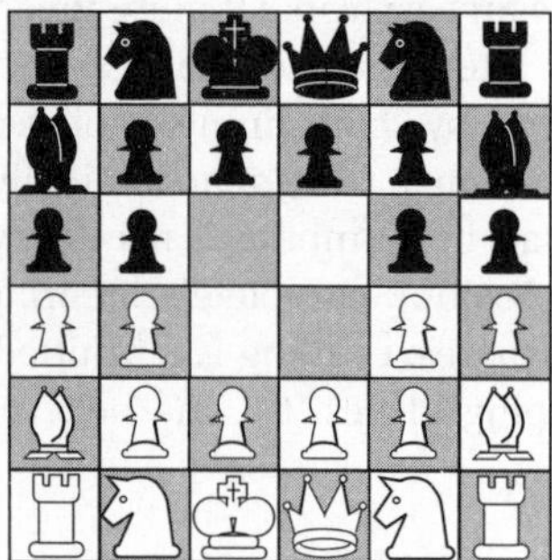

6x6 *Compact Chess* (Dean-Smith, 1988)

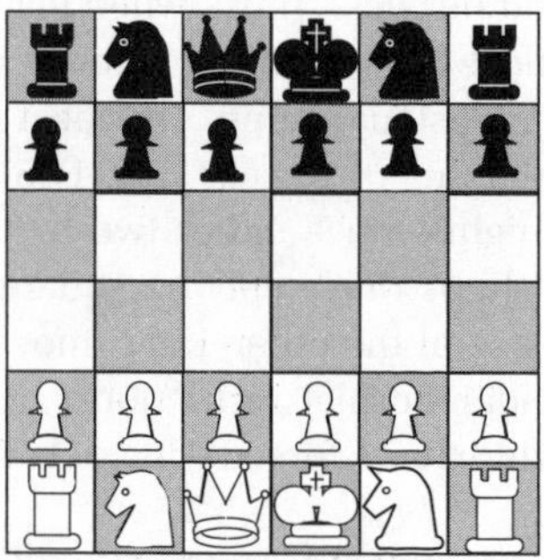

6x6 *Los Alamos Chess* (Kister *et al.*, source undated)

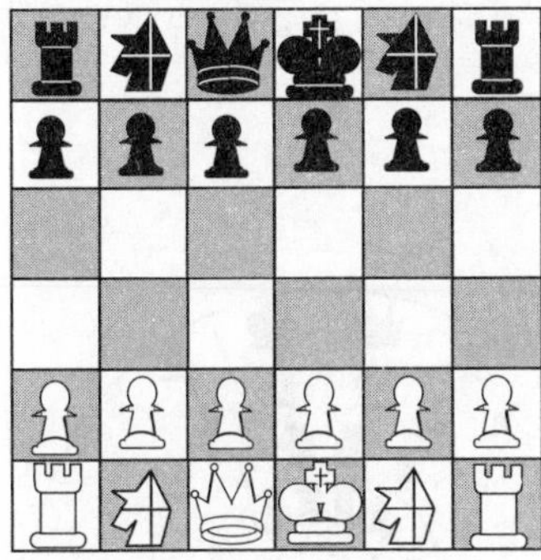

6x6 *Lilliputian Chess* (Dekle, 1986). The unorthodox piece is an archbishop, and moves like a bishop or a knight

5x6 *Petty Chess* (Walker Watson, 1930)

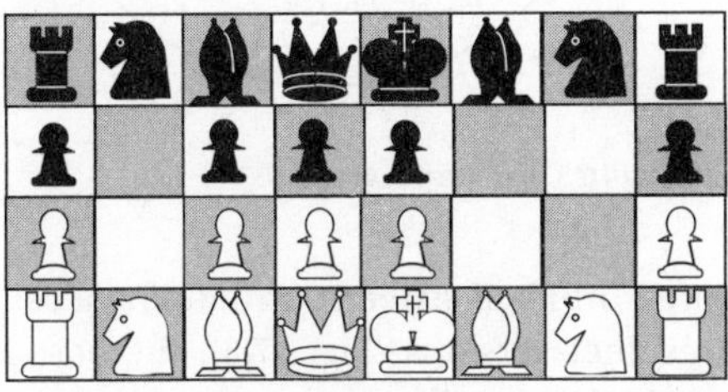

8x4 *Chi-Chi's Chess* (Hackenberg, 1968)

5x5 *Baby Chess* (Gardner, 1989) = Minichess with opposing arrays off-set

5x5 *Minichess* (AISE, 1978), originally Gardner 1969 (with chequering reversed)

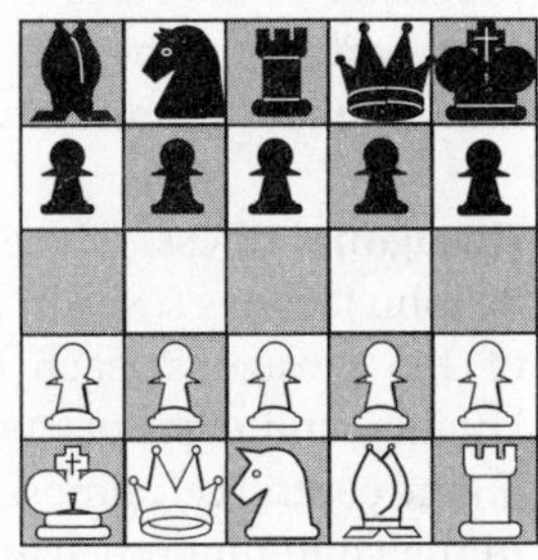

5x5 *Minichess* (Jacobs and Meirovitz, 1983)

Fig. 17.4. Small is beautiful . . .

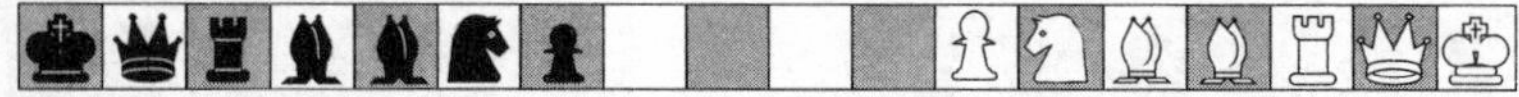

Fig. 17.5. One-dimensional Chess (Glimne).

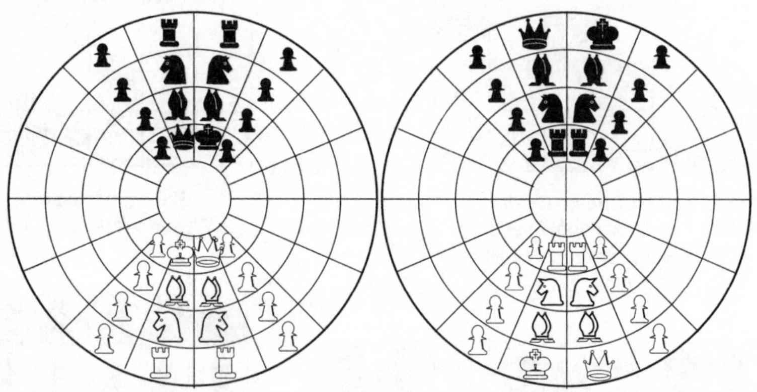

Fig. 17.6. *Left*: Byzantine round Chess. *Right*: The Citadel version.

'squares' arranged in four concentric orbits of sixteen surrounding a central boss. In the second of two distinct versions (Fig. 17.6), the boss is divided into four quadrants called citadels, and if a king succeeds in posting itself on a citadel the game is drawn. A reference to it in Twiss's *Chess* (1789) led to a revival of interest in London and Germany, and the game was practised to the rules of original Shatranj and of modern Chess. Gollon gives some specimen games. Circular Chess periodically reappears on the market under proprietary names, often as three- or four-player variants.

Hexagonal Chess. The earliest seems to have been Hexagonia, published by John Jacques & Son in 1864.[10] Played on a symmetrical field-centred grid of 125 hexagons, each force consisted of one king, two cannon, four knights, and eight pawns. The aim of establishing one's king unopposed on the central cell almost takes it out of the realm of Chess, likening it more to the contemporary game of Agon. In 1912 Sigemund Willesch devised a 91-celled board to accommodate the symmetrical requirements of three-handed Chess. This was more Chess-like, but lacked bishops, apparently because Willesch failed to grasp the concept of diagonal movement on a hexagonal grid. In 1929 H. D. Baskerville published a booklet on a form of hexagonal Chess as close as he could get to the real thing. It suffers from being *too* close. The hexes (patriotically red, white, and blue) are arranged in a virtual square, with eight ranks of eight files enclosing seven ranks of five. Both white bishops played on white squares only, both black ones on blue only, rendering them immune from mutual attack, and leaving red cells totally unepiscopated.

The best-established hexagonal Chess is that developed by Wladislaw Glinski in 1936, and first published in Britain in 1949. Certainly it is the most logical and natural adaptation of square Chess to a hexagonal format. The board has ninety-one cells, and each side has the normal complement of pieces plus a ninth pawn and third bishop (Fig. 17.7). The move of each piece is translated exactly into hexagonal terms. The king, for example, moves one hex orthogonally or diagonally, giving access to twelve in all. Pawns can move forwards two steps initially, and promote upon reaching an opposing base line, which is always six steps away. There is no castling. Glinski's Game has thousands of followers in eastern Europe. The first British championship took place in 1976, to be followed by a European and a World Championship.

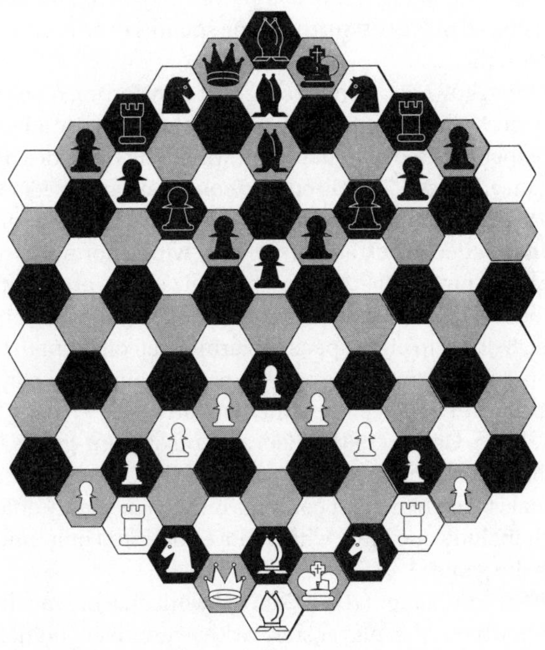

Fig. 17.7. Glinski's Hexagonal Chess.

Other geometrical variants include Balbo's Game (1974), played from diagonally opposite corners of a trellis or 'jagged edge' grid of sixty squares; Paletta's Rhombic Chess (1980), on a board of seventy-two rhombuses, twenty-four each of three colours, in the overall shape of a hexagon; and a variety of spirals.

Variant Pieces. Turning from board to piece variants opens up too vast a domain to summarize adequately. A piece is defined primarily (though not solely) by how it moves and how it captures, and almost any novel move or form of capture you can think of has almost certainly been thought of already. Just three particularly amusing flights of fancy may be mentioned in passing. The gorgon (V. R. Parton, 1970) moves like a queen, but, instead of capturing, petrifies any piece that falls under her gaze, rendering it incapable of movement until released. (Compare Abbott's immobilizer.) Gutzwiller's bishop, named after a player who delivered mate in a Cincinnati League match after making such a move by mistake, shifts to any vacant adjacent orthogonal square before moving diagonally, thus giving it access to all squares of both colours. The bomb (Suttles, 1973) moves like a king. Instead of making a move, a player may detonate one of his two bombs, causing all pieces on surrounding squares to be removed from play, the bomb with them.

More exciting, however, is the prospect of transferring redefinitions from individual pieces to the armies they comprise.[11] For example, Ralph Betza (1980) has experimented with games in which the two sides deploy different but balanced forces. To this end he computer-analysed a vast array of possible pieces to produce a numerical evaluation of each one's working potential. In practice, Black and White play with a normal complement of chesspieces on a normal 8 × 8 board, but only pawns are identical on each side, each of the other pieces being distinctively predefined by move and capture. Betza drew up eight specimen armies, all different in composition but equal in overall strength, enabling experimenters to play any one of fifty-six games with balanced but unequal forces.

Similarly, Bruce Gilson (1984) offers a menu of point-graded pieces from which each player compiles an army, such that (*a*) neither exceeds 200 points in total value, (*b*) neither contains more than twenty different pieces, and (*c*) both include one king, which moves one step only, and whose loss determines the game.

R. Wayne Schmittberger (1980s) started work on a prospective 'Generalized Chess' in which each player starts with a number of points from which to buy different pieces from a common pool—some eighty-eight were initially specified—such that a piece bought by one player became unavailable to the other. If it were adopted, 'the value of each piece, initially assessed by [existing] detailed analysis...would be constantly under review, based not on further mathematical calculations but according to the law of supply and demand in major events' (Pritchard).

Abbott's Ultima. A notable chesspiece variant devised by Bob Abbott in 1961, and published as a tailpiece to *Abbott's New Card Games* (New York, 1963), was originally called 'Baroque'. Enthusiasts dubbed it 'Abbott's Ultima', leading one to wonder why they did not go all the way and call it 'Ulti-Mate'.

Ultima uses a standard 8×8 board and pieces, except that the rooks represent different pieces, requiring one of them to be distinguished in some way, such as by being upturned. Winning is by mate or stalemate. The point of the game derives from the observation that while chesspieces have different methods of movement, they all have the same method of capture. But what if they had the same powers of movement (more or less) and different of capture? And what capturing methods are there to choose from? The resultant pieces are defined as shown in Table 17.1.

Table 17.1. Methods of capture in Abbot's Uttima

name	represented by	move	capture
king	king	1*	replacement
withdrawer	queen	n*	withdrawal
chameleon	bishop	n*	reflection
longleaper	knight	n*	leaping
immobilizer	rook 1	n*	paralysis
co-ordinator	rook 2	n*	co-ordination
pawn	pawn	n+	custodianship

The initial array is that of the standard pieces by which they are represented, the king's rook being the co-ordinator and the queen's marked in some way, or turned upside down, to distinguish it as the immobilizer. Most pieces move like queens, but pawns move like rooks, and kings as normal. Only kings capture by simple replacement. The withdrawer captures like a piece in Fanorona, the chameleon by whatever capturing method defines the piece it captures—a withdrawer by withdrawing from it, a longleaper by leaping it, and so on. It cannot, by logic, capture another chameleon. The longleaper captures by jumping a single piece, like a long queen in Polish Draughts.

The immobilizer does not actually capture, but paralyses any and all enemy pieces lying orthogonally or diagonally adjacent to it. (Immobilizing a king, therefore, does not check it.) Paralysed pieces remain immobile until the immobilizer moves away. Adjacent adverse immobilizers paralyse each other, rendering either immobile until the other is captured or commits suicide. Under the suicide rule, a player on his turn to play may remove from the board any single piece currently paralysed by the adverse immobilizer. This counts as a move. Note that a chameleon moving adjacent to an immobilizer thereby paralyses both of them. The co-ordinator captures a piece lying at either diagonally opposite corner of a rectangle whose other diagonal is defined by the co-ordinator and its king. It can therefore capture two at once. Pawns capture by the custodianship, as in Latrunculi, but using any friendly piece—not necessarily a pawn—as the other custodian. Up to three pieces may be so captured simultaneously. Pawns do not promote.

Abbott revised the game in 1968. Subsequent extensions include Thayer's Ulti-Matem (1967) and Matthew Montchalin's Renaissance (1975), played on a 9 × 9 board.

Losing Chess. Given that negative card games date from the sixteenth century, it is surprising that negative Chess is not recorded earlier than Walter Campbell's game of Take Me (1876).

Typically, the winner is the first to lose all his pieces or be stalemated. Players are obliged to capture if possible, but may choose freely among several possibilities. The king is an ordinary piece: it cannot be checked, but can be captured, and a pawn can promote to a king. Under-promotion is so advatangeous that some prefer a variant in which pawns may promote only to queens. Another variant preserves the king's royalty: escape from check takes precedence over making a capture, and a player left with a bare king wins. Whether checkmate wins or loses depends on prior agreement.

Losing Chess—also called Losums, Give-away Chess, Killer Chess, Take-All Chess, and so on—has become one of the most popular of all Chess variants and been the subject of intensive analysis, especially by G. Braca of the AISE.

Kriegspiel (Blind Chess). Two players sit at either end of a long table divided into three sections by means of two screens, or back to back at two individual tables separated by a third. Each has his own chessboard, with pieces in their initial array, and with his own colour foremost. Between them, invisible to both, stands a master board operated by an umpire. White moves; the umpire records it on the master board and announces 'White has moved'. Black moves; the umpire records it on the master board and announces 'Black has moved'; and so on. Throughout play, the true overall position appears only on the master board. Each player knows for certain only the positions of his own pieces, and seeks to deduce those of his opponent from such information as is presented to him by the umpire. Such information states no more than whether or not an attempted move is possible, the square on which a capture has been made (but not the identity of either piece involved), and the direction of a check (rank, file, long or short diagonal, or by a knight).

This justifiably most popular of Chess variants enjoys the distinction unique among board games of being more fun for the onlookers than for the players. It is, indeed, as much an entertainment as a game, and is at its best when the three participants—including the God-like umpire—have sufficient character and aplomb to throw themselves whole-heartedly into the role of theatrical performers. At the same time, it is nowhere near as haphazard as it may sound from the description. Kriegspiel is a game of imperfect but developing information, and, as such, appeals particularly to card-players.

Kriegspiel as now known is generally credited to Henry Temple, who introduced it to the Knights Lights Club, London, in 1898, though it is said to have been played at the Hampstead Chess Club in 1890.[12] It has been the subject of many articles, booklets, and special issues of Chess magazines ever since, and played in many clubs. It remained a staple part of the diet at the Gambit Chess Rooms, London, until their closure in 1950. Here, says Pritchard,[13] 'The habitués developed a language of their own, akin to that of the Bingo halls; thus 'He's in your angle near the door' meant a capture on a8.'

Kriegspiel evolved in a roundabout way, passing through a phase of games known collectively as Kriegsspiel (with two esses, correctly). An oft-quoted ancestor is a series of games described by Christoph Weikhmann in *Neu-erfundenes Grosses Königs-Spiel* (1664). This illustrates boards consisting of circles joined by lines, which is merely a cosmetic modification of squares, numbering 195, 217, 415, and 697 for games for, respectively, two, four, six, and eight players. Upon them are played versions of an enlarged Chess with fourteen different pieces, including one king and a variety of military and civil ranks. (See also board war-gaming, in Chapter 17.)

Number of Players. Four-handed Chess has been played in India for about a thousand years. In 1030, the Islamic traveller al-Biruni described a Punjabi Chess game played by four and with the aid of dice. It is also mentioned in the *Rajatanrangini* (*c.*1148–9), a metrical chronicle of the kings of Kashmir, and described in more detail in Raghunandana's *Tirthayatratattva*, a

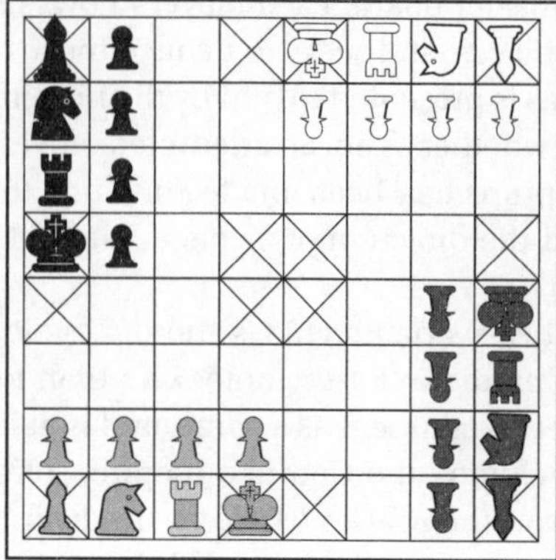
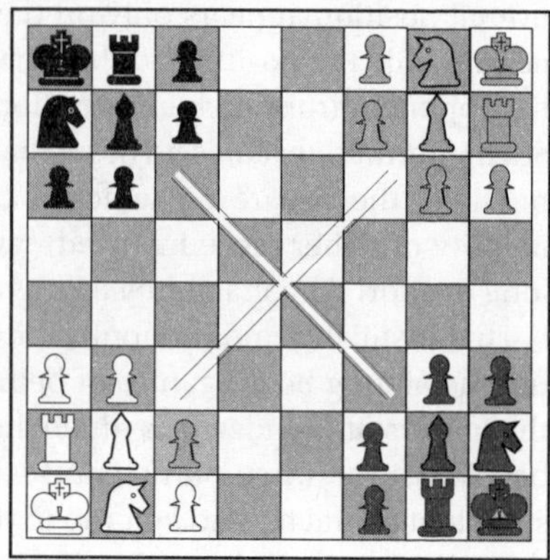

Fig. 17.8. *Left*: Chaturaji. (Indian four-hand dice Chess, after Bell.). King moves (m = 1*), rook denotes a piece moving (m = n+), horse moves (m = 1/2), corner piece moves (m = 2×), pawn moves (1>). From top left anti-clockwise the forces are black, red, green, yellow. Diagonally opposite players (Red-Yellow, Black-Green) are loosely allied. *Right*: Four Seasons Chess (*Acedrex de los quatro tiempos*), played on a specially marked board.

sixteenth-century Sanskrit legal text from Bengal. The game is often referred to as Chaturaji, from a technical term denoting the highest possible victory, namely, the capture of all three opposing kings—which, of course, casts some doubt on the degree of partnership involved and on the essence of the game, in that checkmate is not the object of play. In fact, since the pieces have point-values and the object of play is to capture material rather than force mate, Chaturaji is more a gambling game than one of intellectual conflict, a fact given further emphasis by the original involvement of dice (now long since abandoned). The original rules are unclear. Gollon follows R. C. Bell's admirable reconstruction, and commends the game for its enjoyability.[14]

A four-hand variant described in the Alfonso manuscript of 1283 under the name Four Seasons Chess (*Acedrex de los quatro tiempos*) has obvious affinities with the Indian game. The players are designated Green (spring), Red (summer), Black (autumn), White (winter), and play in that order, counterclockwise. Each attacks the following player and defends himself against the preceding one, a circumstance which probably encouraged some sort of informal alliance between diagonally opposite players, at least until one of them was eliminated by the capture of his king. Thereafter, his conqueror took over both armies, and so on, until only one player remained, who swept the pool. Various payments are specified for captures, checks, and mates.

Modern four-handers are usually partnership games designed for serious players, as distinct from gamblers. The earliest mention (1772) is of a Russian variety probably equivalent to that subsequently identified as Fortress Chess.[15] The sixteen squares to each player's right (Fig. 17.9) are his fortress, accessible only to him, and initially occupied by an extra rook, bishop, and knight, on any desired squares. The queen has the additional power of moving hippogonally, as was customary in Russian Chess of the time. The six holes on each side held pegs indicating the number of games won. Partners sat crosswise, played clockwise, and aimed to mate both opponents. The forces of a mated player were removed from the board, leaving the other to play on alone. Unless on the brink of mating an opponent, thereby reducing the game to one against one, he rarely survived. A London club devoted to Fortress flourished in the 1850s.

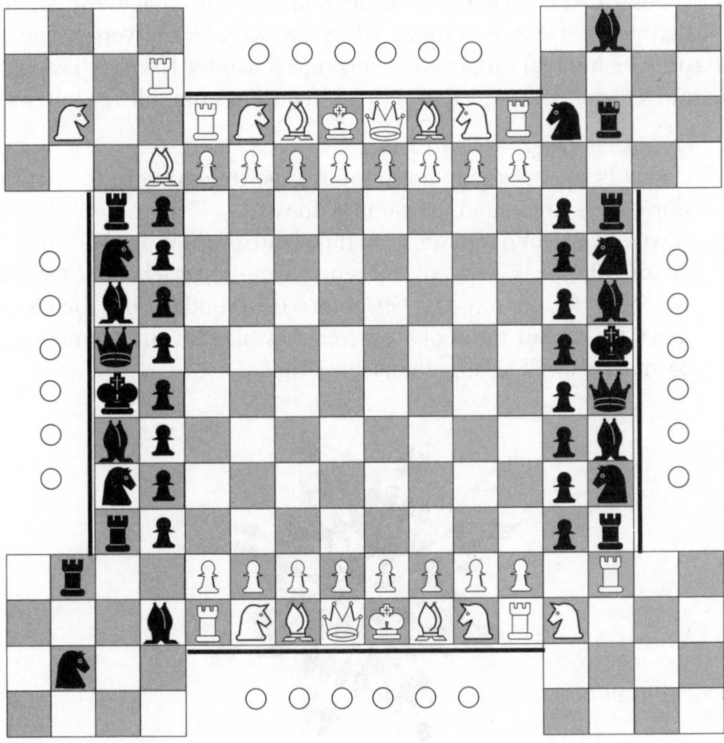

Fig. 17.9. Fortress Chess.

Experimentation blossomed in the nineteenth century, with occasional bizarre results. For example, Baltic Four-Hand Chess, invented by L. Kieseritzky around 1835 and published in the first Lett-language Chess book (1855), was played on a board of 128 chequered rhomboids in the form of an eight-pointed star (Fig. 17.10), and enjoyed some vogue in Germany and the Baltic States. In 1899, a monstrosity involving four chessboards occupying the outer quadrants of what looks like a Pachisi board was the subject of a patent application by a man called Moncrieff.[16] Of the more sensible developments, however, most adopted the format of an 8 × 8 board with an additional wing of two or more rows of eight attached to each of its four sides. The earliest of this type, with wings of 2 × 8, appears in an anonymous pamphlet, *Gesetze des Schachs zu Vieren*, 1779, which has been attributed to Duke Ernst II of Gotha-Altenburg. The earliest English-language work on four-handed Chess is the anonymous *Rules for playing the game of Chess en quatre*, London, undated, but based on a game with wings of 3 × 8 described in a German booklet published in 1784. Many varieties are described in George Verney's *Chess Eccentricities.*[17] Verney himself devised a four-handed variant with wings of 3 × 8 in 1881, which is regarded by many as the classic of its type. Pritchard outlines the rules as follows:

1. Opposite players are partners.
2. Object is to checkmate both opponents. Unless both of a partnership's kings are mated the game is drawn.
3. Pawns move one square at a time and promote (to Q only) on opponents' back rank. (E. Falkener (*Games Ancient and Oriental*, 1892) and J. Gollon (*Chess Variations*, 1974) both favour the pawn-2 move for all but the rooks' pawns; they also favour promotion on partner's as well as opponents' back ranks.)

Fig. 17.10. Board for Baltic four-handed Chess.

4. When a pawn is blocked by a friendly pawn it can leap over it to a vacant square immediately beyond even if both pawns are moving in the same direction.
5. A pawn reaching the rear rank of partner reverses direction (and is marked to indicate this), and again if reaching the first rank of the player, and so on.
6. The men of a player whose king is mated are inert. They do not exercise any power (e.g. they cannot check) and are immune from capture.
7. A player may release an opponent from mate, but in doing so may not capture one of the mated player's men.
8. No castling.
9. The partnership that does not have the move may change seats before or after White's first move.
10. The turn of play rotates clockwise.

Three-handed Chess is a contradiction in terms. A three-handed game of strategy tends to an inbuilt imbalance according to the self-perceived relative strengths of the three players. If two perceive themselves as weak, they will tend to an alliance in order to eliminate the strong player before taking on each other. If two perceive themselves as strong, they will tacitly agree to eliminate the weak player to leave themselves a clear field; otherwise, each lays himself open to the danger of the weak player's deciding to assist the adverse strong opponent. The only logical way to overcome this problem is to specify as each player's objective that he mate the player on his left (assuming clockwise rotation) while defending himself against his right-hand opponent. Curiously, only one modern inventor seems to have taken this route to a solution. Basic geometry presents another problem, to which the obvious, but rarely elegant, solution is to devise a tessellation of triangles or hexagons, or to place three square boards in a corner-to-corner arrangement enclosing a triangular area, which itself is filled with triangles, hexagons, or distorted rhomboids.

A Chinese three-hander called San-kuo-qi, an extension of Xiang-qi, traditionally represents the War of the Three Kingdoms (AD 221–64), but the date of its invention is unrecorded. The earliest European three-hander seems to be that of Filippo Marinelli, described in his *Guioco delli Scacchi fra tre*, Naples, 1722. It was played on an 8 × 8 board with three wings of 2 × 8. Each of the players Yellow, Black, Red started with the normal complement of pieces on his own wing, Black occupying the central one, and with each king sited to the right of its queen. A few of the two or three dozen three-handers published in the last quarter of the twentieth century rate at least a mention *en passant.* Noris-Schach, a proprietary game by Treugut and Böttcher (1974), is played on a board consisting of ninety-six triangles, each player having, in addition to the normal complement, an extra pawn and a cardinal, which moves like a queen but cannot capture. It was widely played in Germany for several years. Vernon Parton, doyen of unorthodox Chess inventors, made at least two novel approaches to the problem. Mad Three-Party (1971) is played on a 10×10 board, each player having a distinctly coloured set consisting of eight pieces, an extra but differentiated king, and no pawns. Each in turn places a piece on any vacant square, kings being placed last and, by law, not in check. Play proceeds in rotation, each player aiming to mate the marked king of his right-hand opponent and the unmarked of his left. No-one may check a 'wrong' king. The first to mate wins. Triscacia (1974) is played on a standard 8×8 board with a reduced complement of pieces, and exhibits the sensible rule that each player may attack only the king of the player whose turn to play immediately follows his own.

Pritchard's *Encyclopedia of Chess Variants* also mentions various team games (Caterpillar, Double Bughouse, Sociable Chess, Tandem, etc.), and games for six (Chexx), seven (a variety of Xiang-qi), and eight (Octopus).

NOTES

1. Quoted by D. Pritchard, *Encyclopedia of Chess Variants* (Godalming, 1994), p. x.
2. R. Eales, *Chess: The History of the Game* (London, 1985), 108; the note about Philidor's prowess from Pritchard, *Encyclopedia.*
3. In his *Encyclopedia of Chess Variants* (indispensable and heavily drawn on here).
4. The *dababa* (modern transliteration, but 19th-cent. *dabbaba(h)* is still perpetuated) was a manned war machine on wheels, incorporating a battering ram; compare Roman *vinea*, medieval *sow.*
5. Details in Murray, *History of Chess*, Pritchard, *Encyclopedia*; see also John Gollon, *Chess Variations* (Rutland, Vermont, 1968; rev. 1974).
6. David Hooper, and Kenneth Whyld, *The Oxford Companion to Chess* (Oxford, 1984), s.v.
7. Pritchard, *Encyclopedia of Chess Variants.*
8. R. C. Bell, *Discovering Old Board Games* (Aylesbury, 1973), 29–31. Pritchard also describes it and gives additional sources.
9. Personal communication. First published in *Games & Puzzles* (1977).
10. Date verified by Pritchard, contrary to the 1860 of some reports.
11. For further details of the games mentioned here, see entries in Pritchard, *Encyclopedia of Chess Variants*, for Betza's Chess, Free Choice Chess, Generalized Chess.
12. By Richard Griffith, according to *The Oxford Companion to Chess.* Pritchard says this is unsubstantiated.
13. Pritchard, *Encyclopedia of Chess Variants*, 166.

14. Bell, *Board and Table Games*, i. 52–7; Gollon, *Chess Variations*, 31–40.
15. From Cox's account of his visit to Russia in 1772, reported in Twiss, *Chess* (London, 1789) i. 27 (cited by Murray, History of Chess, 859). Fortress was described by A. v. Petroff in *Schachzeitung* (1850), 377. For details of play, see Pritchard, 1994.
16. See Pritchard for details of Baltic Chess (s.v.) and s.v. 'Patents' (pp. 219–20) for Moncrieff's game.
17. See also Murray, *History of Chess*, 859–60.

The Thought that Counts

Rithmomachy—the Philosophers' Game

The ordinary recreations which we have in Winter... are Cards, Tables and Dice, Shovelboord, Chess-Play, the Philosophers Game.

Robert Burton, *The Anatomy of Melancholy* (1621)

It was my wish to have subjoined a general outline of the method of playing, but the author is so exceedingly obscure in his phraseology, and negligent in his explanations, that I found it impossible to follow him with the least degree of satisfaction.

Strutt, *Sports and Pastimes of the People of England* (1801)

To his eyes 2-4-6-8-10 was a thing of beauty; 3-6-9 had an exotic charm. And he would carry the sequence 1-2-4-8-16 on and till he had covered pages, for sheer love of the magic of the thing.

Ben Ames Williams, 'Coconuts', in *The Saturday Evening Post* (1926)

One of the most extraordinary board games of all time sprang apparently from nowhere in eleventh-century western Europe, enjoyed the patronage of the educated classes for well over half a millennium, and eventually died without issue in the early eighteenth century. The nature of game is indicated by its several names, of which the chief is Rithmomachia, a quasi-Latin word derived from Greek *rithmos* 'number' and *mache* 'battle'. This became naturalized as Rithmomachy in English and its equivalents in other countries. In some Latin contexts it is *pugna* (or *certamen*) *numerorum*, a literal translation of 'battle of numbers', and from quite early on it was also known as the Philosophers' Game—in the medieval sense of the word, that is, equivalent to what we might nowadays call scientists, or perhaps mathematicians.

Many descriptions and accounts of the game survive, of varying degrees of completeness and lucidity, of which no two agree in detail except where one is a translation of another. Historically, the two most important are those of 1482 by John Shirwood, Bishop of Durham, and of 1616 by 'Gustavus Selenus' (Augustus II, Duke of Brunswick), itself a German translation of an Italian work of 1472.[1] Since the very variety and notorious inadequacy of sources render it impossible to describe any specific set of rules as most typical, let alone definitive, the following description is highly generalized, and should not be regarded as referring to any one particular version of the game.

The Game. Rithmomachy is played on a chequered grid of 8×16 squares, equivalent to two conjoined chessboards, and so placed that the two players, nominally White and Black, face each other across the shorter distance. Each player's right-hand half counts as his home board and the other's adverse board, and each starts with the army of his own colour arrayed on his home board.

Pieces. Each side has a theoretical twenty-four pieces in three distinctive shapes called rounds, triangles, and squares, each bearing a number. White's twenty-four pieces are based on the even numbers 2-4-6-8, Black's on the odd series 3-5-7-9. The numbers marked on each side's remaining twenty pieces are derived from its four base numbers by a method that may be formulated as shown in the last columns of Table 18.1. The actual method was based on an arcane algorithm designed to show how all numbers are logically generated from unity. Most varieties of the game require each piece to bear its number on both sides, but in the opposite colour on the reverse.

In practice, White actually has twenty-nine and Black twenty-eight pieces. White's square 91 is omitted, and is replaced by a pile of six additional pieces, namely (from top to bottom), rounds numbered 1 and 4, triangles 9 and 16, and squares 25 and 36. Black's square 190 is omitted, and is replaced by a pile of five pieces, namely (from top to bottom), round 16, triangles 25 and 36, and squares 49 and 64. The total value of each pile is that of the omitted square piece—that is, 91 for White and 190 for Black. Each pile is called a pyramid, or, in the guise of a proper name, Pyramis.

Table 18.1. Values of pieces in Rithmomachy.

shapes	W	B	W	B	W	B	W	B	formula	or ($m = n + 1$)
rounds	2	3	4	5	6	7	8	9	n	n
	4	9	16	25	36	49	64	81	n^2	n^2
triangles	6	12	20	30	42	56	72	90	$n(n+1)$	nm
	9	16	25	36	49	64	81	100	$(n+1)^2$	m^2
squares	15	28	45	66	91	120	153	190	$(2n+1)(n+1)$	$2m^2 - m$
	25	49	81	121	169	225	289	361	$(2n+1)^2$	$(n+m)^2$

The opening array of the earlier game is shown in Fig. 18.1. In the later game each of the two forces was initially arranged two ranks further back, against the shorter edge of the board. The relative positions of the numerals on each side are by no means random, but follow several arithmetical principles. The most significant of these, because necessary for the strategy of play, is the concept of numerical progressions, or harmonies. Three integers $a<b<c$ are said to be in

arithmetical progression if	*(b-a)/(c-b) = a/a*	e.g. 2-3-4, 91-190-289
geometrical progression if	*(b-a)/(c-b)= a/b*	e.g. 2-4-8, 100-190-361
harmonic progression if	*(b-a)/(c-b) = a/c*	e.g. 2-3-6, 72-90-120

(A table of all possible progressions in Rithmomachy is appended to this chapter.)

Movement. All accounts agree as to the *distance* of movement, namely: rounds one step each, triangles two, squares three. A pyramid may move according to the power of any piece it contains (designated 'any' in Table 18.2), with the logical consequence that when it has lost both components of a given type, it no longer enjoys that type's power of movement. If these numbers seem inappropriate, it should be remembered that, to the medieval mind—as to the classical—the initial square was considered part of the move. Thus in original descriptions of the game a round is *said* to move two spaces, a triangle three, and a square four, which of course sounds more logical.

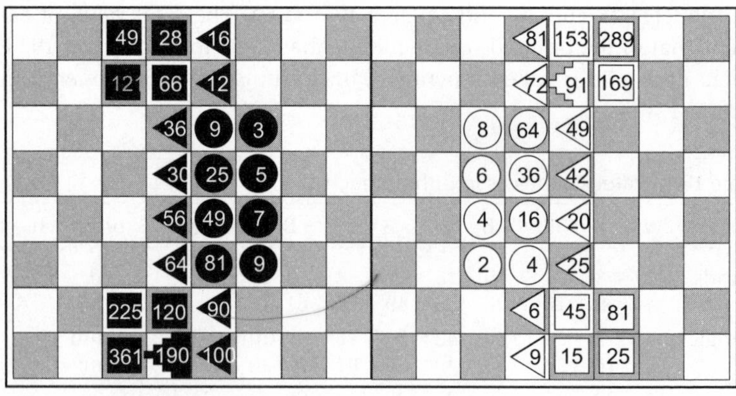

Fig. 18.1. Rithmomachy.

Direction. As to the *direction* of travel—whether forward only, orthogonal, diagonal, or both—sources vary considerably, as indicated in the table below. Invariably, there is no jumping: intervening spaces must be vacant. Some include special or privilege moves, typically of an hippogonal variety. Bossière (1556), for example, permits every piece except the pyramid one knight-move during the course of a game, provided that this does not result in a capture.

What follows is based on the reconstruction of Illmer *et al.*,[5] whereby rounds move orthogonally, triangles diagonally, and squares either, ad lib.

Capture and Conversion. There are two types of capture: by blockade and by arithmetical relationship. If double-sided pieces are used, captured pieces can be turned over and used in the formation of triumphs (Shirwood), or re-entered on the capturer's back row and so enlisted into his army (Bossière).

Capture by blockade. If piece A moves to such a position as to render enemy piece B totally immobile—that is, blocked in every possible flight path by a colleague of A or the edge of the board—then B is captured by blockade. It does not count as a blockade, however, if (a) any blockading piece is *en prise* to B, or (b) in at least one direction B is prevented from moving only by a piece or pieces of its own colour. Murray notes that pieces numbered 2, 3, 4, 5, 6, 7, 153, and 190, are capturable only by blockade, but this applies specifically to Shirwood's version (1482), in which the only other modes of capture recognized are those of equality, addition, and distance multiplication.

Capture by arithmetical relationships. A piece A_1 can capture an enemy piece B, either alone or in conjunction with a piece A_2, provided that (*a*) A_1 (and A_2 if present) can legally move to the square occupied by B, and (*b*) a

Table 18.2. Moves in Rithmomachy

Source	●	▲	■	pyramid
Shirwood 1482 (Murray)[2]	1✱	2✱	3✱	any
Bossière 1556 (Murray)	1+	2+	3+	any
Selenus 1616 (Murray)	1 >	2×	3✱	any
Lever 1563, basic (Lewin)[3]	1 >	2+	3+	1,2,3✱
Lever 1563, special (Lewin)	—	1/2	1/3	—
Composite (Illmer *et al.*)	1+	2×	3✱	any

Notes: > forwards only; + orthogonal; × diagonal; ✱ orthogonal or diagonal; 1/2 like a knight; 1/3 like a camel.

specified arithmetical relationship exists between A_1 and B (and A_2 if present). The method of capture varies in different accounts. In the earlier game (Shirwood), A_1 or A_2, if any, ad lib, captures by replacement, moving to the square occupied by B and ousting it from the board. In the later game (Selenus), a piece does not move and capture in the same turn, but may only do one or the other. If, therefore, at the start of a turn, B is *en prise* to one or two pieces A, it is captured and removed from the board, but A_1 (and A_2 if present) remain *in situ*. In some accounts, a piece that could capture is huffed (as in Draughts) if its owner makes a move instead of a capture. In most accounts, double-sided pieces are used.

The specified arithmetical relationships entitling A_1 (and A_2) to capture B might be any of the following, though no individual source gives this list in its entirety.

Equality. Piece A controls a square occupied by enemy piece B. If A and B are equal in value, B is captured by equality, and removed from the board. Such captures are infrequent, as the only numbers common to both sides are the perfect squares from 9 to 81.

Addition, subtraction, multiplication, division, progression. If pieces A_1 and A_2 control a square occupied by B, then B is captured by

- addition, if $B = A_1 + A_2$,
- subtraction, if $B = A_1 - A_2$ or vice-versa,
- multiplication, if $B = A_1 \times A_2$,
- division, if $B = A_1 / A_2$ or vice versa,
- progression, if the three pieces form an arithmetical, geometrical, or harmonic progression (of which B need not be the middle term).

Distance multiplication (and division). Piece A lies in uninterrupted line with an enemy piece B in its direction of travel—that is, orthogonally if A is a round, diagonally if a triangle, either if a square. If B = A multiplied by their distance apart, then B is captured by distance multiplication. The defining distance always includes the squares occupied by A and B, making the lowest possible distance factor two (when A and B are adjacent). Distance multiplication is not permitted if any piece of either colour lies between A and B. In the version described by Barozzi and Selenus, A can similarly capture B if B is equivalent to A *divided* by the intervening distance. (I have not seen all possible sources, but suspect that 'distance' and 'two-piece' multiplication and division were mutually exclusive in any given version of the game.)

Multiple captures. If a piece can capture more than one enemy piece, not necessarily by the same means, it captures them all. Not all sources mention this, but none specifically forbids it.

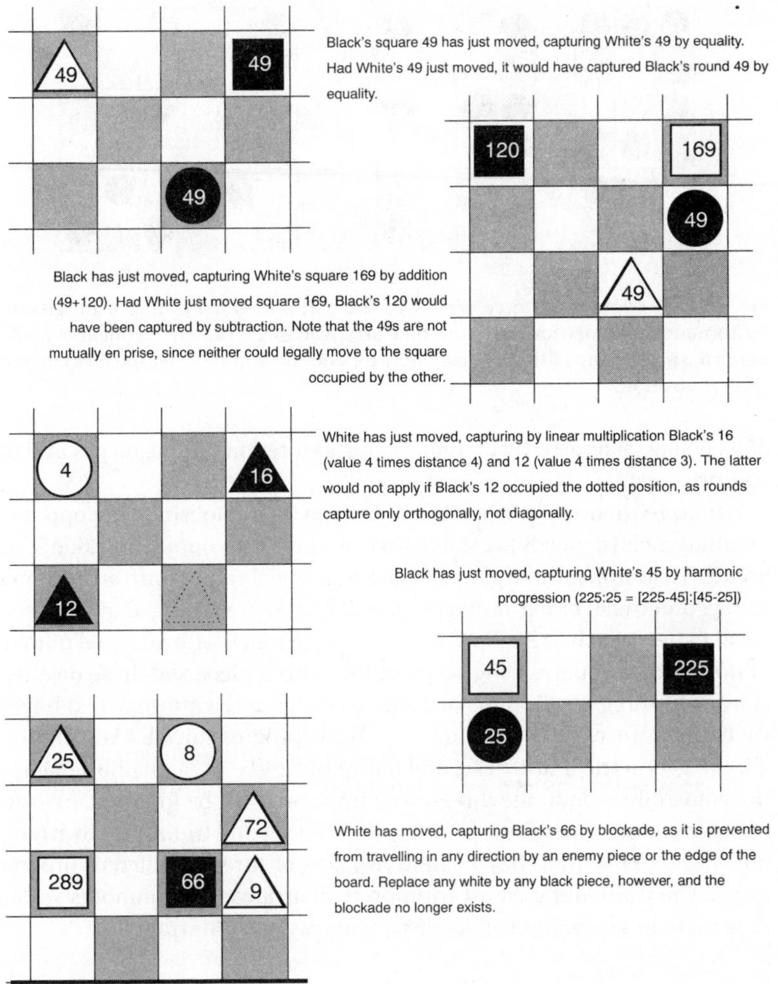

Fig. 18.2. Various types of capture.

Compound captures. If two or more pieces A_1, A_2, etc, control a square occupied by B, and the value of B is the solution of any equation involving each of those pieces (once only) related by any of the permitted operations, then B undergoes a compound capture.

Pyramid captures. The value of a pyramid, whether for the purpose of capturing or being captured, is that of any one of its constituent pieces, or

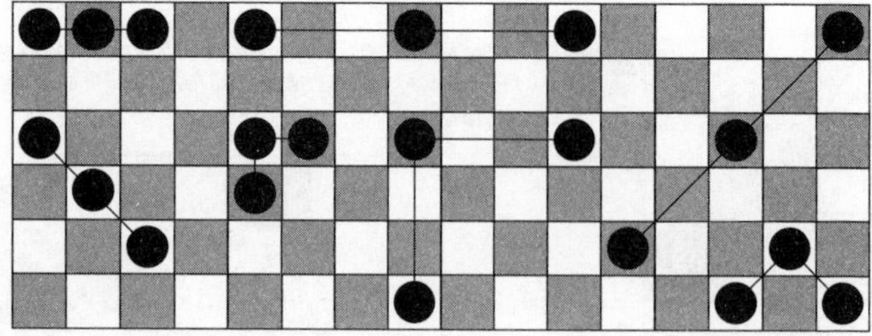

Fig. 18.3. A triumph is three pieces of the same colour forming a progression (arithmetical, geometrical, or harmonic), arranged in a symmetrical linear or angled pattern, such as any of those shown above. The median number must occupy the central position.

of its whole (White 91, Black 190) so long as it retains *all* the pieces initially comprising it.

Triumphs. In order to win after, or instead of, demolishing the opposing pyramid, a player needs to establish a triumph on his opponent's side of the board. A triumph is three pieces whose numerical values form an arithmetical, geometrical, or harmonic progression, and are arranged in a symmetrical pattern, such as in a row, column, or diagonal, with an equal number of unoccupied squares lying between the central piece and those on either side, or forming three points of a square. Given three integers a (x) b (y) c, such that $a<b<c$, $x=b-a$, and $y=c-b$, the progression a,b,c is arithmetic if $x=y$, geometric if $b/a=c/b$, and harmonic if $y/x=c/a$. In one version of the game (Shirwood), the three-piece triumph must be followed, in order, by the creation of two further triumphs: 'The second triumph is to arrange four numbers so that they include two sets of three in different progressions. The third and greatest triumph is to arrange four numbers so that they include sets of three in all three progressions' (Murray).

Origins

Like Draughts, Rithmomachy appears to be a game of European invention. Unlike Draughts, it was even more restricted to Germany, France, England, and Italy, a list from which Spain is notable for its absence. Its point of origin can no longer be guessed at. Murray suggested twelfth-century France, but Illmer offers earlier references emanating from southern Germany in the eleventh century. None of these notices suffice to enable the reconstruction of a definitive set of rules even for one locality, and it is beyond doubt that no two communities played such a complex and esoteric game in exactly the same way. Many early descriptions appear deliberately obscure, as if to assert the cultural superiority of those who were able to come to grips with it. Others suggest that some players and commentators did not themselves fully understand the underlying arithmetical principles, relying instead on lists, rotes, and cribs, of varying degrees of accuracy.

The conceptual origins of Rithmomachy are twofold. One lies in a tradition of philosophical numerology dating back to the school of Pythagoras, and transmitted during the Dark Ages by Nicomachus of Gerasa (*c.* AD 100) and Boethius (*c.* AD 500), whose *De Consolatione Philosophiae* is largely a translation of Nicomachus. The Pythagorean arithmetic of Rithmomachy is essentially integral and proportional. Two numbers are either equal or unequal, and, if unequal, may be so in any of five ways, as shown in Table 18.3. These sets of proportions, together with the base numbers 2-4-6-8 (even and 'feminine') and 3-5-7-9 (odd and 'masculine'), are used to generate the six levels of numbers represented on the Rithmomachy pieces and their arrangement on the board.

The second element relates to that initial array. Rithmomachy is not only a game of numbers but also an abstract representation of warfare, like Chess. The authors of a German study of the game (Illmer *et al.*) point to a parallel between the forces and initial disposition of the game with those of the army of classical antiquity. This is a threefold army, as opposed to the fourfold army of the Indian chaturanga which gave us Chess. As described by the Roman military theoretician Vegetius (fourth century BC), it consists of a relatively immobile central phalanx of well-armed, experienced legionaries, followed by more lightly armoured and faster-moving archers and spear-throwers, and flanked by cavalry, themselves escorted by younger and nimbler archers and other light weapon-bearers. The more battle-hardened Flavius Arrianus (second century AD) describes a similar arrangement. He further specifies their numerical proportions

Table 18.3. Given B>A, n = any integer >1, m = any integer >1 and <A, then:

type	designation	examples expressed as proportions
B = nA	*multiplex*	n:1
B = A + 1	*superparticularis*	3:2, 4:3, 5:4, 6:5, etc
B = A + m	*superpartiens*	5:3, 7:4, 7:5, 8:5, 9:5, 9:7, etc
B = nA + 1	*multiplex superparticularis*	5:2, 7:3, 9:4, 10:3, 11:2, 11:5, etc
B = nA + m	*multiplex superpartiens*	8:3, 11:3, 11:4, etc

as 1 of cavalry to 2 of light infantry to 4 of heavy infantry (the phalanx), and recommends quantifying the forces available in powers of two in order to facilitate their redeployment as the battle progresses. It was with a comparable disposition of forces that Belisar, commander of the east Roman army, defeated the Persians at Dara, Mesopotamia, in AD 530. Illmer *et al.* note with interest the relative powers of movement of the threefold division of Rithmomachy forces into rounds, representing the relatively immobile phalanx; triangles, the more mobile light infantry; and squares, the wider-ranging cavalry, and draw a comparison—literally—between Belisar's battle-formation and the opening array of Rithmomachy (Fig.18.4).

What light this throws on the origin of Rithmomachy remains to be explored. It is clearly a European invention, and probably inspired by the example of Chess; yet this points to a time around the end of the first millennium when few European scholars and clerics (synonymous terms, in effect) can have had either the mathematical competence or the practical knowledge of classical warfare to have devised so complicated a game. Scarcely more credible, and certainly unevidenced, is the possibility of its origin in late antiquity and transmission through the European Dark Ages. More intelligible is its demise around the turn of the seventeenth–eighteenth centuries. By this time Chess was becoming established as the foremost game of intellectual appeal rather than as the social accomplishment it had hitherto been, while the sort of mystical numerology on which Rithmomachy rang the changes fell increasingly out of date as mathematics began to serve more practical and scientific ends. The example of Chess, by this time, must have shown up Rithmomachy as complicated rather than deep. By 1738 a major German encyclopaedia described it as obsolete.

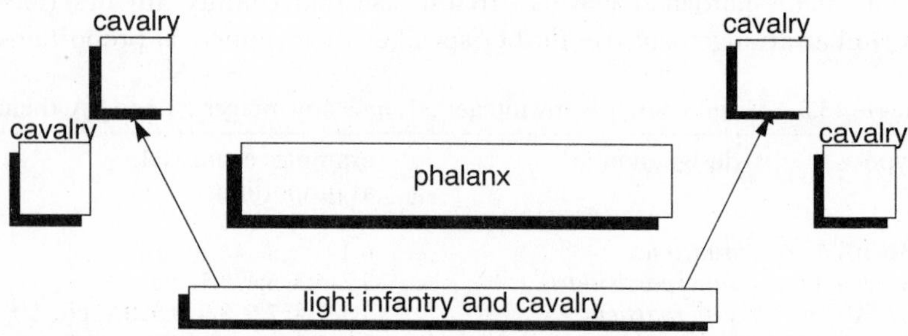

Fig. 18.4. Possible military origin of Rithmomachy array.

Table 18.4. Table of all possible progressions in Rithmomachy*

Arithmetical						Geometrical			Harmonic		
2	3	4	8	12	16	2	4	8	2	3	6
2	4	6	8	25	42	2	12	72	3	4	6
2	5	8	8	36	64	3	6	12	3	5	15
2	7	12	8	49	90	4	6	9	4	6	12
2	9	16	8	64	120	4	8	16	4	7	28
2	15	28	9	12	15	4	12	36	5	8	20
2	16	30	9	45	81	4	16	64	5	9	45
3	4	5	9	81	153	4	20	100	6	8	12
3	**5**	**7**	12	16	20	4	30	225	7	12	42
3	6	9	**12**	**66**	**120**	5	15	45	8	15	120
3	9	15	12	20	28	**9**	**12**	**16**	9	15	45
3	42	81	**12**	**56**	**100**	9	15	25	9	16	72
4	5	6	12	42	72	**9**	**30**	**100**	12	15	20
4	6	8	15	20	25	9	45	225	15	20	30
4	8	12	15	30	45	16	20	25	25	45	225
4	12	20	15	120	225	**16**	**28**	**49**	30	36	45
4	16	28	**16**	**36**	**56**	16	36	81	30	45	90
4	20	36	20	25	30	20	30	45	72	90	120
4	30	56	20	28	36	**25**	**30**	**36**			
5	6	7	20	42	64	25	45	81			
5	**7**	**9**	28	42	56	36	42	49			
5	15	25	**28**	**64**	**100**	**36**	**66**	**121**			
5	25	45	30	36	42	**36**	**90**	**225**			
6	7	8	42	49	56	**49**	**56**	**64**			
6	9	12	42	66	90	49	91	169			
6	36	66	42	81	120	64	72	81			
7	8	9	49	169	289	**64**	**120**	**225**			
7	**16**	**25**	56	64	72	**81**	**90**	**100**			
7	**28**	**49**	72	81	90	81	153	289			
7	49	91	81	153	225	**100**	**190**	**361**			
7	**64**	**121**	91	190	289						

* Those in outline cells can be made entirely with white pieces and so be used to form white triumphs (25 possibilities); those in shaded cells can be used to form black triumphs (19 possibilities, none of them harmonic). All others must be, and a few of those designated triumphs can also be, formed with pieces of both colours, and so be used for capture by progression.

NOTES

1. Substantial sources include Richard de Fournivall, Chancellor of Amiens (attrib.), *Vetula*, an imitation of Ovid's *Ars Amatoria* (13th cent.); a 1470 manuscript of Chess problems and Rithmomachy in the Ashmolean Museum, Oxford; 1482 Shirwood's *Tractatubus de ludo Arithmomachia* (MS Bibl. Casanatense, Rome, 7910); 1496 Jacobus Faber Stapulensis, *Rithmomachia*, an appendix to a book on arithmetic by Jordanus (Paris); 1554/6 Claude de Bossière *Le très excellent et ancien jeu Pythagorique, dict Rhythmomachie*; 1563 Lever Rafe [so Lewin, but Murray says W.F. = William Fulke] *The most noble auncient and learned playe, called the Philosophers Game*, a translation of de Bossière; 1572 Francesco Barozzi; 1616 Selenus, *Das Schach- oder König-Spiel*, derived from Barozzi.
2. Murray, *History of Board Games*, 84–7.
3. C. G. Lewin, 'The Philosophers' Game', *Games & Puzzles*, 1st ser. 16 (Aug. 1973), 14–19.
4. D. Illmer *et al.*, *Rhythmomachia* (Munich, 1987), 'based partly on oldest game descriptions, partly on French and German treatises from the Renaissance and C17'.

TODAY'S GAMES

Variations on a Theme

The chances are that somewhere or other any board-game that has ever existed is still played, though possibly in a more developed form.

H. J. R. Murray, *A History of Board Games other than Chess* (1952)

There are in America today individuals and companies who do nothing but apply their ingenuity to the construction and invention of games with which to amuse the public and thereby derive their sustenance. Yet, despite this concentration of effort, the dice-and-board games of today do not differ in principle from those of the Aztecs and the Hindus.

Charles John Erasmus, *Southwestern Journal of Anthropology*[1]

The history of board games stretches longest over those consisting solely of boards, pieces, and sometimes dice: games that are largely positional and abstract, and folk or traditional in the sense of being anonymously composed and in the public domain. But scan the shelves of any modern games shop, or the games department of any superstore, and you will find such games—if at all—in the minority. The vast majority of products now available under the heading 'board games' are thematic rather than mathematic: elaborate, colourful and graphic rather than plain, monochrome, and abstract: proprietary rather than communal: and credited either to named authors or corporately to the manufacturers. It was in the eighteenth century that proprietary games first appeared, and in the nineteenth that major games companies such as Parker Brothers, Waddingtons, and Ravensburger, typically arose as offshoots from companies originally specializing in related activities such as paper products, print production, and publishing. In the twentieth century proprietary games have come at least to equal if not to dominate the games market, especially through the expansion of international trading in a global market, consequently of an increasingly broad international level of popular culture (dominated by America, for self-evident reasons), and, latterly, by the extraordinary explosion of reprographic techniques and facilities, which has brought publishing, whether of books or games, within the reach of the private individual.

A very rough idea of the proportion of traditional to proprietary games-playing at the end of the 20th century emerges from the results of a survey carried out by *Games & Puzzles* magazine. Respondents were asked to state which of the following classes of table games they themselves regularly played, and the percentage of positive replies was as shown in Table 19.1.

Table 19.1. Proportion of traditional to proprietary games played (%)

Game	%	Classification	Game	%	Classification
Scrabble	65	*proprietary*	dice games	28	*traditional*
family board games	63	*proprietary*	Bridge	27	*traditional (if commercialized)*
word games	51	*either*			
Monopoly	47	*proprietary*	various strategy games	26	*proprietary (mainly)*
Backgammon	45	*traditional*			
Trivial Pursuit	41	*proprietary*	Go	24	*traditional*
Draughts	32	*traditional*	role-playing games	19	*proprietary*
board war games	31	*proprietary*			
			Mah Jong	18	*traditional*

Source: *Games & Puzzles*, 2nd ser. 7.

Also listed were computer games (42 per cent), play-by-mail (17 per cent), and miniature war-gaming (8 per cent). If, further, we dismiss role-playing games as not quite falling into the category of table games, note the surprising omission of dominoes from the prompt list, and ignore the extremely unscientific nature of the survey and the smallness of the statistical sample, we find that the play of table games is just about evenly divided between the traditional and the proprietary. Further light is thrown on this topic by the small ads for local games clubs and meetings appearing in the same magazine. Besides 'board games' in general, these mention specifically Backgammon, Diplomacy, Go, Kingmaker, Othello, Scrabble, Trivial Pursuit, and War games. Chess and Draughts clubs are too numerous to justify listing. In this connection it will be relevant to note the existence of the British section of FIDE (Fédération Internationale des Echecs), the British Draughts Federation, The English Draughts Association, the British Isles Backgammon Association, the British Go Association, the British Othello Federation, and the UK Scrabble Clubs movement.

On-Board, Off-Board

A point of interest about modern board games is their gradual shift of emphasis away from the board and into the circle of players. Traditional board games like Chess and Draughts are essentially positional board games. In such games, it is obvious from a diagram of the final position exactly who has won, and why: one player has reached home first, or has completed a pattern or arrangement of his own pieces, or has wiped the board of all enemy pieces. In a game like Monopoly, on the other hand, a great deal of gaming material does not come into contact with the board.

The board is still essential to the play, but the winning is measured in terms of the other material. Wandering further away from the board, we reach a game like Trivial Pursuit and its derivatives, in which all the real play takes place off the board. The board is almost an irrelevance: it does little more than keep a score, like a Cribbage board. Finally, we reach fantasy games, some of which involve a board as a convenience for keeping track of inter-player relationship, but most of which are boardless role-playing games, overlapping with 'play' in its theatrical rather than any other sense of the word.

Board games published at the start of the twenty-first century can be roughly categorized as follows:

Classics. Traditional games such as Chess, Draughts, and Backgammon, and proprietary games such as Monopoly and Scrabble. Signs of their classic status include the existence of clubs devoted to their practice, a significant literature including periodicals or at least fanzines, translation into computer format, and national and international championships and tournaments.

Specialist games. Whether traditional or proprietary, these may be characterized as games of skill and strategy appealing to players broadly describable as adult, serious, educated, intelligent. Many of these share the associated features of classic games, from which category they are only excluded by their appeal to a specialist section of the market.

Family games. Proprietary games designed primarily for children, but playable by adults in their capacity as parents. None are entirely abstract, but some may be recognized as an abstract concept dressed up with a decorative or everyday theme, such as shopping, traffic, holidays, and so on, or on current TV programmes or character merchandizing. Many derive their mechanics from those of traditional race games: throw dice, go there, get stuck, get home first, win most wealth. Depending on the extent to which they are linked to current icons, they are not necessarily as ephemeral as those of the following category, but eventually become outdated as fashions in parenting change. This category includes games described as 'educational', and deliberately simplified versions of classic games—Junior Scrabble, for example.

Pulp games. Borrowing a term from literature, these are ephemeral games designed to cash in on current trends, fads, and fashions, entirely based on TV programmes or characters merchandized from the world of showbiz and popular entertainment. Several sub-categories may be distinguished, including games described as 'adult', in the sense of sexually titillating, and promotional games produced for advertising purposes.

Theme Games

Theme games are board games purporting to simulate or represent some sort of real-life activity. There is an important difference between simulations and representations. Simulations, as the term implies, are designed to enable the participants to exercise as realistically as possible the same sort of skills of judgement and decision-making as are required for the subject in question. They are not 'games', nor are the participants 'players', in the usual sense of the words, since the exercise is designed not for fun, recreation, or social intercourse, but to provide exercise, practice, training, experimentation, and so on, in an important field of real-life endeavour. Simulations include war games as played by the military and business games as played on weekend management courses, and the sort of subjects explored in that branch of mathematics called 'game theory'—which may relate to the 'real world outside', but in fact bear very little relation to anything that goes in in the (paradoxically) 'real' world of games inhabited by genuine games enthusiasts.

Genuinely recreational theme games are therefore better described as representational than as simulatory. Indeed, the less realistic they are, whether due to the creative limitations of the inventor or the inherent limitations of the material, the less representational they become, and the more symbolic or even purely nominal. Monopoly, for example, characterizes itself as 'the property trading game'. No one would regard it as a simulation, but whether it rates as representational, symbolic, or purely nominal, is probably open to conflicting interpretations.

Hardly any field of human endeavour has failed to be translated into a board game. Topics I have encountered in 25 years of writing and reading games reviews include angling, art exhibitions, astrology, the Black Death, escaping (from Colditz, from Titanic), evolution, fire-fighting, gardening, hill-walking, Hollywood film production, libel actions, naturism (nudes *versus* prudes), oil prospecting, organized crime, pirating, safaris, sheep-farming, stamp-collecting, television production, travelling (holiday, business, freight), and underwater exploration, not to mention (yet) the distinctive categories of business games and war games. And if you think the Black Death and the Titanic games tasteless, you have yet to encounter Wicked Willy, a game based on the purchase and implicit consumption of contraceptives, of which the best that can be hoped is that it will, in the nature of things, fail to engender any progeny.

Games at the lower end of this market rely for their underlying mechanism on well-established formulae, the least imaginative being variations on a theme of Goose—roll dice, move there, take chance, miss turn, get home first. Being designed for family fun rather than for genuine games enthusiasts, procedural originality is irrelevant. They rely entirely on their theme for whatever sales potential may be squeezed out of them, and their own makers do not expect a shelf-life longer than the topicality of the theme in question. At the upper end of the market, however, the world's great games inventors—Alex Randolph, Reiner Knizia, Klaus Teuber, Sid Sackson, *et al.*—are more than capable of devising games whose mechanisms include original features and whose themes are timeless rather than currently fashionable. At this level, indeed, the dividing line becomes blurred between theme games with a novel mechanism, and basically abstract games dressed up to look thematic.

For the purpose of the following survey I have distinguished ten thematic groups as follows: Business and trading, Detection and deduction, Crime, War, Fantasy, Alternative histories, Politics, Sports, Word games, Social interaction and quiz games ('trivia'). Another significant topic, Travel, has already been largely covered in the chapter on race games. Another is sex, from which I plead to be excused, as I have a headache.

Business and Trading

A perennially favourite theme of modern board games is that of economics, business, trading, and money-making in general. Such games involve a board on which the positions of players' pieces, whether moved randomly by dice or by strategic control, do not so much indicate their relative spatial relationships with one another as serve to specify their individual current circumstances in terms of opportunities and limitations. They also involve representations of money, and of commodities by which money is to be acquired, and the overall aim is to win by acquiring most money or most of the commodities. How much of the play takes place on the board and how much in interaction between the players varies enormously.

Monopoly. The archetype of trading games, and in many ways of all modern thematic board games, is represented by Monopoly. Yet even Monopoly can be deconstructed into a distant descendant of primitive race games such as Nyout, even though probably no such comparison ever entered the heads of those who contributed to its development.

Monopoly is basically a race game—not one in which the aim is to get home first, since the track is looped and the play unbounded, but one in which it is to be the last one circulating when everyone else has dropped out through exhaustion of energy. Energy is represented by, and measured in terms of, money. Money is acquired by various means. A certain amount is given to each person at start of play, more acquired with the completion of each lap (Salary: collect £200), and some won or lost through the operation of hazards triggered by landing on certain spaces (Chance, Community Chest). Up to this point, Monopoly can be seen as an expansion of the Royal Game of Goose, made by replacing a bounded objective, 'home', with an unbounded objective, 'survival', and introducing off-the-board resources of motive energy (money) which can be ploughed back into continued on-board movement. What gives the game its originality is the introduction of ownership: you can purchase individual squares and charge other players for landing on them. Furthermore, you can invest money in the development of squares (by building houses and hotels on them) to increase the amount of income thereby generated. For this purpose, however, you must acquire them in matched sets (of the same colour), and for this, in turn, unless you want the game to go on for ever, you have to be prepared to trade properties with other players.

Hence, so to speak, the centre of gravity of play has shifted from the board itself to the relationship of the board to the resources available and their distribution among the players. The skill involved is no longer spatial and positional, but psychological and behavioural. Monopoly has become a byword for a successful game—everyone wants to 'invent another Monopoly'—partly through its technical originality (ownership of squares), partly through the new dimension of skill it brought into the play of board games, and largely because its theme is so appropriate to the mechanism underlying it. The spaces of the race track have been translated into real estate. What—in retrospect—could be a more natural development? Who invented it, and why had no one thought of it before?

Well, of course, they had. The story that it sprang fully formed from the brain of an out-of-work heating engineer during the American Depression, who thereby became a millionaire, is one of the most typical creation myths of our times.[2] In fact, the earliest name that can be attached to it is that of Lizzie J. Magie, a Maryland Quaker, who patented what she then called The Landlord's Game in 1904; and its subsequent development into what we now know as Monopoly follows the traditional pattern of any folk game from Nyout to Chess.

The board depicted in the 1904 patent (Fig.19.1) is immediately familiar. It features a square track of 40 spaces, of which 22 are sites purchasable for development, and the others include one railway per side, a lighting franchise on side 2, water works on side 3, and corners marked Jail, Go to Jail, Public Park, and Mother Earth, the latter paying $100 salary when passed. In place of Income Tax, there are 'Absolute Necessity' spaces (Bread, Coal, Shelter, Clothing) for which a tax is paid to the Public Treasury. Movement

No. 748,626. PATENTED JAN. 5, 1904.

L. J. MAGIE.
GAME BOARD.
APPLICATION FILED MAR. 23, 1903.

NO MODEL. 2 SHEETS—SHEET 1.

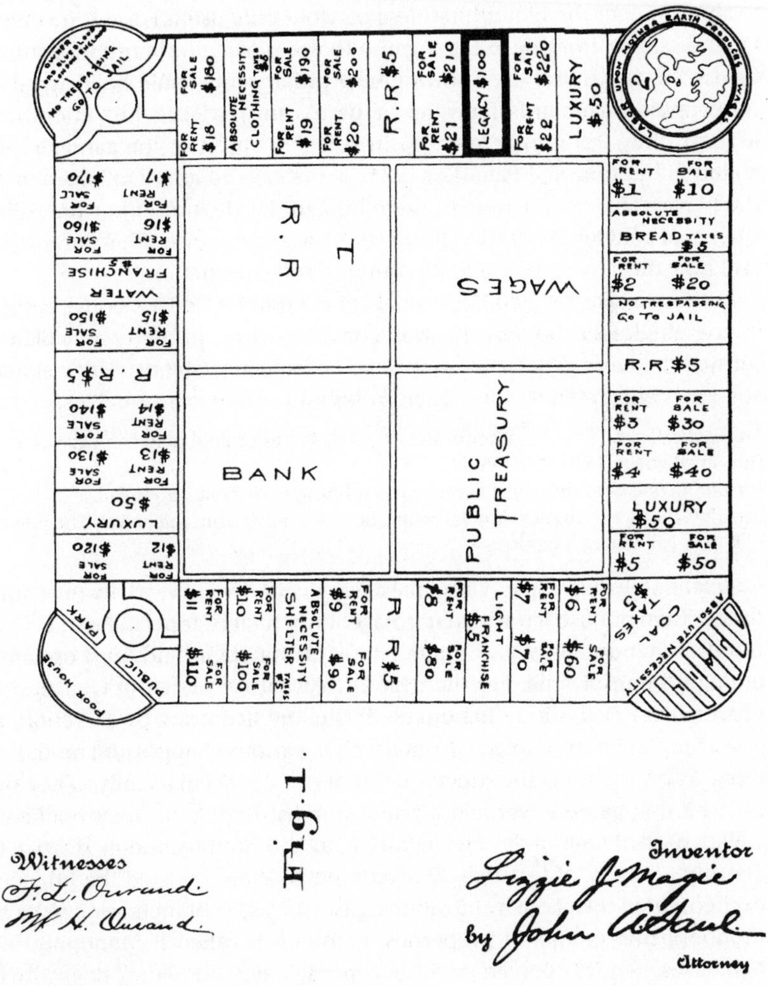

Fig. 19.1. Earliest ancestor of the Monopoly board, from the Patent Specification for The Landlords Game, 1904.

is dictated by rolling one or two dice, lots are bought from the Public Treasury (bank), rent is paid to the owner of a lot when landed upon, jail is exited by throwing a double or paying a fine, money is borrowable from another player, or the bank, or by mortgage. In short, it has all the defining ingredients of Monopoly short of hazard cards and the possibility of increasing rents due by developing lots owned.

Short, too, of the bloodthirstiness of Monopoly itself. For our inventive Quakeress, far from devoting a game to the praise of Mammon, actually devised it as a moral tale showing how unfair rents could be charged by unscrupulous landlords, for which, if there is any justice in the games world at least, they will rightly fetch up in jail. The object of the game, as she stated in her renewed Patent of 1924, 'is not only to afford amusement to the players, but to illustrate to them how under the present or prevailing system of land tenure, the landlord has an advantage over other enterprises and how the single tax would discourage land speculation.'

In this she was following the tenets of economist Henry George, creator of the single-tax theory, who was convinced that property speculation formed the basis of society's economic and social problems. Her vision of society is illustrated by subsequent rules and annotations, such as:

La Swelle Hotel. 'The space represents the distinction made between classes, only moneyed guests being accepted'.
Throwing one with the single die: 'Caught robbing hen-roost – go to jail.'
Throwing a two: 'Caught robbing the public—take $200 from the board. The players will now call you Senator.'

Unfortunately for Magie's principles, this is not how others saw the game. Rather than publish it through normal commercial channels, she sold a few hundred handmade sets through shops in Maryland and (appropriately enough) Pennsylvania. For the next 20 years it circulated in Quaker and university circles, still in handmade form, and acquiring by accretion, as one group or family copied it from another, various changes and modifications. Many renamed the streets after those of their own locality. (They still do. The first game I ever had a hand in constructing, in my schooldays, called itself 'Paranopoly' and centred on the South London district of Tooting.) Others, of less than Quakerly persuasion, boosted the financial excitement of the game by introducing the principle of increasing rents by monopolizing groups of properties. Some even called it Monopoly, but Magie resisted this perversion of her moral vision and stuck doggedly to 'The Landlord's Game' when she renewed her patent with a revised version in 1924. Even so, in this revision we find that 'If one player owns the three local public utilities, Slambang Trolley, Soakem Lighting System, and Ting-a-Ling Telephone Company, he has a monopoly... [and] the rates are raised to $100 for each space.' According to an article in the *Saturday Evening Post* of 6 October 1945, it was George Parker, of Parker Bros, who advised her to renew her patent after his company rejected the game, probably on grounds of complexity, though they had already published another game of hers called Mock Trial. The game continued to circulate in mainly handmade versions, though in 1929 a version entitled Finance was published by a mid-western company.

Enter heating engineer Charles Darrow, of Germantown, Pennsylvania. One evening in 1933 he and his wife were entertaining friends who had brought a home-made set with them. It included Chance and Community Chest, houses and hotels, and had been copied from another one bearing names of streets in Atlantic City, a fashionable seaside and racing resort. Darrow was not the first to be struck by its commercial potential, but he was the first to exploit it successfully—partly through luck, for its time was bound to come, and partly through his professional design abilities, for the board we use today is substantially that which he drew up for submission to Parker Bros in 1934. Once again Parkers rejected it as too complicated, and cited no fewer than fifty-two specific faults. Undaunted, Darrow had five thousand sets made up and sold them at $2.50 apiece through retail outlets from Philadelphia to Boston and New York. Rapid sales persuaded Parkers to re-enter the scene. They published their first edition in spring 1935, and by autumn were taking on extra staff and running weekend shifts to meet the demand for 200,000 per week. Darrow's first royalty cheque was for $7,000. He subsequently became a multi-millionaire, retiring at 46 to devote his life to orchids and photography, and dying in 1967.

The American edition still exhibits Atlantic City street names, right down to 'Marvin Gardens', a misspelling of 'Marven Gardens' perpetrated in the original home-made set prepared by Darrow's friends. The British edition also appeared in 1935, and with equal success, published by Waddingtons under licence to Parkers. Before publishing, however, Victor Watson, then head of the company, took the precaution of Anglicizing it, for which purpose he charged his secretary with walking around London to root out some suitable names. At the same time, railroads became railways and dollars became pounds sterling, though jail did not become gaol. Other countries followed suit, France basing her edition on Paris, Spain on Madrid, with a Catalan regional variant on Barcelona, and so on. Nazi Germany proscribed the game on obvious grounds, as did Stalin; at time of writing, it is still officially banned in China, North Korea, and Cuba.

There is a postscript to the Monopoly story that might have appealed to Lizzie Magie in all save financial respects. For many years the official line was that Charles Darrow was the 'onlie begetter' of the game, and Allphin's

Table 19.2. How Atlantic City became London following a Waddington secretary's walkabout.

Atlantic City	London	Atlantic City	London
Go: $200 salary	Go: £200 salary	Free Parking	Free Parking
Mediterranean Ave	Old Kent Road	Kentucky Avenue	Strand
Community Chest	Community Chest	Chance	Chance
Baltic Avenue	Whitechapel Road	Indiana Avenue	Fleet Street
Income Tax	Income Tax	Illinois Avenue	Trafalgar Square
Reading Railroad	Kings Cross Station	B & O Railroad	Fenchurch St Station
Oriental Avenue	The Angel, Islington	Atlantic Avenue	Leicester Square
Chance	Chance	Ventnor Avenue	Coventry Street
Vermont Avenue	Euston Road	Water Works	Water Works
Connecticut Avenue	Pentonville Road	Marvin Gardens	Piccadilly
Jail	Jail	Go to Jail	Go to Jail
St Charles Place	Pall Mall	Pacific Avenue	Regent Street
Electric Company	Electric Company	N. Carolina Ave	Oxford Street
States Avenue	Whitechapel	Community Chest	Community Chest
Virginia Avenue	Northumberland Ave	Pennsylvania Ave	Bond Street
Pennsylvania Railroad	Marylebone Station	Short Line	Liverpool St Station
St James Place	Bow Street	Chance	Chance
Community Chest	Community Chest	Park Place	Park Lane
Tennessee Avenue	Marlborough Street	Luxury Tax	Super Tax
New York Avenue	Vine Street	Boardwalk	Mayfair

attempted debunking of that myth in a 1975 issue of *Games & Puzzles*, based on personal recollections of a version he played in 1923 and supported by Sid Sackson's unearthing of Magie's original patent,[3] was met with vigorous assertions of mistaken identity. In 1973, however, Ralph Anspach, a San Francisco professor of economics, published a game called Anti-Monopoly, as a deliberate reaction against all those business games that glorified the monopoly principle—an unconscious reversion, in fact, to Magie's original intention. Needless to say, this gave rise to a conflict of commercial interests, and various courts found themselves strewn with the litter of legal battles for some ten years or so. The final outcome was twofold. Anti-Monopoly won its right to independent existence, and hitherto hushed-up aspects of Monopoly's history came to light. In particular, they showed that Darrow's application for a patent in 1935 had been thwarted by the discovery of patents for the all-too-similar Landlord's Game. To overcome this problem, and so preserve the status of the modern creation myth, Parker Brothers purchased the rights to both The Landlord's Game and Finance, its 1929 spin-off, and bought up all the sets of either game that they could find. Out of this stupendous deal, the game's earliest inventor, Lizzie Magie Phillips (as she had become by marriage), got a final pay-off of $500.

Acquire. True business-gaming enthusiasts still speak highly of Sid Sackson's game of Acquire, first published by 3M in the early 1960s, and look deprecatingly on those of lesser discernment who liken it to the relatively simplistic Monopoly for the mere similarity of building hotels. Reduced to essentials, each in turn places a tile representing a hotel on one of the 108 squares of the board. A player getting two or more hotels on orthogonally connected squares thereby forms a chain, identifies it as one of seven possible named chains of varying values, and acquires a block of stock in that chain. Stock can also be bought in any chain on the board, regardless of its founder. When a tile is placed that connects two chains, the smaller is merged into the larger. When a chain contains more than ten hotels, it cannot be taken over. Play ceases when one player, calculating that it is advantageous to do so, calls a halt, which he may only do if one chain contains at least 40 hotels or all chains contain at least ten. Bonuses accrue to the players holding the two largest blocks of stock, then everyone sells out to the Stock Market and 'It will come as no surprise [writes Sackson][4] that the player who has accumulated the biggest pile of dollars is crowned the victor. However, it is surprising how often the crown will go to a player who has quietly and unsuspectingly brought his scheme to fruition while others, apparently in the lead, fought each other to exhaustion.'

While the material format of Acquire resembles that of games of alignment and configuration, it is typical of modern board games in that the strategy of positional play is governed by that of (quasi-financial) considerations taking place above and beyond the board rather than vice versa. Sackson insists that there is no board in the usual sense, and explains how he developed the game from a form of solitaire played with cards derived from Lotto (Bingo).

Ransom. 'The back stabbing, money grabbing game!' (Phil O'Neil Games) may be taken, at random, to show how this theme has progressed since what now seems like those halcyon days of the Depression. 'Here's your chance to wheel and deal in the property development market while lying, cheating, and, of course, holding your opponents to ransom', runs Tony Hetherington's review.[5] 'Between two and six tycoons invest in land, bricks and labour while competing for contracts to build some of the best known parts of the New York skyline . . . A fun game in which players can be as sneaky and underhand as they like.'

Thanks. You can keep it.

Detection, Deduction

Detective games followed close on the golden era of the detective novel. Whipple and Smith produced several based on the Dick Tracy character in the 1930s, while the board accompanying Selchow and Righter's game, Mr Ree (say it quickly several times over), bears more than a passing resemblance to its more famous successor...

Cluedo. This classic deduction game requires no description, beyond, perhaps, pointing out that it is more of a card game than a board game. It can easily be played without the board, whose only real function is to slow the game up by insisting that you must be in the room in which you assert the crime to have been committed. Sleuth, a comparable but more elaborate card game, was, in fact, devised by Sid Sackson in the 1970s.

Cluedo was invented by Anthony E. Pratt in 1944, demonstrated to Norman Watson, Waddingtons Chief Executive Officer, in 1946, and sold outright, though post-war shortage of materials delayed its publication until about 1950.[6] The board design remains essentially that of Mrs Pratt, a gifted amateur painter. It was not an immediate best-seller, but gradually attracted a following which boomed some ten years later with publication in other countries. Like Monopoly, its names and characters vary. The Americans would not have appreciated the pun on Ludo, as the latter has always been known to them as Parcheesi. As Clue, this game enjoys the remarkable distinction of having had a film based on it (Paramount 1985, with Eileen Brennan and Tim Curry), instead of the other way round.

A similar game published by Milton Bradley added, to the three elements of whodunnit, what with, and where, a fourth, 'motive', resulting in a game called Why? (One would like to think that, when charged with plagiarism, they produced a business game called Why Not?)

A great exponent of the deductive theme is Eric Solomon. In The Sigma File, players representing spies employ a combination of deduction and bluff to determine who really controls a case of secret documents. In Black Box, a two-player abstract, one player seeks to deduce the position of four 'atoms' placed by the other on an 8×8 grid by shooting orthogonal 'rays' into it. If a ray does not hit an atom it is merely 'absorbed' and never seen again; if not, it is deflected, and the experimenter bases his deductions on the point from which it emerges.[7]

Crime

Deduction and detection overlap with crime, which in turn naturally overlaps with business and trading. No undoubted criminal classic has emerged of comparable status to Cluedo, though there is much to be said for Scotland Yard, winner of Germany's Game of the Year Award in 1983. This takes place on a somewhat fictionalized map of London, with prominence given to three topographically linked transport systems: underground, buses, and taxis. One player operates 'Mr X', a criminal on the run, and the others each a detective who seeks to capture him by landing on the same space at the same time. This task derives its deductive property from the fact that Mr X's exact position remains secret, except on specific occasions when he is obliged to reveal himself. The game was designed by a group called Projekt-Team and published by Ravensburger.

Of out-and-out crime games, three may be described as classics. The object of The Godfather Game, set in Manhattan and appropriately packaged in a purple-lined 'violin' case, is to gain control of as many rackets as possible. These comprise bookmaking, extortion, bootlegging, loan-sharking, and hijacking, but, unrealistically, neither drugs nor prostitution—'too immoral for a family game', as David Pritchard accurately remarks.[8] Despite the dice and cards, Godfather involves a fair balance of chance and skill. More to our historical purpose, Pritchard adds 'The fight for racket control in a neighbourhood is based on the game of Go, though the connection is not stated in the rules. Control is achieved when more than half of a neighbourhood is occupied or governed. In this part of the game, Go players will have a decided, though not a decisive, advantage.'

Organized Crime, invented and marketed by Jim Koplow in 1975, is described by Steve Jackson as a cross between The Godfather and Diplomacy.[9] The latter is evoked by the fact that, before he can move into a racket, a player must obtain the approval of the National Commission, on which he requires a seat, for which purpose he needs to be voted in, which in turn involves negotiation, not to mention bribery and corruption. The basic aim of the game is to survive—not an easy task, when any player rich enough can hire a hit-man to rub you out.

Related crime games of merit include Chicago, Mafia, The Brotherhood, Assassin! and The Mob (a.k.a. Capone, and, like Cluedo, more of a card game than a board game), whose titles may be left to speak for themselves. The third classic, barely known outside Scandinavia, is Tjuv och Polis—equivalent to 'Cops and Robbers'—invented by a teenager and first published 1943 in Sweden, where it continues to enjoy a rating equivalent to that of its British contemporary, Cluedo.

War

Almost any board game represents conflict to the extent that winners and losers are determined by activities taking place on a game-board, itself symbolic of a theatre of war. (And one can only note, in passing, the reverse connection between 'theatre' and 'play'.) The term 'war game', however, has several more specific senses, which may be listed in order from least to most realistic:

1. Abstract or symbolic games now divorced from any sense of realism (Chess).
2. Representational board games whose theme is war (Risk, Tri-Tactics, Diplomacy).
3. Board war games, i.e. on-board re-creations of historical battles (Anzio, Gettysburg).
4. Miniature war games using models (mainly of infantry and cavalry).
5. Simulations used by the military for study and training.

Abstracts having already been surveyed, and miniatures and simulations being irrelevant to our theme, let's start with board war games.

Board war-gaming, in its recreational sense, is an historically recent phenomenon. It can be dated back to the establishment of the American war games company Avalon Hill in 1958 and its subsequent publication of such classics as Gettysburg, Stalingrad, and Squad Leader. The world of war games has since expanded to such a degree as to form an independent section of the games market, with its own publishers, clubs, magazines, and specialist shops.

A typical board war game is for two players. The minimum essential equipment is a board and pieces, dice, and a Conflict Resolution Table (CRT). The board represents a scaled map of the theatre of battle, the scale varying according to the real-life area needing to be covered and the degree of simplification which the author considered appropriate for a game of reasonable playing time—20 moves, perhaps; but anything up to 400 is not unheard of, albeit best suited to players with nothing else to do. It is overlaid with a grid of (mostly) hexagonal cells whose purpose, like the squares of a chessboard, is to denote specific positions occupiable by pieces. Hexes are preferred, however, because they increase the number of orthogonal directions from four to six while avoiding the anomaly of diagonal moves, each of which is unrealistically equivalent to two orthogonals. The pieces are usually squares punched out of cardboard and bearing abbreviated information as to which side they belong to (by colour), their nature and type, their combat factor, and their speed of movement. The last two are denoted by numbers from 1 to 6 or more, depending on the dice used. More elaborate games have three numbers, the first two denoting respectively offensive and defensive combat factors.

The initial disposition of forces is determined either by rule, deriving from historical accuracy, or by strategic pre-placement. A move is equivalent to an appropriate real-time period measured in weeks or months.

Theoretically, both sides move simultaneously; in practice, however, it is more convenient to alternate, since a move consists of moving not one piece, as in Chess, but (potentially) every element of one's forces on the board. Each normally moves one space, but some, notably those representing transport, may move further. The movement phase is followed by one of combat. A die is rolled for each member of a pair of forces opposing one another along orthogonal lines. The number rolled is related to its combat factor, and the result of that element of conflict is resolved by reference to the appropriate part of the CRT, resulting in the loss or retreat of one force, or a stand-off.

This outline of the basics of board war games suggests a parallel with traditional abstracts such as Chess. Shorn of the historically realistic elements which characterize them individually, they may be regarded as extensions of Chess in which the greatest conceptual advance is that of moving one's whole army in one turn, rather than just one element of it. Correspondingly, and in contrast to those who regard them as little better than frustrated warmongers, those who play board war games are best regarded as Chess players who (like card players) prefer the massed uncertainties of real life to the artificial, cause-and-effect linearities of Chess.

Indeed, to some extent the roots of board war games can be traced back historically to German expansions of Chess.[10] Many regard as their first true ancestor Christoph Weikhmann's Grosses Königs-Spiel of 1664, played by up to eight players on a board of up to 697 cells with fourteen different pieces. Larger still was a game invented in 1780 by Helwig, a court official to the Duke of Brunswick, involving a board of 1666 plain squares and 120 combat units including infantry, cavalry, and artillery. In 1798 a military writer from Schleswig, Georg Venturinus, developed this into a board of 3,600 squares overlaying a map covering part of the Franco-German border, and incorporating such features as military supplies and communication lines. In 1824 one Lieutenant von Reisswitz, of the Prussian army, so impressed General von Muffling, then Chief of Staff, with a game involving detailed maps, elaborate rules, and an umpire to arbitrate on aspects of conflict resolution, that the latter had every regiment issued with a set for training purposes. By a further development of 1876, Colonel von Verdy du Vernois placed increased emphasis on the umpire, and this mainstream line of development produced military war game simulations nowadays facilitated and arbitrated by computer. Of recreational gaming offshoots, the first was umpire-assisted Kriegspiel, as surveyed above in Chapter 17 (on Chess). That of modern board war-gaming derives more directly from ideas and practices developed in the field of miniature war-gaming. The translation of models or figurines into flat pieces on a more manageable board was initiated by an abstract military game, Tactics, devised by Charles Roberts in 1953. Roberts had 2,000 copies made up, and was sufficiently encouraged by its success to concentrate professionally on games design by setting up the company still known as Avalon Hill.

L'Attaque Family. A distinctive series of tactical war games has been published by Gibson Games since the end of the First World War. The original was an imported French military game, l'Attaque, to which Harry Gibson and his brother added a naval variety, Dover Patrol (formerly Jutland), and an aerial companion, Aviation. In 1935 the series was extended by the addition of a combined operations game entitled Tri-Tactics. At time of writing, it is represented in Britain by a revision of the original military game under the title Sharpe's Attack, with reference to a television drama series, and elsewhere under the name Stratego. Underlying all these games is a basic mechanism which, with little imagination, can be likened to a form of Blind Chess, or Kriegspiel, but requiring no umpire. An outline of Sharpe's Attack, shorn of its historically realistic embellishments, will serve for them all.

Two players, representing England (red) and France (blue), each operate an army of thirty-six pieces on a board of 10 × 10 squares (actually rectangles). Besides historical identities, the pieces bear combat values in the following proportions:

value	1	2	3	4	5	6	7	8	9	10
quantity	1	8	4	4	4	4	2	2	1	1

There are also five non-combatant pieces consisting of one spy and four redoubts. The game is one of placement and movement, and the winner is the first to capture the enemy 'colours', depicted on the piece of unit value, or the player with the greatest value left on board in case of stalemate. Each player starts by deploying his pieces ad lib on his own side of the board. The stand-up pieces are so designed as to present blank backs to the opponent's view, so that at start of play neither knows the exact disposition of enemy forces. Thereafter, each in turn moves a piece to an orthogonally adjacent square. If this puts it back to back with an enemy piece, the player who moved may (but need not) announce 'Attack!'. If he does, the two pieces are revealed. If both are of equal combat power, both are removed from play; if not, the lesser is defeated and alone removed. The fact that an attack only occurs if announced and when a piece moves means that it is possible to avoid loss by moving a weaker piece up to a known stronger piece and refusing to attack.

One distinctive element of the series is therefore that of memory and, to some extent, deduction. Another is that of graded capture, whereby the stronger capture the weaker. This has appeared in several modern games, and may perhaps be traced back to the Jungle Game (q.v.), possibly a Chinese Chess derivative.

Risk. A long-popular family game, Risk is played, preferably by six, on a board representing a map of the world divided into forty-two areas. It is a game of placement, movement, and conflict, the object being to gain the most territories by occupying them with armies. To start, each in turn places an army in any vacant territory until the specified initial number of armies, related to the number playing, is used up. Thereafter, play consists in acquiring new armies and attacking occupied territories. Armies are acquired partly by a formula related to the number already held and partly by getting three of a kind in the draw of cards. Dice rolls determine the outcome of conflict between adjacent enemy armies. As a player's armies grow, rendering him more dangerous, so does the amount of territory he has to defend, rendering him correspondingly more vulnerable. The game builds to a climax in which one player bids to sweep the board. If he fails by even a fraction, the counter-attack can mean disaster, because his attack will have left him spread out and vulnerable.[11] The others may informally co-operate against such a player, but there is no provision for negotiation as there is in Diplomacy. Risk, therefore, may not appeal either to military strategists or to diplomatists, but enjoys an enduring appeal due to its fine balance of chance and skill and to its variety and unpredictability.

The invention of French film director Albert Lamorisse, Risk was first published in 1957 as La Conquête du Monde. When Parker Brothers took it up they simply translated it as World Conquest, but soon retitled it out of deference to American war veterans. Legend has it that R, I, S, K were the initials of the four grandchildren of the company director who suggested it.[12]

Diplomacy. The Diplomacy board represents a map of Europe in 1900 divided into a grid of about eighty contiguous cells. These are not regular polygons as in abstract games or board war games, but realistically represent the named regions of seven major countries, a number of minor ones, and areas of sea or ocean. The game is designed for seven players, each representing one of the major powers Austria-Hungary, France, Germany, Russia, Great Britain, Italy, Russia, and Turkey. Each starts with three forces (Russia with four) representing armies or navies as appropriate to its geography. The aim of the game is to emerge as the dominant power by knocking out all the others. Play consists of a number of moves, each representing a six-month period starting spring 1900, autumn 1900, etc. At each period each player writes down secret instructions directing each of his forces either to stay put or to move to an adjacent cell of the appropriate type (land or sea). When all are ready, the instructions are revealed and the moves enacted, if possible. Certain cells are designated supply bases. A player who occupies a supply base unopposed acquires a new army or navy, and, if that base is situated in an unoccupied minor country, occupies that country too. Conflict arises where the armies or navies of two or more powers seek to occupy the same area, and set rules determine whether the result is victory, defeat, or a stand-off.

So far, in abstract terms, Diplomacy is an extension of abstract games of capture by replacement, but with simultaneous instead of alternating moves, and with the movement of all one's forces at a time as in board war games. As a multi-player game, its chief distinction from board war games is that players spend most of their real time engaged in making and breaking alliances with one another. Anything relevant to the play may be negotiated—for example, an agreement that both should attack a third country, or that each should acknowledge the other's sphere of influence, or merely even that both should share such information as they may glean from negotiations with third parties. At start of play a 30-minute period is recommended for initial strategic planning, followed by moves to be made at a minimum of 15-minute intervals; but these arbitrary times naturally lengthen as the number of on-board forces increases and the balance of power shifts from one country or alliance to another. Full-blown Diplomacy needs to be played over a weekend rather than in one evening, and, of course, lends itself admirably to postal play.

Diplomacy was developed by Allan B. Calhamer in the 1950s, achieving its characteristic form by 1954 and its final revision in 1958. Following the usual pattern of rejection by major games companies, he published 500 sets at his own expense in 1959. In 1960 it was taken up by Games Research Incorporated, and has since become a classic. The game arose from his study of nineteenth-century European history at Harvard, and subsequently of political geography.[13] He relates its underlying mechanism to that of Chess, having started originally with a board of sixty-four squares and thirty-two pieces, subsequently expanded to its present eighty areas and thirty-four pieces equivalent to kings. He had also explored some concepts of temporary alliances by experimenting with the scoring system of nominally non-partnership card games such as Hearts.

Fantasy

Fantasy role-playing games, as opposed to family board games with a fantasy theme, are historically recent activities that amount to a cross between game-playing and theatrical role-playing. Though formally derived from war games, they have now almost entirely dispensed with boards in the usual sense of the word, and so, strictly speaking, fall outside the purview of this book. In view of their historical origins, however, and of the irrational hostility they evoke on the part of those most ignorant of their nature (richly fed by misinformation propagated by the media and entertainment industries) they should not be omitted from our survey.

Fantasy games arose in the early 1970s from non-historical board war games in which some players began to insert supernatural elements derived from myth, legend, and folklore. They can be seen as the gaming branch of a cultural movement whose literary branch is represented by such writers as Peake, Tolkien, and Moorcock, and which may be classed, with New Ageism, as a reaction against the dehumanizing effects of science, technology, and commercially-driven materialism.

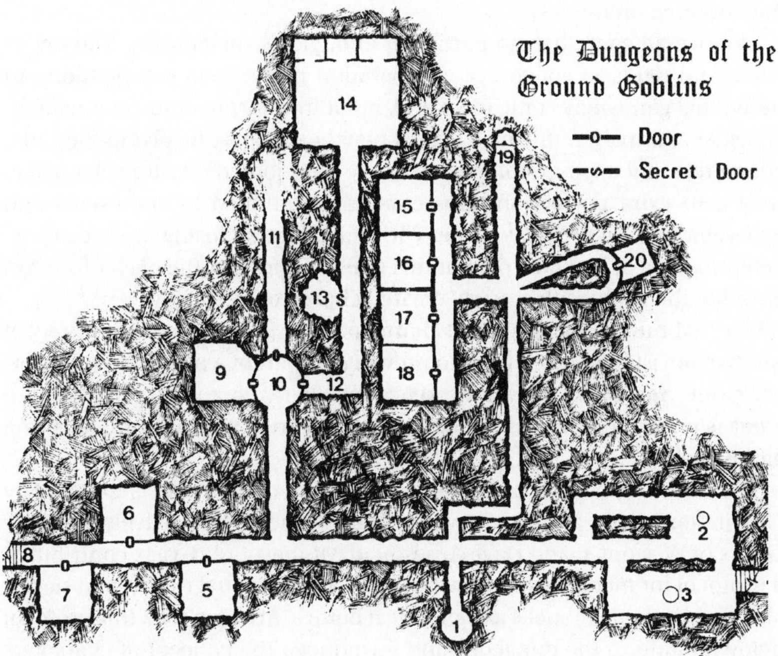

Fig. 19.2. This primitive fantasy board is still a far cry from the chessboard. Chamber 7 houses ten Gnolls guarding a chest containing 100 gold pieces, and chamber 9 a Gorgon guarding 1500 gold pieces, Boots of Levitation, Crystal Ball, Bag of Holding and Curse Scrolls. Enter chamber 10, and the Dungeon Caretaker will answer your questions—for a golden fee. (Illustration from Steve Jackson, 'Dungeons and Dragons', *Games & Puzzles*, 48 (May 1976), 7–9.)

Typically, the players each adopt the role of a mythical being—dwarf, magician, hero, whatever –and are randomly accorded an initial range of powers and abilities by the roll of a die. They are then placed in an opening situation, defined by place, surrounding objects, magical phenomena, and so on. The totality of such details, however, is known only to a non-player known as the Games Master (GM), equivalent to the umpire at Kriegspiel or Blind Chess. At each turn of events the GM imparts some information as to the current situation and the players respond by deploying their powers in whatever way seems strategically suitable. The GM, from his vantage point of ludic omniscience, and in accordance with the published rules of the particular game being played, determines the outcome of such interactions, and evolves a new situation. The general aim is to survive and prosper, especially by acquiring treasure and increasing one's powers through successful conflict with various traps and monsters that may be encountered on the way.

The overall game has no particular end, yields no winners or losers as such, and tends to encourage co-operation rather than competition. An individual game may come to an end, but it may form part of an indefinite series or 'campaign', in which case a new one begins, involving the same characters and any newcomers who may have joined. Existing characters may gain extra powers and possessions determined by the events and experience of the previous game. The equivalent of 'losing' is that a character may die or be killed off, but this does not prevent the player from re-entering the game with a newly created character.

The GM must have maps and charts to follow, which may be entirely of his own devising or designed and provided as part of a published proprietary game, and the players may sketch speculative maps as a visual aid to what is going on, but this is normally the nearest approach there is to a game board.

The basic ingredients of fantasy role-playing games were elaborated by two independent groups of war-gamers, headed respectively by Gary Gygax of Wisconsin and Dave Arneson of Minnesota.[14] Gygax contributed a protocol for medieval battles which, besides the usual castles and sieges, also involved magic spells and mythical beings. Arneson took this protocol below ground to the dungeons and introduced the concept of characters with abilities determined by die rolls. The two pooled their ideas in a campaign called Greyhawk, whose popularity spread in true folk tradition (like Lizzie Magie's game of Landlord) largely in high-school and university circles, and through the Diplomacy postal-play network. Turned down by all the usual manufacturers, they invested their resources in a new company called TSR (Tactical Studies Rules), and in 1974 published Dungeons and Dragons, which today remains the classic and archetype of the fantasy gaming world.

Alternative Histories

Another offshoot of board war-games, besides fantasy games, may be called 'alternative histories'. Diplomacy, nominally a war-game, is the archetype, in that players start with a Europe as it was in 1900 and finish with what it might have been several years later if negotiations had followed different lines. Typically, they are games for three or more players, each of whom represents an historical race, nation, or culture. The board represents a map of the appropriate region or continent, and the aims include migration, conflict, settlement, prosperity, and general overall dominion. In Britannia,[15] four players control some of the seventeen ethnic groups that battled for Britain from the early Roman invasion to the Norman Conquest. History of the World describes itself as 'the boldest board game concept yet attempted, capturing in a few hours play the entire sweep of the human race across 5,000 years of history, and the entire face of the globe'. Civilizations, highly regarded by aficionados of the genre, is set in the cradles of civilization surrounding the Levantine Mediterranean. Here Greeks, Egyptians, *et al.*, seek to rise from the most primitive levels of Palaeolithic endeavour, through agriculture and political stability, eventually into the higher reaches of art, music, and philosophy. An even bolder sweep of time was essayed in a now defunct game called Infinity,[16] which invited players to recreate the heavens and earth in under an hour in the privacy of their own homes. Against the background of an inchoate universe, players evolved galaxies, planets, life, civilization, etc., in a way that frankly owed more to Rummy than to Genesis. By all accounts it was on the way towards becoming a cult game in certain circles, but was abandoned by many when Dungeons & Dragons appeared on the scene. History also provides themes for thematic board games other than those of war-gaming format. Kingmaker, invented by Andrew McNeil and first published in 1975, is based on the fifteenth-century Wars of the Roses: each player represents a noble family of the time and seeks to establish his favoured candidate on the throne by eliminating rival pretenders. History also overlaps with business games. Two popular games based on a theme of building railways appeared within a short time of each other. Railway Rivals, by David Gwynn Watts, replaces a single board with eight hexagonal grids needing to be coloured in, each based on a railway of Britain or North America, and providing a series of educational games designed to acquaint players with the more-or-less real-life problems of building a network.[17] Francis

Gresham's '1829' is basically an historical game simulating the establishment and expansion of the major railway companies in nineteenth-century England.[18] Medieval Europe provides subject matter for Fugger Welser Medici, played on a board depicting the trade routes of that period. In the longest version, taking up to eight hours of play, 'you not only climb the social ladder but earn enough to buy a country estate and build a sizeable family fortune'.[19] The object of Plague is to be the first to collect and bury 99 plague victims.[20]

Politics

Games based on politics—a cross between crime, fantasy, and alternative history—go back a long way, but have yet to produce a classic. The Race for the Presidency predates 1897, The Way to the White House appeared in 1927, and, in the early 1980s, Jack Jaffé came up with one retitled Save the President! (after doubts were expressed about his original idea, Kill the President!) Class Struggle, by Bertel Ollman (1978), attracted much attention in the American press; but perhaps more nostalgic in this line, in the light of subsequent events, was Police State, which Dan Glimne describes as 'A rather bloody satire about life in Soviet Russia, where you had to denounce the other players and get them sent off to Siberia so you could take over their flats. There was a shortage of *everything* in the game, except back-stabbing . . .'. One of the funniest, while at the same time attractive to serious games-players, was Junta (1979), by Vincent Tsao and others. 'Who will be the next El Presidente of la Republica de los Bananas?' it asks; and the answer eventually emerges when players have followed rules classified under such headings as The Constitution of the Republic, The Bank, the Swiss Bank Account, The President's Brother-in-Law, Assassinations, etc.

Perhaps the greatest British contribution to this topic, arcane as it may have appeared to the rest of the world, was Election (David Drakes *et al.*, Intellect Games, 1974), in which players representing up to six political flavours— Conservative, Independent, Labour, Liberal, Nationalist, Socialist—toured a map of the United Kingdom making speeches, promises, and bribes, securing the support of various social groupings, and tracking their popularity on a poll chart. Not until all the support spaces were filled was the election itself called, and it took a great deal of excitingly realistic counting to find out who had actually won. Clever elements of realism made it, for example, difficult for the Conservative candidate to secure much support in Scotland, and desirable for all to appeal to the retired classes of the West Country.[21]

A splendid game called Propaganda, published by Wff'n'Proof in the 1970s, might nowadays have fared well under the 'social interaction' heading. Unfortunately, it was way ahead of its time, and too intellectual for the average gamer in the street. 'Democracy', as G. B. Shaw so accurately observed, 'substitutes election by the incompetent many for appointment by the corrupt few'.[22]

Sports

Practically every activity classifiable as a sport has been translated into board-game format, and the more popular the sport—football, baseball, golf, horse-racing—the more numerous the publications. Many a would-be games-inventor starts by basing something on his favourite sport, which is entirely self-defeating, as it is the least favourite theme of games manufacturers. The subject has produced few, if any, classics, and added nothing of earth-shattering significance to the stock of underlying board-gaming ideas. Two long-standing British favourites are Wembley (soccer) and Totopoly (horse-racing).

Word Games

Given the popularity of board games and word games down the ages, it is perhaps surprising that no one seems to have thought of combining the two before the end of the nineteenth century. But then, it still comes as a surprise to be reminded that it was only in 1913 that the crossword puzzle first appeared.[23] The earliest boxed word game known to R. C. Bell, who knows more than there exists to know about such things, is a set of square bone tiles engraved with capital letters on one side and minuscules on the other, dating from 1850 or perhaps earlier, and apparently of French origin in view of the accents that some of them bear. His collection also includes a board with a pattern of simple loops on which are placed a number of wooden discs (56 are illustrated) bearing various capital letters and one ampersand. It is, he reports, 'marked Pat. Feb. 16 '86, and is a mixture of puzzle and game; suitable for teaching children their alphabet and also for a form of solitaire in completing words or phrases in a given time'.[24] A boxed game of the 1920s entitled Word Making and Word Taking consists of square letter-cards of cheap cardboard, usable for a variety of games, none of them requiring a board. It, or something very similar, appears at a critical point in Hitchcock's film *Suspicion* (RKO 1941), when Joan Fontaine nearly frightens herself to death by accidentally constructing the word MURDER. Among the more successful boxed word games are Lexicon, a card game patented by David Whitelaw in 1925 and subsequently published (on and off) by Waddingtons, and Boggle, a dice game invented by Alan Turoff and first published in the early 1970s. Of board-based word games, the following are noteworthy.

Scrabble could be described as the Chess of word games, as attested by its national tournament status in the UK, USA, and Australia, and by the vast amount of literature and articles devoted to it.

The main equipment is a board of $15 \times 15 = 225$ squares and 100 letter tiles, of which 98 are marked with a letter and a point-value, as shown in the upper row of Table 19.2, and two are blanks. Blanks count as any letter and score nothing.

Table 19.2. Scrabble letters.

letter	**E**	**A**	**I**	**O**	**N**	**R**	**T**	**D**	**L**	**S**	**U**	**G**	**B**	**C**	**F**	**H**	**M**	**P**	**V**	**W**	**Y**	**J**	**K**	**Q**	**X**	**Z**
quantity	9	8	8	8	6	6	6	4	4	4	4	3	2	2	2	2	2	2	2	2	2	1	1	1	1	1

Up to four can play, but two is best. Each in turn plays one or more tiles to the board to make words in crossword-interlocking fashion, and draws a like number so long as any remain. Each word made or extended scores the total point-value of its constituent letters. Certain so-called 'premium' squares increase the score by doubling or tripling an individual letter or a whole word.

It is the existence and arrangement of such squares that brings to the word game the added dimension of positional strategy. Given that the opening word must cover the central square, the arrangement is designed to favour the gradual expansion of words in all directions outwards, with the more valuable squares lying towards the extremities. Thus the first skill of the game is rooted in your vocabulary, and in the ability to visualise words constructible from tiles on your own rack. The second lies in manœuvring your way towards premium squares, while simultaneously trying to deny them to your opponent. It is this degree of player interaction that places Scrabble in the league of deep strategic games.

All of which is a far cry from the simple and unpublished game of Lexico invented by an out-of-work Connecticut architect in the Depression year of 1931. A study of the games market led Alfred Butts to pick on words as the basis of a new development. Lexico itself was not unlike its near-namesake Lexicon, in that the equipment consisted simply of tiles with letters, but no board. Following a procedure akin to Rummy, a fad card game of the time, the winner was the first to complete a seven-letter word and lay it face up on the table. For variety, Butts later accorded point-values to the letters, and when one player went out the others could subsequently score for making words of four or more letters. He offered it in this form to several manufacturers, but without success.

Architect Butts naturally went back to the drawing board, and duly came up with the idea of adding a board to the equipment and playing tiles to it in the manner of crosswords, which had then only recently become a craze. Now renamed 'It', the game was offered again to the manufacturers, and again turned down as being 'too intellectual', no doubt on the popular but conveniently unprovable business theory that 'No one ever lost money by underestimating the intelligence of the public.' The new title may not have helped matters. 'It' had been coined by romantic writer Elinor Glyn in the previous decade as a synonym for sex, especially as embodied in silent film star Clara Bow. The game was evidently not as sexy as it sounded—which is perhaps ironic, in view of today's use of 'playing Scrabble' as a phrase rich in euphemistic suggestiveness.

In 1939 Butts was introduced by a mutual friend to James Brunot, who had been looking for a suitable business to develop away from the city lights and rat-race. Brunot liked the look of what was now called Criss-Cross Words, and started experimenting with it himself. War intervened to hold this up, and by 1942 Butts and his wife were making up game sets and marketing them through one Chester Ives, a bookshop owner in Danbury, Connecticut, who undertook the manufacture of the boards. This came to nothing, or nothing to write home about, and for a while it seemed as if Butts's brainchild would remain for ever the Peter Pan of the games world.

In 1947, however, James Brunot re-entered the picture by returning from Washington, where he had been the wartime executive director of the President's War Relief and Control Board. Brunot had made one or two changes to the game, including the rule about starting across the middle instead of up in the top left corner, and, perhaps more inspirationally, changing the name of the game to Scrabble. No particular significance attached to the word: it just happened to be one of several nice-sounding possibilities that research showed had not already been registered as a trade name. (But would the game have been so successful had it been published, as it nearly was, under the title Logo-Loco?) Under a new arrangement between the two, Brunot would manufacture and market the newly named game through his business facility, the Production and Marketing Company.

In the three years from 1949 to 1951 sales of Scrabble remained at the disappointingly low level of under 10,000 per annum. It was only in 1952, when Jack Strauss played and enjoyed it on holiday, that the game found the break it had been looking for. Strauss was surprised on returning to work to learn that Scrabble was not on sale at New York City's famous department store, Macy's. Fortunately, he was the Chairman of Macy's. Once there, everybody who was anybody started buying it. The game caught on and became a national craze. Within two years, Brunot's company had sold over four million sets.

Shortly after, Brunot sold to Selchow and Righter (who had long ago rejected Criss-Cross Words) the rights to the manufacture of the standard set, retaining for himself those for non-standard and speciality editions. He kept these until 1971, eventually selling out his entire interest to Selchow and Righter. Scrabble was introduced to Australia in 1953, being published there by T. R. Urban, and in 1954 to the UK through J. W. Spear and Son, who continue to market and promote the game.

In 1971 Scrabble achieved the status of national tournament play through the enthusiasm of games fanatic Gyles Brandreth. Brandreth had been struck by the popularity of the game in British prisons, on which he was then writing a book. Intrigued by its tournament possibilities, he put an advertisement in *The Times* newspaper to assess possible support. The response was overwhelming, and, with the ready co-operation of Spears Games, the British National Scrabble Championships have become an annual event attracting thousands of competitors.

Upwords bears a superficial resemblance to Scrabble, but differs in significant respects, and many word-gamers prefer it for its classic simplicity. It has the rare merit of being as satisfactory for three or four players as for two. The latest version involves a board of 10 × 10 squares and 100 square letter-tiles. (The original had 8 × 8 squares and 64 tiles.) Each in turn plays to the board one or more tiles from his rack of seven in such a way as to make or extend one or more words connecting in crossword fashion, and scores for the number of tiles used—the letters do not have individual point-values.

The original feature of Upwords, as implied by its title, is that you can build words not only from left to right and from top to bottom, but also in the third dimension from ground level *upwards.* In brief, you can change words by piling letter tiles on top of one another. For example, you can change NOVEL to HOVEL, or NAVEL, or NOMAD. Or you can build and extend it to make, for example, ENAMEL or INNOVATE—or even, with AIINNOT in your rack, INNOVATION, thereby gaining a bonus for using all seven tiles.

Upwords was invented in 1982 by Elliot Rudell, of Torrance, California, using modified pieces of equipment from a game then published under the name Chinese Chess. The publisher Milton Bradley immediately expressed

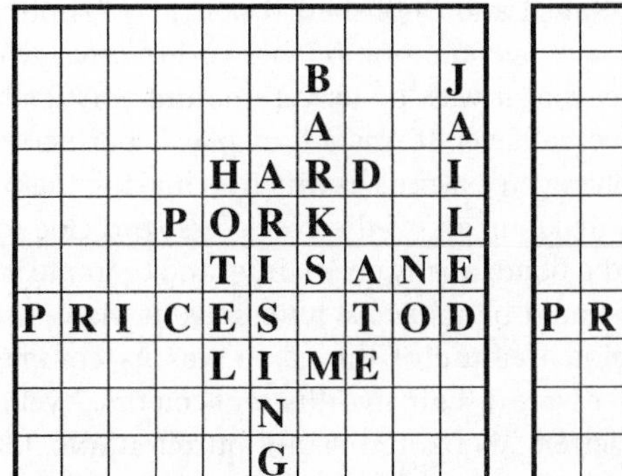

Fig. 19.3. Upwords. *Left*: A typical foundation of words at ground level before any building has been done. The last move was the addition of M to LI, making LIME and ATE for a score of 14. (A word scores double if every one of its letters is at ground level.) The next player started building by playing six letters to the vertical word HOTEL, scoring 11 for COMBATED, 5 for BARD, 5 for PARK, and 5 for DIME, total 26. Shaded squares indicate changed letters standing two high.

interest, but reported a tendency of players to keep building upwards to such an extent that the game became physically unstable and failed to develop properly in the basic two dimensions. Rudell countered this by the simple device of limiting stacks to five tiles and awarding double points to words entirely at ground level. In this form it took off with success that, in true Californian tradition, the inventor now has UPWORDS as his personalized car number-plate. The game seemed less successful on the UK market and was withdrawn after a few years. However, 1995 saw its relaunch in the 10 × 10 form developed in-house by Hasbro UK, which ought to give it a new lease of life.

Rudell reports[25] an interesting history lineage note as follows: 'Alfred Butts invented Scrabble. Alan Turoff invented Boggle. I invented Upwords. Alfred Butts's nephew babysat Alan Turoff. My first job in the toy industry had me working in the office next to Caroline Poole, who subsequently married Alan Turoff.' It's a small world, even in the USA.

Word for Word, a game by Paul Lamond (Creative Games, 1993), is one of the better derivatives of the Trivia family, in which players aim to complete circuit of the board by responding to challenges about words. The standard challenges are to provide synonyms, rhymes, or definitions for a given word, and the procedure is spiced up with additional tasks involving acronyms, antonyms, rhyming slang, collective nouns, and so on.

Montage, invented by Djoli Kansil and published (briefly) by Gamut of Games in 1974, might well have become one of the world's great word games were it not for the fact that it was, by its very nature, ineluctably pitched at too high an intellectual level. It was a four-player partnership game based on the idea of solving crosswords as much as making them.[26] Each in turn was required to make up an off-the-cuff crossword clue to a word that could be made on the board at any given time, and to frame it in such a way that his partner would be more likely to solve it than either opponent. The all-too-ingenious feature of the game was its complete absence of letters! In their place were discs in five different colours. A yellow disc represented any of the letters ABCDZ, red EFGHJ, purple ILMNK, blue OPRSQ, green UTVWXY. Thus a sequence of red-yellow-purple-red could represent HALF or FANG, but if clued 'Recreation for a sporting bird' could only mean GAME.

Social Interaction and Quiz Games ('Trivia')

The perennial popularity of quizzes renders unsurprising the discovery that most of the retail shelf-space devoted to boxed games is occupied by quiz games, especially in non-specialist games shops. Many are well-known television quiz games done into board or card game format, and are not worth mentioning; some amount to boxed-up quizzes *about* popular television programmes—the less said about these, the better; and at least one tests your knowledge not of television programmes, but of the commercials that keep interrupting them—a concept so appalling as to defy belief. Of the others, two worthy of mention are Trivial Pursuit and Pictionary.

Trivial Pursuit. There were quiz board games before Trivial Pursuit, just as there were trading games before Monopoly, but this was the one that hit on the right formula at the right time and so became the archetype of them all. The measure of its success is the amount of imitation it has spawned, and the entry into the language—even the dictionary—of *trivia* as a synonym for any general knowledge quiz or competition. Simplicity itself, Trivial Pursuit is a looped race game in which players move around the board in accordance with the throw of dice, land on spaces indicating any of six departments of knowledge, answer a question in that category that someone else reads from one of hundreds of cards, acquire credits for answers, and aim to be the first home with a statutory number of credits.

Trivial Pursuit was devised by Scott Abbott and brothers Chris and John Haney, of Montreal, in December 1979. In 1980 they finished compiling the questions and produced a few prototypes to show Canadian and American manufacturers, who, as in all the best stories (cf. Monopoly, Scrabble, Diplomacy, etc.), dutifully turned it down. In 1981 the inventors sank the last of their savings into production of a thousand or so sets for sale by mail order and in the few shops that would take them despite the relatively high asking price. The response was underwhelming, but picked up slightly towards Christmas. They exhibited the game at the New York Toy Fair in February 1982, and this, too, started out unpromisingly—'they were stuck in a room at the far end of a distant corridor, and most of the people passing by were actually looking for the bathroom'.[27] It was not until the game appeared on a television chat show, with the host reading questions to the guests, that people began to sit up, take notice, and, more importantly, place orders. In 1983 it was licensed to several European countries. Since then it has appeared in more than fifty countries and twenty languages, selling well over 75 million sets. The whole success story was re-enacted as a television film by the Canadian Broadcasting Corporation in 1987. Perhaps the greatest mark of its success has been the generic use of the word 'trivia' to stand for 'unimportant factual information (as) used in the game of Trivial Pursuit' (*Shorter Oxford English Dictionary*, 1993).

Trvial Pursuit has produced its own spin-offs on a variety of subjects, and inspired an even greater number of imitations based on more or less esoteric subjects. More interestingly, albeit less successfully, it has engendered a series of open-ended games of social interaction, in which the questions posed are matters of opinion or speculation rather than fact. Some flavour of such games may be imparted by such titles as Scruples and the (now defunct) I Think You Think I Think...

Pictionary. In this more original offshoot of the trivia branch forward motivation is provided by recognizing, deducing, or just correctly guessing, the word on a card drawn from a pack. The players are divided into two teams, each of which appoints one of its number to act as their draughtsman or illustrator. The word on the card is revealed only to the illustrator, who draws a pencil sketch to illustrate the randomly selected word. Fairly straightforward when presenting picturable objects like OSTRICH or (ambiguously) STUDS, the game gets more challenging when it comes to verbs such as SOAR or PAVE, and abstractions like STRENGTH or LIFE.

NOTES

1. 'Patolli, Pachisi, and the Limitation of Possibilities', *Southwestern Journal of Anthropology*, 6 (Winter 1950), 369–87 (reprinted in E. M. Avedon and B. Sutton-Smith, *The Study of Games* (New York, 1971), 128).

2. The following section is based on two major articles on the subject: Willard Allphin, 'Who Invented Monopoly?', *Games & Puzzles*, 1st ser. 34 (March 1975), 4–7, with critical comments by the then Marketing Vice-President of Parker Bros; and Dan Glimne, 'Monopoly: The TRUE Story', *Games & Puzzles*, 2nd ser. 6 (Sept. 1994), 6–8.
3. Sid Sackson, *A Gamut of Games* (London, 1974, text 1969), 8–9.
4. Sid Sackson, 'Acquire', *Games & Puzzles*, 1st ser. 11 (Mar. 1973), 4–5.
5. *Games & Puzzles*, 2nd ser. 14 (May 1995), 11 and 13.
6. Information by courtesy of Dan Glimne, who has researched origins with the kind assistance of Waddingtons Games.
7. See *Games & Puzzles*, 1st ser. 63 (Aug. 1977), 14–15.
8. Divid Pritchard, 'The Godfather Game', *Games & Puzzles*, 1st ser. 7 (Nov. 1972), 4–5. Publisher not stated.
9. By Steve Jackson, reviewing the game in *Games & Puzzles*, 1st ser. 44 (Jan. 1976), 14.
10. This section, and especially this paragraph, leans heavily on Nicholas Palmer, *The Comprehensive Guide to Board Wargaming* (London, 1980), who in turn acknowledges Martin Campion and Steven Patrick, 'The History of Wargaming', in *Strategy and Tactics*, 33, the magazine of Simulations Publications Incorporated (SPI).
11. This observation is taken verbatim from Barry Buzan, 'Risk', *Games & Puzzles*, 1st ser. 2 (June 1972), 10.
12. Steve Jackson, personal communication.
13. Allan B. Calhamer, 'The Invention of Diplomacy', *Games & Puzzles*, 1st ser. 21 (Jan. 1974), 8–13, includes strategic analysis. See also Calhamer, 'Diplomacy', *Modern Board Games* (London, 1975), 26–44.
14. Information derived from J. Eric Holmes, *Fantasy Role Playing Games* (London, 1981).
15. Britannia, History of the World, and Civilisations, are published in Britain by Gibsons Games.
16. Reviewed and described in *Games & Puzzles*, 1st ser. 36 (May 1975), 27, and 52 (Sept. 1976), 8, both by David Parlett, the first under a pseudonym.
17. Reviewed by John Deans in *Games & Puzzles*, 1st ser. 35 (Apr. 1975), 24.
18. Reviewed by Steve Jackson in *Games & Puzzles*, 1st ser. 39 (Aug. 1975), 25–6.
19. Tony Hetherington, *Games & Puzzles*, 2nd ser. 14 (May 1995), 18. German game published by 'Doris and Frank'.
20. B&B Productions, Weymouth. Information supplied by Dan Glimne.
21. See David Parlett, 'Election' (review), *Games & Puzzles*, 1st ser. 31 (Dec. 1974), 19–20, also feature article, 1st ser. 45 (Feb. 1976), 6–8.
22. George Bernard Shaw, 'Maxims for Revolutionists', appended to *Man and Superman* (1903).
23. The first crossword, then called Word Cross, was devised by Arthur Wynne, a British journalist, and published in a 1913 edition of the *New York World*.
24. R. C. Bell, 'Word Games', *Games & Puzzles*, 1st ser. 31 (Dec. 1974), 14–16.
25. Elliot Rudell, personal communication.
26. Review and feature article by David Parlett in *Games & Puzzles*, 1st ser. 24 (May 1974), 20 and 30 (Nov. 1974), 17–19.
27. Dan Glimne, personal communication.

Index of board games

General Index

PICTURE ACKNOWLEDGEMENT

The author and publisher wish to thank the following who have kindly given permission to reproduce the figures indicated:

4.4 © British Museum; **5.2** British Patent 5586 of 1893; **7.3** Photo: Reunion des Musée Nationaux, Paris/Jean Schormans; **12.18** Courtesy of the Trustees of the Victoria and Albert Museum.